D. H. LAWRENCE

Daniel J. Schneider

DHLDHLDHLDHLDHLDHLDHLDHLDHLDHLDHLDHLDHLDHLDHLDHLDHLDHLDHLDHLDHLDHLDHLDHLDHLDHLDHLDHLDHLDHLDHLDHLDHLDHLDHLDHLDHLDHLDHLDHL

D. H. Lawrence

THE ARTIST AS PSYCHOLOGIST

DHLDHLDHLDHLDHLDHLDHLDHLDHLDHLDHLDHLDHLDHLDHLDHLDHLDHLDHLDHLDHLDHLDHLDHLDHLDHLDHLDHLDHLDHLDHLDHLDHLDHLDHLDHLDHLDHLDHLDHL

UNIVERSITY PRESS OF KANSAS

Published by the University Press of Kansas
(Lawrence, Kansas 66045), which was organized
by the Kansas Board of Regents and is operated
and funded by Emporia State University, Fort
Hays State University, Kansas State University,
Pittsburg State University, the University of
Kansas, and Wichita State University

Library of Congress Cataloging in Publication Data

Schneider, Daniel J., 1927–
D. H. Lawrence, the artist as psychologist.
Bibliography: p.
Includes index.
1. Lawrence, D. H. (David Herbert), 1885–1930—Knowledge—Psychology. 2. Psychology in literature.
I. Title.
PR6023.A93Z866 1984 823′.912 83-21361
ISBN 0-7006-0241-0

Printed in the United States of America

Again, for Jeanne

Contents

Preface

Over the past three decades our understanding of what D. H. Lawrence was doing in his art has been deepened and clarified by critics who have viewed the fiction through the lens of Lawrence's psychological ideas. Lawrence's essay "The Crown" is one of the basic sources of Colin Clarke's important *River of Dissolution: D. H. Lawrence and English Romanticism;* Aidan Burns's fine study, *Nature and Culture in D. H. Lawrence,* uses *Studies in Classic American Literature* as the lens to reveal what Lawrence was doing in his art; Peter Balbert's interesting little study *The Psychology of Rhythm in D. H. Lawrence: The Meaning of Form in "The Rainbow"* takes Lawrence's two books on the unconscious as its starting point; Richard Swigg's *Lawrence, Hardy, and American Literature* uses "Study of Thomas Hardy" to enable us to see what Lawrence was doing; and that important early study by H. M. Daleski, *The Forked Flame: A Study of D. H. Lawrence,* is heavily indebted to the essays.

Although these and other studies draw on Lawrence's essays to illuminate his fiction, no one has yet done a comprehensive study of the principles of Lawrence's psychology or a systematic analysis of the problems Lawrence confronted as he sought to work his psychological laws into his fiction. My purpose here is to examine thoroughly Lawrence's psychology as it affects the forms of his novels. I begin by defining the principles of psychology Lawrence took to be primary and by showing how these principles arose from the climate of intellectual opinion of his formative years. The industry of a number of scholars, notably Émile Delavenay, has provided the groundwork for this further exploration of the affinities of Lawrence's thinking with that of the foremost scientists and philosophers of his time, particularly Herbert Spencer, Ernst Haeckel, William James, Arthur Schopenhauer, and Friedrich Nietzsche. Next I consider the artistic problems Lawrence wrestled with as he strove to incorporate his psychological laws in his "realistic" and didactic novels. In what ways did his psychology determine the structure of his fiction? How adequate are his solutions to the problems presented by his unique intentions? Finally, I compare his psychology with prominent psychologies of his own time and of today: is it possible to say that his ideas constitute a unique contribution to knowledge?

In analyzing Lawrence's psychology, I have made use of all of his discursive writings, especially *Psychoanalysis and the Unconscious* and *Fantasia of the Unconscious.* His fiction provided him, he said, with the living data, the passional experience, from which his "subjective science" was deduced. But if he deduced his laws of psychology from life, "life" as it appears in his fiction is seen always through the lens of these laws. The relationship between his art and his psychology is indeed so intimate that it is hard to know where to place the emphasis: on the artist as psychologist, or on the psychologist as artist? As psychologist, he was driven to invent new forms of fiction, adequate to present without falsification his insights into the realities of a divided psyche and its dynamic process. As artist, he had to find ways to adapt his psychology to the requirements of his fiction—requirements issuing from his moral and religious evaluation of experience—his didactic aims—and from his mimetic intentions.

A host of problems arose, and the brilliant fusion of psychology and art in a novel like *Women in Love* was extremely difficult to achieve. Many times Lawrence failed to resolve the tension between his psychology and his art; and because he was an experimental writer, always devising new forms to present his naturalistic and mystical vision, continually making new beginnings, creating new problems to solve, refusing to accept the easy solutions of conventional form, he was bound to write imperfectly. He loved his novels as he wrote them, relishing their freshness, spontaneity, and truth to life; and even his extensive revisions of his original drafts usually had to be done spontaneously, the whole novel being reconceived, never spliced with paste and scissors. But that very insistence on fidelity to life was a part of his artistic problem. His respect for experiential realities, his refusal to falsify the data, together with his desire to see *all* facts in relation to his "philosophy," which was at least half a psychology, often made it necessary for him to disappoint the conventional expectations that he half encouraged. His determination to be an accurate and honest *psychologist* presented new problems in plotting, characterization, point of view, and diction.

Thus I shall consider, for example, the problem of characterization. The artist may want a hero; but in an age when, as E. M. Forster has remarked, psychology has fractured the self and infected us all with profound doubts about human integrity, an age in which, as Byron says at the outset of *Don Juan,* we discover that every new hero, "cloying the gazettes with cant," is "not the true one," the hero is likely to become antihero, Underground Man, cockroach or K, or "our ancient friend Don Juan." The artist may wish to present the deeply moving spectacle of a brave man fighting indefatigably for his dark gods in a dehumanized secular civilization, but what if the psychologist sees the brave man, like Richard Somers of *Kangaroo,* as a "despicable little brat," a "preacher and a blatherer"?

The tension between the artist and the psychologist arose inevitably as Lawrence sought to define, in novel after novel, the actualities of his own psychic oscillations and struggle for balance from 1910 to 1930. In novels of two decades, he recorded with maximum fidelity to his own experience the difficult passages from adolescence to a young manhood marked by idealistic fervor and hope, to a grim crisis of middle age after his humiliating experiences during the First World War, to those last soberly affirmative explorations of alternative ways of living for man in "a tragic age." He was himself the indispensable hero of much of his fiction; but he knew his weaknesses well: his tendency toward "reaction," his tendency to escape, or to be the preacher and blatherer rather than the man of action, his misanthropy, his sexual anxieties, his failures as a man in the world of men. How make a hero of that unstable flux of emotion that one calls one's self?

I shall consider, too, problems of plotting faced by this novelist-psychologist. The plot must present actual psychic process. But it must also present the moral and religious vision of the didactic writer; and it must present with mimetic fidelity the behavior of his characters. If the writer becomes interested in "allotropic states" and in the inhuman determinants of behavior, he runs the risk continually of sacrificing mimetic fidelity to his theory of psychology; and if, as a naturalist of the soul, he refuses to judge his characters but insists, rather, on their being taken as the innocent agents of the deep forces that determine their conduct, how can he arrive at persuasive moral evaluations? The psychologist and the artist-prophet are potentially at odds.

Or consider, again, the construction of the action in a novel that seeks fidelity to psychic process. Refusing to put his thumb on the scales and thus to force his plot to an imposed conclusion, Lawrence conscientiously eschewed the artificiality of conventionally comic or tragic endings, of conventional climaxes, and of conventional ways of maximizing pity and fear or joy and the sense of fulfillment. His tragicomic art embraced the instability and raggedness in human experience: ambivalence, incompleteness, process. But the novel built on the assumption of instabilty, mutability, and inconclusiveness in human experience is always in danger of becoming a record of the sheer welter of human feeling, with "undisciplined squads of emotion" that are anathema to the formed and ordered experience of conventional art.

Because of these often conflicting aims, it is not surprising that Lawrence's novels fail to satisfy many of his readers. Yet the strange forms his fiction assumed were invariably the product of his prolonged meditations on the nature of the psyche and the psychic struggles of our time. Even his artistic failures are faithful records of the inner debates of modern men and women. And even his worst writing shows those qualities that Longinus identified almost twenty centuries ago as being indispensable to literary excellence; a firm grasp of ideas, and vigorous and inspired emotion. It shows, too, a remarkable detachment—the detachment of a generalizing intelligence that fed avidly on ideas from a great variety of sources. In naturalists like Charles Darwin, Herbert Spencer, Ernst Haeckel, and T. H. Huxley; in philosophers like Plato, Heraclitus, Schopenhauer, and Nietzsche; in anthropologists and students of religion like Leo Frobenius, Jane Harrison, Sir James Frazer, and Gilbert Murray; in psychologists like William James, Siegmund Freud, C. G. Jung, and Trigant Burrow; in mystics like William Blake and Madame Blavatsky; in novelists like Dostoevsky, Hawthorne, Melville, and Hardy; and in a score of other sources, he found ideas that stimulated his reflections on the nature of the psyche.

His curiousity was inexhaustible. Divining the affinities of all living things in the inhuman sources of life, he looked hard at the uniqueness of being in its immense diversity, everywhere seeking clues to the nature of that strange creative force that manifested itself in a poppy, a cow, and a man.

He generalized swiftly and easily from the particular, but he seldom lost sight of stubborn, recalcitrant realities that his generalizations overrode. His mind was naturally abstractive and synthetic, but it was also profoundly analytical. His imaginative divinations, which sprang from careful observation, were matched by an unparalleled ability to diagnose in himself the deep causes of his behavior.

He brought to psychology, too, an uncanny poet's "negative capability," which enabled him to grasp truths inaccessible to objective observation; but his intuitive powers were so well balanced by common sense that his sympathetic awareness of the inclinations and needs of others was devoid of sentimentalism. He was, in short, well equipped to grasp the deep needs of the psyche and the nature of psychic process. Curious, imaginative, wide-ranging, and original, he arrived at conclusions undreamt of until recently, in the work of some existential psychologists.

To examine his art in relation to his psychology is to appreciate freshly F. R. Leavis's defense of the sane and healthy Lawrence. It was Leavis who first emphasized Lawrence's detachment, Lawrence's remarkable ability to stand at a distance, contemplating experience even while presenting the immediacy of personal involvement. The justice of that insight has grown upon me as I have studied Lawrence. Now, after some thirty years' immersion in his writings and after violent swings in my attitudes—from worshiper to despiser to sobered admirer—I believe Leavis's case for Lawrence's essential health and wisdom can be made even stronger. This study of the artist as psychologist will show, I trust, why that belief is justified.

ACKNOWLEDGMENTS

I am grateful to The National Endowment for the Humanities and to The Office of Graduate Studies and Research of the University of Tennessee for stipends that gave me time to read in psychology, to write the final chapter, and to revise the entire manuscript.

A grant from the John C. Hodges Better English Fund, administered by the English Department of the University of Tennessee, enabled me to work at the Humanities Research Center of the University of Texas in Austin. I appreciate the generous and gracious assistance provided by the Humanities Research Center.

For helping me to secure assistance in my research and writing, I am indebted to two fine teachers and scholars under whom I studied, Richard Ellmann and James K. Robinson; to my unfailingly supportive colleagues, John Hurt Fisher and Joseph T. Trahern; and to that excellent scholar and editor William T. Stafford.

It is a deep pleasure to acknowledge the incomparable help and support of James C. Cowan, editor of the *D. H. Lawrence Review*, whose careful reading and wide erudition have helped me to avoid errors and to be aware of omissions.

Finally, I must mention some friends who helped me at a time when the writing of a book like this seemed unlikely: Jean Hagstrum, Wallace Douglas, Bruce Park, George Peck, Maurice Beebe, and the inimitable Robert T. Fitzhugh, now deceased.

Portions of this book have appeared, in slightly different form, in three scholarly journals. Chapter 2 is a revision of two articles: "Schopenhauer and the Development of D. H. Lawrence's Psychology," *South Atlantic Review* 48, no. 1 (January 1983): 1–19; and "D.

H. Lawrence and Nietzsche's *Thus Spoke Zarathustra,*'' *South Carolina Review* 15 (Spring 1983): 96–108. Chapter 8 is a revised version of ''The Laws of Action and Reaction in *Women in Love,*'' *D. H. Lawrence Review* 14 (Fall 1981): 238–62. A part of chapter 8 appeared as ''Art and Psychology in D. H. Lawrence's *Kangaroo,*'' *D. H. Lawrence Review* 14, no. 2 (Summer 1981): 156–71. I am much obliged to the editors of these periodicals for permission to reprint this material.

When one has worked on a writer for some thirty years, the ideas of a number of scholars inevitably become a part of one's thinking. It perhaps goes without saying that the strengths of this book depend, in large part, on others and that the weaknesses are my own.

List of Abbreviations Used in Citing Works by D. H. Lawrence

AR	*Aaron's Rod* (Harmondsworth, Eng.: Penguin Books Ltd., 1950)
CL	*The Collected Letters of D. H. Lawrence*, ed. Harry T. Moore (New York: Viking Press, 1962)
CSS	*The Complete Short Stories*, 3 vols. (Harmondsworth, Eng.: Penguin Books Ltd., 1980)
FU	*Fantasia of the Unconscious*, in "*Fantasia of the Unconscious*" and "*Psychoanalysis and the Unconscious*" (Harmondsworth, Eng.: Penguin Books Ltd., 1977)
K	*Kangaroo* (New York: Viking Compass, 1976)
Letters	*The Letters of D. H. Lawrence*, ed. Aldous Huxley (New York: Viking Press, 1932)

LIST OF ABBREVIATIONS

LCL *Lady Chatterley's Lover* (New York: Grove Press, Inc., 1957)

MEH *Movements in European History* (Oxford: Oxford University Press, 1925)

MM *Mornings in Mexico*, in *"Mornings in Mexico" and "Etruscan Places"* (London: William Heinemann Ltd., 1956)

PS *The Plumed Serpent* (New York: Vintage Books, Inc., 1951)

PU *Psychoanalysis and the Unconscious*, in *"Fantasia of the Unconscious" and "Psychoanalysis and the Unconscious"* (Harmondsworth, Eng.: Penguin Books Ltd., 1977)

R *The Rainbow* (Harmondsworth, Eng.: Penguin Books Ltd., 1976)

SCAL *Studies in Classic American Literature* (Harmondsworth, Eng.: Penguin Books Ltd., 1977)

SL *Sons and Lovers* (Harmondsworth, Eng.: Penguin Books Ltd., 1979)

SP *D. H. Lawrence: Selected Poems*, ed. Kenneth Rexroth (New York: Viking Compass Book, 1959)

LIST OF ABBREVIATIONS

T — *The Trespasser* (London: William Heinemann Ltd., 1955)

TI — *Twilight in Italy*, in *D. H. Lawrence and Italy: "Twilight in Italy," "Sea and Sardinia," "Etruscan Places"* (New York: Viking Press, 1972)

WL — *Women in Love* (New York: Random House, Modern Library, 1950)

WP — *The White Peacock* (London: William Heinemann Ltd., 1955)

1

Lawrence's Psychology, I: Materialism

The man who does disinterested work is [considered] abnormal.
—D. H. Lawrence

The view of Lawrence as a healthy and detached intelligence is not the prevailing one. He has been attacked so often for his romantic espousal of Feeling against Reason—that is, for his "irrationalism"—and his art has been seen so often as a reflection of his personal instabilities that the contrary view of Leavis has virtually been forgotten. As criticism refines our awareness of what Lawrence was saying and doing, attention has been diverted increasingly from the manifest content of his art to a latent content defined in terms that he himself would hardly have recognized. Marguerite Beede Howe's *The Art of the Self in D. H. Lawrence,*[1] with its allegorical readings of the fiction, is only one of the more recent examples of this tendency to reduce Lawrence's novels to compulsive irrational fears. Gavriel Ben-Ephraim, in *The Moon's Dominion,* regards the authorial voice in Lawrence as a "defense mechanism" which is "untrustworthy."[2] Ann Englander regards Lawrence's technique generally as evasion of the conflicts that he could not deal with in his schizoid state of mind.[3] Colin Clarke's impressive *River of Dissolution: D. H. Lawrence & English Romanticism,* which concludes with the assertion that Lawrence's rejection of sensationalism was balanced by "an equally decisive, if less direct, *commitment* to sensationalism—that is, to disintegrative sex and the machine-principle," employs a similar strategy: latent content is proclaimed as Lawrence's true message, manifest content is relegated to comparative unimportance.[4] Paradoxes easily resolved by Lawrence's synthesizing imagination—the paradox, for example, that the way of death can also be the way of life—are treated as instances of contradictions that are evidence of the incoherence of his thinking.

Pointing out contradictions that Lawrence was presumably unaware of and unable to resolve has been the strategy of much recent criticism.

Indeed, so much folly, madness, and inconsistency has been discovered that one wonders why Lawrence was ever taken seriously in the first place. Lawrence, Clarke argues, "is under an evident compulsion to make *incompatible* statements about voluptuousness or dissociated sensuality" (*River of Dissolution,* 63). In a similar vein, Émile Delavenay, in one of the best-informed studies of Lawrence as man and as artist, implies again and again that Lawrence adopted uncritically the queer ideas he picked up from such men as Houston Chamberlain, Otto Weininger, Max Nordau, and Edward Carpenter; and Delavenay finds that the key to Lawrence's life and work is escapism.[5] Thus, Lawrence's sensitive, inquiring, flexible intelligence is reduced to simple-minded compulsiveness or to paranoia or schizophrenia. As Yudhishtar observes in his *Conflict in the Novels of D. H. Lawrence,*[6] absolutely essential passages in Lawrence's works—especially passages concerned with the importance of "dynamic balance" in the psyche—are either ignored or are treated as superficial pronouncements contradicted by the real content of the novels.

In face of the accumulating *argumenta ad hominem* and the accumulating discoveries of latent homosexuality, misogyny, ontological insecurity, and outright schizophrenia in Lawrence's work, F. R. Leavis's case for a healthy, detached, and highly intelligent Lawrence may now appear naïve, superficial, or sententious. One hopes, however, that it is not being sententious to remind psychoanalytic critics that any writer who seeks to reveal the truth about his deepest desires and fears exposes himself inevitably to the charge that he is unbalanced, sick, or confused. The most bizarre delusions of the schizophrenic are those of normal consciousness in its dreaming state; and it is the business of the psychological novelist to dream "being awake": to discover those deep conflicts and regressive tendencies that, as Freud saw, arise in all human behavior; and to use them in creating his vision of life.[7] Thus the novelist must look within, as Conrad counseled, must contemplate pitilessly all latent fears and desires if he is to make them available for our contemplation and our understanding. This does not mean, however, that the novelist's aim is to present his inner turmoil. The novelist's concern, as the Freudian Edward Glover has remarked, "should be to express the artistic truth which lies entangled in his own mind. Otherwise, more likely than not he will entangle the mind of his reader in psychological confusions."[8]

Now doubtless Lawrence could not always find adequate moral and psychological premises to explain and find a way out of the confusions of his inner life. And humanists or Christians have generally sound reasons, from their perspectives, for rejecting his "religion of the blood." What is disturbing, however, is the view that Lawrence's thinking is incoherent, compulsive, self-defensive, or just plain silly—a view that ignores his detachment, his power of observation, his intelligence, his prolonged efforts to define and account for the deep psychological and moral problems of our age, and his prolonged meditation on the sources of renewal of individual and social health. He worked unremittingly to define the deep inner problems of modern men and women: the problem of submitting to a social system that is not life-promoting or life-enhancing; the problem of seeking in "reduction" and "sensationalism" a cure for inner impotence and emptiness; the problem of meaningless work and abstraction in modern life; the problem of making Love into the be-all and end-all of existence, while inwardly we are consumed by Nietzschean *ressentiment*; the problem of balancing the sympathetic and voluntary promptings of the psyche; and the problem of achieving some relatedness to the cosmos. He grasped these problems so completely that his work continually cleanses the mind of superstition, idolatry, sentimentalism, and bad faith.

His psychology is complex. Aldous Huxley defined Lawrence's position as "mystical materialism"; T. S. Eliot said that Lawrence wanted life to be "a kind of religious behaviorism."[9] These two phrases suggest Lawrence's indebtedness both to deterministic and reductionist thought of the late nineteenth century and his effort to go beyond materialism toward a position that has been defined variously as Gestaltist, existential, or, quite simply, mystical.[10] For on the one hand he regards human beings as manifestations of the underlying will of nature: creatures whose vital impulses arise as correlatives of the natural forces of attraction and repulsion which seek equilibrium. In this sense he appears as a materialist or a behaviorist. On the other hand, he denies that life can ever be explained in mechanico-material terms. Life is a thrusting into being, blind in its origins but acquiring, with its increasing differentiation, a purposive nature, characterized by vital striving or aspiration. The deepest desire of man, in his thrusting into individuation, becomes the desire for purposive activity; his deepest motive the religious or creative motive. Thus, as several critics have pointed out, Lawrence anticipates existential psychology with its stress on freedom and responsibility, on human "becoming" and the "project" of life, and on the problem of making one's essence or identity not only in oneself but in relatedness to the Other.

Yet freedom and responsibility are not grounded, for Lawrence, in man's existential situation but in his vital, spontaneous striving for being. The roots of human purposiveness remain biological, not metaphysical. In this respect, Lawrence avoids a fundamental difficulty facing existential psychology: namely, the tendency to revert to an essentially pre-Freudian position. Affirming freedom and man's ability to "make himself," existential psychology tends to deny the unconscious and its biological roots; it also tends to deny the psychic mechanisms of repression and the social causes of neurosis. A timeless human condition is substituted for the individual historically conditioned, and neurosis is explained as a moral failure—the failure to have the courage to be or to be authentic. Lawrence, in his thinking about the social causes of neurosis, never persuaded himself that personal therapy, or "mind-cure," is enough, or that freedom is within the reach of most men. A healthy humanity, he knew, cannot exist in a sick society. Social and political rebellion are a precondition of psychic health. The mass of men he viewed with a Nietzschean contempt as a herd conditioned to collective neurosis by the combined forces of Christianity, capitalism, and modern rationalism—the worship of "the Ideal" in all of its forms. Most men, he declared, "have no souls"; most are half-created or "uncreate," have not yet come into being. Only a few—the most highly individuated—are endowed by nature with the power to attain to freedom and responsibility and with the capacity to do disinterested work. These few alone are capable of heeding the voice of the whole, or integral, self that he called the Holy Ghost.

Thus freedom and responsibility are the most recent and the highest development of the will of the Unknowable Source. The "higher man" arises—that is, the individual, who is "still the earth's most recent creation," as Nietzsche said; and it is this higher man who must lead mankind to build the rainbow bridge into the future, not by cutting man off from his biological roots, but by planting one foot of the rainbow in the dark Source. In such a man, the will to power is neither suppressed nor warped into a sadistic ambition to dominate and control. It flowers as the creative, religious motive: the desire to destroy dead forms of social organization and to build a new heaven and a new earth. If usual religion is a mass delusion, as Freud contended, it is not that for the handful of men and women who are genuinely religious; and the instinctive passions of the unconscious are not dangerous in these rare individuals but are the sources of their healthy striving for being-in-the-infinite.

Lawrence's view on acting impulsively has been misunderstood. Instinctive impulses cannot be denied. Like Blake, Lawrence accepted that "he who desires but acts not, breeds pestilence." But Lawrence did not believe, as so many critics have claimed, that to act impulsively is to act healthily. Wisdom and the balancing will of the integral self (the Holy Ghost) are needed to check the blind pattern of impulsive "action and reaction," which is characteristic in our age. Healthy satisfaction of our deep love and power impulses occurs only when the two are balanced. The aggression of the power impulse cannot be suppressed without disaster. But it can be balanced by satisfying the love impulse, and the balancing can prevent those extremes of sadism that arise from the contemporary overemphasis on the ego and on ideal consciousness. The problem, as Lawrence believed, is to devise educational, political, and social methods and institutions to promote balance. A few individuals, acting as individuals, can go part of the way toward health; but Western man will never satisfy his deep "sympathetic" impulse or his deep "voluntary" impulse until he overcomes the egoism and alienation fostered by capitalism and the "love and benevolence ideal" inculcated by Christianity and romanticism.

That overcoming can occur only when men "realize," or incorporate into themselves, their being in the All; when they realize that their individuality is derivative and is an illusion in the last analysis. The paradox at the root of all of Lawrence's thought is that we must die if we would live: the old self, the absolute ego, must die by surrendering to the will of the Source before the new self, an organic whole deriving its energy from the Source, can come into being. Achievement of the maximum of being implies the realization of the nothingness and of the Allness of self in the Whole of Being. The proper study of psychology is man not only in himself and in his relatedness to other men but also in relation to the deity. As Nicholas Berdyaev has said, "to rediscover man is to rediscover God."

Grounded in a Schopenhauerian metaphysics reinterpreted in the light of vitalist notions of striving and aspiration, Lawrence's psychology thus exhibits crucial features of Freudian psychology anticipated by Schopenhauer. In his novels Lawrence suggests most of the psychic mechanisms that operate to prevent vital striving (regression, repression, introjection, projection, displacement, sublimation, etc.) and many of the anxieties or illnesses that result from the failure to "come into being." Implicitly he raises in every novel the question of how one can recover from the near-disastrous effects of a society hostile to life and then move toward healthy balance. Repression of the deep love or sympathetic impulse, effected by the systematic strengthening of the false goals of egoistic success or domination, production, and conscious control, has produced a "race of decent godless men" haunted by dread, unable to trust one another or join together in collective purposive action and seeking in "sensationalism" and "reaction" their cures for their inner emptiness and isolation. The repression of the deep spontaneous power impulse, effected by the systematic inculcation of the ideals of love, benevolence, equality, democracy, and the common good, has bred a race of men and women who are unable to affirm "I am I," lacking integral selfhood, unable to act from an inner core of purpose. The frustration of these deep impulses has led to intensified aggression not only against others but also against the self.

The cure, for Lawrence, is both social and individual. One must fight to change society. And one must discover the causes of one's illness, asking not only "Why am I behaving as I am?" in the manner of Freudian psychoanalysis, but also "For what reasons am I living?" in the manner of existential psychology. To answer this latter question, however, is to seek the ground of being. Not the ego's will-to-power but the divine will-to-creation-of-the-new and to destruction-of-the-old must be affirmed before one can come fully into being. Thus Lawrence departs fundamentally from an existential psychology rooted in atheism that affirms "the self" as conscious controller and decision maker, the little god in the machine. For Lawrence, the goal of life—the goalless goal of mankind—is to live in harmony with the creative and destructive will of the great Source.

Viewing Lawrence's career as a prolonged search for a way of life in which people can grow sanely, with a "natural mind-body harmony," we see his restlessness, his incessant traveling, his "escapism," in an altogether different light from that of the critics who have diagnosed his schizophrenia, his latent homosexuality, his misogyny, his anti-Oedipal reaction, or his romantic naïveté. Whatever his personal problems might have been, there remains the *disinterested* Lawrence, whose life was a prolonged effort to find in his own and in other cultures the social, racial, and religious conditions that enable an individual to achieve balance, to fulfill all of his deepest needs, and to live in healthy relatedness to others and to the inhuman world. He wanted, Frieda says, to write a book about each continent[11]—wanted to make his research as complete as possible. In an age in which "the love and benevolence ideal" had led Europeans and Americans to surrender their integral selves to a bullying mass psyche, he searched for a society, or a group of individuals, to right the balance by fusing the sympathetic impulses toward unison and the "power" impulse of male authority and mastery. He did not find the healthy civilization he sought or the companions he wanted; he found, at most, only clues to the health he envisioned for the individual and society and for the individual in society. He knew that however deeply he might yearn to return to the innocence and spontaneity of a primitive culture, civilized men could no longer "cluster round the drum." As a white European with an individualized consciousness, he could never return to the homogeneous collective will of tribal life; and indeed he distrusted any attempt to return even as he distrusted any surrender to the Magna Mater (to Nature personified) or to the mindless "African" supremacy of sensation. From Frobenius, Lawrence had learned about an essential hostility between the civilized European and the "savage." Yet Lawrence had the good sense to recognize the value of primitive tribal life—the satisfaction of deep needs of the sympathetic center in tribal unison and the satisfaction of the deep needs of the voluntary center in submission to a "greater man."

He insisted that the healthy individual and the healthy society must always reckon with time and change. Both God and the self are continual creations, not memories; both are realized only in a living response to changing realities. From Heraclitus—and perhaps also from Bergson—Lawrence had learned that it is impossible to omit time and process in the construction of man's relationship to the universe. One must learn to *listen* to the dark gods. They, as Ursula Brangwen knows, "with the clarity of ultimate knowledge," will transmute "the integral spirit" "unless I set my will, unless I absolve myself from the rhythm of life, fix myself and remain static, cut off from living, absolved within my own will" (*WL*, 219).[12] The fixation of the will is a disease of the Western psyche. The integral spirit, or the whole self, in its relatedness to the surrounding cosmos, can never be fixed wholly upon a single objective. Healthy living is learning to accept the deep changes within the self in response to the deep changes without. The healthy self must learn, periodically, to give up the old ego, to welcome its death. By "dipping into" the darkness of the unconscious source of life, the soul can discover those energies and the deep joy and peace that spring from the realization of oneness with the All; and the energized, renewed self, emerging from that fecund darkness, is prepared to adventure again into the light of individual awareness. In Lawrence's mystical language, the "flowing together" is inseparable from "the flowing apart." The two motions constitute the God rhythm and the life rhythm. The death of the old self in the primal unity, followed by the resurrection of the new self in a new awareness, is the precondition of building a new world, new values, and a new religion.

To trace the development of Lawrence's psychology is thus to trace the gradual refinement of his notion of health and the gradual sharpening of his answers to the question that presided over his entire career:

how can man achieve health and wholeness in a world that denies the unconscious sources of his behavior? In this and the next two chapters I will trace the reasoning by which he arrived at the answers to that question, which I have summarized roughly in the preceding pages. I want to suggest how he worked with, reshaped, and amplified ideas he found, for the most part, in his early reading of philosophy and psychology. In doing this, I shall focus on five influential thinkers—Herbert Spencer, Ernst Haeckel, William James, Arthur Schopenhauer, and Friedrich Nietzsche. Other influences, both early and late, have been considered admirably by a number of scholars, notably Émile Delavenay, William York Tindall, and Colin Clarke. But the convergence in Lawrence's thinking of many closely related ideas that fall roughly under the rubric of materialism has not, I think, been generally understood. In other words, the "scientific" Lawrence has not been understood. And that is unfortunate. For to view Lawrence's thinking in relation to that of five highly respected authorities whose ideas kindled young imaginations during the period of Lawrence's early intellectual development is to discover a critical intelligence whose keenness and detachment everywhere call into question the received idea that his thinking is a species of romantic irrationalism.

MATERIALISM

His intellectual awakening began, it seems safe to say, with his reading of Schopenhauer and Nietzsche, together with his avid interest in the biology of Darwin, T. H. Huxley, and Haeckel. These thinkers were to Lawrence what G. E. Moore was to Bloomsbury: they made possible the revaluation of all values.

Not surprisingly, his thinking during these years (roughly from 1905 to 1912) originates in rebellion or, to use Lawrence's word, reaction. In reaction to the chapel morality that throughout his adolescence bred fear, shame, and guilt, Lawrence was to announce defiantly: "I say only that is wicked which is a violation of one's feeling and instinct."[13] In reaction to preachings of right and wrong, he proclaimed with a Nietzschean contempt: "With *should* and *ought* I have nothing to do." Against the tender-minded velleities of "spiritual" women like Jessie Chambers, he hurled a defiant realism—"Je suis grand animal." As Émile Delavenay has pointed out, Lawrence's antagonism to the spiritual is suggested in *Sons and Lovers,* where Paul quotes from Baudelaire's "Le Balcon," his voice "growing almost brutal," "showing his teeth, passionately and bitterly": " 'Tu te rappeleras *(sic)* la beaûté *(sic)* des caresses.' "[14] Rejecting "the orthodox creed," he embraced the doctrines of T. H. Huxley, Ernst Haeckel, Herbert

Spencer, and William James: according to Jessie Chambers, "he tried to fill a spiritual vacuum by swallowing materialism at a gulp."[15] He turned also to vitalist thought—to Edward Carpenter and Bernard Shaw—for the freedom he sought from "the mind-forged manacles" of the Midlands. In defiance of the conformity of Eastwood, his hometown, he turned to Nietzsche or Carlyle for models of strong, heroic individuals. In short, his mind fed avidly on almost any idea that would support his attack on "spirituality"—on prudery, pudency, and the general terror of the pudenda.

Whatever influences may have dominated his thinking, rebellion against the "spiritual" was constant. So it is not surprising that he turned, for a time, to materialism, not, as Jessie Chambers said, to fill a spiritual vacuum in his soul, but to fill what might be called with greater justice the physical vacuum in the society. To understand the stress he placed on "the blood," one must grasp at the outset the immensity of the freedom, the release, that "materialism" and related doctrines held out to the delicate young man (the "prig" as he later called himself) who had been reared to self-consciousness by a spiritual woman in a spiritual age. One should also bear in mind that in its origins his psychology reflects the thinking of tough-minded empiricists and naturalists, not the fancies of theosophists and mystics. Later on, when he read theosophy, he seized on ideas and images that would complement and expand his early ideas; and he discovered, to his delight, that in Madame Blavatsky or in yoga, as in science, the notions of a *principium individuationis*, of attraction and repulsion, and of balance are of central importance. Thus science might be wedded to occult ideas. But in 1918 he said that "magic, astrology, anything of that sort" was "antipathetic" to him, though "interesting" (*Letters*, 440); and in 1922 he stated that he did not like mysticism, though he "no longer" believed in the "ideal plausibilities" of science, which he had accepted for "twenty years" (*FU*, 151).

The development of Lawrence's psychology was so profoundly linked to those materialists whom he swallowed "at a gulp" that examination of their major ideas sheds considerable light on his early thinking. Scholars have accepted that when he read Huxley, Darwin, Spencer, and Haeckel, he was influenced chiefly by seeing man in an evolutionary context, in his "place in nature," as one of Huxley's books has it. That is certainly true; but materialism was engaged in a war on several fronts, one of which was psychology, and its enemies included not only Christian theology but also prevailing notions about the nature of the mind and its powers. It seems likely that Lawrence accepted many of materialism's important psychological implications along with its general perspective. In any case, one finds in the writings of the materialists four ideas that assume major importance in Lawrence's psychology.

The first is the idea of the physiological or chemical basis of life and consciousness, an idea that would issue in Lawrence's treatment of the soul as "carbon."

The second is the idea that the force or energy in nature, which is manifested in attraction and repulsion, always seeks a balance: the fundamental rhythm of nature is that of alternation, oscillation, or action and reaction.

The third is the idea of the instrumental nature of thought—an idea that Lawrence would emphasize as part of his general view that thought always "hovers behind" the actuality of being and is in the service of the body as the latter seeks its unique ends.

The fourth is pantheism, matter and spirit being regarded as attributes of the undivided divine substance: an idea that leads inevitably to the conclusion that the self is "a oneness with the infinite."

Looking at the writings of the materialists whom Lawrence read, I shall have occasion to remark a number of other ideas that Lawrence assimilated in his thought-adventures during the decade of his early intellectual development. These four, however, are so important that they constitute the foundation of all Lawrence's subsequent thinking about the laws of psychology.

The idea of the physiological or chemical basis of life and consciousness can be found everywhere in scientific writings at the turn of the century. In his review of the development of psychology during "the last years of the nineteenth century and the early years of the twentieth century," L. S. Hearnshaw points out that "evolutionary biology introduced a new way of looking at minds, as something functional and dynamic, subject to the laws of heredity and variation, and developing from simple to complex by stages."[16] Led by William James, psychologists protested against "the static, analytic, isolated study of consciousness, divorced from the matrix of nature and society" (230). William McDougall, James Ward, G. F. Stout, and others joined to voice a common theme:

> Activity, conation, effort, striving, will, attention—call it what you like—was of the essence of mind. All this tuned in not only with certain philosophical trends then in the air, and expressed by philosophers like Nietzsche and Bergson, but also with the teachings of evolutionary biology. Impulse, not reason, was king, or, according to McDougall, a cluster of basic instincts which we share with other members of the animal kingdom. The more

> elaborate superstructure of human mentality was in the end merely subservient to these same instinctive drives. The savagery of the 1914–18 War, the apparent breakdown of rational and civilized behaviour in the accepted sense, the revelations of Freudian psychoanalysis and of the new art forms, all seemed to confirm the basic rightness of McDougall's viewpoint, and "hormic psychology," as it was termed, became extremely fashionable. The speculative nature of many of its proposals was overlooked. [230–31]

Anthropology and sociology were invoked to provide additional evidence of the derivative or subservient nature of the mind. As the ideas of Comte, Marx, and Durkheim and of late-nineteenth-century anthropologists such as Tylor and Levy-Bruhl began to be felt, McDougall, E. A. Ross, and Graham Wallas wrote books on social psychology, which became "a recognized branch of psychology." The term *behavior,* introduced in 1900 by Lloyd Morgan, and defined as "the reaction of that which we speak of as behaving, in response to certain surrounding conditions or circumstances which evoke the behaviour," was picked up in 1905 by McDougall in his *Physiological Psychology* and, migrating to America, became "the central defining concept of psychology, ousting all earlier claimants, experience, consciousness, and mind" (Hearnshaw, 233).

These key ideas exerted their influence during the period of Lawrence's most active intellectual growth. By 1912, when he became acquainted with Freud, Lawrence would find still another version of a "hormic" psychology that emphasized innate drives. The Freudian libido resembled the Schopenhauerian will and the Bergsonian élan vital; and as Hearnshaw observes, "the distinction between 'primary' and 'secondary' processes" (i.e., between energy striving for discharge and the blocking of discharge by preconscious or conscious resistance) fitted neatly not only onto the Freudian picture of the psyche but also onto the whole "doctrine of levels, propounded by Herbert Spencer, Hughlings Jackson, and the neurologists" (238). Consciousness, as Spencer argued, was concerned with "the establishment of correspondence" between organisms and their environments (a point Lawrence would repeat in *Psychology and the Unconscious*). Thought was instrumental, was a function of organic adaptation; and it was in the service of primitive organic needs. As Schopenhauer maintained, thought was a secondary activity.

It is within the context of this emphasis on "drives," or "will," or "instinct" that Lawrence's psychology may be most clearly understood in its early development. Later on, by the time he wrote *Fantasia of the Unconscious,* he appears to have rejected many of the "speculative'' proposals of hormic psychologies. In particular, he rejected a mechanistic materialism that denied the creative, religious impulse in man; and he rejected evolution on similar grounds, preferring to believe in "the strangeness and rainbow-change of ever-renewed creative civilizations'' (Foreword, *FU*, 14). But that the basic principles of his psychology were shaped by his reading of materialists seems indisputable when a number of his key ideas are viewed in relation to the whole context of materialist and hormic thought.

HERBERT SPENCER

The climate of opinion that influenced Lawrence's thinking is perfectly exemplified in Herbert Spencer. In Spencer, as in Schopenhauer, Lawrence would have found the idea of psychic activity as a play of those forces that Lawrence described as inhuman. Whatever the reservations Lawrence had later about Spencer's idea of "force,'' we must remember Jessie Chambers's statement that Lawrence "swallowed materialism at a gulp.'' In truth, a number of ideas in Spencer's *First Principles* must have appealed to Lawrence.

Not the least perhaps was Spencer's very idea of a synthetic philosophy. In seeking the goal of philosophy, a "universal synthesis comprehending and consolidating [the] special syntheses [of all sciences]''[17]—in seeking, that is, a law to subsume all other laws in all other sciences—Spencer provided a model of the very procedures that Lawrence would follow in developing his own "philosophy.'' As Spencer traces the relationships of matter, motion, and force in all phenomena and seeks to exhibit everywhere—in physics, in chemistry, in biology, in sociology, and in psychology—those analogues, or correspondences, that testify to the operation of his first principles; so Lawrence, driven by the same rage for a supreme fiction, was to view all phenomena as manifestations of the God-stuff, which is polarized into fire and water, male and female, voluntary and sympathetic principles, and whose operation is manifested in the psyche, in society, and in the cosmos.

Spencer's whole discussion of force as an effect of "the Unknowable'' is paralleled by Lawrence's idea of the inhuman Source and the "unknown'' that lies behind all of our known world. When Spencer speaks of "that Reality which is behind the veil of Appearance'' and argues that man is "one of the works of the Unknown Cause; and when the Unknown Cause produces in him a certain belief, he is thereby authorized to profess and act out that belief'' (*First Principles*, 120, 133), one recalls Lawrence's deep conviction that man, as part of nature, must learn how to act "dynamically, from the Great Source'' and that he must act spontaneously on his deepest impulses, in unison with the great processes of which he is a manifestation. When Spencer argues, further, that the theologian and the scientist can agree in the recognition of "an Inscrutable Power manifested to us through all phenomena" and goes on to say that this recognition is "an essentially religious [position]—nay, is *the* religious one" (118, 119), one is led to see a strong parallel between Spencer's materialism and Lawrence's affirmation of the "Pan principle."

Yet again, there is Spencer's firm declaration that because homogeneity is unstable, "supremacy and subordination must establish themselves, as we see they do, throughout the structure of a society" (420). This view, strongly reinforced by Nietzsche, became an article of faith that Lawrence did not question: the foundation of Lawrence's idea of a "natural aristocracy."

Most striking, however, is Spencer's central notion of psychic activity as the correlate of physical forces—an idea that anticipates the view that Lawrence was to take in his analysis of psychic activity. Beginning with the postulate of "the persistence of force," Spencer argues that "each manifestation of force can be interpreted only as the effect of some antecedent force: no matter whether it be an inorganic action, an animal movement, a thought, or a feeling" (227). Psychic or mental energies are not self-created; they are correlates of physical forces. And since attraction and repulsion, or action and reaction, constitute the only forms "under which the workings of the Unknowable are cognizable by us" (230), Spencer is led to look for a "rhythm of motion" or oscillation throughout the whole of the universe. For rhythm, he argues, "results wherever there is a conflict of forces not in equilibrium. If the antagonist forces at any point are balanced, there is rest" (258). Thus rhythm, or action and reaction, becomes a law of life. It is observable in the periodicity of planets and of climatic conditions, in geologic upheavals and submergences, and in the rise and fall of species; within human society, it is seen in the rhythms of war and peace, in "the action and reaction of political progress," in the alternating "exaltation and depression" of religious attitudes, and in commerce in "industrial actions and re-actions . . . continually alternating" (271, 272, 503). In short, "it needs but to contemplate this repeated action and reaction, to see that it is, like every action and reaction, a consequence of the persistence of force" (274); "given the co-existence everywhere of antagonist forces . . . and rhythm is an inevitable corollary from the persistence of force" (275).

The idea that psychic activity is another such action and reaction of antagonist forces is naturally implicit in this principle. And the idea of action and reaction is linked to the idea that nature, or the Unknowable, always seeks a balance. The rhythms or oscillations throughout nature indicate a striving, over a period of time, for equilibrium. Thus in the human body, according to Spencer,

> there are rhythms which exhibit a balancing of opposing forces at each extreme, and the maintenance of a certain general balance. This is seen in the daily alternation of mental activity and mental rest—the forces expended during the one being compensated by the forces acquired during the other. It is also seen in the recurring rise and fall of each desire: each desire reaching a certain intensity, is equilibrated either by expenditure of the force it embodies, in the desired actions, or, less completely, in the imagination of such actions. [497–98]

All oscillations, all actions and reactions, at all levels of experience can be seen as the blind striving of the Unknowable to bring about a balance; and man's "feelings," Spencer argues, must be "in equilibrium with the external forces they encounter" (506). Man's freedom "must result from the complete equilibration between man's desires and the conduct necessitated by surrounding conditions" (506–7).

What is the most signifcant in this for our understanding of Lawrence's developing psychology is that the idea of balance is derived, as it had been derived by early Greek philosophers and physicians, from nature itself, and not from an Aristotelian concept of a golden mean. I say "significant" because increasingly it has appeared to me, as I have read critical studies of Lawrence's ideas, that "balance" has become, for the critics, a metaphysical abstraction or an ideal norm rather than an organic phenomenon, a striving of nature. Yet the striving for balance is a constant preoccupation of Lawrence's well-rounded characters. Characteristically, these characters oscillate, realizing that they have been too submissive or too independent, too soft or too hard, too trusting or not trusting enough, too sensual or too spiritual, too sympathetic or too proud, too selfless or too selfish. And as normal consciousness is preoccupied with the problem of achieving balance, so Lawrence came to insist, in *Fantasia of the Unconscious*, upon the premental centers' struggle for balance.

Lawrence's derivation of the psyche from the great physical "centers"—the solar plexus and the lumbar ganglion, the cardiac plexus and the thoracic ganglion—is certainly, as James C. Cowan has pointed out, "anatomical nonsense"; but as Cowan observes, these centers all have *regulating* functions. As metaphors, they provided what Lawrence was looking for in the psyche. (He professed no "scientific *exactitude*," he said, "particularly in terminology" [*PU*, 234–35].)

Nature, Lawrence argues, has provided us with an automatic balancing system, both physical and psychic. Left to itself, the body always seeks a balance; left to itself and not forced, the psyche also seeks a balance. Any imbalance breeds illness or a destructive reaction, as nature struggles blindly for an equilibrium. Hence it is necessary to learn how not to interfere with the deepest impulses and how to find a way of life in which opposed desires may be satisfied. Thus Lady Daphne in "The Ladybird" learns to live during the daytime with her conscious, spiritual husband and at night with Count Dionys, the lord of the underworld and of the destructive principle. In *Fantasia of the Unconscious* Lawrence reminds us that man, "in the daytime, must follow his own soul's greatest impulse, and give himself to life-work and risk himself to death," but that in the evening "the mind changes its activity," becomes passive, or is liberated from "the laws of idealism," released into passion or "blood-consciousness" (100, 172–73). The day self and the night self, the ideal and the non-ideal, non-mental selves, must exist separate but in equilibrium, just as man and woman, polarized, must remain separate but in conjunction. It seems fair to add that Lawrence sought this healthy balance in his own life: he enjoyed both his writing and his domestic chores, his reading and his gardening, criticism and horseback riding. As Frieda observed, "He worked hard as a relaxation and wrote for hard work" (*"Not I, But the Wind . . .,"* 153).

I have noted that in Spencer the idea of action and reaction and the seeking of a balance extends to the history of society. Spencer's tracing of the alternating rhythm of war and peace—"War, exhaustion, recoil—peace, prosperity, and renewed aggression:—see here the alternation more or less discernible in the military activities of both savage and civilized nations" (271)—is closely paralleled by Lawrence's view, in *Movements in European History,* of two dominant motives operating throughout history: "the motive of peace and increase, and the motive of contest and martial triumph. As soon as the appetite for martial adventure and triumph in conflict is satisfied, the appetite for peace and increase manifests itself, and *vice versa.* It seems a law of life" (344). Indeed, Lawrence's whole view of "the great, surging movements which rose in the hearts of men in Europe" stresses the alternation of "togetherness" and "apartness": the "great, surging movements" of history sweep "human beings together into one great concerted action, or [sweep] them apart for ever on the tides of opposition. These are movements which have no deducible origin. They have no reasonable cause, though they are so great that we must call them impersonal" (*MEH,* xi–xii). In short, history deals with "the unknown powers . . . that well up inside the hearts of men'' (xii–xiii), the great ''sympathetic'' and ''voluntary'' premental forces that Lawrence sees as originating in the unconscious.

The idea of action and reaction extends to Spencer's formulation of the supreme law of his philosophy. The universal synthesis that Spencer sought—a synthesis to be discovered, he argued, in ''a law of the continuous redistribution of matter and motion''—is the law of Evolution and Dissolution. The law may be stated briefly: ''Loss of motion and consequent integration, eventually followed by gain of motion and consequent disintegration'' (284). The integration of matter occurs from a ''diffused, imperceptible state, to a concentrated, perceptible state'' (284). Evolution at all levels—whether of the solar system, of organisms, or of society—is defined as ''an integration of matter and concomitant dissipation of motion; during which the matter passes from an indefinite, incoherent homogeneity to a definite, coherent heterogeneity; and during which the retained motion [i.e., motion transformed into material forms of force] undergoes a parallel transformation'' (394).

If force evolves in ever more heterogeneous forms (an idea that Lawrence certainly accepted in ''Study of Thomas Hardy''), evolution is itself governed by the rhythm of attraction and repulsion, and the universe must be seen as passing through eras of Evolution and Dissolution. As Spencer says near the conclusion of *First Principles*, ''apparently, the universally-co-existent forces of attraction and repulsion, which, as we have seen, necessitate rhythm in all minor changes throughout the Universe, also necessitate rhythm in the totality of its changes—produce now an immeasurable period during which the attractive forces predominating, cause universal concentration, and then an immeasurable period during which the repulsive forces predominating, cause universal diffusion—alternate eras of Evolution and Dissolution'' (529). The idea of the waxing and waning of the earth and of societies is almost as old as recorded history, to be sure. Lawrence could have got the idea from a hundred sources. But Spencer's vocabulary here, linking evolution to a loss of motion and dissolution to a gain of motion, is paralleled by Lawrence's discussion, in ''Study of Thomas Hardy,'' of the female impulse toward inertia and the male impulse toward motion. And in his discussion of historical epochs, Lawrence contrasts the homogeneity of the female society with the reaction into heterogeneity of the male society, with its emphasis on individuation away from the collective whole. Again, the idea of eras of evolution and dissolution is paralleled by Lawrence's discussion in *Women in Love* of the ''stream of synthetic creation'' and the ''dark river of dissolution.'' Lawrence's idea of the disintegration of our time—the drift down the dark river of dissolution—may thus be traceable, not necessarily to English romanticism, as Colin Clarke has traced it, but to the Law of Laws of Spencer's synthetic philosophy.

It seems reasonable to conclude that Lawrence's ''subjective science''—a phrase that, by the way, he could have found in Spencer—is more strongly indebted to Spencer than we have supposed it to be. But reductionist ideas were in the air, and to appreciate their impact on Lawrence's mind one must look at other materialists whom Lawrence read during his twenties.

ERNST HAECKEL

During his ''materialist'' period, Lawrence also read Ernst Haeckel's *The Riddle of the Universe,* a book that would have confirmed much that Lawrence found in Spencer. Haeckel's book is a fierce, uncompromising statement of monistic materialism and of the inseparability of chemical or material forces and spiritual or emotional facts. Haeckel's view of nature, indeed, suggests several of the ideas that Lawrence developed in his ''Hardy'' essay. Following the speculations of J. C. Vogt, Haeckel sees primitive matter in an ''original state of quiescence'' (''uncondensed'' matter that has ''the same mean consistency throughout'') and then dividing into ''great masses or centres of condensation,'' which he calls ''positive ponderable matter.'' The latter are endowed with ''the feeling of like or desire'' and are ''continually striving to complete the process of condensation''; the former, ''the negative, imponderable matter, on the other hand, offers a perpetual and equal resistance to the further increase of its strain and of the feeling of dislike connected therewith.''[18] In short, ''the whole drama of nature apparently consists in an alternation of movement and repose; yet the bodies at rest have an inalienable quantity of force, just as truly as those that are in motion'' (231). Such a view, with its emphasis on repose and movement, quiescence and differentiation, has striking affinities to Lawrence's discussion, in ''Study of Thomas Hardy,'' of nature's primal homogeneity and its differentiation, of the negative Will-to-Inertia and the positive Will-to-Motion—ideas that Delavenay also finds in Houston Stewart Chamberlain's *Foundations of the Nineteenth Century.*

Even more striking is the correspondence between Haeckel's view of the origins of emotion and Lawrence's idea of the soul as ''carbon.'' According to Haeckel, ''love'' and ''hate'' are manifested at the most primitive levels of matter:

> The different relation of the various elements towards each other, which chemistry calls "affinity," is one of the most important properties of ponderable matter; it is manifested in the different relative quantities or proportions of their combination in the intensity of its consummation. Each shade of inclination, from complete indifference to the fiercest passion, is exemplified in the chemical relation of the various elements towards each other, just as we find in the psychology of man, and especially in the life of the sexes. Goethe, in his classical romance, *Affinities*, compared the relations of pairs of lovers with the phenomenon of the same name in the formation of chemical combinations. The irresistible passion that draws Edward to the sympathetic Ottilia, or Paris to Helen, and leaps over all bounds of reason and morality, is the same powerful "unconscious" attractive force which impels the living spermatozoon to force an entrance into the ovum in the fertilization of the egg of the animal or plant—the same impetuous movement which unites two atoms of hydrogen to one atom of oxygen for the formation of a molecule of water. The fundamental *unity of affinity in the whole of nature*, from the simplest chemical process to the most complicated love story, was recognized by the great Greek scientist, Empedocles, in the fifth century B.C., in his theory of "the love and hatred of the elements." It receives empirical confirmation from the interesting progress of cellular psychology. . . . even the *atom* is not without a rudimentary form of sensation and will, or, as it is best expressed, of feeling *(aesthesis)* and inclination *(tropesis)*—that is, a universal "soul" of the simplest character. [224–25]

Human affinities, as well as human repulsions, are thus grounded in matter and in "the law of substance." Desire and aversion, love and hatred,

> "attraction" and "repulsion" seem to be the sources of will, that momentous element of the soul which determines the character of the individual. . . . Even at the lowest stages of organic life we find in all the protists those elementary feelings of like and dislike, revealing themselves in what are called their *tropisms*, in the striving after light and darkness, heat or cold, and in their different relations to positive and negative electricity. [127–28]

The passions of man are "absolutely amenable to physical laws" (128); and from this it follows that a writer, if he chooses to deal with man as the expression of the greater "inhuman will," as Lawrence wished to deal with him, must trace human feelings to their origins in matter, to attraction and repulsion, and particularly to the nature of carbon, "the chemical basis of life" (4). A "scientific" depiction of the carbon of the soul in its allotropic states has obvious similarities to Haeckel's "law of substance."

The similarities are evident, too, in Lawrence's and Haeckel's metaphysics. Haeckel's dogmatic monism has obvious affinities to Schopenhauer's doctrine of the will. The universe, according to Haeckel, is "eternal, infinite, illimitable. . . . Its substance, with its two attributes (matter and energy), fills infinite space, and is in eternal motion" (13). Thus substance or nature is identical with "God": "We adhere firmly to the pure, unequivocal monism of Spinoza: Matter, or infinitely extended substance, and spirit (or energy), or sensitive and thinking substance, are the two fundamental attributes or principal properties of the all-embracing divine essence of the world, the universal substance" (21). "God" becomes "an *intramundane* being. . . . everywhere identical with nature itself, and. . . . operative *within* the world as 'force' or energy"; from which it follows "necessarily that pantheism is *the world-system of the modern scientist*" (288–89).

Such a world system, because it says nothing about purpose or meaning, might well lead to despair, and when Haeckel points out that man "is but a tiny grain of protoplasm in the perishable framework of organic nature," just as "our mother-earth is a mere speck in the sunbeam in the illimitable universe," one is reminded of Lawrence's final vision of Paul Morel: "One tiny upright speck of flesh, less than an ear of wheat lost in the field," the world of "stars and sun, a few bright grains. . . . spinning round for terror, and holding each other in embrace, there in a darkness that outpassed them all, and left them tiny and daunted" (*SL*, 420). Yet this vision of terror and darkness could also be translated, by an imaginative thinker, into a profoundly affirmative vision of "the unity of affinity in the whole of nature"—a vision comparable in religious power to that of the "orthodox creed" which Lawrence had rejected.

From Haeckel and Spencer it is but a short step to behaviorism. Lawrence finally refused to take that step. But in his early reading, he was obviously much affected by a psychologist whose work has been described by C. H. Judd as "the really significant beginnings of behaviorism." In *Psychoanalysis and the Unconscious* Lawrence referred to him as "the immortal James."

WILLIAM JAMES

It was noted earlier that the idea of the physiological or chemical basis of life and consciousness is found everywhere in scientific writings at the turn of the century. William James is not generally regarded, and did not regard himself, as a materialist; indeed, his "special task," as

Gerald E. Myers has pointed out, was to show "how a psychology, rooted in physiology, can avoid materialism and mechanism."[19] Yet the great intellectual excitement that James stirred in his readers was largely the result of James's endorsement of "physiological psychology." "At present," James wrote in 1910, "Psychology is on the materialistic tack, and ought in the interests of ultimate success to be allowed full headway even by those who are certain she will never fetch the port without putting down the helm once more." Thus James's working hypothesis is that of "physiological psychology," the notion that "mental action may be uniformly and absolutely a function of brain-action, . . . being to the brain-action as effect to cause."[20] James acknowledges that his hypothesis "doubtless is materialism: it puts the Higher at the mercy of the Lower," for, "according to another 'working hypothesis,' that namely of physiology, the laws of brain-action are at bottom mechanical laws." But his protestation that the materialist position does not "in the least explain the *nature* of thought" and that his hypothesis in that sense "is not materialism" seemed unimportant to a number of his readers. Thus C. S. Peirce asserted that James's psychological methodology was "materialistic to the core"; and George Santayana concluded that James had "outdone the materialists themselves" by applying "the principle of the total and immediate dependence of mind on matter to several fields in which we are still accustomed only to metaphysical or psychological hypotheses."[21]

The young Lawrence was quick to grasp the significance of James's idea. Like James and Spencer, Lawrence accepted the view that the mind evolves as an instrument in the service of life ("Study of Thomas Hardy," *Phoenix*, 431). Its function is simply to enable the organism to adapt to the world. As James states: "Our various ways of feeling and thinking have grown to be what they are because of their utility in shaping our *reactions* on the outer world. On the whole, few recent formulas have done more service in psychology than the Spencerian one that the essence of mental life and bodily life are one, namely, 'the adjustment of inner to outer relations.' . . . Primarily then, and fundamentally, the mental life is for the sake of action of a perservative sort."[22] Fairly early in his intellectual development, Lawrence questioned the view that the sole purpose of life is survival, as one sees in his reflections on Schopenhauer; but he embraced without hesitation the view that the mind is "instrumental": it records or projects what the body feels in its instinctive life. "All the emotions belong to the body, and are only recognized by the mind" (*Phoenix II*, 493). Thus Lawrence takes over what came to be known as the James-Lange theory of the emotions. The emotions are the body's visceral states. They do not originate in "mental causes." We do not cry because we are sorry or strike because we are angry; rather, says James, "we feel sorry because we cry, angry because we strike, afraid because we tremble."[23]

Lawrence, however, carries the idea further. The body, as the origin of consciousness and ideals, registers a premental or unconscious knowledge which is not only prior to but also richer and more reliable than any conscious record or projection of the bodily experience. Ideas are formed from and are the result of "the emanation of dynamic impulse and the collision or communion of this impulse with its object" (*FU*, 76). Dynamic impulse—that is, the sympathetic and voluntary strivings of the unconscious—is more complex, subtler, and more variable than mental ideas can possibly suggest. The premental knowledge of the body is "life-knowledge," dynamic knowledge, or, as Lawrence speaks of it in *Studies in Classic American Literature*, "blood-knowledge, instinct, intuition, all the vast vital flux of knowing that goes on in the dark, antecedent to the mind" (*SCAL*, 84). When a man is truly living, Lawrence argues in "Study of Thomas Hardy," he "does not know [mentally] what he does, his mind, his consciousness, unacquaint [*sic*], hovers behind, full of extraneous gleams and glances, and altogether devoid of knowledge [i.e., dynamic premental knowledge]" (*Phoenix*, 431). The unconscious is thus "the fountain of real motivity" (*PU*, 207). And bodily motion is, as Richard J. Kuczkowski has observed, "at the heart of Lawrence's conception of the unconscious."[24] Building on the James-Lange theory of the emotions, Lawrence arrives at his famous statement that his "great religion is a belief in the blood, the flesh, as being wiser than the intellect. We can go wrong in our minds. But what our blood feels and believes and says, is always true" (*Letters*, 94). The blood cannot lie, for its direct living impulses have not been checked or disguised by the conscious ego or by the social self, which masquerades as the true self.

The implications are enormous. Conscious knowledge of the self and of the external world is always about a self and a world that *have just vanished*. And this idea is supported by James. James points out: "The present moment of consciousness is . . . the darkest in the whole series [of passing "selves" or "Thoughts"]. It may feel its own immediate existence . . . , but nothing can be known *about* it till it be dead and gone" (*Principles*, 323). In short, the "self" (which James defines as continuous Thought which appropriates or "repudiates" its various "constituents") can become an *object* for thought only after it is past. But in the present "the absolute original of my conscious selfhood" is simply "the sense of my bodily existence": "The nucleus of the '*me*' is always the bodily existence felt to be present at the time" (324n, 378).

This idea is echoed in "Study of Thomas Hardy," where Lawrence argues that the origin is physical: "the Law is the immediate law of the body"; "the senses, sensation, sensuousness, these things which are incontrovertibly Me, these are my God, these belong to God, said Job. And he persisted, and he was right. They issue from God on the female side" (*Phoenix*, 466, 453). The "me," which lies beneath all the secondary developments of consciousness, remains the living body. But this self can never be known ideally. Any definitions imposed upon its actual dynamic life are belated, futile attempts to seize a physical dynamic reality which is always changing. Thus Lawrence arrives at the conclusion that seemed so preposterous to Bertrand Russell: to know a thing mentally is to destroy it by removing it from the living process of change.

Here I touch on the "stream of consciousness." Lawrence's allusion to James's idea in *Psychoanalysis and the Unconscious* indicates the strength of its effect on his thinking:

> . . . the mysterious stream of consciousness. Immortal phrase of the immortal James! Oh stream of hell which undermined my adolescence! The stream of consciousness! I felt it streaming through my brain, in at one ear and out at the other. And again I was sure it went round in my cranium, like Homer's Ocean, encircling my established mind. And sometimes I felt it must bubble up in the cerebellum and wind its way through all the convolutions of the true brain. Horrid stream! Whence did it come, and whither was it bound? The stream of consciousness! [*PU*, 202–3]

The stream was horrid because its streaming suggests that there is no self, only a flux of thoughts and feelings. James's definition of the inner or subjective self as an appropriating or repudiating Thought, "at each moment different from that of the last moment, but *appropriative* of the latter, together with all that the latter called its own" (*Principles*, 379), thus puts into sharp focus a question that Lawrence had to wrestle with: whether there is a self beyond the passing Thought—that is, a deeper "established" self—or whether one is condemned to live solely as a stream of thoughts mechanically produced by the brain's action.

Lawrence's answer to this question is to take a different tack: to look for the self not in the conscious mind but in the unconscious. Thus in one sense he rejects James's view. Yet the idea that life, both conscious and unconscious, is continuous flow and change is paramount in Lawrence's psychology. One important implication of the idea that self is a stream or flow is Lawrence's idea that evil is fixity or permanence. It is but a step from this to the recognition of a pragmatic attitude as a means of dealing with an open-ended, ever-changing experience.

Pragmatism, as it is commonly understood, is alien to Lawrence's religious consciousness. But as Lawrence accepted Nietzsche's idea that philosophy is always provisional, always in need of revision and reinterpretation, so he came to accept the provisional and open attitudes of pragmatism along with the idea that the criterion for the acceptance of a belief is its "life value" (not its cash value!). When James, in his discussion of "attention," asks, in his pragmatic way, "*just what the effort to attend would effect if it were an original force,*" and then answers that such an effort might be "critical" because prolongation of attention might "make us act; and that act may seal our doom" (*Principles,* 428–29), he anticipates the argument in *Varieties of Religious Experience* (which Lawrence read) that belief is "dynamogenic." The belief in free will has salutary effects. As James says in *Principles of Psychology,* "the whole feeling of reality, the whole sting and excitement of our voluntary life, depends on our sense that in it things are *really being decided* from one moment to another, and that it is not the dull rattling off of a chain that was forged innumerable ages ago" (429). The Lawrence who decried mechanistic materialism would have welcomed such an assertion, while adding that the "effort to attend" is the result of a deep organic desire. In that strange chapter "Cosmological" in *Fantasia of the Unconsciousness,* Lawrence underscores the importance of *directing attention* to life and the living individual as the clue to the universe. Arguing that the cosmos is the product of "the dead bodies and energies of bygone individuals," and that the dead soul is "incorporate in the living soul," he goes on to say:

> How this all is, and what are the laws of the relation between life and death, the living and the dead, I don't know. But that this relation exists, and exists in a manner as I describe it, for my own part I know. And I am fully aware that once we direct attention this way, instead of to the absurdity of the atom, then we have a whole *living* universe of knowledge before us. The universe of life and death, of which we, whose business it is to live and to die, know nothing. Whilst concerning the universe of Force and Matter we pile up theories and make staggering and disastrous discoveries of machinery and poison-gas, all of which we were much better without.
>
> It is life we have to live by, not machines and ideals. [*FU,* 152]

To direct attention toward life and towards the relationship of life to the cosmos is *pragmatically* the wisest course; it pays dividends—by restoring man to the bosom of nature.

There are other ways, too, in which "the immortal James" might have appealed to Lawrence. James's endorsement of materialism is, as we have noted, equivocal. For while James puts the "Higher at the mercy of the Lower," he notes that the materialistic hypothesis does not explain the *nature* of thought. In fact, as Gerald E. Myers has pointed out, James's view does not reduce consciousness to mechanistic materialism. James carefully distinguishes between nervous or mechanical activity and mental or intelligent activity, the latter being marked by the " 'pursuance of future ends and the choice of means for their attainment.' "[25] In short, consciousness is goal-directed. Depending on its interests, it selects or repudiates various "constituents." So, it is possible for James to point out that "characteristic ethical energies" are exhibited in the choice to "keep the foot unflinchingly on the arduous path" (*Principles*. 276). If thought is thus purposive and if, as James assumes, thought is in the service of instinct or deep organic needs, it follows that one of man's deep needs is for purposive action. In this way, James opens the door to the conclusion that Lawrence, with his deep religious passion, had to affirm: that "the ultimate, greatest desire in man is [the] desire for great *purposive* activity" (*FU*, 109).

James's discussion of the "selective industry" that is the life of man's "inner or subjective being" suggests still another idea that became important in Lawrence's analysis of the psyche. Lawrence's notion of "sympathetic or antipathetic" vibrations between the self and the world has been traced to his reading of Madame Blavatsky, James M. Pryse, and other dealers in the curious wares of theosophy and the occult. But the idea is not necessarily mystical. For James, the subjective self is "the home of interest" or "the source of effort and attention." Consciousness is a "welcoming or opposing, appropriating or disowning." Even "primary reactions are like the opening or the closing of the door," as if every item in experience has to pass "an entrance-examination." The subjective self is thus a core of "turnings-toward and turnings-from" (*Principles*, 285–89). The things we feel most deeply are those which are "ours" in the sense that they are supremely interesting to this selective consciousness and provide "excitement" in the stream of thought. James does not invoke "vibrations" to account for the "turnings-toward and turnings-from," but his idea is obviously akin to Lawrence's notion that "between an individual and any external object with which he has an affective connection, there exists a certain vital flow," and this flow is "either sympathetic or antipathetic" (*FU*, 131–32). Primary reactions are receptive or not, as in James. The "spirit of place" may affect one positively or negatively. (For Richard Somers in *Kangaroo*, "sympathetic" Australia is "antipathetic"; for Kate Leslie in *The Plumed Ser-*

pent, "voluntary" Mexico is "antipathetic.") An encounter with another person may cause a "slight disturbance in my own vibration," and when confronting a Negro, a white man may "put up a resistance" or "allow the disturbance [of the blood] to continue, because, after all, there is some peculiar alien sympathy between us" (*Phoenix II,* 618). The idea of sympathetic receptiveness or voluntary resistance to an object is fundamental in Lawrence's psychology. And James's discussion of interest, attention, and the "selective industry" of consciousness also became an important part of the educational theory that Lawrence developed after he encountered Jamesian ideas in education courses at Nottingham University.

Further elaboration of the parallels between James's thinking and Lawrence's would become too speculative. Perhaps James's discussion of "the social self," bound to its mates by feelings of "amativeness" and "sympathy," stuck in Lawrence's mind as he worked out his sharp contrasts between "The Individual Consciousness V. the Social Consciousness" (*Phoenix,* 761–64). Also interesting to Lawrence, as his letter to Louie Burrows on 23 December 1907 indicates, was James's idea of a world soul, or cosmic consicousness. (James says in *Principles of Psychology,* "I find the notion of some sort of *anima mundi* thinking in all of us to be a more promising hypothesis, in spite of all its difficulties, than that of a lot of absolutely individual souls" [328].) Of greatest importance to Lawrence, however, remains James's insistence that feeling and thought cannot be divorced from impulse or instinct: ". . . all the shiftings and expansions and contractions of the sphere of what shall be considered me and mine, are but the results of the fact that certain *things* appeal to primitive and instinctive impulses of our nature." To understand "mind" and "self," one must look at "the survival of the fittest" (*Principles,* 304, 308), at the fact that "interest in things" is the result of organic adaptation. It is "selective interest," originating in organic needs, that makes a self what it is. Lawrence might have been impatient with James's *reduction* of "self" to a "passing Thought" or with James's emphasis on survival; but James's psychology was a strong breeze to swell the sails of a younger Lawrence.

In his study of education at Nottingham University College, Lawrence certainly encountered views very similar to James's when he read the lively, undogmatic essays entitled *The Herbartian Psychology Applied to Education,* by John Adams, president of the Educational Institute of Scotland. Adams refers to James several times, with strong approval. He considers the view that consciousness is a mere epiphenomenon—the view that, as T. H. Huxley maintained, "conscious ness is a mere by-product, a sort of accident, something that has no more to do with the working of the brain than a steam whistle has with the working of the locomotive''; or, as Cabanis held, ''the brain secretes thought as the liver secretes bile.''[26] Adams presents this physiological view of consciousness only to reject it (as James also rejected it), for ''scientific men cannot satisfy even themselves with the theory that ideas are a sort of morbid secretion of specially modified protoplasm'' (37). But Adams notes with interest William James's reversal of ''the usual view of the causal relation between emotion and its expression.'' The usual view is that emotion originates in consciousness; James, however, says that emotion is inseparable from bodily symptoms: ''If we fancy some strong emotion, and then try to abstract from our consciousness of it all the feelings of its bodily symptoms, we find we have nothing left behind, no mind-stuff out of which the emotions can be constituted, and that a cold and neutral state of intellectual perception is all that remains'' (255). Such ''physiologico-psychological theories,'' says Adams, ''have a great deal to do with the real work of teaching''; and he approves Maudsley's conclusion that ''conciousness is the result, not the cause of the excitation'' which arises when we voluntarily direct attention towards an object (255, 257). Adams argues, in consequence, that ''the result of a course of education is no longer to be tested by the amount of knowledge acquired, but by the strength and variety of the interests aroused'' (277), and he concludes that ''only in so far as a man makes the most of his nature does he fulfil his function in the organism of which he forms a part'' (278): ''John must develop, and that according to fixed laws. What those laws are can be discovered only by learning the course of nature. Find what nature wills, says the Froebelian, and do that. John must develop according to the laws of his own nature; his development must be self-development, development from within. Before, therefore, we can educate John, we must know him'' (40). Thus the new education places the emphasis on ''interest,'' on ''self-expression,'' or on ''true selfishness,'' a benign selfishness that means making the most of one's own nature.

In ''Education of the People,'' Lawrence echoes Adams's conclusion by laying down, as his ''ideal for a new system of education,'' the principle that ''every man shall be himself, shall have every opportunity to come to his own intrinsic fullness of being'' (*Phoenix*, 603). Because the inner or subjective life is ''the home of interest,'' as James argued, Lawrence had no doubt that any education which divorces subject matter from the child's interests is bound to fail. In discussing the right way to teach geography, for example, he insists that the child must have an "affective connection" with the material he studies. "The soul must give earnest attention," and "the discipline of the soul's full attention" can occur only when the child makes the material his own—for example, when a child makes a clay landscape "entirely according to its own fancy" (*FU*, 94). The essential point is that consciousness is the result, not the cause, of an excitation of interest. For Lawrence that excitation arises not mechanically but vitally, in the child's creative impulse, in the striving for maximum of being. To explain consciousness, then, science must move beyond mechanical and reductive explanations. As Ursula realizes at the university, life is not merely "a conjuction of forces, physical and chemical"; a pure materialism does not explain the "intention" of the will that urges human beings towards that selfhood which is "a consummation, a being infinite" (*R*, 441). Lawrence would have endorsed heartily Adams's conclusion that one must first "find what nature wills . . . and do that."

More important than Spencer, Haeckel, and James in their influence on Lawrence were Schopenhauer and Nietzsche, whose thought I shall examine in the next chapter. The naturalism of Schopenhauer and Nietzsche entails no fundamental departure, however, from the four premises of materialistic thought that I listed earlier. The thinking of many of the foremost scientists and philosophers of his time converged to reinforce Lawrence's conviction that life is the manifestation of the inhuman will or force that remains unknown; that men, like atoms, are driven by the forces of attraction and repulsion—by the deep "sympathetic" and "voluntary" impulses; that the mind is in the service of impulse, but falsifies by creating a belated and frozen picture of the flux of reality; and that all of nature, in the "systole-diastole" of creation and destruction, is the "God-stuff" objectified.

Not mystics, not dabblers in the occult, but the sternest and most highly respected naturalists were the chief sources of Lawrence's "mystical materialism."

2

Lawrence's Psychology, II: Schopenhauer and Nietzsche

DHLDHLDHLDHLDHLDHLDHLDHLDHLDHLDHLDHLDHLDHLDHLDHLDHLDHLDHLDHLDHLDHLDHLDHLDHLDHLDHLDHLDHLDHLDHLDHLDHLDHLDHLDHLDHLDHLDHLDHLDHL

SCHOPENHAUER

D. H. Lawrence first read Schopenhauer in 1905 or 1906, and as Émile Delavenay has observed, "it must have been refreshing for Lawrence to discover in a writer as respected as Schopenhauer the theory that sexual passion is the primary motivating drive of all human activity."[1] But Schopenhauer's naturalistic vision of life contained something else that the puritanical Lawrence probably would have required in any philosophy he embraced wholeheartedly: in expounding his philosophy of the will, Schopenhauer would have appealed not only to Lawrence's religious doubts, as Delavenay observes, but also to Lawrence's profound religious passion.

When Schopenhauer spoke of "the immortal part" of man, in a passage that Lawrence underlined and that prompted him to add two exclamation points in the margin, and when Schopenhauer called attention to the affinities between his doctrine of the will and Hindu and Buddhist ideas, the German philosopher suggested a naturalistic equivalent to the Absolute of Christianity that Lawrence had rejected. Moreover, Schopenhauer's "sharp distinction of will from knowledge"—a distinction that emphasized "the primacy of the former" and that constituted, Schopenhauer said, "the fundamental characteristic of my philosophy"[2]—was to become so important in Lawrence's thinking that a major part of Lawrence's art can be regarded as a development from the Schopenhauerian antithesis between *will* and *idea*. As Alan R. Zoll has observed, "Lawrence's works can be taken as a progression of working out the implication of Schopenhauer's ideas,"[3] a progression that, in Zoll's analysis, focuses on three important manifestations of Schopenhauerian and of vitalist thought. First, Lawrence emphasizes "the sense of the individuality of the self as a . . . unique manifestation of the universal Will" ("the vitalists' subtle but important modification of the traditional Great Chain of Being into the universal Great Chain of Phenomena'' [4]). Second, Lawrence adopts the idea of sexual *Polarität,* but revises this idea to make polarity ''not only a basis of struggle but, antiperistatically, . . . a basis of renewal for the individual of either sex.'' (''Sexual polarization'' became, for Lawrence, ''the fundamental source'' of the attainment of ''fulness of being'' [6, 10].) Third, Lawrence seizes on the opposition between will and idea, and the consequent opposition of ''*Empfindung,* or sensuous apperception, to the more traditional *Erkennens* [*sic;* read *Erkenntnis*], or strictly intellectual knowledge'' (7).

Zoll's fine analysis of the ways in which Lawrence drew upon and modified Schopenhauer's thought is so comprehensive that further analysis of Lawrence's philosophical indebtedness to Schopenhauer would now seem almost supererogatory. But though Lawrence's philosophical response to Schopenhauer has been sensitively traced, criticism has not yet focused, except in a very limited way, on Lawrence's development from Schopenhauer's ideas of the basic premises of his psychology. It is this development that will be traced here. As I hope to show, the chief question raised for Lawrence the psychologist by Schopenhauer's metaphysics is whether the individual is motivated solely by the will, or whether there are other sources of motivation that Schopenhauer's ideas fail to take into account. And for Lawrence there remained the difficult problem of determining exactly what it is that the will *wills.* Is it simply a will to live? Lawrence' reflections on this question lead him inevitably to emphasize, as Schopenhauer had emphasized, the affinities of the doctrine of the will to the eastern idea of metempsychosis—an idea which, metaphorically, is absolutely central in Lawrence's psychology.

Lawrence's early psychology, as Delavenay and Mitzi M. Brunsdale have pointed out,[4] focuses on a key idea in Schopenhauer's essay ''The Metaphysics of Love.'' With a blind ingenuity, the will, in order to achieve ''the best for the species,'' contrives to ensure that in sexual attraction each partner will select a mate who possesses the characteristics that he or she lacks. To preserve the *type,* nature takes care to ensure that ''the *will* of the man and the *intellect* of the woman are specially suitable to each other'' (90). Woman, Schopenhauer argues, ''is won especially by firmness of will, decision, and courage, and perhaps also by honesty and goodheartedness. . . . Want of understanding does a man no harm with women'' (84); hence, in a passage that Brunsdale quotes: ''One often sees an ugly, stupid, and coarse fellow get the better of a cultured, able, and amiable man with women. Also marriages from love are sometimes consummated between natures which are mentally very different: for example, the man is rough, powerful, and stupid; the woman tenderly sensitive, delicately thoughtful, cultured, aesthetic, &c.; or the man is a genius and learned, the woman a goose'' (84). That Lawrence was impressed by this idea is indicated by his assertion in *Fantasia of the Unconscious:* ''The woman who thinks and talks as we do is almost sure to have no dynamic blood-polarity with us. The dynamic blood-polarity would make her different from me, and not like me in her thought mode'' (*FU*, 175). Moreover, as Delavenay has pointed out, the Schopenhauerian formula explains nicely the union of Lawrence's own parents, and as Brunsdale has noted (though without providing illustrations), Lawrence's early fiction often centers on such attractions.[5] In *The White Peacock*, for example, Lawrence dramatizes exactly such an attraction of opposites and such a love for what one lacks: George Saxton, the man of the flesh, seeks completion in Lettie Beardsall, the woman of highly developed consciousness; Lettie, aware of her loss of a vital connection with nature, is drawn to George, the natural man. As Schopenhauer maintained, ''the physical qualities of two individuals can be such that, for the purpose of restoring as far as possible the type of the species, the one is quite specially and perfectly the completion or supplement of the other, which therefore desires it exclusively'' (90). In such cases, passion ''gains a nobler and more sublime appearance from the fact that it is directed to an individual object, and to it alone''; and where sexual selection is so highly individualized, the intensity of desire ''attains a vehemence that no other wish ever reaches, and therefore makes one ready for any sacrifice, and in case its fulfilment remains unalterably denied, may lead to madness or suicide'' (90). Brunsdale notes that Schopenhauer in this passage might again have suggested to Lawrence the plots of his early fiction. Thus in *The White Peacock* George Saxton, after losing Lettie, makes the profound error of marrying Meg, who is not his temperamental complement, and plunges self-destructively into drink; and in *The Trespasser* Siegmund commits suicide when he realizes that he cannot marry Helena.

But the idea that ''each loves what he lacks'' was only the starting point of Lawrence's reasoning about the nature of sexual motivation. He was quick to generalize the idea: to see that the love of what one lacks is more than a sexual desire; it is also a desire to overcome separation, or divorce, from nature itself, from the whole of the cosmos. Man, confronted existentially by his awareness that he is merely ''derivative,'' merely a fragment of the Whole, seeks to unite himself with the All (all that is ''Not-I'') in the act of loving. His desire is not just to perpetuate the species but to be restored to the primal unity of nature and so to achieve a godlike wholeness and infinitude.

Thus Lawrence appears to have taken seriously Schopenhauer's sardonic observation that the lover imagines "an infinite blessedness which is to be found for him in the union with this female individual" (95). There is indeed a sense in which the lover, in the act of love, approaches infinite blessedness. But Lawrence saw clearly that such blessedness and completion are not made possible solely in the love relationship. The males in *The White Peacock* and *The Rainbow*, imagining that woman will provide "infinite blessedness" and wedding themselves to the Magna Mater (the center of reality that they imagine will give them security), discover that their weddings destroy their individuality, and they become mere slaves or servants of the female. Satisfaction of the "love," or "sympathetic," impulse is not enough: as Schopenhauer had suggested (a suggestion that was strongly reinforced by Nietzsche), there is also a psychological concern for "the individual and its perfection"—that is, a need to establish one's identity. I shall say more about this presently.

While Schopenhauer's thinking about love for what one lacks was thus a strong spur to Lawrence's early reflections on the nature of the desire, even more important to Lawrence was the general Schopenhauerian vision of life as the objectification of the will and the Schopenhauerian distinction between will and idea—between the *Ding an sich* and the phenomenal world. For the psychologist the Schopenhauerian metaphysics raises several important questions. If one grants that men can desire only what nature desires (what the will desires), the question remains, what exactly does the will desire? Is it solely a will to live? What "directions" or chief "promptings" or "impulses" does the will give rise to? Only the sexual impulse? As for the mind, is it totally powerless, totally in the service of the will? Or is it capable of directing life against the blind impulses of the will?

Lawrence obviously was quick to accept Schopenhauer's central contention that the world known to the intellect is, as Kant had maintained, phenomenal and that, indeed, the phenomenal world of multiplicity, time, and change is but maya, while the reality, "the premiss of all premisses," exists prior to knowledge and consciousness. Lawrence's prolonged attack on conscious knowing is clearly derived from Schopenhauer's idea that the will cannot be comprehended by the intellect (38) and that, indeed, all knowing is false. Writes Schopenhauer:

> For as soon as I *know*, I have an idea; but this idea, just because it is *my* idea, cannot be identical with what is known, but repeats it in an entirely different form, for it makes a being for other out of a being for self, and is thus always to be regarded as a phenomenal

> appearance of the thing in itself. Therefore for a *knowing* consciousness, however it may be constituted, there can be always only phenomena. This is not entirely obviated even by the fact that it is my own nature which is known; for, since it falls within my *knowing* consciousness, it is already a reflex of my nature, something different from this itself, thus already in a certain degree phenomenon. So far, then, as I am a knowing being, I have even in my own nature only a phenomenon; so far, on the other hand, as I am directly this nature itself, I am not a *knowing* being. . . . knowledge is only a secondary property of our being. [''On Death,'' 151]

As early as 1906 in his poetry,[6] and then very elaborately in 1911 in *The Trespasser*, Lawrence had seized upon this fundamental distinction between maya and reality. In *The Trespasser* the world of sunlit forms, of individuals and change and motion and time, is an illusion of warmth and tenderness that Siegmund experiences as he blossoms in his love for Helena; but beneath this world is the cold unliving darkness of the sea, a world of matter indifferent to him and cruel. Unable to overcome the blind forces of nature, Siegmund ceases to fight to affirm the flame of life. The sunlit world becomes unreal to him, and he commits suicide, reflecting that life is ''but a flame that bursts off the surface of darkness and tapers into the darkness again'' (159) and that ''if the spark goes out, the essence of the fire is there in the darkness'' (166).[7]

Thus Lawrence very early appears to have taken over the Schopenhauerian contrast between the world as will and the world as idea. The intellect creates a false picture of reality. We can ''go wrong in our minds''; the blood, which is the desire of the will, is always wiser than the intellect. Efforts to force life to take a direction determined by the mind rather than by the inhuman will are bound to cause psychic damage. As Schopenhauer said: ''If [the sexual impulse of the will] is voluntarily suppressed, as we see in rare exceptions, then this is the turning of the will, which changes its course. The will does not transcend the individual, but is abolished in it. Yet this can only take place by means of the individual doing painful violence to itself'' (111). Lawrence accepted this view of repression. The mind may seek to change the course of the will and may apparently succeed for a time in resisting the will's promptings, but the only healthy use of the mind is to act in accordance with the deepest promptings. Here one should note also that because man as knower, as intellect or ego, is not the real man, the *Ding an sich*, Lawrence sought for ways to move beyond conventional representations of the ego and of mental causes in human behavior. As he said in his famous letter to Edward Garnett, in reference to Emilio Marinetti and the Futurists, he was interested in "the inhuman will, call it physiology, or like Marinetti—physiology of matter": he did not care about the *ego* of a woman but about what "she *is* as a phenomenon (or as representing some greater, inhuman will)" (5 June 1914).

The question remains, what *are* the deepest promptings of that greater, inhuman will? Sexual desire is clearly the chief prompting. But beyond sexual desire there is also the animal's desire to defend itself against all hostile forces in the environment. Lawrence takes over Schopenhauer's basic conception of the will as a force that expresses itself both in a "longing for union" and in a resistance to dissolution. The "inner nature" of the forces within matter (in "unorganized nature"), Schopenhauer argues, is discovered in gravitation, "that longing for union which proceeds from the very inner nature of bodies" (63); and even in organized nature, in living things, "all manifestations of this fundamental effort [of self-preservation] may constantly be traced back to a seeking or pursuit and a shunning or fleeing from, according to the occasion" (61). There is a "constant tension between centripetal and centrifugal force," which is the "universal essential conflict of the manifestation of the will" (*World as Will and Idea,* 1:193).

The oscillation of attraction and repulsion—a longing for union and a resistance to union—is precisely what we witness in much of *The Rainbow,* where the "sympathetic" impulse to fuse with another person alternates with the "voluntary" impulse to withdraw and hold oneself intact, independent. A novelist determined to present man as a manifestation of "some greater, inhuman will" would have to seek his motive forces in just such electromagnetic oscillations. To treat of human behavior as the objectification of the will, Lawrence had to work into his novels a pattern of centripetal and centrifugal to-and-fros.

Yet Lawrence was also uneasy about Schopenhauer's conception of the will. His doubt about the adequacy of the conception is revealed as early as 1910 in *The White Peacock,* where Lettie smiles at the Schopenhauerian idea that one is sacrificed for the sake of the species; it is evident, too, in *The Trespasser,* where the Nietzschean idea of striving "beyond oneself" is contrasted with the Schopenhauerian idea of acquiescing passively to nature's will. Then in "Study of Thomas Hardy" Lawrence seeks to define explicitly the nature of the will in relation to the phenomenal world. In his discussion of Hardy's *Return of the Native,* Lawrence first presents Hardy's Egdon Heath as the symbol of the will:

> What is the real stuff of tragedy in the book? It is the Heath. It is the primitive, primal earth, where the instinctive life heaves up. There, in the deep, rude stirrings of the instincts, there was the reality that worked the tragedy. Close to the body of things, there can be heard the stir that makes us and destroys us. The heath heaved with raw instinct. Egdon, whose dark soil was strong and crude and organic as the body of a beast. Out of the body of this crude earth are born Eustacia, Wildeve, Mistress Yeobright, Clym, and all the others. They are one year's accidental crop. What matters if some are drowned or dead, and others preaching or married: what matter, any more than the withering heath, the reddening berries, the seedy furze, and the dead fern of one autumn of Egdon? The Heath persists. Its body is strong and fecund, it will bear many more crops besides this. Here is the sombre, latent power that will go on producing, no matter what happens to the product. Here is the deep, black source from whence all these little contents of lives are drawn. And the contents of the small lives are spilled and wasted. There is savage satisfaction in it: for so much more remains to come, such a black, powerful fecundity is working there that what does it matter?
>
> Three people die and are taken back into the Heath; they mingle their strong earth again with its powerful soil, having been broken off at their stem. It is very good. Not Egdon is futile, sending forth life on the powerful heave of passion. It cannot be futile, for it is eternal. What is futile is the purpose of man.
>
> Man has a purpose which he has divorced from the passionate purpose that issued him out of the earth into being.[8] [*Phoenix*, 415]

Beginning with the eternal will, Lawrence, like Schopenhauer, contemplates the alternation of death and reproduction. Like Schopenhauer, Lawrence sees that being or nature is "devoid of knowledge" and that man's consciousness "hovers behind" the reality of actual being (*Phoenix*, 431). But at this point in his essay, Lawrence turns to an idea that Schopenhauer had not emphasized but that is, as Zoll has pointed out, significant in vitalist thought. Lawrence sees life as a striving toward maximum differentiation, or "maximum of being":

> It seems as though one of the conditions of life is, that life shall continually and progressively differentiate itself, almost as though this differentiation were a Purpose. Life starts crude and unspecified, a great Mass. And it proceeds to evolve out of that mass ever more distinct and definite particular forms, an ever-multiplying number of separate species and orders, as if it were working always to the production of the infinite number of perfect individuals, the individual so thorough that he should have nothing in

> common with any other individual. It is as if all coagulation must be loosened, as if the elements must work themselves free and pure from the compound. [*Phoneix*, 431]

Indeed, the reaction against homogeneity, he says, "has become extended and intensifed," and he imagines a future in which "wonderful, distinct individuals, like angels, move about, each one being himself, perfect as a complete melody or a pure colour" (432).

In emphasizing what might be called a will to differentiation along with the blind will to live, Lawrence thus draws upon the vitalist idea of creative evolution; and he also picks up Nietzsche's notion of a will to power, or to overcome, as a dominant motive force behind appearances. (The idea was in Lawrence's mind as early as 1911, when, in *The Trespasser*, Siegmund's Doppelgänger, Hampson, suggests to Siegmund that man must "strive beyond himself.") This is not to say that Lawrence rejects Schopenhauer's view that the individual exists within the will. To the end of his life, Lawrence would remain convinced that individuality is an illusion (see, for example, *The Plumed Serpent*), that the world created by the mind is false, and that the supreme lesson of consciousness is to learn *not* to know—and how to live in unison with the will. But Lawrence felt it necessary to stress a will to differentiation if only because he believed that mere procreation can never satisfy man's deep need to be "utterly himself" and his need for an Absolute.

His questioning of the Schopenhauerian will to live was thus very close. A significant marginal comment by Lawrence refers to Schopenhauer's contention that the lover is "ready to make any kind of sacrifice" for his beloved because "the immortal part of him is yearning for her." Lawrence, as noted previously, underlined the words "the immortal part of him" and added two exclamation points in the margin, along with the remark, "Is the 'will to live' the only immortal part?" (Brunsdale, 72). Delavenay explains this question as issuing from Lawrence's religious upbringing or from Lawrence's personal experiences with Jessie Chambers and other women; but Brunsdale suggests more plausibly that Lawrence felt "a limitation in Schopenhauer because of a developing notion of vitalistic personal belief" (73). Although Brunsdale does not amplify her remark, she means, I think, that Lawrence had decided that there is, in addition to the will to live, an immortal will to become a "greater man," a will toward transcendence, or a will toward differentiation.

Such an idea, as Lawrence develops it in "Study of Thomas Hardy," is related to Schopenhauer's notion that there is more to sexual union than procreation. For Schopenhauer argues in "The Metaphysics of Love" that the mere sexual impulse is "ignoble," but the "individualising, and with it the intensity of the love, can reach so high a degree that without its satisfaction all the good things in the world, and even life itself, lose their value" (90). In a similar vein, Lawrence says: "In love, a man, a woman, flows on to the very furthest edge of known feeling, being, and out beyond the furthest edge: and taking the superb and supreme risk, deposits a security of life in the womb" (*Phoenix*, 441). He asks: "Am I here to deposit security, the continuance of life," or is this but "a minor function"? What is important, he concludes, is that both male and female "drive on to the edge of the unknown, and beyond" (441). They overcome their incompleteness as distinct sexual beings and discover wholeness of being in their union. Such wholeness Lawrence equates with "the whole consciousness"—that is, a consciousness of being richer than that which the male or female can know in isolation.

Lawrence develops this idea in considerable detail. The universe, he argues, beginning in "one motionless homogeneity," must have "reacted" against "the vast, homogeneous inertia" (432).[9] Here Lawrence may have had in mind Schopenhauer's idea that the condition of "every world that is formed into a globe cannot be rest, but motion," a centrifugal resistance to centripetal force.[10] The reaction and motion are essentially a male reaction against a female inertia or, to put the matter differently, a reaction of spirit, or consciousness, against undifferentiated matter, or unconsciousness. But this reaction, Lawrence argues, though not "frictionless," is not in opposition to the female. Rather, the female is the axle on which the male turns, and "the axle and wheel are one." The male and the female, broken off from the primal unity of the will, can return to that unity, become "two in one, fused," and hence "infinite and eternal" (442–44). Such fusion, which is identification with the will, is "complete consciousness" or the "flower" which is the maximum of being. The individual escapes an illusory individuality as distinct male or as distinct female and acquires, in sexual union, a greater individuality, that of the male and female joined. One becomes, in effect, the *whole* will rather than a fragment of the whole.

Thus a will to differentiation and the will to union are joined or balanced. The male individuality is not sacrificed to the will; on the contrary, the male achieves a greater individuality by "cleaving" to the axle of the female. His male "consicousness" is expanded; it is not mere *knowing*, but, rather, a sort of life consciousness, a consciousness centered on and deriving strength from the Source itself. It is consciousness of relatedness, of man's relationship not merely to women but to "the female" in all forms. It is "vital truth," or knowing in nature—that is, a knowing of vital interconnectedness, of self-in-the-All. In the language Lawrence later employed, a "voluntary" reaction of consciousness is balanced by the "sympathetic" union with the rest of the cosmos. As Lawrence says, speaking of the female Will-to-Inertia and the male Will-to-Motion: "The human effort [must] be always to recover balance, to symbolize and so to possess that which is missing. Which is the religious effort of Man" (447). The male's desire for the female is an admission of deficiency; the female's desire for the male is a similar admission. Each loves what he or she lacks. But when male and female join in union, each attains to "the Absolute, the Eternal, Infinite, Unchanging" (446). In short, each attains to "God"—or to the will, the eternal unchanging reality behind the multiplicity of phenomena. The truth is, Lawrence points out, that the very "division into male and female is arbitrary, for the purpose of thought" (448). For male and female are finally one, as motion and rest are one if viewed "completely"—that is, if we recognize that they are but appearances relative to the observer.

The discussion of motion and inertia is closely linked to the fiction Lawrence was writing during this period. In *The Rainbow,* motion is associated with the desire for "the beyond" (for consciousness, for education, for religion), while immobility is linked with the passive acceptance of "the blood" and the cycles of death and reproduction. In his effort to consolidate his system, Lawrence gradually began to alter certain facts of his personal life. Women like his mother or Jessie Chambers were conscious, or "spiritual," and looked to "the beyond," like the women in the Marsh valley. Men like his father were unconscious, like Tom Brangwen. But as the novel develops, Lawrence takes a more philosophical—or a more Schopenhauerian—view of the sexes. Woman becomes the womb of nature, conserver of life, procreator; man, released from the burden of childbearing, is freed to adventure into the unknown. But man, "a raging activity, change potent within change," needs woman for his "sense of stability." "She supplies him with the feeling of Immutability, Permanence, Eternality" (*Phoenix,* 446). All the males in *The Rainbow* view woman in this way, and each woman realizes that she must find "a hub" for her stability. Without these relationships, "Either the particular woman breaks down before the stress of the man, becomes erratic herself, no stay, no centre; or else the man is insufficiently active to carry out the static principle of his female, of his woman" (*Phoenix,* 447).

All of *The Rainbow* and of *Women in Love* is implicit in such an observation. The males, insufficiently active or conscious, are unable to find a purpose beyond that of serving women; they are insufficiently differentiated, only half-created, half-developed. The females, unable to live with men who have no purpose and no real courage to adventure into the unknown, become erratic, seeking fulfillment in a freedom that is irresponsible and chaotic. Only Ursula and Rupert Birkin in *Women in Love* find the right union and right balance.

But a crucial condition must be met by the Lawrencian lovers before they can achieve that healthy balancing of their deepest urges. The lovers must first accept the death of their old selves. This condition for health and for the achievement of wholeness of being is strongly suggested in Schopenhauer's analysis of the nature of the will and of death in its relationship to the will.

Schopenhauer's vision focuses on the inseparabilty of life and death. What we witness in experience is "the alternation of death and reproduction, which . . . appear only as the pulse-beats of that form which endures through all time." The phenomenal world is a "constant arising and passing away" which, however, "can by no means touch the root of things"—the *Ding an sich*, which remains "imperishable" (105, 129). There is thus in nature what Lawrence called in "The Reality of Peace" a great "systole-diastole." Life and death are inseparable; indeed, life feeds death, and death feeds life. The process is continuous, perhaps eternal. For "in Time and Eternity all is flux." And it is this great process, this bodying forth of the great underlying mystery, that Lawrence contemplated in his earliest poems which, with their emphasis on generation and death, so often suggest the work of Dylan Thomas. A girl with cherries in her hair entices the male; nearby lie three dead blackbirds ("Cherry Robbers"). The calving of a "red heifer" is seen in conjunction with "the sow . . . grabbing her litter / With snarling red jaws" ("Renascence"). A man kills a rabbit, then makes love to a girl, who "dies" in the sexual act and finds death "good" ("Love on the Farm"). The world of sunlight or fire is everywhere contrasted with a darkness that may signify either death or the unconscious instinctive source of all. The same contrasts are richly developed in *The White Peacock* and in *The Trespasser*. Life arises and is cut down; the sunlit world of generation is opposed to the darkness below: the inhuman will, the source to which all things return. Life indeed arises out of the darkness of the womb and returns to that same darkness as tomb; there is, as Joyce says in *Ulysses*, an "allwombing tomb" in the sea, just as there is an "alltombing womb."

If life and death are thus inseparable objectifications of the eternal will (i.e., manifestations of the dark gods behind the phenomenal reality), nature then does not only will life; it also wills death. The great creative impulse requires death as part of its continuous effort to create life. And man, insofar as he is the objectification of the will, can desire only what nature desires. Does it not follow that *if man acts in harmony with the will,* he will desire death as well as life—death as a condition of renewed life?

Certainly Lawrence's acceptance of death as a part of the will's intention and his emphasis on the desirability of death as a precondition of new life recall several of Schopenhauer's sanguine conclusions in the essay "On Death and Its Relation to the Indestructibility of Our True Nature." For Schopenhauer, one's death as an individual (that product of the Kantian intellect) is not a death for one's inner nature, which coincides with the eternal will. The individual dies, but matter is indestructible; hence man, who exists "in and with the whole of nature," is indestructible. Arising and passing away cannot touch "the root of things." "The true symbol of nature," says Schopenhauer (who was later echoed by Nietzsche), "is the circle," "the schema or type of recurrence." Confronting death, then, the wise man will say, " 'What is the loss of this individuality to me, who bear in myself the possibility of innumerable individualities?' " (132, 148). The doctrine of metempsychosis, or palingenesis, makes perfect sense from this point of view: in the *Bhagavadgita* and in Hinduism there is a profound truth acceptable to the naturalist, acceptable even, Schopenhauer points out, to "the excessively empirical Hume" (164). Only "small, limited minds . . . fear death quite seriously as their annihilation"; "persons of decidedly superior capacity are completely free from such terrors" (130). A reasonable man "can only think of himself as without beginning, as eternal, in fact as timeless" (143).

The doctrine is not only consoling; it is positively heartening. For death, the return to "the womb of nature," may be accompanied by the hope of "more favourable conditions of existence" (124). The only way for man to change, to undergo metamorphosis, is to "cease to be what he is" (148):

> Thus for a blessed condition of man it would be by no means sufficient that he should be transferred to a "better world," but it would also be necessary that a complete change should take place in himself; that thus he should no longer be what he is, and, on the contrary, should become what he is not. But for this he must first of all cease to be what he is: this desideratum is, as a preliminary, supplied by death, the moral necessity of which can already be seen from this point of view. [148–49]

To die as a phenomenal self is to return to the womb of nature in which new possibilities of life are born. As Schopenhauer interprets metempsychosis, death is a phenomenon in which

> the will of man, in itself individual, [separates] itself . . . from the intellect received from the mother in generation, and in accordance with its now modified nature, under the guidance of the absolutely necessary course of the world harmonising with this, [receives] through a new generation a new intellect, . . . which alone has the faculty of memory, is the mortal part or the form, while the will is the eternal part, the substance. . . . These constant new births, then, constitute the succession of the life-dreams of a will which in itself is indestructible. [160]

Lawrence picks up this idea in *Fantasia of the Unconscious,* arguing that "the dead soul remains always soul, and always retains its individual quality. And it does not disappear, but re-enters into the soul of the living" (152). The idea is suggested too in *The Trespasser,* where Siegmund reflects that "the essence of the fire is there in the darkness." The idea of rebirth in the womb of nature—metaphorical rebirth—was also demonstrated to Lawrence in his personal experience. In 1911, after his mother's death and his own serious illness, Lawrence said he had died—in his soul; and it was not until he fell in love with Frieda that he could speak of his "coming through," his rebirth, his eagerness to "begin again." Death, then, was linked in his experience with a joyous phoenixlike resurrection. And for the rest of his life he was able to contemplate death not just with equanimity but indeed with a positive assent to nature's great purpose, much like Schopenhauer's wise man, "who surrenders and denies the will to live" and is able "to die willingly, to die gladly, to die joyfully," knowing that "he needs and desires no continuance of his person" (167).

But Lawrence goes still further. In "The Reality of Peace" (1917) he argues that life and death are one, and are in us at all times. Thus:

> We are not only creatures of light and virtue. We are also alive in corruption and death. It is necessary to balance the dark against the light if we are ever going to be free. We must know that we, ourselves, are the living stream of seething corruption, this also, all the while, as well as the bright river of life. We must recover our balance to be free. From our bodies comes the issue of corruption as well as the issue of creation. We must have our being in both, our knowledge must consist in both. . . . The man I know myself to be must be destroyed before the true man I am can exist. The old man in me must die and be put away. [*Phoenix,* 676]

The "great desire of creation and the great desire of dissolution" exist in man as "pure equivalents," as "the systole-diastole of the physical universe" (678). Man can deny neither desire. When he is urged toward death, he must die: as Paul Morel thinks, " 'If I had to die, I'd will to die' " (*SL*, 472). Human desire must coincide with that of the great will. For the will urges man to destroy "the old man" before one can become reborn. The symbolic equation of death and life that Lawrence develops here corresponds perfectly to the equations of darkness and light, female and male. Accepting death, man accepts darkness and the female: that is, he is released from his male ego or consciousness (the light) and becomes one with the womb, which is also the tomb, becomes one with nature. But in such acceptance he is reborn, the old self destroyed in the tomb of the female, the new self arising in the womb of the female. In psychological terms, the self is made whole by accepting its unconscious desires, including the desire of death. Shame and horror are not excluded but incorporated in life; for only by accepting shame and horror can one become whole.

There is nothing in Schopenhauer to correspond to this Lawrencian leap into psychology. Yet Schopenhauer provides many anticipations of these conclusions. As we have seen, Schopenhauer had called attention to the dangers of suppressing—or, as Freud would have said, repressing—the promptings of the will; he had also called attention to the shame that arises from puritanical attitudes:

> But now the act through which the will asserts itself and man arises is one of which all are, in their inmost being, ashamed, which they therefore carefully conceal; nay, if they are caught in it, are terrified as if they had been taken in a crime. . . . the shame . . . extends even to the parts which are concerned in [the act of generation], although, like all other parts, they are given us by nature. [112–13]

Lawrence simply carries the Schopenhauerian idea to its logical conclusions. Suppression of the knowledge of the act of generation is no different from suppression of the knowledge of death; for generation and death are the inseparable objectifications of the will. The "conspiracy of silence" of the Victorian period was a denial of all manifestations of the will. Health is possible only on condition that man accept all of his desires, including the desire for sexual activity and the desire for death.

Thus Lawrence posits, as a basic premise of his psychology, that the will to live must be "balanced" by the will to destroy or to die, this latter desire being inherent in man's condition as a mere slave of matter or of a stagnant society. Rather than be "a cabbage," inert, passive, submissive to an intolerable social system or to a meaningless "tick-tack" of mechanical activity whose sole purpose is survival, man prefers death; for men need above all the Absolute, the Eternal, and will do "anything, anything to prove that we are not altogether sealed in our own self-preservation as dying chrysalides" (*Phoenix*, 406). Rather than "remain secure under the bushel," the mass of men prefer the "sensation" of death; with a Dostoevskyan desire for a supreme assertion of self, they prefer war to meaningless security. In the higher man, the desire for death takes the form of "passionate, purposive *destructive* activity" (*FU*, 187). In his health, the higher man realizes that it is nature's will to destroy a dead society.

Thus Lawrence develops the ideas implicit in the Schopenhauerian germ. Neither the will to live nor the will to die can give man the wholeness he seeks. All of Lawrence's psychology issues from the assumption that health is a balancing of the will to unity and the will to differentiation, of the female impulse and the male impulse, of darkness and light, of spirit and flesh, and of death (the dissolution of selfhood in the "allwombing tomb" of Nature) and life (the creation of selfhood in the "alltombing womb" of Nature).

We are in a position to summarize, then, the principles of psychology that Lawrence developed as he meditated upon and reshaped Schopenhauerian and vitalist thought:

1. Man, as the objectification of the will, can desire or shun only what "nature" desires or shuns. As nature is both creative and destructive, both synthetic and reductive, both a putting together and a pulling apart, both a life impulse and a death impulse, so man carries within him these two primal impulses: the unitive impulse to create or synthesize and the divisive impulse to separate, dismember, and destroy the unity. Another way of saying this is that the will to live takes two forms: the form of attraction (a "sympathetic" impulse) and the form of repulsion (a "voluntary" impulse).

2. The unitive or sympathetic impulse is a desire to become one with the All, to join oneself with the whole of the universe. It is manifested in sexual union, in communal action, and in art, in which the artist becomes one with what he presents. It is therefore inseparable from the impulse to die, for identification with the All is not possible unless one dies as a separate, independent self and surrenders the will of self to the greater will.

Corollary: The individual desires to die when he discovers the meaninglessness of his isolation: "Without God . . . we are nothing."

3. The divisive or voluntary impulse is an impulse to achieve the maximum of individuality, to create or produce the individual self. It is thus a reaction against the self-obliterating oneness, an effort to free oneself from blind nature and to act purposively and creatively. As a reaction against unity, it is destructive. But a maximum differentation of self is not possible unless one first surrenders the self to the infinite or the All. Only in surrender to the female in the cosmos can the male discover true wholeness of being; only in surrender to the male in the cosmos can the female discover true wholeness of being. One must die in order to live. The old self (distinct male, distinct female) can become a greater self only by uniting with its opposite. Such union is the death of the old self and the rebirth of a new self.

Corollary: Individuality is finally an illusion; men and women are but fragments of the whole and can discover wholeness only by uniting.

4. The mind creates a false picture of the world—a phenomenal world. But the mind, insofar as it is in the service of the body or of nature, may bring to awareness the real promptings of the unconscious—that is, of nature. The mind may serve either a part of the psyche or the whole psyche. When it serves either the sympathetic or the voluntary motive forces exclusively, it interferes with the desire of the whole, or integral, self and turns man against nature. Only when the mind is in the service of the whole self is it healthily employed. "Consciousness" must become "consciousness-in-nature," the intuitive recognition of all phenomena as objectifications of the will.

To these four principles, we must add one additional idea implicit in the Lawrencian, and Schopenhauerian, perspective: There is no goal in life save to act in unison with the will. To live in accordance with the deepest promptings of the will is to realize that the present is the sole reality, the *nunc stans*, in which, as Schopenhauer said, "the two infinities"—time past and time future—become one. To live in the present, at every moment in unison with the whole will, is to achieve "being," the goalless goal of life. For every moment, without beginning and without end, is an objectification of the eternal, which is imperishable.

The improvisations that Lawrence played on themes he discovered in the materialists, in Schopenhauer, and in vitalists are bold and original: most critics would call them mystical. Yet even in his affirmation of the mystical paradox that one must die in order to live, he obviously tries to ground his psychology in reliable scientific and philosophical principles, and the analogues, or correspondences, between physical laws and psychic laws also exist, as we have seen, in

Spencer, Haeckel, and Schopenhauer. The four propositions listed above are fundamental; most of Lawrence's psychology is a working out of the implications of these propositions. But in Nietzsche, Lawrence found ideas distinct enough to merit separate attention.

FRIEDRICH NIETZSCHE

Lawrence's indebtedness to Nietzsche has been recognized by a number of scholars.[11] It is indeed so profound that to trace all of the parallels in their thinking would require a book comparable to Delavenay's *D. H. Lawrence and Edward Carpenter*. The repudiation of Christianity and the celebration of Dionysian life affirmation; the attack on the herd, together with the praise of the aristocrat or the Overman; the rejection of democracy, socialism, and the notions of love, equality, brotherhood, and "idealism"; the calling for a revaluation of values—a "new naturalism in morality" which would be "dominated by an instinct of life";[12] the attack on rationalism and the interpretation of human conduct as a manifestation of an unconscious *Wille zur Macht* —all of these parallels in the dialectics of Nietzsche and of Lawrence are so strong that no account of Lawrence's psychology would be adequate if the Nietzschean influence were not given particular attention.

Looking carefully at Lawrence's psychology, one finds four ideas that have striking affinities to Nietzschean notions about man's deepest motivations and the nature of psychic health. First, the religious or creative motive is seen as the deepest instinct of the higher or greater man. Second, love and marriage are found to be in conflict with the "power-motive." Third, the self is divided, its division being manifested particularly in the phenomena of rationalization and reaction. Fourth, health entails acceptance of mutability and laughter. In tracing these correspondences between Lawrence's thought and Nietzsche's, criticism should also note the temperamental basis for Lawrence's response. Both Nietzsche and Lawrence were puritans who sought to announce to mankind "the end of the longest error" and the beginning of noon, "the high point of humanity" (486). Both, in reaction to the repressions of Christianity and of nineteenth-century propriety and "reason," sought to shed their sicknesses by incorporating Dionysus into a vision of healthy life.

The Religious or Creative Motive. What is perhaps most striking in Nietzsche's treatment of "the higher man" is that such a man's noble motives are everywhere contrasted with the base motives of the mob, the rabble, the "all-too-human," the "superfluous" plebeians who are motivated by *ressentiment* and desire for "power and first the lever of power, much money'' (162). The Nietzschean dialectic, like that of Lawrence, continually contrasts the bullying but servile mob with the creative, purposive desires of a Zarathustra or of a Don Ramón. The higher man may be motivated by the *Wille zur Macht,* but clearly his power-will is not egotistical. On the contrary, it is a generous desire to give of himself, to use his energies to create a new world, a new heaven and a new earth. Thus the deepest motive of the higher man is analogous to what Victor Frankl calls a will to meaning, or what Lawrence calls the essential religious or creative motive. Zarathustra, like all of Lawrence's veritable heroes, desires to create not only a new selfhood, for the individual is ''still the [earth's] most recent creation'' (171), but also new values: ''The noble man wants to create something new and a new virtue. The good [i.e., those who deny life] want the old, and that the old be preserved'' (156). The goal of this noble man is to liberate himself from the state and the mob, from the tyranny of base men and the tyranny of plebeian *ressentiment:* ''For *that man be delivered from revenge,* that is for me the bridge to the highest hope, and a rainbow after long storms'' (211). The higher man, liberating others from both Christ and Casesar, can lead mankind to full acceptance of the earth, full development of human potentialities, and acceptance of man's life in relation to eternity—''the eternal return of life; the future promised and hallowed in the past; the triumphant Yes to life beyond all death and change; *true* life as the over-all continuation of life through procreation, through the mysteries of sexuality'' (561).

But to become fitted for his great mission, the higher man must first be able to accept the death of the old self. As Lawrence, after his own psychic death and his rebirth through love, had focused on the phoenix to symbolize both eternal recurrence and continual palingenesis, Nietzsche stressed the importance of dying and rebirth as the condition of achieving true nobility. The metaphor of ''going under,'' announced at the beginning of *Thus Spoke Zarathustra,* is bound up with the idea of death and rebirth. The sun must set, or ''go under'': man must die. The sun must rise again: man must be reborn as the Overman. Because ''the worst enemy you can encounter will always be you, yourself,'' the higher man must learn how to die: ''You must wish to consume yourself in your own flame: how could you wish to become new unless you had first become ashes!'' (176). The creator must submit to ''suffering'' and ''much change'': ''Indeed, there must be much bitter dying in your life, you creators'' (199). And when the time comes to die, the higher man must not cling rotting to the branches of life; he must learn to die ''the death that consummates'' (183).

As we have seen, Lawrence, in the same vein, insists that the soul must die continually, passing away into the great darkness of the infinite source, then arising with a new being and a new life, determined to create "a new heaven and new earth." Only the living dead cling to life instead of accepting their death and transfiguration. Only the great herd of insulated egos refuse to acknowledge death in the understanding and to accept that death and corruption are a part of themselves.

Love, Marriage, and Power. As the higher man must repudiate the values of the rabble, so he must turn against the engulfing darkness of the female. Night, for both Nietzsche and Lawrence, is associated with the female and with love; day, with the male's creative activity in the building of a new world. In "The Night Song" Zarathustra sings:

> A craving for love is within me; it speaks the language of love.
>
> Light am I; ah, that I were night! but this is my loneliness that I am girt with light. Ah, that I were dark and nocturnal! How I would suck at the breasts of light! . . .
>
> But I live in my own light; I drink back into myself the flames that break out of me. I do not know the happiness of those who receive. [217–18]

As giver and creator, Zarathustra longs for the night in which his soul might become a fountain. But the light and the darkness, the fire and the water, are opposite principles. Zarathustra is tempted to surrender to the darkness, to take, like an infant, the light supplied by others. But he cannot; he must strive for the "high noon" of reality. "I am carried away, my soul dances," the Drunkard proclaims in "The Drunken Song": "Day's work! Day's work! Who shall be the lord of the earth?" (432).

It is this sort of oscillation in Nietzsche—between the craving to surrender oneself to the female and the opposite craving, to assert one's proud and separate selfhood as creator and "lord of the earth"—that Lawrence would probably have noted with particular attention. The rhythms of Zarathustra's life are significant. From the solitude of his cave he ventures out, bringing his "light" to the "underworld," his "fire into the valleys" (122). He seeks "living companions" and reminds himself that " 'out of love alone shall my despising and my warning bird fly up, not out of the swamp' " (289). But in seeking comrades he must guard against his strong love for others. For he is "trust-overfull" and is "ready to love" "every monster" (266–67). "Love is the danger of the loneliest; love of everything if only it is alive. Laughable, verily, are my folly and my modesty in love" (267).

Again, he reflects that "consideration and pity have ever been my greatest dangers" (297). Fearful of the mob in whom "everything is betrayed" (297), he returns with joy to his solitude, his silence. But his love prompts him to "go under" again, and he warns himself against his nausea, his negative spirit that may reject the earth and its joys. "Does one have to curse right away, where one does not love?" (405).

Love and the will to power are thus mixed in Zarathustra. He is ambivalent, drawn out of love to others, withdrawing in disgust and repudiation from the tyranny of the "outside-myself" (329). "With malice and love" Zarathustra shakes his friends' hands; and if he enjoys their companionship, he is "overcome by a slight aversion and by scorn" (415, 422) and is glad to slip outside the cave and into the open, with his animals. For "all great love," he reasons, "does not *want* love: it wants more" (405); "higher than love of the neighbor is love of the farthest and the future" (173). Day's work—the building of new values and a new world—must never be compromised for the sake of love.

It is perhaps unnecessary to insist on the similarity of this ambivalent Zarathustra to several of Lawrence's heroes. The fact is that the oscillation between love and the will to power is so central in Lawrence's psychology that in novel after novel the experience of the hero becomes a prolonged to-and-fro of sympathetic (or love) impulses and voluntary (or power) impulses. And Lawrence, like Zarathustra, must warn himself repeatedly against too much sympathy. Like Zarathustra, Lawrence's heroes all yearn to surrender to the female night and to have companions, or blood brothers; like Zarathustra, these heroes recoil in revulsion, warning themselves repeatedly against giving themselves away to others, against too much love.

It is hardly surprising, then, that both men are distrustful of conventional love and marriage, which threaten to destroy the heroic soul in the "greater man." Both men, following Schopenhauer in regarding woman as the instrument of the blind life force, serving above all a procreative urge, are fearful of being devoured by her and associate her with the tyranny of the mob. The only proper role for woman in marriage, both agree, is that of submission to male authority. Says Zarathustra: "The happiness of man is: I will. The happiness of woman is: he wills. . . . woman must obey and find a depth for her surface" (179). In the same vein, Lawrence argues in *Aaron's Rod* that "the woman must submit," not to "any foolish and arbitrary will," but to "the soul in its dark motion of power and pride," "submit livingly, not subjectedly," discovering her fulfillment in an acceptance of the "mode of power" instead of the "love-mode" which has enslaved men in our time. For conventional love and marriage crush all male creativeness. Says Zarathustra:

> Marriage: thus I name the will of two to create the one that is more than those who created it. Reverence for each other, as for those willing with such a will, is what I name marriage. Let this be the meaning and truth of your marriage. But that which the all-too-many, the superfluous, call marriage—alas, what shall I name that? Alas, this poverty of the soul in pair! Alas, this filth of the soul in pair! Alas, this wretched contentment in pair! Marriage they call this; . . . these animals entangled in the heavenly net. [182]

It is exactly the same protest as Lawrence raises against the dreadful *egoisme à deux* of married couples: "The hot narrow intimacy between man and wife was abhorrent. The way they shut their doors, these married people, and shut themselves in to their own exclusive alliance with each other, even in love, disgusted him. It was a whole community of mistrustful couples insulated in private houses or private rooms, always in couples, and no further life, no further immediate, no disinterested relationship admitted: a kaleidoscope of couples, disjoined, separatist, meaningless entities of married couples" (*WL*, 226). As sex turns a man into "a broken half of a couple," "a prisoner," his individuality obliterated in dreadful fusion, so Nietzsche comments on the male's annihilation in marriage:

> Worthy I deemed this man, and ripe for the sense of the earth; but when I saw his wife, the earth seemed to me a house for the senseless. . . .
>
> This one went out like a hero in quest of truths, and eventually he conquered a little dressed-up lie. His marriage he calls it. . . .
>
> That one sought a maid with the virtues of an angel. But all at once he became the maid of a woman; and now he must turn himself into an angel. [182]

The true purpose of marriage, says Nietzsche, is "not merely to reproduce, but to produce something *higher*" (323). As Lawrence stressed that the nuclei of the egg and the sperm combine to produce a new individual, so Nietzsche places the stress on the creative possibilities of marriage. Both, too, are puritanically horrified by the two beasts who "find each other" in marriage, the "merging, the clutching, the mingling of love" (*Zarathustra*, 183; *WL*, 227). And both counsel chastity when the soul, recoiling from "the bitch sensuality," is visited by the desire for chastity. Zarathustra asks: " 'What is chastity? Is chastity not folly? Yet this folly came to us, not we to it. We offered this guest hostel and heart: now it dwells with us—may it stay as long as it will!' " (167). So Lawrence's Mellors writes to Connie: "I love this chastity, which is the pause of peace of our fucking. . . . Now is the time to be chaste, it is so good to be chaste, like a river of cool water in my soul. I love the chastity now that it flows between us. It is like fresh water and rain. How can men want wearisomely to philander? What a misery to be like Don Juan . . . impotent and unable to be chaste in the cool between-whiles, as by a river" (*LCL*, 374). In such a passage, and in much of Lawrence and Nietzsche, there is a deep acceptance of the rhythms of man's life, of a flux in desire that the wise man must heed. But more of that later.

The Divided Self: Rationalization and Reaction. It is clear from this analysis of Lawrence's and Nietzsche's views of love and power that both men saw a deep division within the psyche, a division that both had discovered in Dostoevsky's Underground Man and his Raskolnikov, who oscillate between extremes of compassion or love and power or self-assertion. It was also perhaps in Dostoevsky that Lawrence and Nietzsche discovered two other important ideas of their psychology: the idea of rationalization, the offering of "good" reasons to disguise one's "real" reasons; and the idea of the reaction from excessive spirituality into pure bestiality.

Nietzsche's analysis of rationalization and reaction in *Zarathustra* issues from his deepest insight: that what man really wants, as opposed to what he thinks he wants, is power. In truth, Nietzsche argues, "There are no mental causes at all"; and motive is "merely a surface phenomenon of consciousness, something alongside the deed that is more likely to cover up the antecedents of the deeds than to represent them" (495). The true causes of human behavior are either a collocation of events too numerous to be defined or animal instinct. The mind is merely instrumental; it is in the service of the body's will. Says Zarathustra: "The awakened and knowing say: body am I entirely, and nothing else; and soul is only a word for something about the body. The body is a great reason. . . . An instrument of your body is also your little reason, my brother, which you call 'spirit'—a little instrument and toy of your great reason" (146). From this it follows that beneath all talk of "the spiritual" or the "higher," beneath all talk of "selflessness" and "loving one's neighbor," beneath all the romantic liberal talk of "equality," "brotherhood," and "the rights of man," and beneath all Platonic jibbering about "the Good," the "ideal," the *ens realissimum*, lies the hairy brute, the predator, the animal seeking domination or omnipotence. As Dostoevsky, in *Notes from Underground*, points out that what man really wants is an independent will, free from all restraints, free even of the laws of nature, and as

Dostoevsky traces the inevitable plunge from love or self-sacrifice into the abyss of depravity and cruelty, so Nietzsche, in diagnosing the psychology of the "higher man," comments: "The more he aspires to the height and light, the more strongly do his roots strive earthward, downward, into the dark, the deep—into evil" (154). The higher men really want "more thrills, more danger, more earthquakes. You desire, . . . you higher men—you desire the most wicked, most dangerous life, of which *I* am most afraid: the life of wild animals, woods, caves, steep mountains, and labyrinthian gorges" (414). And if the higher man, like the eagle, gazes into "his *own* abysses" and longs to "pounce on *lambs*, . . . hating all lamb souls," hatred and cruelty are no less to be found in the plebeian preachers of equality. "Underneath all *romantisme* lie the grunting and greed of Rousseau's instinct for revenge" (411, 514). When they speak of justice, the preachers of equality (the tarantulas, Zarathustra calls them) want the world to "be filled with the storms of [their] revenge"; they say, " 'We shall wreak vengeance and abuse on all whose equals we are not' " (212). "Aggrieved conceit" and "repressed envy" will "erupt . . . as a flame and as the frenzy of revenge" (212). Thus the human will, seeking always to transform "It was" into "Thus I willed it," is perverted from creativeness to the desire for punishment. Impotent, it desires omnipotence at any cost.

Here Nietzsche defines what was to become a central insight of Lawrence's fiction. The "higher" people (the word "higher" is recurrent in *Women in Love*) all talk of socialism, of equality, and of love. But the talk at Hermione Roddice's Breadalby is like "a rattle of artillery," and beneath the professions of human love and compassionate liberalism (the talk of Bertrand Russell and of John Maynard Keynes) Lawrence sees the lust for cruelty, the lust of the superwarrior who, like Plato, uses dialectic to gain power. They are all, these higher people, like the "insane" Halliday: "On the one hand he's had religious mania, and on the other, he is fascinated by obscenity. Either he's a pure servant, washing the feet of Christ, or else he is making obscene drawings of Jesus—action and reaction—and between the two, nothing. He is really insane" (*WL*, 107). Lawrence saw that he, too, in the role of Richard Somers of *Kangaroo*, wanted to "erupt" like a dormant volcano, that he too desired not love and sympathetic unison with his neighbors but rather to destroy the whole society with its "love and benevolence ideal," as, during the war, he had wanted to kill millions of Germans. Indeed, the entire society, as he saw it in *Aaron's Rod* and *Kangaroo*, wishes only to react against the love ideal and to plunge into a bloody revolution—the bloodier, the better.

Hollow men and hollow women will do anything to smash the existing system, in which they feel themselves to be impotent, purposeless, "nullified." So World War I, Lawrence believed, was simply the inevitable reaction of the mob of egos who, unable to bear their "cabbage" existence, preferred death to living in a society in which, instinct being crushed and regarded as disease, life was declining, lapsing into the dark river of dissolution.

Yet both Lawrence and Nietzsche also recognized the possible virtue—the life-giving power—of the carrying of reaction to an extreme. Nausea, says Nietzsche, "creates wings and water-divining powers" (317). "The greatest evil is necessary for the overman's best" (400). Zarathustra, summoning his higher men to join him, summons also his "most abysmal thought" and urges the abyss within him to speak, for "I have turned my ultimate depth inside out into the light" (328). He welcomes Nausea, because it is only by accepting the worst within him that he can become whole. In the same vein, Lawrence could say that acceptance of corruption and death in the understanding is the essential precondition of growth and rebirth as a new man. To accept that corruption and death are within us is to cleanse the self, to cast out the festering *ressentiment* and the spirit of revenge spawned by the Christian and romantic overemphasis on love, selflessness, and self-sacrifice. Paradoxically, the plunge into "sensationalism" and "reduction," into "corruption and death," may unloose the soul, free it from the fixed objectives of the egoistic will, and open it to new possibilities of life, or to the desire to build a new heaven and earth. Like Nietzsche, Lawrence recognizes that there can be no separation of the individual psyche and the whole of the universe. The force behind the universe is both creative and corruptive, a will to creation and a will to destruction. Those wills exist within man, and man can never learn to live healthily, in harmony with the deeps that are within him, until he has learned to accept the abyss along with the mountaintop, the darkness of the unconsciousness along with the light of the spirit.

For this reason, both Lawrence and Nietzsche affirm the necessity of accepting all instincts. Says Nietzsche in *Zarathustra:* "With knowledge, the body purifies itself; making experiments with knowledge, it elevates itself; in the lover of knowledge all instincts become holy; in the elevated, the soul becomes gay" (189). For the same reason he can say " 'Do whatever you will, but first be such as are *able to will*' " (284). It is precisely this view that Lawrence embraces when he announces, "I shall accept all my desires and repudiate none" and when he calls for acting on one's "deepest impulse." " 'It's the hardest thing in the world,' " says Rupert Birkin, " 'to act spontaneously on one's impulses—and it's the only really gentlemanly thing to do—provided you're fit to do it' '' (*WL*, 36). It is the man of character, the gentleman or the higher man, who alone is capable of acting responsibly on his impulses. In him, as in all men, the mind is merely instrumental, is in the service of an unconscious will. But in him it is in the service of a higher will than that of the egoist: the deepest impulse of the higher man is "the inherent passion . . . to produce, to create, to be as God" (*Phoenix*, 429). That higher will to power, manifested in the purposive destruction of all life-denying institutions and ideas and in the bold construction of a new world, is entirely different from the will to power of the plebeian acting out of *ressentiment* and the spirit of envy. Higher men, recognizing the dangers of subjugating life to such a base will, accept all of their desires because they know that the creative passion is so strong that it can subdue all other passions in them.

This distinction between a base will to power and a higher will to power is obviously important in both writers; for both must distinguish carefully between the terrible bullying of the mob, the "superfluous" herd of power-seeking egos and the noble creative and purposive desire of a Zarathustra or a Don Ramón. In Nietzsche, as in Lawrence, the definition of the virtues of the higher man is always coupled with an attack upon the proponents of the base will to power. In Nietzsche, it is abhorrent that the mob seek to become masters: "What is womanish, what derives from the servile, and especially the mob hodgepodge: *that* would now become master of all human destiny. O nausea!" (399). So in *Aaron's Rod* Lawrence repudiates with disgust and rage the bullying "female" society that demands subservience to "the life-centrality of woman" and allegiance to its dead and putrid ideals of love and self-sacrifice.

There was, nevertheless, Lawrence believed, an important difference between this "deep power urge," as he conceived it, and Nietzsche's higher will to power. In *Aaron's Rod*, Rawdon Lilly defines the essential difference:

> "We've got to accept the power motive, accept it in deep responsibility . . . . It is a great life motive . . . . Power—the power-urge. The will-to-power—but not in Nietzsche's sense. Not intellectual power. Not mental power. Not conscious will-power. Not even wisdom. But dark, living, fructifying power. . . . The urge of power does not seek for happiness any more than for any other state. It urges from within, darkly, for the displacing of the old leaves, the inception of the new." [*AR*, 345–46]

Here Lawrence attacks Nietzsche's conception of the will to power because, as Lilly argues, Nietzsche's will to power "was the conscious and benevolent will, in fact, the love-will'' (346). John B. Humma has argued that Lawrence misinterprets Nietzsche's *Wille zur Macht*, and Humma is perhaps correct;[13] but Humma does not distinguish between the shallow and the deep power impulses. For Lawrence ''the deep power-urge is not conscious of its aims: and it is certainly not consciously benevolent or love-directed'' (*AR*, 346). It is an urge to act in unison with the great Source, the creative mystery. For Nietzsche, this deep power urge is hardly distinguishable from an egoistic will to make all things conscious, a will ''that everything be changed into what is thinkable for man'' (198). When Nietzsche writes, ''I love him who lives to know, and who wants to know so that the overman may live some day'' (127), we may well imagine Lawrence's rejoinder: ''The supreme lesson of human consciousness is to learn how *not to know*. That is, how not to *interfere* . . . how to live dynamically, from the great Source, and not statically, like machines driven by ideas and principles from the head, or automatically, from one fixed desire'' (*FU*, 76). The difference between Lawrence's ''deep power urge'' and Nietzsche's higher will to power is thus profound, if we accept this Lawrencian contention that Nietzsche overemphasized consciousness.

Yet the similarity of their conceptions of the higher will to power remains impressive. For Nietzsche, like Lawrence, clearly recognizes the limitations of the will of his higher men. In his analysis of the ''ascetic of the spirit,'' Nietzsche examines carefully a man with a ''heroic will,'' who, feeling contempt and nausea, has ''subdued monsters, . . . solved riddles.'' But this man, however ''sublime,'' is condemned because he is all will—a ''tense'' soul whose ''knowledge has not learned to smile and to be without jealousy'' (228, 230). Such a man, Zarathustra says, must learn to relax:

> No violent will can attain the beautiful by exertion. . . .
>
> To stand with relaxed muscles and unharnessed will: that is most difficult for all of you who are sublime.
>
> When power becomes gracious and descends into the visible—such descent I call beauty.
>
> And there is nobody from whom I want beauty as much as from you who are powerful: let your kindness be your final self-conquest.
>
> Of all evil I deem you capable: therefore I want the good from you. [230]

The ''soul's secret,'' Zarathustra concludes, is that ''only when the hero has abandoned her, she is approached in a dream by the overhero'' (231). In short, the relinquishing of the fixed will of the soul is a necessary condition for true elevation: ''The ether itself should elevate him, the will-less one'' (230). Such a man does not merely ''subdue monsters''; he can ''redeem his own monsters and riddles, changing them into heavenly children'' (230); the darkness within him can be converted into light. Thus Nietzsche would appear to be suggesting, as Lawrence also suggested, that only by relaxing the will can one become filled with the deep promptings to become the overman, instead of the mere despiser. One must wait for the influx of generous, life-affirming impulses. The analogy to this, in Lawrencian language, is the idea that one must surrender oneself to the great current of life, must wait and listen for the deepest promptings and must allow the dark gods to enter the clearing of the known self (*SCAL*, 117–22).

The Flux and Laughter. It may be, then, that Lawrence's disagreement with Nietzsche is not quite so profound as Lawrence thinks it is. In any case, both finally join in their belief that health is possible only when man learns to accept change and to laugh at himself. Both men condemn those with ''fixed will'' who ''want the old, and that the old be preserved'' (Nietzsche, 156). Heraclitus, whom Nietzsche regards with ''the highest respect'' (480), is also, for Lawrence, a great teacher: ''In Time and in Eternity all is flux'' (''The Crown''; *Phoenix II*, 413). Hence, like Nietzsche, Lawrence distrusts all systems: there is ''no eternal system, there is no rock of eternal truth'' (413). God, like the rainbow, appears and vanishes and reappears, ''always different.'' Man must recognize that ''this desire for constancy, for fixity in the temporal world'' is evil (414). Man must learn to accept the ''transmutation'' of his ''integral spirit'' (*WL*, 219). And he must learn to laugh at himself. The deepest self in man, the integral self that Lawrence called the Holy Ghost, prompts us

> not to be too egoistic and wilful in our conscious self, but to change as the spirit inside us bids us change, and leave off when it bids us leave off, and laugh when we must laugh, particularly at ourselves, for in deadly earnestness there is always something a bit ridiculous. The Holy Ghost bids us never be too deadly in our earnestness, always to laugh in time, at ourselves and everything. Particularly at our sublimities. Everything has its hour of ridicule—everything. [*SCAL*, 79]

Not the spirit of gravity, not the dour sublimities of ''those who are sublime,'' but the laughter of the higher men (422–23). It is through laughter and the dance that Nietzsche's higher men drive out nausea, then convalesce and move toward true health. So Lawrence—surely one of the most earnest writers who ever lived—cautions himself against the bitterness that threatens to drive him into wholesale reaction and the desire for revenge against the dead society.

Each of these two earnest puritans needed to remind himself to laugh. Each, in his striving to be "hard" against the flaccid, passive acceptance of intolerable evils by his sentimental contemporaries, was always in danger of being ovecome by nausea, in danger of becoming a mere despiser. Each, in his intense emphasis upon the responsibility that man assumes when he declares, "All is permitted," was in danger of cutting himself off from society and friends by launching prolonged diatribes against the human race, which would condemn the condemner to solitary isolation from his kind. Each, in his intense strivings to overcome puritanical repressions and to liberate himself from the tyranny of a life-denying idealism, was in danger of becoming more puritanical than the Puritans, more strict with himself, more demanding, and more intolerant of personal weaknesses. Each, as a psychologist, recognized clearly, I think, that his prolonged commitment to his work, his mission, could cause him irreparable physical or psychic harm. One must learn to relax the will; one must learn to accept the flux of desire as part of the great flux of the earth. Only in a complete naturalism—a naturalism that would accept all desires as holy—could the two of them find health and wholeness, the health that is possible only when one can forgive oneself or laugh at oneself if one has failed to become a higher man.

Beyond Lawrence's obvious indebtedness to Nietzsche for the stance of his whole "philosophy," two principles of Lawrencian psychology emerge from his meditations on Nietzschean ideas. These must be added to the four principles developed in his reflections on Schopenhauer:

5. The deepest desire of man is the creative or religious desire to destroy dead forms of life and to build "a new heaven and a new earth." This is the deep power urge, in contrast to the will for personal or egoistic power.

6. Overemphasis on one desire of the psyche breeds a reaction to an opposite desire. An excess of sympathy (or love) breeds a reaction into voluntary self-assertion. An excess of willfulness (or power) breeds a reaction into sympathetic connection. Thus nature seeks a balance. But the violent swing from one extreme to the other is unhealthy; a steady balancing of sympathetic and voluntary impulses, in accordance with the natural flux of desire, is necessary.

Corollary: Healthy living means accepting the flux of desire. No way of life should be perpetuated beyond its time.

The implications of the law of action and reaction are fully developed, both in the novels, beginning with *The Rainbow* and *Women in Love,* and in Lawrence's systematic analysis of the psyche in his two studies of the unconscious. The law became one of the chief structuring principles of his fiction after 1914. But before turning to the novels, I must look carefully at the theory of the psyche developed in *Psychoanalysis and the Unconscious* and *Fantasia of the Unconscious*.

3

Lawrence's Psychology, III: Theory of the Unconscious

DHLDHLDHLDHLDHLDHLDHLDHLDHLDHLDHLDHLDHLDHLDHLDHLDHLDHLDHLDHLDHLDHLDHLDHLDHLDHLDHLDHLDHLDHLDHLDHLDHLDHLDHLDHLDHLDHLDHLDHL

Desire and anger are from God.
—D. H. Lawrence

Lawrence's theory was not explicitly set down until 1921, and as William York Tindall has shown, Lawrence's thinking at that time bears the obvious imprint of Hindu and theosophical ideas, particularly those of James M. Pryse.[1] Richard J. Kuczkowski has further shown parallels between Lawrence's thinking and that of the theosophist Helen Blavatsky.[2] But if Lawrence's use of the cakras of Yoga makes "anatomical nonsense," as James C. Cowan has shown, and if his "cosmophysiology," as Kuczkowski calls it, depresses even ardent Lorenzoists, Lawrence was obviously developing ideas he had long held and had presented as early as "Study of Thomas Hardy," "The Crown," and "The Reality of Peace." The anatomical terminology is of no real importance; nor is the cosmophysiology, which is a poetic invention designed to return the reader to an ancient sense of unity with the world. Lawrence liked theosophy and occult ideas because he found in them ideas and metaphors that helped him to amplify his own ideas, much as Yeats used automatic writing for images in his poetry. As Kuczkowski observes, Lawrence read theosophy and the occult "for confirmation or expansion of his intuitions, for hints to spark his imagination."[3] Many of those hints would easily be correlated with ideas he had found in Schopenhauer, Spencer, and others. Moreover, Lawrence follows Jung, whose *Psychology of the Unconscious* Lawrence probably read in 1918,[4] in regarding mystical ideas as manifestations of the unconscious, to be examined for the light they throw on our deepest impulses.

It is important in this connection to note that in *Psychoanalysis and the Unconscious* Lawrence sets out deliberately to be "scientific."[5] Later, when writing *Fantasia,* he decides to present his system simply as his own, declaring defiantly that he no longer believes "one-fifth" of what science has told him about the sun and moon and stars. He has believed the "ideal plausibilities" of science for twenty years, he says, but now he refuses to accept them; "for *my* part," he writes, "I know that life, and life only is the clue to the universe" (*FU*, 153). Yet, in this same book, after announcing his belief in the souls of the dead, he adds: "I'm sorry, because I don't like mysticism. It has no trousers and no trousers' seat: *n'a pas de quoi*. And I should feel so uncomfortable if I put my hand behind me and felt an absolute blank" (23). Satiric, defiant, presenting himself as a man and not a scientist, he says in effect: "Yes, of course I know much of this sounds silly. Just can't help it. I'm right, though, if you can see beyond the words to the facts." What is important is the new way in which he analyzes the relationship of sympathetic and voluntary, objective and subjective (or spiritual and sensual), female and male impulses within the unconscious.

The diagram clarifies Lawrence's thinking about the deep divisions in the psyche. The psyche is divided both vertically and horizontally, and Lawrence views these divisions "into polarized duality" as being both "psychical and physical" (*FU*, 37). The original egg cell, which is created by the fusion of the two parent nuclei, first divides vertically, into sympathetic and voluntary subjective, or "sensual," centers. The two sensual centers then divide horizontally to create the objective or spiritual centers, one sympathetic, one voluntary. The psyche is thus divided in its very origins. "There are two ways [sensual and spiritual] of love [or sympathy], two ways [sensual and spiritual] of activity in independence [or power]" (*FU*, 46). Health consists in "some sort of equilibrium between the two modes," the equilibrium or balanced polarity of sympathetic and voluntary urges, sensual and spiritual. "The two sympathetic centres are always, or should always be, counter-balanced by their corresponding voluntary centres" (*FU*, 47–48). Illness occurs in the human being when the centers are not properly "polarized," when, for example, the sympathetic center is not balanced by the voluntary, or the spiritual by the sensual. Human beings may be too sympathetic or too voluntary, too spiritual or too sensual. And while Lawrence reminds us (*FU*, 47) that "there is not and cannot be any norm of human conduct," since some people "must be too sympathetic, and some must be too proud," it is always the norm of balance or equilibrium to which he returns when he analyzes the neurotic behavior of men in our time.

The fundamental hypothesis of this theory is that instinctual energy is directed toward self-realization, or maximum of being. The unconscious is defined as "that essential unique nature of every individual

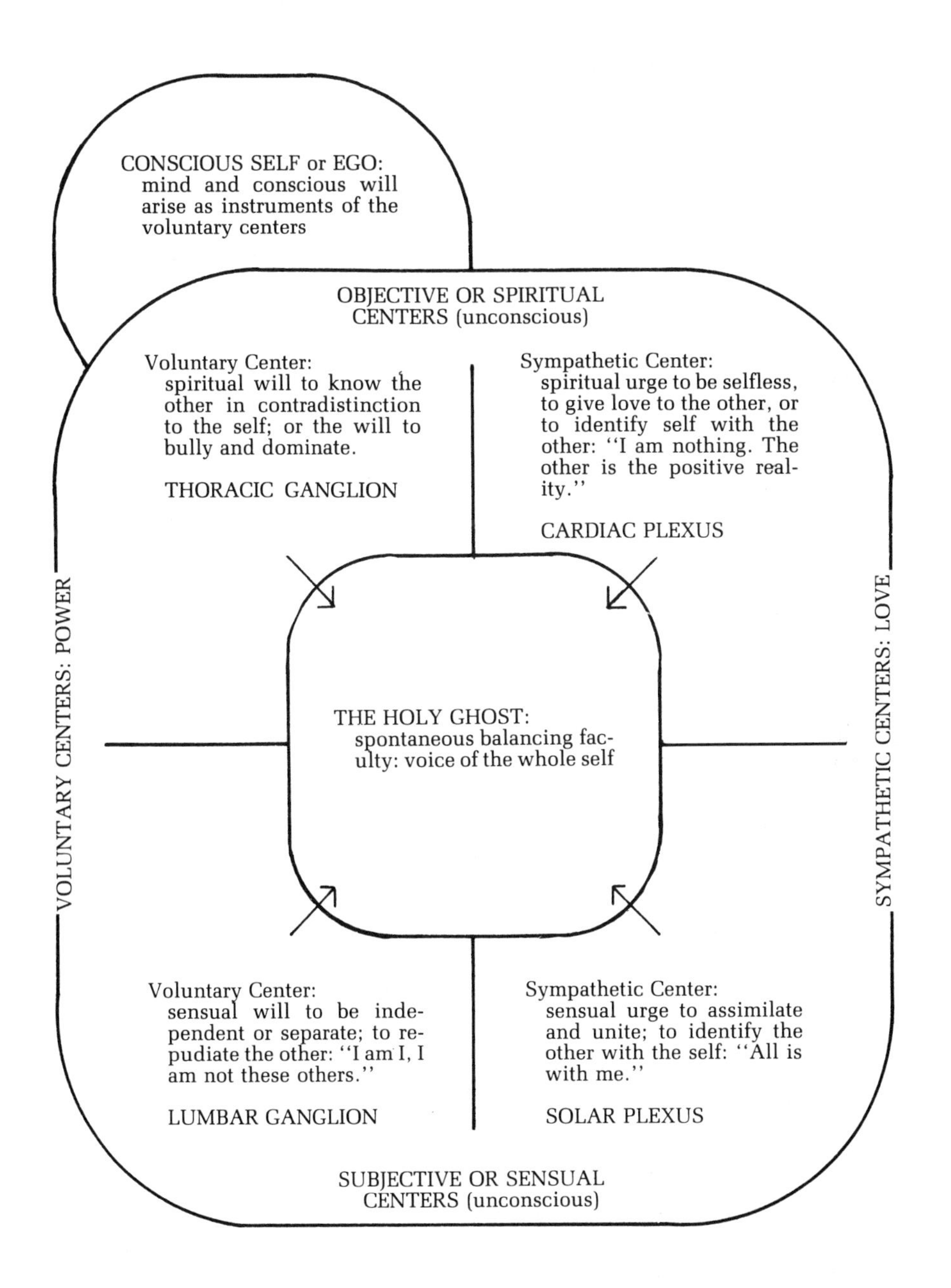
CONSCIOUS SELF or EGO:
mind and conscious will arise as instruments of the voluntary centers
OBJECTIVE OR SPIRITUAL CENTERS (unconscious)
Voluntary Center:
spiritual will to know the other in contradistinction to the self; or the will to bully and dominate.
THORACIC GANGLION
Sympathetic Center:
spiritual urge to be selfless, to give love to the other, or to identify self with the other: "I am nothing. The other is the positive reality."
CARDIAC PLEXUS
VOLUNTARY CENTERS: POWER
SYMPATHETIC CENTERS: LOVE
THE HOLY GHOST:
spontaneous balancing faculty: voice of the whole self
Voluntary Center:
sensual will to be independent or separate; to repudiate the other: "I am I, I am not these others."
LUMBAR GANGLION
Sympathetic Center:
sensual urge to assimilate and unite; to identify the other with the self: "All is with me."
SOLAR PLEXUS
SUBJECTIVE OR SENSUAL CENTERS (unconscious)

creature, which is, by its very nature, unanalysable, undefinable, unconceivable'' (*PU*, 214). In seeking to come to perfection or to unfold its individuality, the healthy self is directed by an inherent purposiveness. Not the pleasure principle but the will to individual perfection, or to maximum of being, governs. Thus the deepest premental knowledge is the physical or sensual knowledge that ''I am I''; even as it sucks at the mother's breast, the infant ''knows'' its own power, its selfhood.

In the striving for self-perfection, two deep unconscious impulses arise: the ''love'' impulse, which is essentially a striving for an enlarged selfhood through communion with others, and the ''power'' impulse, a striving for selfhood through repudiation of others. Thus Lawrence's system of instinctive energies is, like Freud's, basically dualistic. As Freud postulated Eros and Deros instincts—both derivable from a principle of constancy or a deep desire to avoid extremes of tension—Lawrence postulates Love and Power, both derivable from the deep desire for self-realization. Note that both Eros and aggression arise, in Lawrence, as healthy instinctive strivings for maximum of being.

Now the origin of the unconscious, according to Lawrence, is the solar plexus, a sympathetic center; and in defining the nature of its energies, Lawrence works with the idea that the newborn infant realizes its own nature in its premental knowledge that the self, or subject, is the All. The ''great prime knowledge'' of the infant is the knowledge that ''I am I, the vital centre of all things. I am I, the clue to the whole. All is one with me. It is the one identity'' (*FU*, 35).

In *Psychoanalysis and the Unconscious,* Lawrence makes it clear that this unconscious mode of knowing is that of ''assimilatory unison'' (*PU*, 226). The infant ''rejoices in the mother and its own blissful centrality, its unison with the as yet unknown universe'' (36). In other passages, Lawrence stresses that ''to an infant the mother is the whole universe'' (*FU*, 32); the infant seeks to return to the womb, the origin; it cleaves to ''the old source'' or seeks ''the old oneness'' (*PU*, 222, 220). So the solar plexus is the center of ''unification, or at least unison'' (222), the center that establishes sympathetic connection, ''the profound intake of love or vibration from the living correspondent outside'' (*FU*, 47).

This unconscious desire to assimilate the All may provide ''unspeakable effluence and inter-communication'' (*PU*, 221); but if the unique single self of the infant were to dissolve in the All, it would be obliterated. Thus the effort to assimilate the whole threatens selfhood and individuality. And the infant recoils from the All, which it has tried to take into itself—recoils, that is, from the female, the mother. The voluntary center awakens—the center of "assertive individualism," "our positive centre of independence" (*FU*, 35). The child discovers its "new, separate power" and screams in "revolt from connection, the revolt from union" (*PU*, 222). The knowledge of the lumbar ganglion is this voluntary knowledge: "I am I, not because I am at one with all the universe, but because I am other than all the universe. It is my distinction from all the rest of things which makes me myself. Because I am set utterly apart and distinguished from all that is the rest of the universe, therefore *I am I*" (*FU*, 35). The sympathetic center assimilates, seeks connection, and takes in; the voluntary center repudiates, recoils, and is associated with negation and excretion.

The development of the objective, or spiritual, centers is the next phase of the unconscious striving for maximum of being. In contrast to the subjective or sensual knowledge of the lower centers, objective or spiritual knowledge is not of the "I" in its love and power modes, but of that which is "not I"—the object. The self, in its striving for perfection, seeks unconsciously to know the object as distinct from the self, and its knowledge arises either in the mode of love or of power. In the love mode, the object appears to the self as so precious, such an amplification of being, that the self gives to the object its total love: the self is indeed identified with the object; whereas, in the subjective sympathetic center, the object is identified with the self. In the power, or voluntary, mode, the object is regarded in contradistinction to the self: it defines the limits of the self. The object is now distinguished from the subject; whereas in the subjective voluntary center, the subject distinguishes itself from the object.

The self is supreme on the subjective or sensual level; the object as "self-object" is supreme on the objective level. "Spiritually," the individual comes to perfection through a premental realization of a reality greater than the self (an object of which the self is a part) or different from the self, hence awakening the premental knowledge of the limits of the self. "Sensually," the individual comes to perfection through the premental realization of a selfhood that is either the whole of reality or acquires its reality in contradistinction to the Other.

The self develops healthily—or moves towards maximum of being—as long as all four centers exist in dynamic balance. For the voluntary centers (the subjective and the objective) healthily balance the sympathetic urge toward assimilatory unison or selfless identification; they healthily prompt the individual to reject any unison with his beloved or with his tribe that might destroy the self. But if these centers are not, in turn, checked and balanced by the sympathetic centers, the individual will seek self-realization only in a destructive repudiation or reaction, will sever all connections with the Other, and will hence drive himself into an unendurable separateness and solitude. Again, the sympathetic centers may healthily balance the voluntary tendency toward separation and reaction; they may healthily bring the individual into organic connection with others, with nature, and with the infinite. But if they are not balanced by the voluntary centers, the human being will become the passive slave of a beloved or of a collective will that will violate his integrity.

Similarly, the objective, or spiritual, centers healthily balance the individual's subjectivity: they check what might be called the primary narcissism of the lower, or sensual, centers. They awaken the individual to the reality beyond the self and urge him into healthy relatedness with that reality. But the spiritual centers must be balanced by the sensual centers, for any overemphasis on the object weakens the dynamic power of the subject—its subjective integrity. If the object is everything, the subject is nothing. By the same token, if the subject is everything, the object is nothing. Imbalance produces either the selfless idealist or the self-intoxicated megalomaniac—St. Francis or Napoleon.

What prevents the overemphasis of sympathetic, or voluntary, impulses is that the unconscious is, by hypothesis, a self-regulating system with compensatory functions which are automatically invoked in the interests of self-realization. Thus when the infant recoils from "assimilatory unison," its effort is "blind, almost mechanistic" (*PU*, 223). The automatic self-regulation of the psyche is correlated, in fact, with the physical regulatory systems of the body: "For at every point psyche and [organ] functions are so nearly identified that only by holding our breath can we realize their *duality* in identification" (*PU*, 243). The body is "mechanico-material": its behavior, like that of inorganic matter, is determined by the laws of mechanical action and reaction; the psyche, on the other hand, is "vital-creative," a vital force arising within matter. Thus life and death are joined in the body. But both body and psyche are self-regulating, since the general law of the universe is a law of homeostasis, or equilibrium.

If permitted to function without interference, the self-regulating mechanisms of the unconscious would ensure perfect health. But in its dealings with the external world, the psyche is always threatened by forces that can disturb the dynamic balance. Thus it became necessary for Lawrence to postulate another mechanism, or "faculty," which, like the Freudian ego, adjusts the deep instinctive demands of the psyche to the realities of the world. This new entity is the voice of the entire self, a "*spontaneous* will," Lawrence says, which "reacts at once against the exaggeration of any one particular circuit of polarity." This will is "a great balancing faculty, the faculty whereby automatization is *prevented* in the evolving psyche" (*PU*, 248). He adds that this "faculty for self-determination" is identical with "conscience" in the premental state. In *Fantasia*, less "scientific," Lawrence calls this faculty the Holy Ghost, or the individual "in his totality of consciousness, in his oneness of being" (*FU*, 133). As such, it is "pure conscience" (*FU*, 134), apparently similar to the Freudian superego. But it performs some of the functions of the ego as well. First, it recognizes the need for healthy change. As Lawrence says in "Reflections on the Death of a Porcupine," the Holy Ghost "seeks for ever a new incarnation, and subordinates the old to the new" (*Phoenix II*, 471). Thus it opposes "conservative psyche," which is formed by society or by conservative instinct. Second, the Holy Ghost prescribes limits. It teaches us, Lawrence says, not to carry any of our promptings to extremes; it teaches us to laugh at ourselves. It is thus a spokesman for balance, a conscious arbitrator articulating the deep unconscious needs for balance in a world often hostile to such balance. Third, the Holy Ghost passes judgment on one's conduct. Its judgments arise from a life wisdom that surpasses all conventional ethical prescriptions in depth and awareness, a wisdom that Lawrence defines as

> a state of soul. It is the state wherein we know our wholeness and the complicated, manifold nature of our being. It is the state wherein we know the great relations which exist between us and our near ones. And it is the state which accepts full responsibility, first for our own souls, and then for the living dynamic relations wherein we have our being. It is no use expecting the other person to know. Each must know for himself. [*FU*, 53]

Such knowledge issues in morality, which is "a delicate act of adjustment on the soul's part, not a rule or a prescription" (*FU*, 54). The Holy Ghost, aware of the nature of mind and of conservative psyche, receptive to the deep sympathetic and voluntary promptings of the soul, and guided by the need for both balance and purposiveness, performs the act of adjustment, which is morality. So it strives for "the silence and central appeasedness of maturity," together with the assumption of "a sacred responsibility for the next purposive step into the future" (*FU*, 124). When it says, "I am wrong," it means that one has failed to live in accordance with one's deepest promptings, or has failed to effect the proper balance of these promptings, allowing a part of the self to govern the whole. Its judgments are thus, in a sense, a priori synthetic judgments: a priori in the sense that their essential purposive and creative form is determined by the impulses of the soul; synthetic in that experiential data enter into the final determination of morality.

One is tempted to call the Holy Ghost an "ideal social self," as William James defined it: "a self that is at least *worthy* of approving recognition by the highest *possible* judging companion"—for example, by such a judge as God (*Principles of Psychology,* 301). Freudians would see such a self as a superego, an introjected primal father. For Lawrence, however, the Holy Ghost arises, not from the social matrix or from primal repression, but from the unity of the self, with its intense hunger for purpose. The origin of the Holy Ghost is therefore apparently the desire for purpose and perfection that arises initially in the soul itself; and Lawrence's Holy Ghost, like Freud's ego, arises from the unconscious itself—but from the unconscious defined, not with reference to a pleasure or Nirvana principle, but with reference to a will for meaning. The Holy Ghost may well arise, then, only in religious men and women, in those who spontaneously direct attention to Meaning and Purpose as an expression of the divine will.

It is precisely this direction of attention that makes possible religious action. The Holy Ghost opens the doors of attention to all that is relevant to God's will and closes the doors to all that threatens to trivialize or to secularize life. Disdaining a secular security, affirming only "Thy will be done," the Holy Ghost decides how man's inherent sense of purpose may be translated into experience in the here and now. People directed by the Holy Ghost are innately leaders, by virtue of their religious awareness and their disposition to relate all conduct to religious purposes.

Thus the Holy Ghost is virtually identical with the "Self" that, in Jung and in Erich Neumann, listens to a "voice" that speaks only to exceptional people: "The revelation of the Voice to a single person presupposes an individual whose individuality is so strong that he can make himself independent of the collective and its values. All founders of ethics are heretics, since they oppose the revelation of the Voice to the deliverances of conscience as the representative of the old ethic."[6] According to Neumann, the Self, which listens to the Voice, takes the place of "the heteronomous super-ego" and is "installed" as a godlike power, "consciously appointed and recognised by the ego as an authoritative control centre" (123). The role of this Self is to achieve wholeness and to avoid "partial systems" (124). In the Self the divine Voice (the collective unconscious in Jung and Neumann) speaks, and the Jungian "law of compensation" is heeded. Balance is achieved.

From this Self arises a "new ethic," based on acceptance and assimilation of "the shadow," on a revaluation of "good" and "evil," and on acceptance of personal responsibility to "work through" one's own evil.

What is most striking in Jung and Neumann is that "the ego does not possess the ultimate power of decision in the new ethic" (144). The ultimate power arises from the divine. With this, Lawrence would agree. The Holy Ghost is a Director who is Directed. The paradox may perhaps be explained by an analogy between living and writing a novel.

Once a novel is begun, the writer often discovers that it "writes itself." It has its own inherent needs, tendencies, and momentum, and the wise writer realizes that he must allow these to unfold according to necessity and probability. His task is not to interfere. Yet at the same time he maintains a gentle remissive control, alert to the possibility that one of the generative sources of his total composition may assume disproportionate strength or fascination and may assert itself at the expense of other elements in the vital balance of the whole. For example, one character may seek to "take over," may become so interesting or attractive in his own right that the novelist will be inclined to give him free rein; or one line of action may acquire a fatal fascination and seek a development that would upset the proportions of the whole. In these cases, the writer, without doing violence to the unfolding organic whole, must check the impulse toward overemphasis. Yet the checking, or the control, is done not because the writer wills it but because the whole requires it. The writer is the voice of the organic whole, not of a part. He must submit himself to the inherent needs of the whole.

A similar task is performed by Lawrence's integral self—a sort of egoless ego that has no intention of asserting its own wishes but only seeks to allow the deep needs of life to unfold according to their nature and in harmony with the will of nature.[7] "Not I, but the Wind." The wind is the great creative and destructive will manifested in the self. Egoistic assertion—forcing the self to act against its deepest desires—can lead only to psychic mutilation.

An obvious objection to Lawrence's Holy Ghost is that it is a mere sublimation. Given what we know of Lawrence's puritanical Congregationalist upbringing and of his oedipal problem, his insistence on a strong conscience would seem to have derived from guilt. But the guilt might be derived also from an ineluctable existential sense of responsibility. Paul Tillich says, in *The Courage to Be*, that man's being is "not only given to him but also demanded of him. He is responsible for it;

literally, he is required to answer, if he is asked, what he has made of himself. He who asks him is his judge, namely he himself, who, at the same time, stands against him."[8] From an existential point of view, Lawrence's hypothesis is entirely reasonable. It is also reasonable if we hold, with William James, that consciousness is not the "dull rattling off of a chain forged innumerable aeons ago" but is capable of really deciding. Lawrence's Holy Ghost, through its effort of attention, checks or encourages instinctive promptings and intelligently adjusts, without compromising, those promptings to a recalcitrant world. The data of religious experience—James's observation of the dynamogenic nature of belief and the authoritative nature of "peak experiences"—are relevant to our understanding of the "balancing will" of the Holy Ghost. When Freud spoke of religion as mass illusion, he did not take into account George Bernard Shaw's observation that the masses are fundamentally irreligious; only a few people are disposed to listen to the Holy Ghost.

The importance of the Holy Ghost in Lawrence's psychology cannot be overrated. We still hear, on every hand, that Lawrence believed in impulsiveness. But he recognized that the instincts, left to themselves, can bring us to destruction, like that of the dinosaurs. Most men, incapable of listening to the dark gods who come into the clearing of the known self, are indeed driven into blind impulsiveness, the blind pattern of "action and reaction" that Lawrence diagnosed as the psychological cause of the First World War. In most men the Holy Ghost never develops. This is not to say that their instincts are evil. As Kate Leslie reflects in *The Plumed Serpent*, there are, within nature, correctives to evil tendencies, and these will arise provided there are controlling leaders. Also Rupert Birkin in *Women in Love*, we recall, advocates acting spontaneously on one's deepest impulses provided one is fit for it—that is, provided one is indeed a higher man. Evil can flourish only if there is no control at all or if control is exerted by those who perpetuate "partial systems." As Lawrence shows in *Women in Love* and several other works, anarchy is the result of the abdication of responsibility for oneself as a part of the whole. Acquiescence to the "partial" system of Western society breeds destructiveness both without and within. The deep need of the present, therefore, is for intelligent religious leaders.

Most men are ruled not by the Holy Ghost but by what Lawrence calls "conservative psyche." In postulating conservative psyche, which is formed by "tradition" and seeks to "persist in its old motions" (*FU*, 133), Lawrence suggests an artificially induced or conditioned self—a persona—that prevents the spontaneous functioning of the unconscious. If the Holy Ghost is a healthy and spontaneous conscience, conservative psyche is an unhealthy, mechanical, and socially formed conscience. So Lawrence, like Freud, insists on the conflict between innate desire and a repressive civilization (internalized as "conservative psyche") that condemns all instinct as shameful. Civilization in the form of capitalism erects the spurious model of the successful self-made man, a tough competitor, and thus suppresses the instinctive sympathetic impulse toward communal action and fellow feeling. Paradoxically, at the same time the rationalization of production requires that men "fit in," that they become functional units of the great machine; thus, as the economist Joseph Schumpeter has observed, men under capitalism become "rational and unheroic," and their deep instinctive *voluntary* impulses are suppressed. Christianity and liberalism perform similar surgery on the unconscious. Christianity suppresses the sensual sympathetic impulses; liberalism, celebrating the ideals of equality, democracy, the common welfare, and the common man, suppresses the deep voluntary impulses. A false self, the I-persona described by Trigant Burrow, acquires control over the whole psyche. The Holy Ghost, which "prompts us to be real," is not heard (*SCAL*, 79).

Mention of the I-persona directs attention to Lawrence's conception of the conscious self.

Lawrence views the mind as an instrument of the body in its struggle for survival. (Here one might recall William James's endorsement of Spencer's idea that mental life is one with bodily life and is directed toward self-preservation.) The mind, as the instrument of the body, is mechanico-material, not vital. Ideas arise automatically, or mechanically, as "the final concrete or registered result of living dynamic interchange and reactions"—that is, of the living sympathetic and voluntary urges (*FU*, 83). Thus the idea of "freedom" arises as the end result of a dynamic voluntary impulse in the psyche. But the idea is like a reflex action: it can only indicate in the crudest way the feeling state or the unconscious response of the soul. Moreover, if the idea is perpetuated after its dynamic cause has ceased to act, it is false, referring not to a living activity of the psyche but to a dead world, a past world. In the final analysis, then, all ideas are false; symbols do not correspond to existence.

The ego, like the mind, also originates in the body as an instrument for self-preservation. In *Psychoanalysis and the Unconscious* Lawrence says that "the first scream of the ego" is the scream of "asserted isolation" (222), but his use of the word *ego* in this context is misleading, for what he is referring to is rather the subjective voluntary center, an unconscious spontaneous impulse. What he means, I suspect, is that the ego arises from the unconscious, as the Freudian ego arises from the id. But it arises only as a result of the confrontation with the hostile external world. It is not spontaneous: it is an instrument that, like the mind, is formed late in the evolution of life and is mechanical, or automatic; it is formed by the body in its defensive-aggressive motions and is nurtured by a society that emphasizes power and control. Thus the ego is part of "conservative psyche," a "spurious self" that is inherited "*en bloc* from the preceding generation" (*Phoenix*, 710). The ego is indeed the "daily I," whose existence we have been taught to assume is real. The ego is oriented towards action, not towards being. It is directed not towards self-realization but towards domination over others or defense against others or perpetuation of the idea of the self which has been artificially induced by a society that stresses ownership, property, and acquisition—all goals of an individualistic consciousness which is directed toward power or defense, not towards being. As conscious will, the ego directs the mind to "arrogate its machine-motions and automatizations over the whole of life" (*PU*, 247). Such a will, as in Nietzsche, is the base will of the mob, not the spontaneous deep will of the Holy Ghost. In seeking a maximum of protection instead of a maximum of being, the ego thus constitutes a powerful weapon that can be directed against life itself as the Freudian superego may be directed against the libido.

Thus the conscious self—the mind, the ego, and the conscious will—which develops out of the power impulses of the voluntary centers but in the service of the body, not of the soul, is a manifestion of the mechanical. The body and its conscious instruments, being material and mechanical, constitute a destructive or death principle; the soul, being spontaneous and creative, constitutes a life principle. That is why Lawrence speaks of the "*duality* in identification" of body and psyche.

It remains for Lawrence to explain the mechanisms by which the balance of the unconscious self is upset. These would appear to be both constitutional and developmental.

The constitutional causes of imbalance, as Lawrence describes them, have to do with inherited or racial tendencies. One may be "sympathetically over-balanced" or "fierce-willed" (*PU*, 230). One may be "Northern" and white, and hence spiritually inclined, or "African" and dark, hence sensually inclined. These constitutional tendencies are so strong that Lawrence believed the white man's realization of his own being must take a direction entirely different from that of the black man.

As for the developmental causes of psychic imbalance, they arise from trespassing on the integrity of the individual. That is why Lawrence defines morality as "the basic desire to preserve the perfect correspondence between the self and the object, to have no trepass and no breach of integrity, nor yet any refaulture in the vitalistic interchange" (*PU*, 227). In the development of the individual, psychic disorders arise from violations of, or interferences with, the integrity of the self. Generally speaking, one center of the psyche is stimulated, while the other centers are repressed. The key word here is *bullying*, the tyrannical censure and rejection of the deep unconscious impulses. Bullying is built into the entire structure of Western civilization. All institutions conspire to prevent the individual's self-realization and to foster his ideal conception of himself as an individual ego. The family, with the Spiritual Woman as spokeswoman for "the love and benevolence ideal," initiates the process of repression and causes "a dislocation or collapse of the great voluntary centres, a derangement of the will" (*FU*, 52). The schools bully the child into passivity and into acceptance of the Ideal in all its forms. Christianity, "instead of doing as it should, collecting the soul into its own strength and integrity," joins in the attack on the dynamic voluntary centers, leaving men "decomposed and degenerate" (*PS*, 304). Capitalism, which demands submission to money power and forces the individual into alienated work, further cripples the independence of the psyche. Socialism, insisting on equality and collectivism, denies all individuality. Moreover, the deep desire for purposiveness is denied again and again by a civilization that teaches men to live for money and success—that false "purposiveness" of the ego.

Thus the energies of the sympathetic and voluntary centers are denied release. But instinctual energies cannot be abolished; they can only be diverted into new directions. And because it is chiefly the great voluntary impulses that are denied healthy release, displacement occurs in two ways. First, in socially acceptable aggression: that is, in capitalistic domination or in "work," an aggression against material objects. Second, in violent aggression against the self or against others—in short, in reaction. As in Freudian psychology the increasing power of the superego, blocking the release of libidinal energies, issues in aggression against the ego or against the world, so in Lawrence the increasing power of the conscious system, blocking release of both sympathetic and voluntary energies, issues in aggression against the self and against the world. And as in Freud, a number of unconscious mechanisms arise in the self's desperate attempts to deal with the threats to its development.

Lawrence does not provide any clear or systematic account of these unconscious mechanisms, but we see them clearly in the novels. The chief mechanism is perhaps regression (or, in Freudian terms, a pathological increase in narcissistic libido): the desire, arising from the unconscious sympathetic center, to return or sink back into "the old oneness," the female source. This mechanism arises in part from a deep frustration of the desire for purposive activity and in part from a frustration of the sympathetic impulse. Neither the love nor the power impulses are gratified, and the individual, cut off from others and lacking purpose, becomes childlike, seeking an infantile bliss in the Magna Mater, on whom he projects his desire for absolute identification with the All. Another mechanism is repression, which, as we have seen, originates largely in the bullying of the spiritual woman. (Lawrence does not see the "severe" father as an instigator of repression but rather as one who may healthily encourage the child to stiffen the centers of independence.) Still another mechanism is displacement, manifested in the diversion of aggressive impulse into "work" or production. And sublimation of the power impulse is repeatedly exhibited in artists, such as Loerke or Gudrun Brangwen in *Women in Love,* who are drawn to art in reaction to the deep frustration of their sympathetic impulses.

The only cure for such disorders of the self is obviously to find a way to permit the healthy release of the frustrated instinctual energies. Lawrence's final solutions to the problem of mental disorder are as bold as they are Utopian.

First, the method of rearing children must change. The child must be allowed to develop freely; he must not be bullied. Above all, the male's voluntary centers must be strengthened. The child must learn to be manly and independent. Boys should become soldiers—not passive, regimented soldiers but free individuals, disciplined, vigorous, and resourceful. The model for the Lawrencian army might thus be the Boy Scout organization, which encourages each individual to grow creatively through meaningful participation in a purposive organization.

Second, the schools must be closed.

Third, Christianity must be abandoned.

Fourth, capitalism must be abolished.

In sum, all coercive social institutions must be either dramatically altered or abolished.

Beyond this, there remains the problem of releasing aggressive energies in ways that will not lead to sadistic cruelty. Here, as we have seen in discussing Nietzsche, Lawrence is driven to distinguish between two types of power impulses, the conscious or egotistical impulse and the unconscious or religious-creative impulse. The former is indeed dangerous—a will to wield power over others. The latter is power in creative destruction and in the creation of a new heaven and a new earth. Conflict, of course, is inevitable. In *The Plumed Serpent*, Don Ramón, in building his new religion, must fight against the tyranny of the old religion. But Ramón is impelled not only by a reactive desire to root out the tares but also by a creative sympathetic desire to join with others in sowing the wheat. Fight he must. Fighting for life is indeed a healthy and inevitable release of the power impulse; but fighting complemented by the discharge of sympathetic impulses is not sadistic.

Much more could be said about various subtleties in Lawrence's psychology. In the last chapter of *Psychoanalysis and the Unconscious*, for example, Lawrence indicates that the four centers which comprise the "first field of consciousness" (that is, premental awareness) are not the whole of the psyche: there are, in reality, seven centers which, as William York Tindall has shown, are derived from the *cakras* (or *chakras*, as Lawrence spelled the term) of Hinduism. Howard Harper, Jr. points out, however, that Lawrence does not make use of seven centers in his fiction and that to understand his psychology as it figures in his art, it is enough for criticism to grasp the essentials of his analysis of the psyche.

His conclusions, however dismaying they have been found to be by many critics, constitute a coherent psychology with well-defined assumptions and a logical development of the implications of those assumptions. As for the value of this psychology as a contribution to knowledge, that will become the subject of my final chapter.

It is clear that the key word in Lawrence's psychology, as perhaps in most psychologies, is *balance*, and that the word has for Lawrence not only a common-sense meaning (work balanced by rest, etc.) but also a "scientific" meaning derived from speculation on the all-subsuming law of the universe. To indicate the pervasiveness of the idea of balance in his thinking, I want to consider Lawrence's analysis of balance at three levels of being: (1) God or the Unknown; (2) the individual and sexual relationships; and (3) organic nature, society, and history. It will be necessary to retrace some familiar ground in order to emphasize the importance of a central Lawrencian insight: that balance consists in "a flowing together and a flowing apart" and that departures from this deep organic rhythm, or striving for balance, entail illness or destruction.

"GOD"

Lawrence was uneasy about the word "God" and seems to have preferred "the Unknown" or "the fourth dimension" to designate that "something far more deeply interfused" that rolls through all things and in the mind of man. Whatever his vocabulary, however, he sees the "God-stuff" in the universe as governed by the great "law of dual attraction and repulsion, a law of polarity" (*Phoenix*, 692). A flowing together is succeeded by a flowing apart. Thus Lawrence writes in his 1915 essay "The Crown":

> God is not the one infinite, nor the other [i.e., not the darkness or the light, the beginning or the end, the blood or the spirit, matter or spirit], our immortality is not in the original eternity, neither in the ultimate eternity. God is the utter relation between the two eternities. He is the flowing together and the flowing apart.
>
> This utter relation is timeless, absolute and perfect. It is in the Beginning and the End, just the same. . . . It is the Unrevealed God: what Jesus called the Holy Ghost.

Lawrence goes on to say that

> the true God is *created* every time a pure relationship, or a consummation out of twoness into oneness takes place. . . . And a man, if he win to a sheer fusion in himself of all the manifold creation, a pure relation, a sheer gleam of oneness out of manyness, then this man is God created where before God was uncreated. He is the Holy Ghost in tissue of flame and flesh, whereas before, the Holy Ghost was but Ghost. [*Phoenix II*, 410, 412]

God "uncreated" is God latent or potential or undifferentiated—pure matter or pure spirit not yet brought together in the differentiating act of creation. God "created" is the incarnation resulting from the fusion of matter and spirit. God is revealed in the Holy Ghost, which brings together matter and spirit, male and female, the unconscious and the conscious minds. In the human psyche, the Holy Ghost is the great spontaneous balancing power. In the Unknown or in God, it is similar. God is created when matter and spirit flow together; God is also present in the flowing apart—the destructive process:

> There are two roads. There is hot sunshine leaping down and interpenetrating the earth to blossom. And there is red fire rushing upward on its path to return, in the coming asunder. Down comes the fire from the sun to the seed, splash into the water of the tiny reservoir of life. Up spurts the foam and stream of greenness, a tree, a fountain of roses, a cloud, a steamy pear-blossom. Back again goes the fire, leaves shrivel and roses fall, back goes the fire to the sun, away goes the dim water. [*Phoenix*, 689]

In the act of creation, fire mates with water, spirit with matter; then fire returns to the sun, the watery matter divides from the fire, the living creature dies. The God-process is continuous; to repeat, the great law of the universe "is a law of dual attraction and repulsion, a law of polarity" (692).

THE INDIVIDUAL AND SEXUAL RELATIONS

Life itself, Lawrence writes in his 1928 essay "Will Women Change?" "is a flow, a soft curving flow, a flowing together and a flowing apart and a flowing together again, in a long subtle motion that has no full-stops and no points, even if there are rough places" (*Phoenix II*, 541). In healthy sexual union, male and female "flow together" and then flow apart. No longer separate and alone, they enter into "oneness" or "pure relation." This healthy union is not possible unless each gives up the old ego and submits to the "creative destruction" of love. The old self is cast off and "dies." A new and greater self is realized. The deficiency or incompleteness in each (as male, as female) is overcome in the relationship in which oneness is made of twoness.

But the flowing apart is essential. The healthy male, having lost himself or "died" in the darkness of unconscious love, is resurrected to adventure into the unknown of the light. As his creative, purposive spirit is awakened and energized through his descent to the infinite darkness, he knows that he must venture into the light and fight to create a new world. Through love, he realizes that he cannot continue to serve the old, dead world; he must build a world in which the will of God is realized. Thus the rhythm of flowing together and flowing apart is the rhythm of death and new creation.

In unhealthy sexual union, the male and female refuse to surrender themselves to the destructive creation wherein a new and greater self is born. They remain separate egos; they do not flow together. On the contrary, sexual relationships take the form of a veering from the extreme of servitude to the opposite extreme of domination, while the individual remains unchanged by the relationship, an invulnerable ego seeking egoistic triumph. Such unhealthy relationships are marked by "sensationalism" and "reduction": in effect, each partner desires to destroy the other—"reduce" the other to inorganic matter at the disposal of the omnipotent ego. The natural rhythm of flowing together and apart is broken, and the terrible rhythm of "action and reaction"—from one extreme to the opposite (submission to tyranny)—results. Gerald Crich and Gudrun Brangwen illustrate this unnatural relationship. Unwilling to accept death of the old ego and to enter into a relationship in "ultimate trust," each battles to subdue and destroy the other.

In "The Reality of Peace," written in 1917 in an effort to focus attention on the unconscious sadistic impulse behind the war, Lawrence calls for acceptance of the natural rhythm of life and death. He insists that "the first great act of living is to encompass death in the understanding." One must accept corruption and death, must realize that "from our bodies comes the issue of corruption as well as the issue of creation. We must have our being in both, our knowledge must consist in both" (*Phoenix*, 676). To do this is to "lapse upon a current that carries us like repose, and extinguishes in repose our self-insistence and self-will" (671). Surrendering himself to the current of life and death, man becomes "a new being": "When we understand our extreme of being in death, we have surpassed into a new being" (676). In such understanding, the individual can say: "I fear neither love nor hate nor death nor pain nor abhorrence. . . . even the abhorrent I will understand and be at peace with. Not by exclusion, but by incorporation and unison" (677). The "marsh" and the "fire" are inseparable, the marsh flower of the flux of putrescence, and the fire of creation. Similarly, ferocity and strength are inseparable from love and submission. The tiger impulse and the lamb impulse—that is, the destructive impulse of power and the creative impulse of love—complement each other. "In a world of petty Alexanders, St. Francis is the star. In a world of sheep, the wolf is god. Each, saint or wolf, shines by virtue of opposition" (691). Thus Lawrence, in announcing "I shall accept all my desires and repudiate none" (680), affirms both the "desire of life or desire of death, desire of putting together or desire of putting asunder." As he says in "The Crown," "There must always be some balance between the passion for destruction and the passion for creation, in every living activity" (*Phoenix II*, 405). To accept this balance is to be "saved from the vast and obscene self-conceit which is the ruling force of the world that envelops me" (*Phoenix*, 685). Again, it is important to note that Lawrence's submission "to the primal unknown out of which issues the all" (695) is coupled with his attack on the traditional notion that man exists as an independent ego. "We are not created of ourselves," he insists; "I do but conduct the unknown of my beginning to the unknown of my end" (696, 697).

THE BALANCE IN ORGANIC NATURE, IN SOCIETY, AND IN HISTORY

The balance needed in the psyche corresponds perfectly to the balance in organic nature. A herd of deer would multiply beyond limits if unchecked, but "the tiger, like a brand of fire, leaps upon [the deer] to restore the balance" (*Phoenix*, 689–90). He "waters his thirst with the moist fawn" (690). The excess of water (inert "female" matter, associated with the "female" herd that would destroy all individuality) must be checked by "fire"—active male power. So in the human community, when the herd of egos, insulated from the realities of life and death, has multiplied and threatens to crush the fiery individual, a man of power is needed to restore the balance. Confronting the "nauseous herd together," with their "one aim, one will, enveloping them into an obscene oneness," the individual wants to "go forth with whips, like the old chieftain" (685–86). Thus Lawrence suggests, as he had suggested in "Study of Thomas Hardy," that in society, as in the psyche, as in the whole of nature, balance must be maintained. If society becomes too "female," too submissive, too sympathetic, it must be balanced by a male assertiveness. The homogeneous society of the Old Testament, "female" in its passive acceptance of the will of the Father, living thus in a darkness of the senses and of the unconscious (the self finding fulfillment as a member of the tribe), must be countered by the assertion of a male voluntary principle: Jesus affirms his separateness from the tribe and his devotion to the spirit, to that which "is Not-Me"; the individual is thus fulfilled in his realization of a reality beyond the tribe (the "Me"). The lamb in the soul must be balanced by the tiger. Indeed, there is in nature the desire for death whenever the female or the male assumes excessive control. The doe desires to die in the jaws of the lion, Lawrence says, because the doe, as the agent of nature, can only desire what nature desires. Therefore a man, insofar as he acts in harmony with the deep Will of which he is a part, will desire his own psychic death—that is, death of the female promptings if they become too strong, death of the male promptings if they become too strong: "Creative life is the attaining a perfect consummation with death. When in my mind there arises the idea of life, then this idea must encompass the idea of death, and this encompassing is the germination of a new epoch of the mind" (*Phoenix*, 682).

The idea of flowing together and flowing apart is clearly indicated in Lawrence's depiction of his utopian theocracy in *The Plumed Serpent*. The men of Quetzalcoatl "flow together" around the drum, "dark, collective men, non-individual," surrendering their egoistic wills to the leader who is one with Quetzalcoatl; but each man is given "the greater manhood" by this merging and comes into being as an individual. As in sexual relationships, union (and death of the old self) makes possible a rebirth: a new pride is born in the men of

Quetzalcoatl. Having entered into sympathetic unison "in actively making a world," each man acquires a new dignity as an individual. Both sympathetic and voluntary urges are satisfied and balanced.

Less mystically, in *Mornings in Mexico,* Lawrence describes the convergence of the Mexicans to the marketplace for "contact and centripetal flow," followed by the "swerve of repulsion" and individuality:

> They have been part of a great stream of men flowing to a centre, to the vortex of the marketplace. And here they have felt life concentrate upon them. . . . There is no goal, and no abiding-place, and nothing is fixed. . . . the natives curved in a strong swirl, towards the vortex of the market. Then on a strong swerve of repulsion, curved out and away again, into space.
>
> Nothing but the touch, the spark of contact. That, no more. That, which is most elusive, still the only treasure. Come, and gone, and yet the clue itself. [*MM,* 42]

This flowing together and flowing apart, this coming and going, he then associates with the evening star "when it is neither night nor day"—that symbol, in *The Plumed Serpent,* of the reconciliation of flesh and spirit, darkness and light, origin and end.

Again, in describing the dancing of the Indians in *Mornings in Mexico,* Lawrence uses the metaphor of the flowing together and apart:

> What are they doing? Who knows? But perhaps they are giving themselves again to the pulsing, incalculable fall of the blood, which seeks forever to fall to the centre of the earth, while the heart, like a planet pulsating in orbit, keeps up the strange, lonely circulating of the separate human existence.
>
> But what we seek, passively, in sleep, they perhaps seek actively, in the round dance. it is the homeward pulling of the blood . . . . the dark blood, falling back from the mind, from sight and speech and knowing, back to the great central source where is rest and unspeakable renewal. [48–49]

The flowing together in the great Source (or into a kind of collective unconscious) gives "rest" and "unspeakable renewal"—exactly what occurs in the act of coition when the self is given up and renewed by a contact which is almost a merging and a self-obliteration. But the individual remains separate. In the "mime dances," the Indian defends "his own isolation in the rhythm of the universe . . . , dancing in the peril of his own isolation, in the overweening of his own singleness" (49). God is "immersed . . . in creation" (52), and if the Indian is embedded in the mystery, God is embedded, no less, in the Indian.

This brief survey of Lawrence's development of the idea of flowing together and flowing apart is sufficient to indicate the pervasiveness of the insight in his thinking—from his cosmology to his handling of sexual relationships to his analysis of the balance in nature, in society, and in the psyche, where the two great premental centers, the sympathetic solar plexus and the voluntary lumbar ganglion, send forth promptings to "assimilatory unison" and to "recoil" and utter division from the whole. The idea also figures in Lawrence's theory of history, which, as I indicated in the first chapter, exhibits the to-and-fro of human beings sweeping "together in one great concerted action" and then sweeping "apart . . . on the tides of opposition" (*MEH*, xi–xii). As Lawrence says in his essay "Morality and the Novel," "Life is so made that opposites sway about a trembling centre of balance. The sins of the fathers are visited on the children. If the fathers drag down the balance on the side of love, peace, and production, then in the third or fourth generation the balance will swing back violently to hate, rage, and destruction. We must balance as we go" (*Phoenix*, 529).

But perfect balance is rare. It is achieved only when the impulse of attraction is equal to that of repulsion—that is, when the individual, entering into a pure relationship with the Other, yet resists fusion and retains his integrity as an individual. Lawrence's most apt metaphor for this relationship is the orbit. Schopenhauer noted that the orbit of a planet around a central body is the result of a tension between centrifugal and centripetal forces:

> On a large scale [the struggle to live] shows itself in the relation between the central body and the planet, for although the planet is in absolute dependence, yet it always resists, just like the chemical forces in the organism; hence arises the constant tension between centripetal and centrifugal force, which keeps the globe in motion, and is itself an example of that universal essential conflict of the manifestation of the will. [*The World as Will and Idea,* 1:193]

Lawrence holds onto the idea of the orbit while dropping the idea of conflict. When the forces working for attraction or repulsion are equal, the soul is reborn and passes into a perfect orbit around the darkness or the origin. As Lawrence says in "The Orbit," part IV of "the Reality of Peace":

> It is when I am drawn by centripetal force into communion with the whole, and when I flee in equivalent centrifugal force away into the splendour of beaming isolation, when these two balance and match each other in mid-space, that suddenly, like a miracle, I find the peace of my orbit. Then I travel neither back nor forth. I hover in the unending delight of a rapid, resultant orbit. [*Phoenix,* 693]

Such a peace is suggested when Rupert Birkin, fulfilled in his love for Ursula, assumes a trajectory between the two infinities:

> To him, the wonder of this transit was overwhelming. He was falling through a gulf of infinite darkness, like a meteorite plunging across the chasm between the worlds. The world was torn in two, and he was plunging like an unlit star through the ineffable rift. What was beyond was not yet for him. He was overcome by the trajectory.
>
> In a trance he lay enfolding Ursula round about. His face was against her fine, fragile hair, he breathed its fragrance with the sea and the profound night. And his soul was at peace; yielded, as he fell into the unknown. This was the first time that an utter and absolute peace had entered his heart, now, in this final transit out of life. [*WL*, 443–44]

In this passage Birkin is not yet ready for his adventure into the beyond. He is like an unlit star, the light of the male spirit put out in his surrender to the darkness. He breathes, in conjunction with the fragrance of Ursula's hair, the sea and the profound night. He experiences the "peace" of sexual union and of union with the unknown—the divine reality. But the word *trajectory* suggests his orbit between past and future, origin and end. As he embraces the darkness of the origin, he remains a star spirit, though an unlit star at this moment.

Life, for the "truly living," must incarnate the rhythm of the God process. So it is not surprising that Lawrence's definition of life is identical with his definition of God. It is clear that the premises of Lawrence's psychology are implicit in his earliest essays and that his two books on the unconscious are almost entirely in harmony with the ideas developed five or six years earlier.

As his work proceeded, he sought to clarify his thinking. Indeed, in his revisions of his novels one can observe his working to define as sharply as possible the nature of the split between voluntary and sympathetic impulses. In Composite A of the handwritten manuscript of *The Rainbow*, dated 2 March 1915, Lawrence wrote the following passage:

> "Come here," she said, unsure.
>
> For some moments he did not move. Then he rose slowly and went across the hearth. He stood before her and looked down at her. [137]

But Lawrence then inserted this sentence after "went across the hearth": "*It required an almost deathly effort of volition, or of acquiescence*" (emphasis mine). Tom Brangwen's ambivalence here is seen clearly as a split between his sympathetic impulse to acquiesce and his voluntary impulse to resist Lydia Lensky and hold himself single and separate. Not only Lawrence's diction but also the forms of his novels come to reflect the laws of his psychology, as will be seen.

Yet one must also bear in mind Lawrence's statement that his "subjective science" was deduced from his fiction. Many of his laws are implicit even in his earliest novel, *The White Peacock*. His thinking was far more systematic, more coherent, and more detached than many critics have thought.

But it is time to turn to the novels and to the unique problems he confronted as he sought to blend his science and his religious doctrine in persuasive images of life.

4

Problems of the Artist-Psychologist

DHLDHLDHLDHLDHLDHLDHLDHLDHLDHLDHLDHLDHLDHLDHLDHLDHLDHLDHLDHLDHLDHLDHLDHLDHLDHLDHLDHLDHLDHLDHLDHLDHLDHLDHLDHLDHLDHLDHLDHLDHLDHL

What problems did Lawrence encounter as he worked to perfect an art in which his laws of psychology became important determinants of the forms of his fiction? Many of these problems have been identified by Lawrence's critics: "the failure and the triumph" of his art, as Eliseo Vivas calls it, is a theme intricately orchestrated in criticism over four decades. Yet analysis of Lawrence's art still cries out for precise definitions of the forms of his novels and for carefully reasoned determination of what such forms require to be shaped with maximum beauty and power. While it is generally accepted nowadays that the novels are experimental and that we cannot expect of them the sort of characterization, mimetic fidelity, and formal development that we look for in novels more conventionally plotted, the question remains: what should we look for? To argue, with John Worthen, that the novels are "thought-adventures," "self-testing" and "exploratory" is useful but does not enable us finally to decide whether they are well made, or as well made as they might be. My purpose in this chapter, therefore, is to define the nature of the forms that Lawrence invented and then to examine the major problems that Lawrence had to solve if he was to bring his work to formal perfection.

Although each novel is unique and will be considered later in its uniqueness, similar problems arise in all of the novels because they all focus on the same question: how can the individual find a healthy balance of his love and power urges, both spiritual and sensual, and achieve maximum of being in himself, in relation to others, and in relation to the All? This question forces Lawrence to consider in all of his novels the same basic obstacles to health and the same contrasting ways of seeking fulfillment: the right way and the wrong. Lawrence's consolidated conception of the human condition and of the alternatives available to men and women in their search for health forces him to return again and again to similar characters, situations, and plot complications to dramatize the moral and psychological problems arising in the quest for the right path. To consider these strategies common to his work as a whole deepens understanding of the formal problems of each work taken separately and heightens awareness of the means available to Lawrence to bring his work to perfection. The possibilities and perils of his art are laid bare. Criticism is enabled to appreciate the difficulties inherent in his task and to assess the artistic effectiveness of his solutions to his problems from a broader perspective.

THE THREEFOLD PURPOSE

No definition of the nature of Lawrence's art can fail to take into account three essential shaping principles: the didactic, the "scientific," and the more or less conventionally mimetic. Shaping his art in accordance with these principles, Lawrence continually shifts his perspective, moving his camera back, then in, then back again. As a didactic writer, viewing life from his religious point of view, he constructs characters who are moral types, almost allegorical figures, whose conduct is judged in relation to the norms provided by his vision of perfection. Then he moves close in, presenting his characters' experience in all its felt vividness, so that we share vicariously the sufferings and yearnings of their souls. With a Keatsian "negative capability," he identifies himself sympathetically with his characters; the reader feels dread and pity for their sufferings and frustrations or rejoices in their brave defiance of a life-denying world. At the same time, Lawrence traces the patterns of their behavior according to his laws of psychology. In doing this, he tends to regard his characters as psychic abstractions—as oscillating impulses—that exhibit the laws of action and reaction in their behavior.

The result of this admixture of distancing and identification is an art whose unique effects are mixed. On the one hand, sympathy and dread arise because the reader shares the characters' anxieties and desires. Even when the characters are "low mimetic" types, they are seen as "men like ourselves" because they are driven by universal unconscious desires and fears; and the reader dreads the consequences of their mistakes as they take a wrong path to fulfillment. On the other hand, an almost clinical attitude arises, such as one might feel in a laboratory, watching other creatures with the keenest interest to understand the laws of their behavior and the effects of their beliefs upon their conduct. One also takes a moral interest in the characters analogous to that felt in reading a Spencerian or a Dantean allegory. In short, dread and sympathy are joined to a cool scientific and moral attentiveness.

The power of Lawrence's novels derives, generally speaking, from his capacity to accomplish these seemingly contradictory goals. Everything selected for inclusion in such novels is for the sake of (1) maximizing sympathy and dread in an image of felt life, (2) exhibiting with maximum clarity the patterns of behavior implied by Lawrence's laws of psychology, and (3) demonstrating his moral and religious doctrine with the utmost persuasiveness.

Such an art is likely to fail whenever any one of its three purposes (mimetic, scientific, and didactic) is realized at the expense of the other two. It fails, for example, when didacticism violates mimetic fidelity or when mimetic fidelity obscures the didactic and scientific intentions or when the scientific purpose is realized at the expense of moral evaluation or mimetic fidelity, and so on. It is an extremely demanding art, which requires of its creator the most subtle and flexible adjustment of "felt life" to naturalistic law and to religious interpretation. If Lawrence often falters in his art, one must remember the difficulty of the task he set for himself. An extraordinarily far-ranging and highly generalizing intelligence, an extraordinary detachment, a sensibility capable of intense intuitive sympathy for human beings and for life in all of its forms, a highly developed religious consciousness that is sensitive to the moral implications of all behavior—these are the indispensable requirements of a writer who would bring such an art to perfection.

This definition of the general purpose of Lawrence's art must be kept in mind as one examines the problems Lawrence confronted in his handling of the various components of his novels—plot, character, point of view, picture, and rhythm and diction.

PLOTS

In Lawrence's novels, generally speaking, a soul is threatened by forces hostile to its development, or an injured soul, incapacitated by hostile forces, struggles to heal itself and to awaken to new life. The conflict in such novels arises initially from the protagonist's attraction to others who seem to promise liberation and fulfillment and then from the protagonist's fear of annihilation in a destructive love relationship. The plot complications of the novels consist in the protagonist's efforts to resolve the conflict, either by self-assertion, reacting against the love relationship, or by self-nullification, surrendering to it. In short, the unfolding action consists generally in a "frictional to-and-fro" between "sympathetic" and "voluntary" impulses—between the desire for "love" and the desire for "power" and independence. The oscillations build toward a climax through a series of encounters which are either unfulfilling or only partially fulfilling. The climax occurs when the protagonist, brought to desperation, is driven to make a drastic choice, healthy or unhealthy.

When failures occur in the relationship, the protagonist either submits masochistically to the destructive relationship and is "nullified" or reacts and battles to assert his egoistic will over the will of the other person. When a battle for supremacy begins, one of the lovers experiences a Pyrrhic triumph, whereas the other is destroyed, for the struggle moves towards a maximum assertion of egoistic power. All of the following characters are destroyed: Siegmund in *The Trespasser;* William Morel in *Sons and Lovers;* Gerald Crich in *Women in Love;* and Carlotta in *The Plumed Serpent.* Psychic destruction and a disintegration of selfhood occur in other instances: George Saxton in *The White Peacock;* Anton Skrebensky in *The Rainbow;* Gudrun and Loerke in *Women in Love;* Clifford in *Lady Chatterley's Lover.* In other cases, the soul is gravely threatened and approaches destruction but then turns toward balance: Paul Morel in *Sons and Lovers;* Ursula in *The Rainbow;* Birkin in *Women in Love;* Aaron in *Aaron's Rod;* Somers in *Kangaroo;* Kate Leslie in *The Plumed Serpent;* and Connie in *Lady Chatterley's Lover.*

Balance is difficult to achieve, however, not only because of the division within the soul but also because of the society that bullies individuals into accepting only the "love urge" as genuine. When balance is achieved, it is effected partly through the heroism of the protagonist, who nobly resists coercion, and partly through the discovery of a new selfhood, a discovery usually born of the act of love, either sexual love or the love of noble men who join together to build a new world. Balance is achieved by Birkin and Ursula in *Women in Love,* by Alvina Houghton in *The Lost Girl,* by Rawdon Lilly in *Aaron's Rod,* by Cipriano and Kate and by Cipriano and Don Ramón in *The Plumed Serpent,* and by Connie and Mellors in *Lady Chatterley's Lover.* One should note here that Lawrence's scrupulous realism tends to rule out a conventional happy ending. His didactic purpose requires an exhibition of "the right way," but his honest recognition of the flux in human experience and his keen awareness of the difficulties of achieving balance require a certain incompleteness in the closure of his novels.

This brief survey of his plots permits us to consider the problems he confronted in creating actions in which psychology, religion, and mimetic fidelity blend to produce the desired final effects.

In carrying out the didactic purpose of his art, Lawrence needed actions that would provide an adequate demonstration of the need for balance: an action, generally, in which the way of love, the first alternative for the protagonist seeking fulfillment, is shown to be bankrupt, so that the remaining alternatives for the protagonist become the seeking of power or the reconciling of power and love. The sympathetic protagonist, who is comparable to James's "free spirit" surrounded by Jamesian fools, must earn our respect by evaluating properly the nature of the threats he faces and by taking the right course of action. In testing the ways of love and power, as well as the third way, the way of balance and health, Lawrence often requires a contrast of opposite lines of action, a counterpointing analogous to that in Hawthorne's *The Marble Faun* or in Brontë's *Wuthering Heights* or in Dostoevsky's *Crime and Punishment*. Both the characters and their unfolding fates or fortunes are paired: the undeveloped characters disintegrate or die; the highly developed characters "come through," at least in significant ways. The action must show that the choices of the paired characters lead inevitably either to death or to life.

Crime and Punishment may be taken as a model to suggest effective ways of handling such an action. Raskolnikov, a highly developed man, tries the way of power and is horrified by the consequences. The lesson is reinforced by repetitions of the test of the way of power in the behavior of Luzhin and Svidrigailov. Sickened by the consequences of his power philosophy, Raskolnikov turns to Sonia and Christianity. Indeed, he oscillates throughout the novel between Sonia, the proponent of love, and Svidrigailov, the proponent of the will and of power. Testing both ways, Raskolnikov arrives at his final decision to accept Sonia's way.

In his successful novels, Lawrence, testing the effort to find fulfillment solely in love, demonstrates the failures that result when love is considered the be-all and end-all of life. Thus in *The Rainbow*, members of three generations try to find fulfillment in love, without undergoing a corresponding growth in integral selfhood, but they fail. After each failure, the vision of the rainbow defines the true path that humanity must seek. In three generations, as men move from unconscious to conscious development (from the way of Law to that of Love), Lawrence tests each stage of development and shows that balance has not been achieved because men have failed to "come into being" and to accept responsibility as the veritable "sons of God." Ursula, the most highly developed of all the characters, discovers that love unbalanced by the purposive or religious power impulse is bankrupt: it turns into a horrible battle for egoistic domination. At the end of the novel she yearns for the fulfillment that still hovers "beyond," in the "unknown," beckoning humanity to venture ahead toward a higher development in accordance with the deep needs of human nature.

In *Women in Love*, the bankruptcy of "the one way" is even more completely demonstrated by being contrasted with a fulfilling balance that provides health and joy. The demonstration is strengthened by a characteristic feature of Lawrence's plots—an ironic reversal in which the lover becomes a monstrous destroyer. Seeking to force life into the mold of love, either personal or spiritual, five couples react into egoistic willfulness and a murderous struggle for power: Gerald and Gudrun, Birkin and Hermione, Thomas Crich and his wife, Halliday and Minette, and Loerke and Gudrun. Only Birkin and Ursula escape the blind pattern of action and reaction and thus achieve a fulfilling balance. The completeness of the demonstration has led many critics to see *Women in Love* as Lawrence's best novel.

Aaron's Rod and *Kangaroo* fail, however, to provide adequate tests either of love or of power. In *Aaron's Rod* the whole society that subscribes to the love ideal (and to the "life-centrality of women") is neurotic and empty, but the hollowness of these men and women is given, not demonstrated as the inevitable consequence of the love ideal. Aaron, the quester, is too weak to earn our respect; and Rawdon Lilly's talk of a healthy balance is weakly exhibited in his actions. Moreover, Lawrence fails to test his thesis that power is needed to balance the way of love in the modern world. Again, he talks about it; he does not dramatize it.

The error in *Kangaroo* is similar. Lawrence seeks to make the violence in Sydney—the clash of Diggers and Communists—test the two opposed political movements based on the love ideal; but the doctrines of Ben Cooley and of the Communist Willie Struther are not tested, for the violence does not arise as a consequence of the programs of each political leader. Moreover, Somers's idea of a healthy alternative is never translated into persuasive action. Lawrence's insistent realism in these two novels prevents him from imagining concrete alternatives to the love ideal.

In *The Plumed Serpent*, again, Christianity is not given much of a test. The cardboard Bishop is easily knocked down by Don Ramón, and Carlotta is just hysterical. Lawrence does exhibit the bankruptcy of ideal love in Kate Leslie's richly dramatized inner life, but we hardly see enough of Kate's relationships with "spiritual" men to be persuaded that spiritual love must always fail; nor do we see that the way of love is the inevitable cause of the disintegration of the Mexicans.

Sons and Lovers also lacks an adequate test of the love alternative. Paul Morel, crippled in his psyche by his mother, cannot love either Miriam or Clara. But the unanswered question in the novel is whether Paul could love a woman well suited to him. The novel implies, but does not demonstrate, that all love relationships frustrate the integral self seeking wholeness of being.

In truth, Lawrence generally has difficulty in presenting an adequate case for the love ideal because, unlike Dostoevsky, he refuses to accept that a person can be utterly selfless and loving without reacting into cruelty and hatred. He refuses to bend reality as he sees it by creating healthy characters who represent the way of love. There are no Sonias in Lawrence's world, no healthy believers who give themselves to Jesus. Such pure, single-minded people are ruled out by his psychology, which postulates inner division between opposing urges from the moment of conception in the womb and argues that modern civilization, overemphasizing the "love and benevolence ideal," drives men to react into sadistic cruelty.

So far I have focused on Lawrence's didactic purpose; but the adequacy of his didactic demonstrations cannot be separated from a consideration of his mimetic power. In his depictions of the effort to find fulfillment through love, Lawrence always creates a strong presumption that the overemphasis on love must lead to failure, because he exhibits with remarkable vividness the torment and terror arising from frustration of the lover's hopes and expectations. Again and again, the male, seeking completion by wedding himself to woman as his raison d'être, discovers that he has wedded himself to his antagonist. The marriage bed becomes the marriage hearse. The battle of wills for supremacy assumes the most hideous forms, as in the remarkable contest between Will Brangwen and Anna:

> Then she turned fiercely on him, and fought him. He was not to do this to her, it was monstrous. . . . Why did he want to drag her down, and kill her spirit?
>
> . . . .
>
> "What do you do to me?" she cried. "What beastly thing do you do to me? You put a horrible pressure on my head, you don't let me sleep, you don't let me live. Every moment of your life you are doing something to me, something horrible, that destroys me. There is something horrible in you, something dark and beastly in your will. What do you want of me? What do you want me to do?"
>
> All the blood in his body went black and powerful and corrosive as he heard her. Black and blind with hatred of her he was. He was in a very black hell, and could not escape. [*R*, 185–86]

All this occurs after Will and Anna have experienced a consummate bliss and joy in the first days of marriage. Ironic reversals such as this are so much a part of Lawrence's plots that the reader tends to take their power for granted. Yet they are evocative of the sympathetic dread that is peculiar to his art, and they dramatize powerfully the bankruptcy of the unbalanced love ideal.

Such reversals are also fundamental in Lawrence's psychology, which seeks to lay bare the continuous struggle for psychic balance as well as the terrible consequences of imbalance. The scientific Lawrence wishes to present "the trembling and oscillating of the balance" of the soul (*Phoenix*, 529). To do this, Lawrence must eschew conventional plot development, which often focuses on a single-minded effort to achieve a goal and reduces motivation to a single exclusive desire. Lawrence's "exhaustive method" entails a basic departure from conventional storytelling. As Lawrence indicates in his letter of 29 January 1914 to Edward Garnett, the exhaustive method differs essentially from writing "a story with a plot." "Plot" becomes the frictional to-and-fro that works up to a culmination. For Lawrence, peripeteia is a law of psychology, not just an artistic technique.

The effectiveness of the reversals depends on the intensity of the protagonist's hopes or expectations. When the woman is identified by the male as the Infinite—the center of reality and the core of meaning—his discovery that she is his enemy, his destroyer, is particularly dreadful. Lawrence's handling of reversal in Will Brangwen's marriage to Anna is extraordinarily powerful for this reason. A similar power is exhibited in the handling of Gerald Crich's relationship with Gudrun. In the early part of the novel, the couple are seen sympathetically, and we feel the intensity of their need for vital connection. But instead of finding release, they are imprisoned within the hard walls of their egos, and their progression towards sensationalism and reduction acquires a singular dreadfulness when Gudrun turns to the vile Loerke and when the desperate Gerald then seeks to strangle her.

Similarly, Clifford Chatterley's disintegration, his going soft inside, becomes particularly horrifying in the light of his former efforts to maintain order and a kind of spiritual beauty in his life. After reading Racine, he submits to Mrs. Bolton's ministrations in vividly rendered passages suggesting perversity and infantilism. Again, the failure of Siegmund in *The Trespasser* is sharpened by peripeteia. Seeking health and wholeness through love, Siegmund is led to suicide. Similar reversals occur in *Aaron's Rod* and in *Kangaroo,* where Lawrence contemplates whole societies that, following the ideal of love and brotherhood, are plunged into violence and destruction. In *Aaron's Rod* we witness not only the violence of the mob in Milan but also the spectacle of cultivated people—Jim Bricknell, Josephine Ford, and their circle of friends—yearning for revolution and blood; and Bricknell, eating constantly, fears he is starving and dying. In *Kan-*

garoo, the efforts of Diggers and Communists to follow the way of love lead to the violence in Sydney that causes Kangaroo's death; and Richard Somers's desire for collective action is followed by his eruption into violent hatred and repudiation. In all of these novels, warnings and ironic reversals exhibit the terrible bankruptcy of the way of "halfness." And Lawrence intensifies the fear or horror by vividly picturing the dehumanization and ugliness caused by submission to the ideals of "work," capitalistic "efficiency," and the "ethics of production." His panoramic pictures of the miners in *The Rainbow*, *Women in Love*, and *Lady Chatterley's Lover*; his panoramic sketches of the Australians in *Kangaroo*, who are healthy, cheerful people but are essentially hollow; his pictures of the Mexicans in *The Plumed Serpent*—all these deepen our sense of the debasement and disintegration of life as a consequence of the "sympathetic" submission to the collective will.

In devising plots that test the love ideal and present the disintegration of characters who are unable to change the pattern of their lives, Lawrence must also find a way to dramatize or to exhibit a contrasting integration and healthy balance. Providing such a contrast is particularly difficult because there are few models of the sort of healthy balance that Lawrence sought to define. And the difficulty is compounded by Lawrence's naturalism, by his reluctance to invent plot lines that do violence to his psychology and his common-sense realism. Thus there is always a danger that Lawrence may not be able to provide adequate correlatives of the fulfilling alternative to the wrong way. How does one translate a utopian vision into a persuasive image of life?

In his first three novels the healthy alternative is implied but is not translated into action. In *The White Peacock* Lawrence diagnoses the disease but has no clear idea of a cure. In *The Trespasser*, Siegmund's Doppelgänger, Hampson, points to a cure: a man must "strive beyond himself." But Lawrence is concerned here only with Siegmund's failure, and there is no contrasting plot line pointing to balance. In *Sons and Lovers*, again, Lawrence traces a pattern of failure; his hero, at the end, is only beginning his quest for a solution.

In *The Rainbow* and in *Women in Love*, however, Lawrence's contrapuntal plot lines sharply define the nature of a healthy fulfillment. In *The Rainbow* each generation's failure, or its partial achievement of fulfillment, defines the failures or achievements of the other generations. Tom's sensual fulfillment sharpens our realization of Skrebensky's failure. Will's limited progress toward purposive or creative activity defines both Tom's and Skrebensky's failures. Ursula's determination to find a true son of God and fulfillment in the rainbow defines the limitations of all three generations and of the society that has become hostile to balance.

The contrapuntal plotting builds a keen sense of the difficulty of "coming through" in a world hostile to health, and hence a keen sense of dread. In every generation, men and women are confronted not only by problems that arise from their inner divisions but also by a changing civilization that destroys their connection with nature and forces them into submission to a coercive industrial system. In every generation the conflict between men and women is intensified as modern rationalism and capitalism increasingly isolate and alienate the individual. The more difficult the obstacles, the more intense our dread and the more intense our relief and joy when a character stands up against the combination of disintegrative forces.

Perhaps the most serious obstacle to fulfillment is the highly developed man's awareness that he is alone in his fight for a new heaven and earth and that he appears ridiculous to others, a Salvator mundi whose jeremiads are bad form. Lawrence obviously needs choral passages in which a reliable spokesman defines the evils of conformity and the vision of a good life in a good society. But no vision can substitute for an actual accomplishment, and the danger is ever present that Lawrence's heroes will arouse the reader's distrust. Are they simply romantic dreamers whose untested ideas are a species of adolescent escapism?

In *Women in Love* Birkin's courageous defiance of social norms and his efforts to change his life and to create a new relatedness with Ursula and with Gerald provide an adequate translation of vision into experience, though his blithe announcement that he and Ursula must just drop everything and go off on their own cannot but trouble some readers. In *Aaron's Rod* and *Kangaroo*, however, Lawrence cannot find adequate correlatives of his fulfilling alternative. Embittered by the nightmare of the war and unwilling to sacrifice his honest realism or his psychology by resorting to a purely invented solution, he can only employ choral speeches to define his healthy alternative. The most that Rawdon Lilly can offer as a solution is "quietness" of soul. Lacking concrete particulars to exhibit the fulfilling way of life, Lawrence falls back on the consciousness of such a way in the mind of the hero; and he brings about Aaron's rejuvenation in Florence through rhetoric, not through carefully prepared probabilities. In *Kangaroo*, Richard Somers's poetic alternative to the love ideal is also meditated, not carried into life. Not until Lawrence wrote *The Plumed Serpent* and *Lady Chatterley's Lover* did he recover his ability to exhibit a healthy alternative in action.

The great difficulties in plotting arise, then, chiefly as a result of Lawrence's reluctance to invent freely when his own experience does not warrant the creation of hopeful solutions. His honesty, his fidelity to life as experienced, are often at odds with his didacticism—his religious effort to provide strong demonstrations of the balanced life. Even when he invents freely, as in *The Lost Girl* and *The Plumed Serpent*, he runs the risk of forcing his women to act as if mesmerized, their normal scruples and reservations being submerged in the hypnotic trance imposed by the masterful male.

This brings me to the problem of characterization.

CHARACTERIZATION

Insofar as they carry out the didactic purposes of the novels, Lawrence's characters are allegorical types exhibiting moral imbalance: they are destructively spiritual or regressively sensual, too sympathetic or too willful. Only a few achieve moral excellence. As exemplifications of Lawrence's psychology, however, the characters are divided; they tend to oscillate between extremes of sympathy and voluntary self-assertion or between extremes of spirituality and sensationalism. In carrying out the scientific purpose of his work, they tend to become unconscious impulses, acting and reacting. But they must also be persuasively real on a common-sense experiential level; hence their speech and behavior must generally exhibit the sort of normality that we associate with characters in the novels of Arnold Bennett or George Moore.

The fundamental opposition is between developed and undeveloped characters. Some of the undeveloped men and women may be temperamentally incapable of further development (e.g., Tom Brangwen of *The Rainbow*, Ciccio of *The Lost Girl*, the Indians and Mexicans of Lawrence's American stories); others are prevented from achieving maturity by their false social consciousness or by their failure to experience rebirth through a healthy love experience in which the old ego is destroyed (e.g., Hermione, Gudrun and Gerald, Jim Bricknell, Kangaroo, and Clifford Chatterley). With its careful counterpointing of undeveloped and developed people, Lawrence's fiction tends toward pure allegory. Problems arise in handling characters who must function simultaneously as allegorical figures, as oscillating impulses, and as real "men like ourselves."

Very considerable, for example, is the difficulty in constructing heroes who can command the reader's respect and sympathy. Because the scientific Lawrence is unwilling to ignore the divisions within the psyche and to eliminate evidence of ugliness and perversity in his characters, he risks sacrificing sympathy and respect for his heroes. Rupert Birkin, for example, is clearly meant to be whole and healthy, a Greek intelligence playing above his Egyptian sensuality, the sympathetic and the voluntary urges balanced in him along with the spiritual and the sensual. Yet Lawrence's honest naturalism compels him to expose Birkin's perversity, his taking Ursula at "the roots of corruption" and his homosexual inclinations; and many critics have found his behavior indistinguishable from the sensationalism and reduction that Lawrence condemns in Gudrun and Gerald, who take the road of corruption and death instead of the road to life. As psychologist, Lawrence must acknowledge Birkin's inclination toward "corruption"; as moralist, Lawrence must take special pains to show that Birkin is responsible, that his reaction into perversity is a healthy sensual righting of the balance in the Alpine ice and snow, which symbolize the spiritual will. Birkin emerges, I think, as a persuasive hero. But in *Aaron's Rod* and *Kangaroo* Rawdon Lilly and Richard Somers do not exhibit the heroic souls that Lawrence wishes them to have: Lawrence's scientific naturalism and his mimetic realism undercut the heroic in these men. Lilly just talks. Richard Somers, who is first presented naturalistically as oscillating between sympathetic and voluntary urges, becomes, in his talks with Ben Cooley, the proud proponent of "the God-passion"; but the shift from realism to heroic drama is unconvincing. Lawrence asks for an admiration and respect that Somers cannot earn, given Lawrence's psychological naturalism.

In contrast, Don Ramón and Cipriano in *The Plumed Serpent* are always in danger of becoming allegorical abstractions, too statuesque to be persuasively real. A similar problem arises in Lawrence's creation of primitives who function as embodiments of the "lower centers." Ciccio in *The Lost Girl* is almost inhuman; it is hard to see why Alvina is attracted to him. He becomes a principle rather than a man. Tom Brangwen in *The Rainbow*, on the other hand, is so richly human—fleshed out as a farmer, a father, and a timid Victorian, immersed in the particulars of a social life that Lawrence knew intimately—that he compels our sympathy and respect even as he functions as "the unconscious" or as the Sensual Man. Lawrence's primitives function effectively in his art if they act and suffer humanly in a persuasively human world; when they become icons, cut off from the particulars of social life, they may fail to command the sympathetic response and credibility that Lawrence means them to have, unless he presents them as members of a remote society, like the Indians in "The Woman Who Rode Away."

Another problem arises from Lawrence's desire to make his characters exhibit the laws of psychic oscillation. The contemplation of the to-and-fro of psychic impulses may cause us to lose sight of the characters as individuals. Thus a sufficient amount of mimetic density must be joined to the presentation of psychic oscillation. In saying this, one should remember that Lawrence's novels are not always realistic as we commonly understand *realism*. For instance, Helena and Siegmund, in *The Trespasser*, are similar to the characters in Hawthorne's *Marble Faun*, and Lawrence wants us to view them as embodiments of universal psychic forces, the male "fire" and the female "water," the male will toward spiritual development and the female resistance to that will. *The Trespasser* must be read as an allegory of the struggle for supremacy between male and female principles in a symbolic world of day and night, sun and moon, fire and water, sky and sun. The question for criticism is this: in what contexts may the character as psychic abstraction function effectively?

Where the context is from the outset symbolic, a psychic landscape, and where Lawrence follows the psychic to-and-fro and ignores mimetic richness, we may accept abstract characterization and symbolic-didactic dialogue as being consistent with his purposes, just as we accept these conventions in *The Faerie Queene* or in *The Marble Faun*. When, on the other hand, Lawrence establishes the convention of realism, he must take pains to reconcile allegory and mimesis or scientific law and mimesis. His handling of Skrebensky in *The Rainbow* illustrates the problem. In Tom and Will Brangwen, mimesis is so well blended with psychic abstraction that one feels no artificiality in their behavior. For Skrebensky, however, Lawrence provides virtually no background of vital experience, and although Skrebensky acts consistently as a man who has no faith and no inner self, it is difficult to accept that he would inevitably choose the African way of sensation in his reunion with Ursula. Lawrence's psychology—his belief that men who lack "integral selfhood" react into sensationalism and reduction as a cure for their inner emptiness—dictates Skrebensky's action. The psychology is not translated into a sufficiently concrete development of motivation; the psychic laws are assumed, not demonstrated. Similarly, in *Aaron's Rod* Aaron's sexual rejuvenation in Italy is forced; there is no sufficient basis in probability and necessity for the sudden return of his sexual powers.

The task of blending psychology and mimetic realism is closely related to the problem of blending naturalism and intense religious conviction. I have already discussed the difficulty of elevating a character to the status of a hero when the image of life is determinedly naturalistic. A second difficulty is that of adjusting naturalism to moral judgment. If men act in accordance with the laws of their natures, if unconscious desires and fears determine their behavior, why condemn them for failing to become whole? Can the Lawrence who treats his characters with an almost medical attentiveness and respect judge them as failures from a moral point of view? Lawrence's solution to this problem was made possible by a brilliant psychological insight. Like some existential psychologists, Lawrence saw that men feel guilt or shame when they are conscious of failing to develop all of their human powers. So strong are the human needs for identity, for relatedness, and for transcendence that any way of life that frustrates these needs leads to self-hatred: guilt arises from dependence on others or from inability to establish a pure relationship with others or from stifling one's inherent religious craving for purposiveness. Thus Lawrence's characters frequently condemn themselves for their failures; even the hardened Miss Inger and Uncle Tom and the hollow Skrebensky in *The Rainbow* realize that what they have chosen to do is hideous. And their moral failures are also exposed in scenes that reveal the collapse of their integrity. Clifford Chatterley, who has insomnia, indulges his infantile irresponsibility by submitting to Mrs. Bolton's ministrations; Will Brangwen moves into a sterile red-brick suburb; Egbert accepts death in "England, My England"; Jim Bricknell eats compulsively.

One must emphasize, finally, that, as T. S. Eliot said of Henry James, Lawrence was not interested in character as we normally conceive of it. He was interested in what men and women are inhumanly, as manifestations of the universal forces operating throughout nature. Mimetic fidelity in Lawrence is not simply a common-sense realism; it also reflects his laws of psychic process. The conventions of Lawrence's fiction are inseparable from these laws. Thus we realize early in all of Lawrence's novels that a character is ill or unhappy because his or her life is unbalanced and because the imbalance is breeding a tension that will lead to a reaction. We realize too that the deepest source of motivation is the character's desire to achieve integral being and that the most intense psychic and moral suffering arises from the frustration of that desire. The protagonists are trapped, and they must find a way out of the trap or they will go mad. The preoccupations of conventional realism—with money or social status or a conventional marriage or victory over the elements—are incidental in Lawrence's novels: the mere surface of life. His characters dwell in the world of their deepest unconscious fears and desires, and their behavior exemplifies the laws of Lawrence's psychology. But when these laws come into conflict with our common-sense notions of probability or with the implicit didactic requirements of the novels, weaknesses result.

POINT OF VIEW

So powerful are Lawrence's dramatizations of conficts between lovers and his building of dread through ironic reversals that the reader, identifying vicariously with the suffering characters, may fail to appreciate the moral significance of their actions. Hence it is necessary for Lawrence to shift the perspective so that the reader cannot identify completely with the characters and can define objectively their errors in judgment or their deficiencies of soul. This distancing of the events to enable us to understand their ethical significance is linked with Lawrence's characteristic foreshortening of experience, which necessitates summaries and overviews of the characters. Usually Lawrence views human conduct over a period of several weeks, so that the whole tendency and issue of the life urges can be laid bare. To trace the stages of psychic development and of the psychic failure or success, he must move rapidly; otherwise our grasp of the laws of psychic action and reaction might be obscured. As he foreshortens, however, he must not sacrifice the intensity of felt life, and he must not convert his characters into pure "impulses."

The following passage from "England, My England" illustrates Lawrence's characteristic narrative procedure, the procedure employed, though with less foreshortening, in his novels:

> And he began to get bitter, and a wicked look began to come on his face. He did not give in to her; not he. There were seven devils inside his long, slim, white body. He was healthy, full of restrained life. Yes, even he himself had to lock up his own vivid life inside himself, now she would not take it from him. Or rather, now that she only took it occasionally. For she had to yield at times. She loved him so, she desired him so, he was so exquisite to her, the fine creature that he was, finer than herself. Yes, with a groan she had to give in to her own unquenched passion for him. And he came to her then—ah, terrible, ah, wonderful, sometimes she wondered how either of them could live after the terror of the passion that swept between them. It was to her as if pure lightning, flash after flash, went through every fibre of her, till extinction came.
>
> But it is the fate of human beings to live on. [CSS, 2:312]

The narrator's view of Egbert flows almost imperceptibly into Egbert's subjective response, then into the narrator's summary of Winifred's attitude, then into Winifred's subjective rehearsal of their love-making, and finally to the narrator again. Moving with the utmost rapidity to trace the consequences of psychic imbalance, Lawrence still manages to convey felt life and to provide moral evaluation. He understood that in constructing a narrative in which felt life exhibits the laws of psychic unfolding and defines the moral significance of all conduct, he must never sacrifice dramatic intensity to doctrine; and at the same time he must never sacrifice doctrine to "the grace of intensity."

Sometimes he failed. Critics who have attacked his "lapses from psychological realism," as in his handling of Skrebensky in *The Rainbow*, are justified in pointing out that quasi-allegorical figures (the man of the Flesh, the man of the Spirit, the man of the Rational Will) may become unconvincing; but Lawrence's problem in blending felt life, science, and ethics is difficult. His decision to employ foreshortened narratives, when viewed in the light of his threefold intention, was brilliant.

He has been criticized often for writing intrusively didactic passages, for substituting preaching for felt life; but his technique of drawing back to interpret the significance of his images of life is necessary to his complex art. One must not expect mimetic realism that rules out "telling" and endorses only "showing." Even in his finest mimetic passages, Lawrence is always telling, through a symbolism that evaluates human behavior in relation to man's possibilities for wholeness. But symbolism alone is not enough for a writer who wishes to define with the utmost precision the moral and psychological laws of modern behavior. Because Lawrence's characters are so often unaware of the implications of their conduct, Lawrence must provide, from the narrator's point of view, the appropriate ethical, psychological, and philosophical comment. Generally he must do this at every crucial stage of the action—whenever a character takes a right or a wrong turn. Moreover, because his narratives often require foreshortening to exhibit the basic moral and psychological principles, Lawrence must often summarize and comment freely.

But to be effective, didactic passages must not claim more than can be verified directly or indirectly by the action. Sometimes Lawrence tries to say too much, and readers find it difficult to accept a condensed authorial statement of his original thoughts. For instance, in *Kangaroo*, when Richard Somers meets Willie Struthers, Lawrence launches into a comment on the impossibility of the love of "mates" unless such love is "polarized" by "the God-passion." The passage may well arouse skepticism because it is based upon a depth of psychological and philosophical analysis that Lawrence simply cannot reveal in the two pages he allows himself for his comment. The passage makes good sense if we have read *The Rainbow*, *Women in Love*, and Lawrence's essays on psychology. But his thinking is not demonstrated by the action of *Kangaroo*, and the passage seems to reduce complex insights to a simplistic journalese. Often it is because Lawrence wants to say so much that we remain unconvinced. What is objectionable is not the convention of authorial intrusion but the use of passages that claim more than is demonstrated.

Perhaps the chief problem in the handling of point of view is that of balancing sympathetic identification with moral or scientific detachment. In using his own life as the basis for his characterization of Paul Morel, Birkin, Rawdon Lilly, and Richard Somers, Lawrence is always in danger of asking for a sympathy unwarranted by the facts he sets down with characteristic honesty: "Oh, wad somebody the giftie gie us. . . ." It is generally true that Lawrence's novels are self-testing, that Lawrence is detached enough to draw back from his heroes and to challenge their ideas, attitudes, and motivations. But as Leavis has observed in *D. H. Lawrence: Novelist*, Lawrence's detachment sometimes falters. Particularly when he confines himself over a number of chapters to the Jamesian central consciousness, Lawrence's moral discrimination may suffer; or his psychological detachment may be blurred. Critics who claim that Lawrence was schizoid point to his failures to recognize the real motivations of Paul, Birkin, Aaron, Lilly, or Somers; these characters are by no means as healthy, it is argued, as Lawrence thinks they are. Lawrence tried to solve this problem by providing a reliable "reflector"—either another character or the implied narrator—to remind us of the limitations of the central consciousness, or by making the central consciousness aware of his own limitations. But the means are not always adequate.

In his treatment of Rupert Birkin, for example, Lawrence might have allayed the uneasiness of many readers if he had allowed Birkin to acknowledge directly the problem of latent homosexuality or sexual perversity. In fact, Birkin would have emerged as an even healthier hero if he had been portrayed as being aware of his buried inclinations and as confronting the moral and psychological problem they present. Writing close to the bone, Lawrence perhaps feared the consequences of such an admission by a man we are meant to admire; but some of the material in his unpublished Prologue could have been used to advantage without compromising the didactic purpose of the novel.

PICTURE

In his handling of picture, Lawrence's basic problem is to make his images function as correlatives of his moral values, of the fears and desires of the psyche, and as a persuasively rendered reality. He has little difficulty in carrying out this threefold purpose, for his idea of the "spirit of place" is perfectly correlated with his moral and psychological ideas. Places are almost always symbolic in Lawrence's fiction. There are spiritual places (such as mountain tops and the North), and there are sensual places (Africa and Egypt). There are sympathetic places (Australia) and voluntary places (Mexico). There are stagnant places, which are hostile to the development of spirit (Nethermere in *The White Peacock,* the Marsh farm in *The Rainbow*); and there are places that are hostile to sensual or unconscious impulses (the glacier in "The Captain's Doll," the Alps in *Women in Love*). Again, in novel after novel, there are pastoral settings, in which the soul may flourish in its connection with organic life, and urban or industrial settings, which threaten to crush or imprison the soul: the garden versus the machine. Picture must, as in Hawthorne, project the psychic duality between darkness and light, moon and sun, water and fire, death and life, unconsciousness and consciousness, union and division, fusion and individuality. Animals and plants are also moral or psychic symbols: there are creatures of the sensual will (the rabbit Bismarck in *Women in Love* and the horses in *The Rainbow*), creatures that symbolize the wholeness of the soul (the plumed serpent, the phoenix, and the gannets in *Kangaroo,* which plunge into the sea and rise into the air), creatures of corruption or the will to death through reduction (the beetles in *Women in Love*); and there are plants that symbolize either sensuality (the lotus and the marsh flower) or the flowering of being (the iris, the poppy, the rose). Lawrence's vision is so comprehensive that he can discover moral and psychological meanings in an enormous number of facts that for the realist would constitute mere setting. As Robert H. MacDonald has observed, "It is probable that Lawrence does try to incorporate everything into the symbolic system."[1]

At the same time Lawrence wants to avoid the univalent meanings of "allegorical figures," which he associates with bald "didactic argument" (*Phoenix,* 295–96). He does not want to reduce life to allegorical equations; his symbolism must suggest the uniqueness of actual experience and thus awaken the reader to that quality of "livingness" which Anais Nin has identified as central in Lawrence's work and which Lawrence himself stressed in his essay "Morality and the Novel." The reader must not feel that Lawrence's settings are moral or psychological abstractions (like the settings in Hawthorne) but rather concrete realities vividly realized. As token of a concrete reality, the symbol would present, Lawrence hoped, not just *meaning* but also "human *feeling*"—"a complex of emotional experience" (*Phoenix*, 296). Such a symbolism, like the poem for Wallace Stevens, must "resist intelligence almost successfully." If it does not, life is "nailed down" and falsified. That "nailing down" of life is a form of immorality against which Lawrence spoke in "Morality and the Novel" (*Phoenix*, 527–32). Thus in devising his symbolism, Lawrence had to guard carefully against his own gift for systematizing.

Lawrence's ability to blend moral, psychological, and mimetic purposes in his handling of picture may be suggested by his descriptions of Australia in *Kangaroo*. Several critics argue that the novel is half travelogue, but in truth no observation is unassimilated into Lawrence's total moral and psychological vision. Consider, for example, the following passage:

> Bright the sun, the air of marvellous clarity, tall stalks of cabbage palms rising in the hollow, and far off, tufted gum trees against a perfectly new sky, the tufts at the end of wire branches. And farther off, blue, blue hills. In the Main Street, large and expensive motor-cars and women in fuzzy fur coats; long, quiescent Australian men in tired-out looking navy blue suits trotting on brown ponies, with a carpet-bag in one hand, doing the shopping; girls in very much-mad hats, also flirtily shopping; three boys with big, magnificent bare legs, lying in a sunny corner in the dust; a lonely white pony hitched as if forever to a post at a street-corner. . . . two half-naked babies sitting like bits of live refuse in the dirt, but with bonny, healthy bare legs: the awful place called "The Travellers' Rest—Mrs. Coddy's Boarding House"—a sort of blind, squalid, corner-building made of wood and tin, with flat pieces of old lace-curtain nailed inside the windows, and the green blinds hermetically drawn. What must it have been like inside? . . .
>
> The wind was cold enough to make you die. Harriet was disgusted at having been dragged away from home. They trailed to the sea to try and get out of it, for it blew from the land, and the sun was hot. . . . So, in the flat-icy wind, that no life had ever softened and no god ever tempered, they crouched on the sea's edge picking these marvellous little shells.
>
> Suddenly, with a cry, to find the water rushing round their ankles and surging up their legs, they dragged their way wildly forward with the wave, and out and up the sand. Where immediately a stronger blast seized Lovat's hat and sent it spinning to the sea again, and he after it like a bird. He caught it as the water lifted it, and then the waste of water enveloped him. Above his knees swirled the green flood, there was water all around him swaying, he looked down at it in amazement, reeling and clutching his hat. [278–80]

Australia is both beautiful and threatening. The "perfectly new sky" is the correlative of a new land, from which European authority is absent. But the threat of the land is that of "aboriginal *sympathetic* apathy," the apathy of the "fern-world," the primordial world before consciousness and individuality arose, a world dominated by the female sympathetic impulse to unison and tribal unity. The Australian men are "long, quiescent," and wear "tired-looking" suits because they, like the land itself, are apathetic, dissolved in sympathetic unison. The boys have "big, magnificent bare legs," and the half-naked babies have "bonny, healthy bare legs," because, as Lawrence emphasizes repeatedly, heavy legs, like those of the horses in "The Horse Dealer's Daughter," are associated with a slumbering sensual power, the antithesis of a high spiritual development. The land has "not even begun": it still belongs to the aboriginal past. "The Travellers' Rest" is a place for those who desire only rest and peace, sealed off from the world of freedom and the unknown.

The sea is symbolic of the unconscious female forces that threaten Somers, the European with a European consciousness. When a cold wind blows up, the sea becomes threatening to him, as if it might erupt into violence, like one of the "dormant volcanoes" of Australia. Unexpectedly, the sea rushes up in a "green flood" and swirls about Somers's legs. He looks down "in amazement, reeling and clutching his hat." On a symbolic level, it is as if he were clutching for what he can save of his European consciousness. The sea is beautiful, but to Somers it seems "female and vindictive," threatening to drown him and his "civilized consciousness."

Lawrence's mind functions simultaneously at both the surface level of normality ("The wind was cold enough to make you die. Harriet was disgusted at having been dragged away from home") and the level of visionary interpretation (the symbolic wind from the sea does bring a hint of the death that will occur because of a violent reaction against the aboriginal sympathetic impulse). Again, in Somers's view of the gannets that leap into the air and then fall back into the sea, Lawrence symbolizes the balance or wholeness of wedding the spirit and the flesh, the conscious and the unconscious. The tension—to use Allen Tate's word—between the extreme of reality and the extreme of imagination is perfectly maintained.

PROSE RHYTHM AND DICTION

A great deal has been written about the unique prose that Lawrence developed to present psychic process in all its complexity. Jacques Berthoud, for example, has observed that Lawrence's "exhaustive method'' seeks to express not only conscious states of mind but also unconscious pressures and instincts.[2] Berthoud is not convinced ''that the attempt to enact unconscious experience can ever properly succeed,'' for, as he argues, ''by definition, the unconscious is not directly available to the conscious mind: it cannot therefore be treated mimetically'' (p.68). But Berthoud is thinking of an unconscious that is different from the one that Lawrence had in mind. In seeking to present psychic process as an expression of the ''inhuman'' will, Lawrence is interested, not in a ''personal'' unconscious, but in the natural process of attraction and repulsion operating behind and within personal motives. Roger Sale has pointed out that in order to ''break down 'the old stable ego of character,''' Lawrence employs a syntax and a language which refer not only to a specific present but also to the timeless inner processes of being.[3]

This brings us to Lawrence's use of repetition, which, he said, was natural to him and which he associated with a ''frictional to-and-fro which works up to culmination'' (Foreword to *WL*, x). The dangers of his repetitive style are obvious: the repetitions may become mechanical or may even be unnecessary. Yet they are generally required by Lawrence's effort to present the actualities of psychic process. As Peter Balbert has pointed out in *The Psychology of Rhythm in D. H. Lawrence*, the frictional to-and-fro exhibits Lawrence's conception of the dualism in the psyche. It is thus not a purely sexual metaphor but a metaphor for the oscillation of sympathetic and voluntary, or of spiritual and sensual, urges. In short, the to-and-fro is the consequence of Lawrence's psychological law of action and reaction.

Beyond this, repetition serves the purpose of presenting the pressures of psychic necessity. When Gerald Crich, after his father's death, is driven by a blind need to find something to fill the vacuum in his soul, the repetitions suggest a monomaniacal effort to liberate himself from his mounting desperation. Short main clauses and careful repetition of a key word combine to produce the effect of insistent pressure: ''But now, he must take a direction. And he did not even know where he was. But he must take a direction now. Nothing would be resolved by merely walking, walking away. He had to take a direction'' (*WL*, 386). There is a tom-tom rhythm here; the mad persistence of his terror echoed in the repeated ''had to take a direction.'' And the compulsion builds in the hammer-blow clauses until he finds relief in the near rape of Gudrun.

The repetition of key words or phrases fixes attention on the single undeniable need. The repetitions build the intensity until a culmination is reached. Ernest Hemingway's repetitions in *A Farewell to Arms* and T. S. Eliot's in *The Waste Land* suggest analogues. The desperation of Frederick Henry in *Farewell* necessitates his turning to Catherine Barkley. The desperation in *The Waste Land* makes the desire for spiritual rejuvenation inevitable. This movement that Kenneth Burke calls a qualitative shift—from one increasingly oppressive state of mind to an opposite state—is exemplified by Lawrence's pattern of action and reaction. The urgency of the psychic pressure is often suggested, too, by asyndetic parataxis, which seems to preclude a consciously deliberated response to a predicament.

In his handling of diction, Lawrence's great problem was to devise a special vocabulary to present the intensity and to define the nature of unconscious processes. The development of this vocabulary was gradual, and it was not until he wrote *The Rainbow* that he found the diction he needed to register directly the felt life below consciousness.

It is a vocabulary that arises from his psychology, emphasizing the attraction and repulsion of the deepest impulses, and the joy and fear attending the psychic to-and-fro. Clusters of associated terms define the various impulses. The destructive power impulse is associated with seizure, weapons, coldness, and inorganic substances that burn or destroy:

> But hard and fierce she had fastened upon him, cold as the moon and burning as a fierce salt. Till gradually his warm, soft iron yielded, and she was there, fierce, corrosive, seething with his destruction, seething like some cruel, corrosive salt around the lost substance of his being, destroying him, destroying him in the kiss. And her soul crystallised with triumph, and his soul was dissolved with agony and annihilation. [*R*, 320]

The sympathetic love impulse is associated with receptiveness, opening, warmth, flowing: "The warmth flowed through her, she felt herself opening, unfolding, asking, as a flower opens in full request under the sun, as the beaks of tiny birds open flat, to receive, to receive" (*R*, 51). Most of the diction is symbolic. The male sun and the female moon, the male heaven and the female earth, the male fire and the female water, day and night—all vie for supremacy. The contest is marked by pursuit and withdrawal, seizures and surrenders, supremacy and "reduction," attack and counterattack. The battle for supremacy ceases only when the power impulse is checked and the lovers enter into a union "in ultimate trust." The boldness of the metaphors is obviously justified by the intensity of the passion. What is at stake is the very being of the lover: the battle may end in destruction of the soul.

In focusing on the inner division between the sympathetic and the voluntary or the spiritual and sensual impulses, Lawrence needs to make us aware of a continual paradox or irony. In *Twilight in Italy*—much of which employs the techniques of fiction that were to be used, in slightly altered form, in *The Rainbow*—Lawrence describes, for example, "a young man of thirty-two-or-three" named Il Duro, a man whose personal problems, like those of all Italy and all of the modern world, have to do with the conflict between the Father and the Son, the old world of the flesh and the new world of the spirit, the world of the past (in which men lived passively in the unconscious, within the collective tribal will) and the world of the present (in which men seek freedom from the tribe and want money, power, and consciousness). Il Duro, who has been to America, is "very handsome, beautiful rather, . . . with a clear golden skin, and perfectly turned face, something godlike." "*But*," Lawrence adds immediately,

> the expression was strange . . . . His eyes . . . had a sinister light in them, a pale, slightly repelling gleam, very much like a god's pale-gleaming eyes, with the same vivid pallor. And all his face had the slightly malignant, suffering look of a satyr. *Yet* he was beautiful. . . . He walked quickly and surely, with his head rather down, passing from his desire to his object, *yet* curiously indifferent, as if the transit were in a strange world, as if none of what he was doing were worth the while. *Yet* he did it for his own pleasure. . . . he had strangely flexible loins, upon which he seemed to crouch forward. *But* he was separate. . . . He felt he could come near to the strange signori. *But* he was always inscrutable. He was curiously attractive and curiously beautiful, *but* somehow like stone in his clear colouring and his clean-cut face. His temples, with the black hair, were distinct and fine as a work of art.
>
> *But* always his eyes had this strange, half-diabolic, half-tortured pale gleam, like a goat's, and his mouth was shut almost uglily, his cheeks stern. [*TI*, 104–6; emphasis mine]

Over and over the sentences tell us that he lives in "animal consciousness" *and yet* he "liked, above all things, to be near the English signori. They seemed to exercise a sort of magnetic attraction over him" (109). Il Duro cannot help himself, and he is "sad," "very strange," condemned to "static misery," unable to break free of the darkness of unconsciousness, yet drawn helplessly to the light—that is, to Lawrence, the spiritual man. The reader views Il Duro with that compassion and muted dread which I have already identified as characteristic in Lawrence, together with that detached wonder which attends our beholding of the strangeness and intensity of his uncontrolled desires. We are constantly made aware of the discrepancy between Il Duro's appearance and his reality, his public self and the inner self. The appearance is godlike, but Il Duro is miserable. There is a suggestion of a Pagliacci motif: psychic anguish is underscored by the contradiction between the external and the inner realities. This Pagliacci motif is recurrent in Lawrence's creation of spiritual characters, like Hermione Roddice in *Women in Love* or Lady Daphne in "The Ladybird."

Il Duro is not a special case. Like all of Lawrence's characters, he is divided, and his behavior is marked by the incessant to-and-fro of contradictory impulses. The paradoxical language heightens our sense of compassion and dread, and at the same time it distances us from the character, alerting us to contradictions illustrative of universal tendencies. Once alerted to these contradictions, we watch for them, aware of the character's psychic imbalance and wondering how long he can continue in this state of inner division. The repetitive style gives the sense of prolonged psychic torment, of obsession so intense that nothing else can command the attention of the divided soul.

A lyrical gift is also necessary to this novelist who wishes to present "the changing rainbow of our living relationships" (*Phoenix*, 532). However, lyricism in Lawrence's novels is never "pure" in the sense of what Robert Penn Warren calls "pure poetry," and must not be. It must be tied to his laws of psychology and to his moral evaluations. Seeking to capture "true and vivid relationships" (*Phoenix*, 530), Lawrence characteristically fuses an immediate, physical impression of an object with the soul's deep sympathetic attraction to, or recoil from, the object. As I have indicated, Lawrence wishes to present "the trembling and oscillating of the balance" of the soul (*Phoenix*, 529). In presenting this "trembling and oscillating," Lawrence seeks not only psychological accuracy but also moral discrimination, for "morality" in Lawrence's novels is the sensitive registering of approaches to and deviations from a healthy balance. As Lawrence says in "Morality and the Novel," morality consists in "that delicate, for ever trembling and changing *balance* between me and my circumambient universe" (*Phoenix*, 528). In short, Lawrence seeks to present the *whole* response of the soul. In his finest lyrical passages, there is no "pure poetry":

> The light on the waves was like liquid radium swinging and slipping. Like radium, the mystic virtue of vivid decomposition, liquid-gushing lucidity.
>
> The sea too was very full. It was nearly high tide, the waves were rolling very tall, with light like a menace on the nape of their necks as they bent, so brilliant. Then, when they fell, the fore-flush

> rushed in a great soft swing with incredible speed up the shore, on the darkness soft-lighted with moon, like a rush of white serpents, then slipping back with a hiss that fell into silence for a second, leaving the sand of granulated silver. [K, 347–48]

The beauty of the night and the moon, like the beauty of Il Duro, fuses with the ominous. The light of the female moon has the "virtue of vivid decomposition." It is a menace. The waves, hissing like snakes, recall the snake-infested marshes that Lawrence associates with the fern world before the emergence of civilized consciousness. The sea is "like a woman with unspeakable desire," but it is inhuman; and the wild ponies that Somers encounters nearby, eating in the moon dusk, are "glad a man was there" (348). The terror and beauty of the inhuman Source and Origin are rendered in a richly sensuous language that defines both the attraction and the revulsion of Somers: the sympathetic urge toward unison and the voluntary recoil from engulfment. The human response is joined to the detached contemplation of this "God without feet or knees or face" (348).

Lawrence finds it so easy to write splendid lyrical passages that he sometimes risks using rhetoric to substitute for carefully planned moral and psychological motivation. The problem becomes obvious in *The Plumed Serpent*, when Kate is mesmerized by Cipriano's "Pan-power"; tapestry takes the place of motivation or "true relatedness." At his best, however, Lawrence remains flexible and blends the tones and attitudes of mundane social intercourse with the lyrical intensities of deep unconscious motivations. In *Kangaroo* he shifts easily from the ordinary ("Harriet was disgusted that she had been dragged away from home," which captures the inflections of her voice as she complains) to the splendid lyricism of the passage quoted above, to cool intellectual analysis. His handling of dialects, particularly in scenes of tender love-making, his capturing of Italian speech rhythms and phrasings in English, his shifts from the lean objective style of a Hemingway to the most rhapsodic subjective responses—all this stylistic flexibility is precisely what is needed in works that simultaneously present felt life, psychological analysis, and religious evaluation.

This survey of the problems that Lawrence faced is too brief to do more than suggest the chief sources of power and of weakness in his complex art. Yet the overview should clarify our notions of what Lawrence is doing and of what he fails to do. As I indicated at the beginning of this chapter, criticism of Lawrence, for all its penetration, still needs adequate definitions of the nature of his work, definitions on which responsible aesthetic judgments can be based. This survey, despite its general nature, can help to refine our ideas of the forms of individual novels and can sharpen our awareness of how each novel can be shaped with maximum beauty and power. In the next several chapters, by following the development of Lawrence's art in relation to his psychology, I wish to show how much the forms of his novels owe to the laws of psychology that he clarified and extended gradually from 1910 to 1930.

5

Psychology and Art in the Early Novels

The theme of conflict between the individual and society is so pervasive in postromantic writing that we have come to expect a writer's first novel to focus on freedom from the blind impersonal forces that make the individual a "pawn of fate" or from an enslaving society that crushes the natural possibilities of life. Developing out of romantic protests against tyranny, together with Byronic protests against "cant" and bourgeois respectability, the theme of freedom to live took the form, by the middle of the nineteenth century, not only of a protest against a capitalism that enchained the workers of the world but also of a concerted attack on propriety and convention, an attack exemplified in Flaubert's laconic observation that hatred of the bourgeoisie is the beginning of virtue. The prison—with its symbolic associates, the net or web, the wall or barrier, the cage, the pit, the trap, the octopus, or the boa constrictor—became the symbol of a whole society and of a whole cosmos bent on crushing the individual and destroying his spontaneous life. And the novel, focusing on marriage, the foundation of bourgeois society, examined the horrifying consequences of an entrapment that constituted, for Marxists, legalized prostitution and, for the less radical, the tyranny of respectability, of Grundyism, of a beastly hypocrisy.

The plight of woman became symbolic of the general problem. In America, Nathaniel Hawthorne led the way with his depiction in *The Scarlet Letter* of Hester Prynne, cast out by a puritanical society and imprisoned in the jail, which Hawthorne contrasts with a wild nature of warm and sensuous, though lawless, freedom. Henry James, following Hawthorne, painted his dark *Portrait of a Lady*, ground in "the mill of the conventional" and entrapped in Gilbert Osmond's Palazzo Roccanera, "the house of darkness, the house of suffocation, the house of death." Mark Twain, William Dean Howells, Frank Norris, and Stephen Crane played variations on the theme of entrapment, a terrible music with the recurrent motif of the destruction of the individual's natural goodness and natural potentialities. Theodore Dreiser's Sister Carrie and Jennie Gerhardt swelled the gallery of trapped women. In France, Flaubert, Maupassant, the brothers Goncourt, Daudet, and Zola presented the ugliness of bourgeois conformity or proletarian victimization. Emma Bovary, Madame Loisel, Gervaise, Germinie Lacerteux, the workers of *Germinal*—all are prisoners and victims, vainly struggling to break free. In Russia, Tolstoy dramatized the ugliness of Anna Karenina's marriage to Alexei and her vain pursuit of life with Vronsky; in *Crime and Punishment* Dostoevsky revealed the horror of Donia's and Sonia's entrapment. In Norway, Ibsen dramatized the tragic fate of Nora Helmer and Hedda Gabler. In England, Dickens exposed the entrapment of Lady Dedlock, and in *Little Dorrit* he drew a picture of a society the central symbol of which was the prison. George Eliot dramatized the horrors of Dorothea Brooke's subservience to the sterile Casaubon, and of Gwendolyn Harleth's to Grandcourt. Trollope followed with his portrait of Lady Paliser; Galsworthy, with his portrait of Irene Forsyte, entrapped by the man of property. George Moore, Arnold Bennett, H. G. Wells, and George Bernard Shaw continued to hammer out the dismal cacophony of entrapment. And Thomas Hardy presented the conflict that Lawrence defined as central not only in Hardy's tragic fiction but in life itself:

> the tragedy of those who, more or less pioneers, have died in the wilderness, whither they had escaped for free action, after having left the walled security, and the comparative imprisonment, of the established convention. This is the theme of novel after novel: . . . be passionate, individual, wilful, you will find the security of the convention a walled prison, you will escape, and you will die, either of your own lack of strength to bear the isolation and the exposure, or by direct revenge from the community, or from both. This is the tragedy, and only this: it is nothing more metaphysical than the division of a man against himself in such a way: first, that he is a member of the community, and must, upon his honour, in no way move to disintegrate the community, either in its moral or its practical form; second, that the convention of the community is a prison to his natural, individual desire, a desire that compels him, whether he feel justified or not, to break the bounds of the community, lands him outside the pale, there to stand alone, and say: "I was right, my desire was real and inevitable; if I was to be myself I must fulfil it, convention or no convention," or else, there to stand alone, doubting, and saying, "Was I right, was I wrong? If I was wrong, oh, let me die!"—in which case he courts death. [*Phoenix*, 411–12]

In Hardy above all, but also in scores of other writers, Lawrence discovered the psychological problem of entrapped men and women and "the division of a man against himself." And Emily Brontë's *Wuthering Heights*—that great early psychological novel which Lawrence admired—provided another striking example of the conflict. As Brontë structured her novel to exhibit the conflict between Wuthering Heights and Thrushcross Grange, between the fire of the wild, dynamic, passionate Earnshaws and the frost of the tepid, restrained, rational, and passive Lintons, and as Brontë placed her heroine, Cathy, between the dark, sensual Heathcliff and the fair, cultured Linton; so Lawrence, in his first novel, *The White Peacock*, placed his heroine, Lettie, squarely between the man of the flesh, George Saxton, and the more cultured Leslie Tempest. Lettie's inner conflict as she is torn between the two men and between her contending desires—the desire for sensual connection and the desire for "culture"—was to become recurrent in Lawrence's fiction, a conflict dramatized again and again in Lawrence's treatment of the quest for escape from the bondage of convention in order to achieve the "maximum of being." In another parallel, which Lawrence would have found in William Blake too, Brontë's depiction of the terrible consequences of Heathcliff's frustration—the long pursuit of revenge and destruction—was to become one of the great laws of Lawrence's fiction: "the flower, if it cannot beat its way through into being, will thrash destruction about itself" (*Phoenix*, 403). This law is exemplified in the pathetic disintegration of George Saxton.

The White Peacock, then, is in a sense a typical young man's novel. The very first paragraph of the novel establishes the conflict that informs the entire action. The gray, shadowy fish that "slide through the gloom of the mill-pond" are "descendants of the silvery things that had darted from the monks, in the young days when the valley was lusty"; but now "the whole place was gathered in the musing of old age." Life stagnates, bemused, incapable of developing. The rural community of Nethermere, with its symbolic overtones of submergence in the dark waters, is "the hollow which held us all," says the narrator, Cyril; and as Lettie says to the "primitive man," George Saxton, in an early choral passage:

> You are blind; you are only half-born; you are gross with good living and heavy sleeping. . . . You never grow up, like bulbs which spend all summer getting fat and fleshy, but never wakening the germ of a flower. As for me, the flower is born in me, but it wants bringing forth. Things don't flower if they're overfed. You have to suffer before you blossom in this life. When death is just touching a plant, it forces it into a passion of flowering. [*WP*, 27]

But the characters of the novel do not flower. All are trapped. All desire to "break free," want something "fresh," want to come alive. But all are victims of life's blind momentum, which sweeps them into relationships that condemn them to destruction, either psychic or physical.

Early in the novel, Cyril's father dies, destroyed in part by his wife's cruelty. Annable, the gamekeeper, dies in the quarry; and Lawrence suggests obliquely that Annable's effort to defy society and to live his own life as an "honest animal" has been thwarted by nature itself. Trying to climb out of the quarry, he is thrown back by the wall: " 'He'd be about half way up—ay—and the whole wall would come down on him' " (*WP*, 154). George Saxton, awakened to the possibilities of a new life by Cyril and Lettie, turns, after Lettie has married Leslie Tempest, to the sensual Meg, a sort of earth goddess; and as Meg becomes "mistress and sole authority," "a beautiful, unassailable tower of strength," George becomes her servant and, deeply frustrated, unable to make himself "whole and complete," drinks himself toward certain death (272, 289, 235). As for Lettie—the white peaçock, the independent woman who has wished over and over again to "break free"—she allows herself to be married off to Leslie and is condemned to live "a small indoor existence with artificial light and padded upholstery" (287). The volatile, restless Alice marries a clerk, and "all her little crackling fires were sodded down with the sods of British respectability" (312). Emily, who has sought to free herself through her relationship with Cyril, marries a stolid Englishman and retreats into the "shadows" and "ease" of traditional life: "Emily had at last found her place, and had escaped from the torture of strange, complex modern life" (316). As the coal miners of the district are "imprisoned underground" (315), so the middle-class men and women are all imprisoned and "netted" by life. All become servants of the Schopenhauerian or Hardyan will. Their potentialities as individuals are drowned in the great ocean of life. The Great Will, the Life Force, fulfills its blind purposes. Beauty and cruelty, life and death, generation and destruction—all are intertwined; and all men become the servants, the slaves, of this Force—all, that is, except the narrator, Cyril, who removes himself from the battle, contemplates the spectacle, and is left, at the end, in an ambiguous position, not subservient to the Magna Mater, but isolated, detached, and apparently still yearning to escape his "rooted loneliness." He alone is not the mere victim and pawn of the Immanent Will. But the unresolved questions that hover over the novel are these: Can anyone escape bondage to the Great Force? Can one "flower"? If so, how?

These questions Lawrence was to explore for the rest of his life. What are the roads to freedom? Can man escape his servitude to the blind

Life Force? Or is man—seen in the context of Nature, as Lawrence sees him throughout this novel—destined to carry out the Great Will from which he derives? Is he but the instrument, the agent, of the underlying reality? If so, has nature given him the power to act purposively as a free agent, not directed but the director, not lived by nature but the living, active creator?

The questions took the form, in Lawrence's formative years, of the great debates between mechanists and vitalists, between Schopenhauerian pessimism and Bergsonian or Shavian optimism, between the reductive monism of the naturalists and materialists and an idealistic liberalism that affirmed "progress." The youthful Lawrence, who sees man as divided within himself, is impressed by both sides of the debate.

As naturalist, Lawrence contemplates the great impersonal rhythms of nature. Again and again he carefully juxtaposes creative and destructive energies, life and death. A plum tree "which had been crucified to the wall, and which had broken away and leaned forward from bondage," produces "great mist-bloomed, crimson treasures, splendid globes"; but in the next paragraph Cyril looks at a "dead pool" which is "moving with rats" (52–53). In chapter 4 there is a fair "in full swing," with active, vigorous life; then the church bell sounds "through the din": Cyril's father is dead (33–34). Flowers yearn "for the sun," in a Blakean desire for fulfillment; but, three paragraphs later, Cyril hears "the scream of a rabbit caught by a weasel" (21). Over and over Lawrence reminds us of the admixture of sunlight and shadow, of creative and destructive force. Lapwings offer "a glistening white breast to the sunlight, to deny it in black shadow" (155). Cyril and his friends trail their "shadows across the fields, extinguishing the sunshine on the flowers as [they] went" (206–7). In Nottingham "the castle on its high rock stood in the dazzling dry sunlight; the fountain stood shadowy in the green glimmer of the lime trees" (244); in London the Life Guards march in scarlet and silver, "like a slightly wavering spark of red life blown along." But "the whole of the city seems a heaving, shuddering struggle of black-mudded objects deprived of the elements of life" (278). At Christmastide a cart passes "gay with oranges" and "scarlet intrusion of apples, and wild confusion of cold, dead poultry" (99). Thus, throughout the novel, descriptive passages suggest an allegorical world of light and darkness, fire and water:

> It was a windy, sunny day. In shelter the heat was passionate, but in the open the wind scattered its fire. Every now and then a white

> cloud, broad-based, blue-shadowed, travelled slowly along the sky-road after the forerunner small in the distance, and trailing over us a chill shade, a gloom which we watched creep on over the water, over the wood and the hill. [204]

A page later, the chicken that Mrs. Saxton has placed "on the warm hob to coax it into life" toddles into the fire and "there was a smell of cooked meat" (205).

In developing his allegorical language, Lawrence everywhere focuses not only on light and darkness but also on the antithesis of heights and depressions. In Nethermere, Cyril says, "we felt ourselves the centre of the waters and the woods that spread down the rainy valley." The valley is opposed to the hills, the quarry to the land above, the earth to the heavens. Presenting a natural world of creation (the upward impulse toward maximum of being) and of destruction (the impulse to return to the bosom of nature), Lawrence very carefully makes human life a part of the natural Heraclitean rhythm. Men, too, bloom and are cut down by the scythe of time; men, too, make love—and kill. And women join in the cruelty, the *bellum omnium:* Emily kills a dog, and Lettie digs her nails into George's thumb (30); women, says Leslie, are also "cruel," like "Napoleon" (51, 45). If men are likened to bulls, savages, Indians, or wild beasts, women are like spiders (in their parlors); women, too, become "wild," and the beautiful Meg is, as we have seen, "a beautiful, unassailable tower of strength that may in its turn stand quietly dealing death" (289).

In a world presented throughout as a remorseless process of creation and destruction, there would seem to be no room for free will. Yet Lawrence, as he beholds the great process, does not endorse blind submission to the laws of nature. On the contrary, he makes clear that the plight of all of these people is owing to their failure to assume responsibility. The central choral passage on this theme deals with Lettie's submission to Leslie:

> Having reached that point in a woman's career when most, perhaps all of the things in life seem worthless and insipid, she had determined to put up with it, to ignore her own self, to empty her own potentialities into the vessel of another or others, and to live her life at second hand. This peculiar abnegation of self is the resource of a woman for the escaping of the responsibilities of her own development. Like a nun, she puts over her living face a veil, as a sign that the woman no longer exists for herself: she is the servant of God, of some man, of her children, or may be of some cause. As a servant, she is no longer responsible for her self, which would make her terrified and lonely. Service is light and easy. To

> be responsible for the good progress of one's life is terrifying. It is the most insufferable form of loneliness, and the heaviest of responsibilities. [280]

And if Lettie has failed to assume responsibility for her own life and has ignored her own "potentialities," the same comment is made implicitly on George Saxton and Leslie. Lettie, in her "seething confusion of emotion," turns to George repeatedly, waiting for him to make a decision. They are not, she tells him, "trees with ivy" but rather "fine humans with free active life"; so it is insane to act simply as nature's instrument: " 'You, for instance—fancy *your* sacrificing yourself—for the next generation—that reminds you of Schopenhauer, doesn't it?—for the next generation, or love, or anything!' " (209). But George is too weak to act in his own right. Pathetically he begs Lettie, " 'Tell me what to do.' " "With terror and humility," he pleads: " 'No, Lettie; don't go. What should I do with my life?' " (215). Thus, like Tom Brangwen, George remains immersed in the marsh, unable to assume responsibility for his life. Like Tom, he looks to marriage to make him "whole and complete" (235), and once cut off from Lettie, who is "like the light" to him, he is "dark and aimless" (300). He has "nothing to be proud of" in his life (65).

The same mistake is made by Leslie, who functions as a sort of Edgar Linton, contrasted with the Heathcliff of George. Leslie, too, is like a "moth" fluttering about the light of Lettie. Like George, Leslie too is "a child" (194, 196); and he ends by serving Lettie, just as George serves Meg and as Tom Renshaw serves Emily as "the rejoiced husband and servant" (320). Only Annable and Cyril, among the males in this book, escape servitude. But Annable is killed, and Lawrence makes it clear that Annable's determination to rear his children as healthy animals has disastrous results: Annable's wife, Proserpine, is desperate, and Annable's son, Sam, becomes a thief. Thus Lawrence implicitly condemns the man whose motto is "Be a good animal." At the end, only Cyril remains to exhibit the "right" way—the way of developing one's "potentialities" and of assuming responsibility for one's own life. Cyril, however, does not act; he stands outside of life and contemplates it in a spirit of detachment.

What, then, is the way to "flower"? Submission to the will of nature means death of the soul; acceptance of one's total animality brings disaster, and submission to social conventions is equally stifling. Is there a way to avert disaster?

The answer to this last question is implicit in the structure of the novel, and it is the answer that became central in Lawrence's thinking to the end of his career. There must, obviously, be some balance. The animal man is incomplete, only half-developed. As George Saxton comes to realize, it is not enough to be a "fixed bit of a mosaic," "a toad in a hole" (64). Somehow the sensual man must emerge from unconsciousness—the dark waters in which the gray fish glide—and must connect himself with the "light" of consciousness and of spiritual development. At the same time, it is not enough to be a conscious being. Creatures like Emily and Lettie have lost the "meaning" of the snowdrops, which "belong to some old wild lost religion." The snowdrops, Lettie realizes, " 'belong to some knowledge we have lost, that I have lost and that I need. I feel afraid. They seem like something in fate. Do you think, Cyril, we can lose things off the earth—like mastodons, and those old monstrosities—but things that matter—wisdom?' " (129). As she recognizes later, it is not just her independence or her having her own way that she wants: " 'When I've had my way, I *do want* somebody to take it back from me' " (210). It is her personal deficiency that prompts her to turn to George Saxton, to seek in the animal man the sensuality, or the connection with nature, that she has lost. Balance is needed. George and Lettie should complement each other.

We can see, in the light of this discussion, why Lawrence included Annable in the final version of his novel. Annable, as spokesman for animality, is the polar opposite of Cyril, the man of the spirit, the artist, the detached observer. Neither Annable nor Cyril finds an acceptable answer to the "strange complex problem of modern life." Annable's reversion to animality looks healthy when compared with Leslie's submission to society and to the white peacock; but as in *The Scarlet Letter* Hester's defense of "nature" ends in lawlessness, so Annable's way ends in animality. Cyril's detachment looks attractive when compared with the bondage of the others, but his isolation is a negative freedom *from* the world, not freedom *for* anything. The novel implies that spirit and flesh must be balanced in a new "responsible" way of life. But Lawrence cannot define this healthy alternative. Perhaps the greatest deficiency of the novel, then, is that in the last analysis Cyril remains unevaluated. While Lettie, George, Leslie, and the others are condemned for failing to assume life responsibility and while Annable's choice of animality is disastrous, we do not know how we are to judge Cyril's life. Lawrence does not wrestle with the question of whether Cyril can connect himself with another person without sacrificing himself; nor does Lawrence have a clear idea of what is entailed in the assumption of responsibility.

Yet Lawrence has already found the premises of his philosophy and of his psychology. The motive forces in *The White Peacock* are two: the sexual desire to connect with another person, thus carrying out the will of nature; and the desire to break free from the great process of nature, to realize one's potentialities for progress in one's own life. Lawrence sees clearly that these desires conflict. Although he is not able as yet to invent scenes in which these motive forces are exhibited in direct conflict, he does show in several scenes the attraction and withdrawal of lovers. Again and again Lettie teases George and then, having roused him, puts him off. Generally, the contrary impulses of the psyche are presented in dialogues in which the characters speak in symbolic equations that define the contending forces—the desire for spiritual development versus the desire for sexual connection; the desire for freedom versus the desire to surrender oneself to another person; the desire for "art" or culture versus the desire for nature. The language is philosophical, though *Geist* and *Natur* are presented, as in Hawthorne, in psychological terms. The following passage is representative:

> "This Atalanta," [Leslie] replied, looking lovingly upon [Lettie], "this Atalanta—I believe she just lagged at last on purpose."
> "You have it," she cried, laughing, submitting to his caresses. "It was you—the apples of your firm heels—the apples of your eyes—the apple Eve bit—that won me—hein!"
> "That was it—you are clever, you are rare. And I've won, won the ripe apples of your cheeks, and your breasts, and your very fists—they can't stop me—and—and—all your roundness and warmness and softness—I've won you, Lettie."
> She nodded wickedly saying:
> "All those—those—yes."
> "All—she admits it—everything!"
> "Oh!—But let me breathe. Did you claim everything?"
> "Yes, and you gave it me."
> "Not yet. Everything though?" [84]

Lettie next asks Leslie to suppose that she is an angel, "like the 'Blessed Damosel,'" to whom he would pray; he answers:

> "Hang thin souls, Lettie! I'm not one of your souly sort. I can't stand Pre-Raphaelites. You—You're not a Burne-Jones—you're an Albert Moore. I think there's more in the warm touch of a soft body than in a prayer. I'll pray with kisses."
> "And when you can't?"
> "I'll wait till prayer-time again. By Jove, I'd rather feel my arms full of you; I'd rather touch that red mouth—you grudger!—than sing hymns with you in any heaven."
> "I'm afraid you'll never sing hymns with me in heaven."

"Well—I have you here—yes, I have you now." [84–85]

The language, as in Hawthorne, is pictorial: paintings or mythological figures are woven into the dialogue so that the split between spirit and flesh may be contemplated. At the same time, a psychological conflict is developed, the contest for supremacy between the spiritual woman and the sexually aroused man. If Leslie thinks he has "won," Lettie promptly puts him "below" her, as worshiper. She simultaneously offers herself to him, teasingly, and withdraws herself in a struggle to preserve her independence. But to present psychological conflict in allegorical language is to place a distance between the reader and the characters, the sort of distance that a writer like Hawthrone, given his didactic intentions, wanted to maintain. Lawrence, however, obviously more interested in felt life than is Hawthorne, runs a grave risk: that his readers will condemn his characters as being hopelessly artificial.

One of the great problems Lawrence does not solve is that of blending didactic allegory and real life. Sometimes the language is persuasively mimetic—as in Lettie's outburst " 'Oh!—but let me breathe.' " But in the next breath, Lawrence returns to the factitious Hawthornese. What he needs is a symbolic language to present the philosophical and psychological problem even as he presents felt life with intensity. He needs symbolic correspondences, not allegorical counters.

The wedding of felt life and allegory is so difficult that it continued to be a problem throughout Lawrence's career. The difficulties are suggested by *The Marble Faun,* in which we see Hawthorne working now with deliberate allegory, now with a symbolism that preserves our sense of a solid reality. In *The White Peacock,* Lawrence is as awkward as Hawthorne. In creating dialogue, Lawrence is often forced to ignore normal reticences or normal inarticulateness. The contrast between the conventions of allegory and those of realism is jarring:

> "Look!" [Lettie] said, "it's a palace, with the ash-trunks smooth like a girl's arm, and the elm-columns, ribbed and bossed and fretted, with the great steel shafts of beech, all rising up to hold an embroidered care-cloth over us; and every thread of the care-cloth vibrates with music for us." [214]

With this one may compare her remark on the next page: " 'I can't tell you—so let me go' " (215). Even if Lettie must be seen as "the white peacock," preferring her dreams to the brutal reality, the symbolic passages seem intolerably affected. It took time for Lawrence to learn how to blend the two voices. Before arriving at a synthesis, he tries first to drive out the realistic in *The Trespasser* (to invent an almost purely symbolic world) and then to drive out the allegorical in *Sons and Lovers*. Neither of these strategies is quite what he was looking for. Yet each novel, in its own way, lays bare the laws of psychology that preoccupied Lawrence before the great period of his "coming through." And a coherent vision of life is exhibited in the action and characterization of both. When one sets the flaws of these novels against the power of their plots, negative criticism dwindles into unimportance.

THE TRESPASSER

The Trespasser is a stronger novel than it has generally been taken to be. Its power derives from the boldness and classic simplicity of its strong allegorical structure. The form Lawrence creates is designed to exhibit the clash of male and female impulses; and the plot, moving with peripeteia to the moral failure and suicide of the hero, exhibits the hero's defeat as an instance of a remorseless pattern in nature that he is not strong enough to overcome. The novel is impersonal; the author is detached. The *pattern* of the conflict and the inevitability of the outcome are what Lawrence wishes us to contemplate.

Freudian critics have tended to reduce the novel's content to an Oedipal problem; the Jungian critic Samuel Eisenstein views the novel as a portrait of the male condemned to "uroboric incest" with the Magna Mater, who controls and destroys him because he lacks the strength to "fight his way back up out of this 'heart of darkness' of the womb."[1] According to John E. Stoll, "the tale of Helena and Siegmund illustrates what the passive male should not do to retain his masculine identity and survive."[2] But Lawrence's symbolism and his psychology in *The Trespasser* are complex, and the pattern of male/female interaction is part of a general vision that these interpretations do not quite imply.

In truth, the novel presents, in a fairly well developed form, many of the major insights that Lawrence articulated later in "Study of Thomas Hardy," in "The Crown," and in his mature fiction and psychological writings. Moreover, the symbolism of light and dark, sun and moon, day and night, spirit and flesh, sky and sea, and fire and water is subtly employed to dramatize the central question of the novel—can the relationship between the antagonistic male and female result in fulfillment or only in destruction? The symbolism isolates for contemplation the elemental fears and desires of the psyche, and the relationship between man and woman is evaluated with such precision as is made possible only by a symbolic language. Certainly some of the negative criticism of *The Trespasser* is justified: sometimes the novel becomes pretentious, and from time to time it is difficult to take Helena seriously, because she seems childish. But once we accept, with Stoll, that the novel is essentially allegorical psychomachia, we can scarcely object that it lacks the mimetic density of a realistic novel or that the prose is "ostentatious" or "written to impress."[3] That's like expecting the characters of *The Marble Faun* to step out of their allegorical framework and to act like the characters in Henry James; and it's like complaining, as some do complain, that Hawthorne's symbolic descriptions, which project psychic duality into the natural world, are just padding. Like much of Hawthorne's fiction, *The Trespasser* is a psychological romance in which our attention is focused on elemental motive forces and on elemental patterns of psychic interaction. It lays bare these forces and interactions with a didactic, even a "scientific," clarity. That clarity is the strength of the novel. The many harsh evaluations of the novel generally fail to recognize its uniqueness and the complexity of the psychic interaction of Helena and Siegmund as revealed in the symbolism.

I had better begin by setting down the psychological and metaphysical principles that inform the novel.

1. The first principle is Schopenhauerian:[4] the Life Force, or the Will to Live, is impersonal, implacable, and cruel; and the female, as the instrument of this force, does not hesitate to use the male for the realization of life's ends. This principle, at least, is Lawrence's starting point; but the Schopenhauerian insight was modified by Lawrence in the light of his personal experience. Unlike Schopenhauer, Lawrence wished to deal, not just with the elemental female, but also with the sensitive spiritual female of his own time and society. As Stoll and others have pointed out, such a female, as Lawrence sees her, sublimates her primal sexual energy by creating a world of fantasy in which she can ignore the brutal realities of the male's animal being and can transform him into a godlike spirit that alone can satisfy her craving for completion.

2. The male, like the female, is incomplete in himself, "derivative," "an outcast" who is without support until he can wed himself to the female. Hence he is driven by a blind desire to make the female everything, his raison d'être. At the same time, however, Lawrence accepts the Nietzschean idea that the male fiercely desires to strive "beyond himself," to become a heroic soul, proud and brave in his manhood, able to act independently against public opinion and conventions. Failure to follow this creative, purposive prompting entails psychic destruction; the inability to resist conventional opinion results in psychic death.

3. In their striving for wholeness of being, both male and female become antagonists. Each strives to triumph over the other, and when one triumphs, the other is nullified. The relationship becomes that of dominance and submission, "pride and subservience," rather than a healthy relationship of independent individuals in conjunction, neither being "nullified" by the other.

4. Life and death are inseparable. Life flowers into magnificence like the poppy, then falls back into the great source from which it derives. But life is also a creative striving toward individuation and light, an effort to escape the bonds of matter and death by adventuring "into the unknown" and by achieving "maximum of being." Schopenhauer's pessimism is thus modified in Lawrence by a Bergsonian emphasis on creative evolution; and the man fails who gives up his struggle to achieve maximum of being, who denies "the strain of God" in him, or who accepts fatalistically his helplessness and insignificance in the cosmos.

In tracing Lawrence's dramatization of these principles, the critic must be particularly sensitive to the meaning of the dominant symbols, for the pattern of psychic conflict is presented in a pattern of symbolic oppositions. Stoll argues that for Lawrence the female is light and the male is dark. But this contention forces Stoll repeatedly to argue that the symbolism is employed ironically. For example, after quoting Helena's remark " 'I saw the sunshine in you,' " Stoll writes: "Let the reader tentatively accept 'sunshine' as one of the metaphors used to signify her all-consuming possessiveness, and seeing the sunshine in Siegmund will immediately suggest Helena's success in molding him to her own desire" (47). Such a reading must ignore, first, the context of Helena's remark, which plainly indicates that Helena is, at this point in the action, battling "with her new subjugation to Siegmund." Second, Stoll must ignore the fact that sunshine, when introduced in the second chapter of the novel, is clearly associated with Siegmund's coming to life and selfhood after his long submission to duty, and that Helena repeatedly wishes to get out of the sun, to shade herself from it and to shade Siegmund from it. Third, the sun is almost explicitly identified with the male spirit on pages 95 and 96 of the novel, where Helena wishes to see "God at home in his white incandescence." Fourth, Lawrence associates the male with the sun in *The Rainbow* and in his explicit formulations of his symbolism in *Fantasia of the Unconscious*. The female he invariably associates with the moon and the sea.

As for the sea, its meaning is complex. R. E. Pritchard, in his *D. H. Lawrence: Body of Darkness*, points out that the sea is "akin to the underground cold, the great 'brute force' that is the unliving source and destroyer of life.''[5] I agree with this interpretation; but it is important to note that the attributes of the sea that are singled out for attention are also reflections of the state of mind of the observer: both Siegmund and Helena view each other as being ''like the sea''; both yearn for but fear the sea. On one level, the sea is identified with the female origin or source and with Helena. On another, it is identified with the brute power that Helena associates with Siegmund's animality. The common denominator, however, is the brute primal energy of the undifferentiated (neither male nor female) Schopenhauerian will, which is both creative and destructive. When Siegmund bathes in the sea, he bathes symbolically in Helena, in the primal energy; Helena also bathes in Siegmund. Such bathing may be either rejuvenative or destructive, just as coition, in Lawrence's fiction generally, may issue either in rebirth, after death of the old self, or in death (the self obliterated by love, by the unconscious). As ''the unconscious,'' the sea is contrasted with the sky and the sun. The female water is opposed to the male light or spirit. Life, originating in the darkness of the water, struggles to climb, or rise, into consciousness; but it is always pulled back by the destructive forces of nature, and the adventurous male spirit undergoes ''death by water.'' We shall see, as we proceed, how carefully Lawrence works with these oppositions as he contemplates the ''frictional to-and-fro'' of his lovers.

At the beginning of the action, after the framing chapter in which we see Helena after Siegmund's death, Lawrence raises the question that became recurrent in his fiction: can a nullified or imprisoned individual find freedom and rebirth through sexual union? Siegmund, who ''for years . . . had suppressed his soul, in a kind of mechanical despair doing his duty and enduring the rest'' (9), is in the grip of the life urge toward freedom and ''maximum of being.'' He turns instinctively for fulfillment to Helena, who is associated symbolically with the moon and the sea. Siegmund ''lifted his face to the moon'' (9), the moonlight enters his drawing room, ''and he thought the whiteness was Helena'' (10). It is she who lies ''at the core of the glamour'' of the night, ''like the moon''; and she is also associated with the sea: ''Helena, with her blue eyes so full of storm, like the sea, but, also like the sea, so eternally self-sufficient, solitary'' (13).

Thus the first note of warning is sounded: Siegmund, the imagery suggests, may find this female sea uncaring. Nevertheless, the prospect of seeing Helena fills him with joy, and in chapter 3, as he journeys to the Isle of Wight, the key phrase becomes ''morning sunshine.'' Lawrence works very delicately in this chapter with a buried metaphor that will become explicit: the sunshine, the glitter, and the morning are the world of life and the individuation of living creatures who, in their innocence, are unaware of the unliving, undifferentiated darkness beneath the outward forms (the maya of the world). "Siegmund's shadows" vanish in the glittering sunshine, and as he journeys toward the sea, "All his body radiated amid the large, magnificent sea noon like a piece of colour" (15). At this point he has forgotten the dangers of the warlike earth, dangers suggested by the "grim and wicked battleships" near Helena's island. But presently clouds "cast over him the shadows of their bulk, and he shivered in the chill wind" (16). It begins to rain, and the rain puts out the sun. The symbolism, which associates "the blue sea" and "the blue haze" with Helena's "blue eyes," fuses the ideas of a destructive watery principle and of a destructive spirituality that Lawrence associates with "blue-eyed" or "northern" people. Helena is not warm or receptive. When Siegmund encounters her, she is "shivering with cold" and her arms are "blue." She becomes the cold female water and the cold female spirituality threatening his male flame and sunshine: "He only knew her blue eyes were rather awful to him" (17). Although he senses immediately that "she was blind to him," his passion impels him to believe that he can "blind himself with her" and "blaze up all his past and future in a passion worth years of living" (18). But Lawrence suggests ironically that the male fire will not prevail: Siegmund is "in her charge" (19), and, again ironically, he is grateful for the mist that shuts out the harsh realities of his situation as husband and father.

Elated, he tells Helena, "There is nothing else but you, and for you there is nothing else but me—look!" (19). But because this remark implies a limitation of her freedom and a loss of her self-sufficiency and because she is "quite alone with the man, in a world of mist," she flings herself suddenly "sobbing against his breast" (19). Fearing to lose herself to him, she also resents his separateness from her. When Siegmund "dreamed by himself," Lawrence observes, "this displeased her. She wanted him for herself. How could he leave her alone while he watched the sky!" (21). As the male turns his face to the sky and the creative sun, the female wants him to be earthbound.

The situation is familiar to readers of the later novels. Male and female are attracted to but fear each other. A to-and-fro of attraction and withdrawal defines their relationship; this is an oscillation, in the language of *Fantasia of the Unconscious*, between sympathetic and voluntary urges. Each wants total possession of the other and resents the other's separateness and self-sufficiency; each fears his or her own obliteration in love. The lion and the unicorn fight for the crown, not knowing that the victory of one over the other means death.

The problem is bound up with Helena's spirituality, her sexual fears. When, in chapter 4, Siegmund is aroused until he becomes "hot blood . . . without a mind; his blood, alive and conscious, running towards her," Helena's "heart leaped away in revulsion" (23). For a moment the lovers seem to "melt and fuse together," but Helena wants only the dream of Siegmund, not the actuality, and "she sank away from his caresses, passively, subtly drew back from him" (23). Her withdrawal, her fear of his blood lust, immediately makes his heart sink and his blood grow "sullen" (23). Then she seeks to mollify him, justifying her withdrawal by telling him that she is cold. On a symbolic level, this coldness—like the coldness of the moon and sea—again threatens his male fire.

In chapter 5 the fire rises: Siegmund's eyes, we learn, "sought her swiftly, as sparks lighting on the tinder. But her eyes were only moist" (25). Fire and water contend. Her "white dress . . . showed her throat gathering like a fountain-jet of solid foam to balance her head," her lace is "dripping spume," and it is only by degrees that the flame of his love and of the firelight induce her to offer "him herself to sacrifice" (28). There commences then the first phase of their love, in which Helena is "subjugated" to Siegmund.

Given peace by Helena's abandonment of herself to him, Siegmund now feels completed. As we might expect, the imagery suggests completion in the union of the female water and the male "morning": Siegmund becomes "like the sea, blue and hazy in the morning, musing by itself" (28). " 'I feel at home here,' " he tells her, " 'as if I had come home, where I was bred' " (29). He is no longer "an outcast" but has returned to the female Source, has become one with the female, "like the sea." Yet Helena, "very hot, feverish and restless" in his arms, resents his possessiveness and turns "to look at the night. The cool, dark, watery sea called to her" (29). She longs to be restored to her solitary female self-sufficiency and is pained because he, sated, "was beyond her now and did not need her" (29). The two are incapable of creating a relationship that is not threatening to one of them, and the scene anticipates Lawrence's later treatment of this dilemma: for example, in *Women in Love,* where Gudrun envies Gerald's peace after she has yielded to him. Like Gudrun, Helena feels left out; and when Siegmund tells her that " 'the darkness is a sort of mother, and the moon a sister, and the stars children, and sometimes the sea is a brother: and there's a family in one house, you see,' " Helena's immediate response is to ask: " 'And I, Siegmund?' " She, he says, is " 'the key to the castle' "; but he feels on his cheek "the smart of her tears" (30).

A general law of psychic life in Lawrence's fiction is that love, under the right conditions, transforms the individual: the old self dies in the darkness of the unconscious, and a new self may be born, eager to adventure into the unknown and to achieve maximum of being. That Lawrence had this law in mind as early as 1911 becomes clear when we follow the next stages of Siegmund's relationship with Helena. Having thrown off the dead mechanical nullity of his old life and having been completed by Helena's love, Siegmund wakes "with wonder in the morning," "transported to a new life, to realise my dream" (30). It is again morning, the time for the flowering of the male spirit, or the light; and Siegmund, transformed, looks at "the poppies . . . blown out like red flame"—the symbols used in "The Crown" to represent the individual's maximum of being. Laughing, Siegmund swims in the sea, only to catch his thigh "on a sharp, submerged point." The "sudden cruelty of the sea" surprises the male, but he puts it out of his mind and, "delighted in himself," feels a new pride, though he is troubled that Helena "rejects me as if I were a baboon, under my clothing" (32).

The conflict, muted, continues as Helena goes down to the sea and, alone, feels a complete "sense of satisfaction" as she creates her private world of dream and fancy, trying to wash away "the soiling of the last night's passion" and, like the sea, feeling "self-sufficient and careless of the rest" (34). Siegmund, however, still rejoicing in his completeness ("with Helena, in this large sea-morning, he was whole and perfect as the day" [35]), now wants the male sun: " 'I like the sunshine on me, real and manifest and tangible. I feel like a seed that his been frozen for ages. I want to be bitten by the sunshine' " (38). He seems about to take the Lawrencian course from rebirth in sexual union to purposive, creative activity in the sunlight of the public world. But Helena shrinks from the extreme of heat and turns again to the sea, approaching so close to the edge of the cliff that she frightens Siegmund. Her counterassertion of the female principle against his male triumph is short-lived, however. At the end of this chapter she is "frightened" by the thudding of Siegmund's heart, which she associates with that of "a great God thudding out waves of life, . . . unconscious" (38). Siegmund has become for her the unconscious heart of the cosmos, the blind will, and she, the spiritual woman, is threatened by the tyrannical God.

In chapter 7 Lawrence extends the symbolism of the sea as a brutal principle in nature. Siegmund's peace is shattered when "the muffled firing of guns on the sea" suggests the brutality and cruelty of a world in which men must fight to survive. He is like Kubla Khan in Xanadu.

Proceeding along the shore with Helena, he is suddenly afraid of becoming "trapped and helpless" as the sea moves in. Yet he is also "elated" by the danger, the threat of the "brute sea," "the great battle of action." But Helena sees the danger in this male lust for power. Seeing him "smiling brutally," she hates "the brute in him" and, "turning suddenly," leaves him (41). Later, when he catches up with her and kisses her, he again feels completed: he is "sea and sunlight mixed" and Helena is "moulded to him in pure passion" (42). But she, having lured him away from the scene of male battle, having won him back to her, feels a "strange elation and satisfaction" and says, " 'It might as well have been the sea as any other way, dear' " (42). It is a queer speech in which she seems to subscribe, fatalistically, to a romantic *Liebestod;* but death-by-water is death in the female element, so that her speech says in effect: "If you must die, better to die in me, not in male battle." Whatever the motivation for her speech—and she herself does not understand why she speaks those words—she is at least half in love with a death that can release her from the tyranny of the brutal world; and her words again foreshadow Siegmund's death. After they have given a light bulb that they have found on the shore to some children, the chapter ends ominously with a reminder of his family: "he was thinking of his own youngest child" (42). The symbolism is fairly obvious: As Siegmund watches Helena "lifting her fingers from off the glass, then gently stroking it, his blood ran hot" (42). The bulb is the penis and is associated with male light and fire. Helena gives the bulb away, indifferently. The symbolism repeats that of chapter 3, where Siegmund's light is threatened by cold, rain, and mist.

Siegmund's dominance over Helena continues into chapter 8, where she, feeling "destroyed," her soul "blasted," sees all things as "made of sunshine more or less soiled" (45). Apparently the male sun has triumphed, and her "pride battled with her new subjugation to Siegmund" (44). But Siegmund, now full of life, ventures "recklessly in his new pride" and swims again in the sea, which ominously drinks "with its cold lips deeply of his warmth" (46). He turns "his face to the sun," becoming the "happy priest of the sun"; and though he is dimly aware that "under all, was this deep mass of cold, that the softness and warmth merely floated upon" (47), he feels "like Adam when he opened the first eyes in the world" (49). Helena, too, sees "the sunshine in [him]," and the chapter is indeed all sun. But the darkness of hostile reality cannot be forgotten. When Siegmund asks Helena whether she does not " 'feel as if it were right—you and me, Helena,' " he finds "her eyes full of tears" (49).

So the oscillations continue beneath the surface of the relationship. In chapter 9 a brief interlude of tranquillity occurs. A late-afternoon lethargy, a "large, fruitful inertia," falls upon the lovers, and in a "twilight of sleep," their passion "softly shed," they are liberated in dreams. "New buds were urged in their souls as they lay in a shadowed twilight, at the porch of death" (50). But of course they are unaware of death; it is the narrator who reminds us that the poppies bloom, that their seed falls "into the hand of God," that then "new splendid blooms of beauty" are born. The lovers are part of the great process of life and death. Sleeping "at the porch of death," they are mysteriously renewed, revived; but the process is impersonal, and the lovers do not comprehend the strange rhythms of life and death and life resurgence in which they act out their lives. It is not until chapter 10 that Siegmund shows uneasiness about being a helpless part of the great process. As the sun sets, he asks Helena, " 'Don't you think we had better be mounting the cliffs?' "—a remark that in the symbolic context bespeaks his desire to free himself from the tyranny of matter and the great impersonal will. And when Helena, "smiling with irresponsible eyes," answers him, " 'Why should we?' " (52), he feels again "the distance between them," her "child-like indifference to consequences," which he contrasts with his own awareness of "the relentless mass of cold" beneath the "delicious warm surface of life," "the mass which has no sympathy with the individual, no cognisance of him" (52). Siegmund, prompted to act purposively against nature's blind processes, is at the same time in love with his enemy. He knows he must act purposively, but he is unable to assert his male will.

Night follows day in this poem of psychic conflict, and after the "sun chapters," chapter 11 is a "night chapter," in which the roles of Siegmund and Helena are dramatically reversed. The lovers walk through the meadows and wild lands and copses until it is late at night and they are lost. Helena is naturally pleased by the immersion in darkness: "She asked for the full black night, that would obliterate everything save Siegmund" (55). And Siegmund also feels joy in the oneness provided by the night. " 'You seem to have knit all things in a piece for me,' " he declares. " 'Things are not separate: they are all in a symphony' " (56). Whereupon Helena feels "triumphant and restored" (58). In her possessiveness, she creates her dream lover and her Zauberland under the moon, uttering phrases of "whispered ecstasy," her soul moving "beyond life," "a little way into death" (60). Siegmund has relinquished himself to her and to the night; but her gloating over him in this ecstasy of possessiveness poisons the relationship. "Suddenly she became aware that she must be slowly weighing down the life of Siegmund" (60). "Stunned, half-conscious," he murmurs, " 'Hawwa,—Eve—Mother!' " (61). And he becomes the child, her child, under the moon and the sway of the female night. Indeed, he is almost destroyed as a self-responsible individual: he feels "rather deathly," "half gone away," and Helena's "strange ecstasy over him" has been "like a pure poison scathing him" (63). She walks on "in triumph" under the moon (65), "pleased with her fancy of wayward little dreams." But Siegmund, demolished as a man, associates himself with the crucified Christ and thinks: "Let me get under cover. . . . Let me hide in . . . the sudden intense darkness. I am small and futile: my small, futile tragedy . . ." (66). The life and pride he has felt in the sunlight have been smashed, and he is now small and insignificant, swallowed by the devouring Mother.

At this point, Lawrence, having exhibited Siegmund's failure to act purposively after the rejuvenating passion, inserts the chapter in which Siegmund meets his Doppelgänger, Hampson. The purpose of the chapter is to objectify Siegmund's problem, the problem of a man who cannot go beyond sympathetic union with woman to achieve full manhood in purposeful activity but must seek his raison d'être in destructive passion, or in "vivid soul-experience." Hampson defines the error of making woman the be-all and end-all of life. Men attracted to " 'supersensitive' " women, he argues, become " 'their instruments' "; the supersensitive woman " 'can't live without us, but she destroys us. These deep, interesting women don't want us: they want the flowers of the spirit they can gather of us. . . . they destroy the natural man in us—that is, us altogether' " (70). The frustration of the male's sexual pride causes destruction of his capacity to flower in purposive striving. Hampson suggests the way to achieve freedom and fulfillment: he says that he strives beyond himself; and the remark is so penetrating that it prompts Siegmund to reflect: " 'You make me feel—as if I were loose, and a long way off from the myself' " (70). A short time later, when Siegmund encounters Helena, he defines his problem: " 'I know I'm a moral coward,' " he says, and asks, " 'What is myself?' " Having failed to strive beyond himself, he confesses weakly that he cannot throw off public opinion, which hovers about them in the form of the conventional landlady.

Now, as if desperate, Siegmund turns again to the sun, declaring that he wants a "sun-soaking," though Helena, who longs for shade, wants him to put on a hat (76, 74). Still casting about for a release from his problem, Siegmund yearns for the simple animal life of a farmer and takes satisfaction in the intense sun, a "furnace" that causes his hands to become "full of blood" and "swollen with heat" (76). But Helena, seeing his satisfaction, feels "very lonely" and resents having "to play to his buoyant happiness, so as not to . . . spoil one minute of his consummate hour" (78). His happiness leaves her "unnecessary to him," and she turns to her fancy of a Mist Spirit that shuts out "the outside" (78). Then, as Siegmund continues to brood on his moral cowardice (81), Helena is unable to contain any longer her revulsion from his animality. Seeing him as "a stooping man . . . something of the 'clothed animal on end,' like the rest of men," she suffers a sudden "agony of disillusion" (83). Her repugnance toward his "brute embrace" and her feeling that she is imprisoned by him drive her into a sudden wild sobbing that stuns him, so that "a death [takes] place in his soul" (84). Even as he enfolds her in his arms, he is "quite alone" and cannot be helped by the woman who would save "him from searching the unknown" (85). It is, of course, her very effort to keep him from searching the unknown that is destroying him.

At this point, seeing his withdrawal from her, Helena suddenly dreads losing him and determines to "get him back." Once again she becomes the mother, soothing him "till he was child to her Madonna" (87). But he recognizes clearly now that he has not the courage to "compel anything, for fear of hurting it" (88). He will not be able to defy convention; and Helena, aware of his wife and his children, cannot help him. Dimly aware at this point that she has "done wrong" by rejecting his animal desire, she tries to take refuge in him "as a child does when it . . . hides in the mother's bosom" (90). Thus *she* becomes the child to *him,* as he had earlier become the child to her. Both, like Gudrun and Gerald, seek to discard their responsibility as adults; but they can find no mature way to love, and "the sense of the oneness and unity of their fates was gone" (90).

The movement of their relationship, from illusion to disillusion, is recapitulated in the symbolism of chapter 17, where Siegmund first finds the morning kind and tender and then, after injuring himself again on the rocks of the sea, recognizes that the kindness is an illusion (93). The morning, too, with its bright sunshine, is an illusion: the warm flowers of life rest upon the coldness of the sea with its "sea-women . . . striving to climb up out of the darkness into the morning" (93). Nature remains cruel and impersonal; and Siegmund, looking at the sea, reflects: " 'I am nothing. I do not count. I am inconsiderable' " (94). To him the sea is destructive, impersonal, female. To Helena, however, it is "a great deal like Siegmund, . . . the sea as it flung over her filled her with the same uncontrollable terror as did Siegmund when he, sometimes, grew silent and strange in a tide of passion" (95). Only when the sea is "blazing with white fire, . . . transfused with white burning, while over it hung the blue sky in a glory, like the blue smoke of the fire of God,'' only when she can see ''God at home in his white incandescence, his fire settling on her like the Holy Spirit,'' can she worship and adore. The fire of the Spirit must burn ''among the waves'' (95-96). She rejects the brute nature of the sea, just as she rejects Siegmund's flesh and blood.

Unaware of how deeply she has injured him in his pride and self-esteem (101), she is ''happy'' as the time for their departure draws near. Siegmund, his illusions gone, sees sharply that '' 'she is sufficient to herself—she doesn't want me' '' (100). '' 'She is alone and a law unto herself: she only wants me to explore me, like a rock-pool, and to bathe in me. After a while, when I am gone, she will see I was not indispensable' '' (100). He no longer believes in the ''strain of God'' in him. The sun, burning into him, is, he thinks, ''certainly consuming some part of me'' (103). Now it is as if, unable to identify himself with the creative, purposive flame of God, he can only submit himself to God's destructive fire. When Helena reminds him that it is time to leave, he almost hates her (109).

The journey homeward intensifies the pathos of Siegmund's condition. Ironically, he, who most needs help, gives help to Helena. When she, tormented by ''the heat of her neighbour's body'' in the train, turns to Siegmund for ''his strength of nerve to support her,'' he submits ''at once, his one aim being to give her out of himself whatever she wanted'' (112). As his last strength is sucked up by her, he contrasts himself with a gentleman who acts bravely and quickly to save his launch from disaster. And he sees again ''the shadow'' through the petals of the day:

> I can see death urging itself into life, the shadow supporting the substance. For my life is burning an invisible flame. The glare of the light of myself, as I burn on the fuel of death, is not enough to hide from me the source and the issue. For what is a life but a flame that bursts off the surface of darkness and tapers into the darkness again. [115]

Thus in language that strongly anticipates that of ''The Crown,'' Siegmund realizes that he will return to the undifferentiated source in which individual identity is abolished, the source of death and of life, the female darkness. His sole consolation is that ''the death that issues differs from the death that was the source'' (115); he can ''enrich death with a potent shadow, if I do not enrich life.'' So he sees himself in the context of the universal process, as one of the bees, rushing ''out of the hive . . . into the dark meadows of night.'' And he consoles himself:

"If the spark goes out, the essence of the fire is there in the darkness" (122). After returning to Beatrice and his children, he arrives at the knowledge that life is "implacable in its kindness," beyond human pity (159). As life's child, he is glad to have parents stronger than himself.

On the last morning of his life, he witnesses the conflict of sun and moon. The sun, a cat, stalks the mouse-moon and destroys it. The passage is typical of the "descriptive writing" that readers often condemn in the novel. But the imagery is of course symbolic and is designed to heighten the pathos. Throughout the night Siegmund has lain in bed, his body sweating, "a terrible, heavy, hot thing over which he had slight control" (155). His "outrage" at the horrible heat of his body "and the exquisite torture of the drops of sweat" reflects his disgust with the tyranny of matter, the animal body and passion that have driven him into helplessness. Then, when he sees lightning in the sky, he watches "with wonder and delight," as if he were witnessing the advent of the spirit, of that light which can triumph over the darkness. The day destroys the night, and the moon becomes "a dead mouse which floats on water" (157). He has witnessed a cosmic triumph over the female night, the body, the sea, the unconscious. But that one brief vision of triumph only underscores his own desperation and helplessness; once day has prevailed, it proves to be "unreal" to him: "Everything out of doors was unreal, like a show, like a peep-show. Helena was an actress somewhere in the brightness of this view. He alone was out of the piece" (157). In the end he can see only the shadow, not the substance—death, not life. He commits suicide.

Helena, as he predicted, has not found him indispensable. Though she grieves for a year after his death, she turns at last to Cecil Byrne, and Lawrence suggests that this new relationship will be, in one way or another, a remorseless repetition of her relationship with Siegmund. " 'I might as well not exist,' " Byrne reflects bitterly, " 'for all she is aware of me' " (183). As the scar of Helena's sunburn wears off—token of her forgetting of Siegmund—she seeks "rest and warmth" in Byrne; but at the same time she makes "a small, moaning noise, as if of weariness and helplessness" (186). Condemned by the Life Force to seek out the male, she resists to the end her total subjugation to his passion. She does not want to be burned by Byrne. Thus Lawrence's allegory of the conflict of elemental male and female forces concludes—not anticlimactically, as Stoll and Eisenstein argue, but rather with a scene that underscores the pathos of Siegmund's defeat and the remorselessness of the will, which urges male and female into connections that threaten the "integral selfhood" of each. The synthesizing principle of the novel is this: whatever is included is for the sake of exhibiting with maximum clarity and pathos the remorselessness of the great impersonal process that urges male and female into destructive union.

The cosmic to-and-fro goes on. Lawrence's vision is almost purely Schopenhauerian. The will, that great elemental sea, casts up a world of living creatures, fair appearances in the sunshine, and it calls them back to itself, implacable. It creates, moreover, a war of each against the other—the war of sun and moon, day and night, sky and sea, male and female. Lawrence sees that in this cosmic war there are no winners. If darkness triumphs over light, or light over darkness, destruction occurs. Each principle needs the other for its completion. The female darkness calls to the male light, and the light to the darkness. A vital harmony and reconciliation is needed. But polar opposites cannot *fuse,* for fusion means annihilation. The two principles can be connected only when established in their separateness; in Birkin's language, they can become separate but in conjunction. Only in such a relationship are they free to realize "maximum of being." Siegmund is destroyed because he seeks maximum of being in the woman, at the expense of his male selfhood. Identifying with the darkness, he denies the "strain of God" in him; and a moral coward, he surrenders all life responsibility. The only solution for Siegmund—the only solution for any of Lawrence's male heroes—is to affirm a proud integral selfhood, to fight against the dead world of convention and the blind forces of nature, and to adventure into the unknown. At the same time, this adventure must be based on a healthy connection with the female, on healthy sexual fulfillment in the great Source. Once that fulfillment is achieved, the male can acquire the courage to "trespass."

This analysis reveals that Lawrence had thought through, in 1912, several of the basic articles of his philosophy. In *The Trespasser* he daringly created a prose poem in which the to-and-fro of antagonistic forces is exhibited and analyzed in carefully wrought symbolic language. Far from indulging in "fine writing" in this book, Lawrence everywhere works intelligently to define the psychological dilemma of modern man and woman. *The Trespasser* is not a turgid outpouring of melancholy youth but the early experimental work of an intelligence in full command of a metaphysic and a psychology that, for many readers, define accurately the realities of their inner lives.

SONS AND LOVERS

As Lawrence amplified and consolidated his vision of life, he continued to confront in his art the basic question that arose in his first two novels: how is it possible to lay bare the laws of psychic interaction without doing violence to life in its full concreteness and complexity? In *The Trespasser* he abstracts from the multifarious richness of experience those basic desires and fears that are eternally exhibited in the relationships between men and women. But to abstract "those principles and passions by which all minds are agitated" is to ignore "the streaks of the tulip," the variegated textures of ordinary life that elude schematization. *The Trespasser* is therefore a "pure" poem of the soul's elemental attractions and repulsions, a poetry of opposed symbols. Such a novel, excluding everything that might blur the focus on the elemental passions in conflict, lacks the mimetic density that an age of realism and naturalism has come to expect. It is too self-contained, too neat; and despite the symbolism's wide implications, the reader feels the confinement, the hothouse atmosphere of the prose poetry. Lawrence, perhaps intimidated by Ford Madox Ford's criticism of *The Trespasser*, turned from poetry to the sensuous realism of *Sons and Lovers*.

He had no intention of abandoning his efforts to define laws of psychology. In *Sons and Lovers*, as in *The Trespasser* and *The White Peacock*, he traces the subjugation of the male to the female, the obliteration of the male's selfhood and freedom as his soul is sucked up by Woman—either the spiritual woman or the possessive sensual woman. Indeed, Lawrence is interested in expanding his understanding of this subjugation to the love urge. By increasing the number of characters and by plotting his action over two generations, he gives himself the freedom to explore, above and beyond the Oedipal problem, many variations of the more general problem that dominated his thinking during the period when he was struggling to "come through."

Early criticism of the novel, which focused on autobiographical content, on the Oedipal problem, or on "destructive or counterfeit loves," tended to ignore the comprehensiveness of the pattern that Lawrence was tracing in the lives of his characters. Within the past decade, however, Richard Swigg and Stephen J. Miko have called attention to the more general pattern informing the action. Swigg, in his *Lawrence, Hardy, and American Literature*, points out that Lawrence was working with the struggle of life to rise "above the mass, above all the unconscious, formless, unresolved things which imprison [Paul's] developing 'on and on, nobody knows where.' "[6] And Miko shrewdly observes that the novel focuses on the problem of how a "fundamental vitality can be embodied or released, what will restrict its growth, and what will encourage self-realization."[7] I think this is exactly right: the pattern that Lawrence traces everywhere in *Sons and*

Lovers is a pattern of life thwarted because of a person's subjugation to others or to capitalist society. Thus the novel reveals Lawrence's early meditations on the question that had become, by 1912, an obsession: How can the individual, single, separate, unique, enter into any relationship with other human beings and with society without sacrificing his individuality and without destroying his creative, purposive energies?

The conflict, at bottom, is not only between nature and culture but also between love and power, though Lawrence did not use the term "power" at this point in his life. The individual, motivated by an impulse to surrender himself to another person—and ultimately to the collective will of society—discovers that his sympathetic impulse, his love urge, threatens his very being as an individual. Paul's surrender to his mother cripples him and afflicts him with that "ontological insecurity," that fear of engulfment, which Marguerite Beede Howe views as the central concern of Lawrence's fiction. But all of the people in the novel are threatened by a kind of "engulfment" or by a thwarting of their potentialities as individuals. Howe's view that the novel exhibits the effort of an ontologically insecure hero to defend his ego against destruction and to return, through "uroboric incest," to the "state of grace from which we have fallen into the alienation of individuality"[8] is psychoanalytically acceptable, but Lawrence was dealing not merely with the problem of his hero but with a more general problem that all people—both the secure and the insecure—confront in their relationships with others. To avoid the death of the soul, one must find a way to live in which the self is not absorbed or "nullified" by others or by society.

This idea is worked so strongly into all parts of the novel that one reads on to discover not only whether Paul will escape but also whether the others will be able to avoid the crippling effects of their love. All are well-meaning people; all are viewed naturalistically as innocent creatures thrown, through no fault of their own, into situations that "cramp" or "clog" or "block" or "imprison" their natural vitality. Indeed, the images in *Sons and Lovers,* issuing from the recurrent conflict between life and life constriction, fall into a simple pattern of oppositions. Life is quick, open, free, flowing, running, loose, alert, natural, easy, or spontaneous. When life is thwarted, it is gripped, held, clogged, tight, blind, tranced, cramped, slow, heavy, ill, hurt, awkward, unreal, bound, or imprisoned. These antinomies arise everywhere as Lawrence follows the fortunes of his characters; and the unique power and beauty of the novel are, to a large extent, the result of Lawrence's ability to move beyond superficial problems and to dramatize with directness and immediacy the underlying and fundamental human problem, which is ultimately the problem of almost all novels: our fear of the impairment of our life energies and of the thwarting of our deep desire to live fully and spontaneously, unimpeded by the pressures of society or of other people. Every one of Lawrence's characters faces not so much an immediate and practical problem as the fundamental "life issue"; and every one of them is seen both as a creature of possibilities—the heir or heiress of magnificent life—and as the victim of forces that suppress and poison the sacred fount.

The relationship of the father and mother—those unforgettably real and unforgettably archetypal figures—initiates the pattern of thwarted life and introduces the note of apprehension and dread that informs the entire novel. Both Morel and Gertrude, as we see with compassionate dread, are crippled by marriage and by the economic and social circumstances of their lives. Yet Morel, when he is alone, standing in what Lawrence might later have called "a proud noble selfhood," is vigorously alive. When Gertrude Coopard meets him, she watches him with fascination (as Miriam, later on, will watch Paul): "He was so full of colour and animation, his voice ran so easily into comic grotesque, he was so ready and so pleasant with everybody." His humor is "warm, a kind of gambolling" (9). And the "sensuous flame of life . . . flowed off his flesh like the flame from a candle" (10). Life runs and flows and flames in the man: these metaphors are recurrent in this novel. Morel rises early, piles "a big fire," and sits down "to an hour of joy"; alone, he is "happy" (27). Being natural and healthy, he loves nature, and his vitality is not daunted even by the mine: "He loved the early morning, and the walk across the field. So he appeared at the pit-top, often with a stalk from the hedge between his teeth, which he chewed all day to keep his mouth moist, down the mine, feeling quite as happy as he was in the field" (28). Again, Lawrence stresses that Morel is quick with the quick of life: "As she heard him sousing heartily in cold water, heard the eager scratch of the steel comb on the side of the bowl, as he wetted his hair, she closed her eyes in disgust. As he bent over, lacing his boots, there was a certain vulgar gusto in his movements that divided him from the reserved, watchful rest of the family" (42). His spontaneous life energy is most sharply realized when he is working, fulfilling his deep male creative desires. Hammering the glowing iron on his "goose," Morel is "jolly." He sings, too, when he mends boots "because of the jolly sound of the hammering"; he is happy mending his pit trousers, happy when he makes fuses, and happy when, in his "warm way," he tells stories about the pit, about the horse Taffy and the mice that somehow thrive in the darkness.

But the spontaneous life of the man, however robust, cannot continue to flow under these circumstances. If the pits do not kill him, they cripple him; and his "wonderfully young body, muscular, without any fat," bears "too many blue scars, like tattoo-marks, where the coal-dust remained under the skin" (197). But the deepest crippling occurs, of course, in his marriage. Cast off by his wife and children, he becomes "more or less a husk" (46); "he could not live in that atmosphere" (47); and he falls into "a slow ruin" (113). Indeed, "his body . . . shrank," and the contraction of his life prepares obliquely for the life constriction to be repeated in his son's life. What Gertrude does to Morel, Miriam will do to Paul.

The pattern of thwarted life is continued in Lawrence's handling of Mrs. Morel. At the outset Lawrence tells us that her life is "baffled and gripped into incandescence by thought and spirit" (10), but the truth is that Mrs. Morel, like her husband, is very richly alive when she is not being suffocated by her husband's presence. Indeed, Lawrence takes pains to emphasize her quickness and vitality:

> She spat on the iron, and a little ball of spit bounded, raced off the dark, glossy surface. Then, kneeling, she rubbed the iron on the sack lining of the hearth-rug vigorously. She was warm in the ruddy firelight. Paul loved the way she crouched and put her head on one side. Her movements were light and quick. It was always a pleasure to watch her. [66]

Her vitality is manifested in a number of ways. She loves her marketing, and when she returns "triumphant," her "step in the entry" is a "quick light step" (74). She rejoices in the florists in Nottingham and exclaims at the abundance and beauty of the fuchsias (98). Paul sees her face as "bright with living warmth," and he draws from her "the life-warmth, the strength to produce" (158). To the end of her life, when she is dying of cancer, Mrs. Morel responds with enthusiasm to living things: " 'Anna,' she exclaimed, 'I saw a lizard out on that rock!' Her eyes were so quick; she was still so full of life" (378). Looking out of the window, she cries, " 'There are my sunflowers!' " In all these passages, she is anything but "baffled and gripped into incandescence by thought and spirit." She is as joyfully alive as her husband is, but only when she is apart from him.

Her contraction, her "clogging," occurs because of her middle-class ambition and their poverty. "Her still face, with the mouth closed tight from suffering and disillusion and self-denial, and her nose the smallest bit on one side, and her blue eyes so young, quick, and warm, made [Paul's] heart contract with love. When she was quiet, so, she looked brave and rich with life, but as if she had been done out of her rights'' (66). In her disillusionment, she turns the children against their father; all become ''reserved, watchful,'' and ''hushed'' as the miner enters the house (42). The years of battling create in her a ''hardness'' (97). Her mouth is ''always closed with disillusion,'' and as she grows frail, her face and eyes are ''fixed, reflecting the relentlessness of life'' (240). So her only hope in life is that her sons will do great things.

All of the children are deeply affected by the tension between the parents, and the imagery defining the effects of the parental strife is built upon the basic pattern of the contrast between life and life constriction. When they are very young, they lie abed ''with their hearts in the grip of an intense anguish'' (60). Their father is ''like the scotch in the smooth, happy machinery of the house,'' and when he enters, there is a ''fall of silence,'' ''the shutting off of life'' (62).

Very deliberately, Lawrence works with imagery of quickness and constraint. William as a boy ''could run like the wind'' (52); his face is ''extraordinarily mobile. Usually he looked as if he saw things, was full of life, and warm; then his smile, like his mother's, came suddenly and was very lovable, and then, when there was any clog in his soul's quick running, his face went stupid and ugly'' (88). The conflict within him when he becomes engaged to Gipsy makes him ''unnatural and intense'' (133); his health fails; he dies of erysipelas.

Arthur, too, is quick—''a quick, careless, impulsive boy, a good deal like his father''; he is ''full of life,'' but his ''fiery temper'' becomes ''uncertain'' as he grows older. He enlists in the army; then he marries; and he is ''caught'': ''It did not matter how he kicked and struggled, he was fast,'' ''he belonged to his wife and child'' (258). The imagery of bondage and imprisonment occurs everywhere in this novel, and Arthur is but one of many whose natural life and freedom are violated by society.

Lawrence's handling of Paul follows the pattern already established. Even though Lawrence suggests, shortly after Paul's birth, that this infant, who ''boiled'' in his mother's womb, has been ''stunned'' at ''some point in its soul,'' though Lawrence emphasizes that the damage to Paul's vitality has been done before birth and notes ''the peculiar knitting of the baby's brows, and the peculiar heaviness of its eyes, as if it were trying to understand something that was pain'' (36), though there is this very deliberate preparation for his later difficulties, Paul is, in truth, like the other children, quick and full of life. Annie, we learn, ''raced wildly at lerky with the other young wild-cats of the Bottoms. And always Paul flew beside her'' (57). Like his father, Paul "loved being out in the country," and he "scoured the coppices and woods and old quarries, as long as a blackberry was to be found" (68). As a lad, he is "quick, light, graceful" (143); "his eyes were quick and bright with life" (145). He responds eagerly to others: the Leivers "kindled him and made him glow to his work," and "he worked all through hay-harvest with them" (149). His tread is always "quick and firm" (155); he jumps up; he exclaims; when he mounts the swing, "every bit of him" goes "swinging, like a bird that swoops for joy of movement" (150); "it was almost as if he were a flame that had lit a warmth in [Miriam] whilst he swung in the middle air" (141). In his youthful gusto, he asserts that Mary Queen of Scots did not deserve imprisonment because "she was only lively" (168). And when he paints, it is life that he wants to capture: "the shimmering protoplasm in the leaves and everywhere, and not the stiffness of the shape. That seems dead to me. Only this shimmeriness is the real living" (152).

All the images of life blockage mark the dreadful threat to this soul, and most prominent are those of imprisonment, immobility, and stillness. When he goes to collect his father's wages, he is "jammed behind the legs of the men," "pushed against the chimney-piece." " 'They always stan' in front of me, so's I can't get out,' " he complains to his mother. When he applies for the job at Jordan's, he is again threatened by entrapment. On the way to Jordan's, he feels "something screwed up tight inside him" (92). Entering the factory, he passes "under the archway, as into the jaws of the dragon," and except for the yard, "the place was like a pit" (93). In the interview, words refuse to come; he stammers and is "stuck" (95). Yet, like his father, he brings his flaming vitality into this pit, and we learn that he "always enjoyed it when the work got faster" (112).

His natural environment seems to be the motion of life. But when he meets Miriam, a serious threat to his vitality appears. He seeks the girl out "as if for nourishment. Together they seemed to sift the vital fact from an experience" (148). But seeking nourishment, he is slowly starved. Miriam, the "maiden in bondage," is "gripped tight" or "in a trance" (145, 153); she is afraid to move, her body is "not flexible and living" (151, 153). "There was no looseness or abandon about her. Everything was gripped stiff with intensity" (154). She "held herself in a grip" (156); her face is "blind" or "closed" (157, 280). Ashamed of her desire for Paul, she is "tied" to "a stake of torture," her soul "coiled into knots of shame" (171). And so she makes Paul feel "anxious and imprisoned" (160). " 'She is one of those who will want to suck a man's soul out till he has none of his own left,' " Paul's mother warns (160). And gradually "his natural fire of love" is "transmitted into the fine stream of thought" (173); she "killed the joy and warmth in him" (280); she "spoilt his ease and naturalness" (179). Forcing Paul to be "spiritual," she threatens to destroy the young man as Gertrude has destroyed Morel. Paul is split in two, "unable to move." After he and Miriam make love, "life seemed a shadow, day a white shadow: night and death, and stillness, and inaction, this seemed like *being*. To be alive, to be urgent and insistent—that was *not-to-be*" (287). It is not until he leaves Miriam, securing "three days that were all his own," that the life energy returns: "It was sweet to rush through the morning lanes on his bicycle" (288). Like his father, he can live only when he is freed of the incubus of the spiritual woman.

Clara Dawes, when Paul meets her, is another person whose natural vitality has been impaired. She has left Baxter Dawes because "it's a question of living. With him, she was only half-alive; the rest was dormant, deadened" (317). Condemned to daily toil at her spinning jenny, Clara is a woman in bondage: "Her arm moved mechanically, that should never have been subdued to a mechanism, and her head was bowed to the lace." Her eyes look "dumb with humiliation, pleading with a kind of captive misery" (262). But Lawrence suggests that Clara, like Miriam and like Gertrude, also threatens to suck up Paul's soul—to awaken herself by drawing upon his vitality. She sees him as "a vigorous slender man, with exhaustless energy"; his eyes "seemed to dance" (306). Although for a time Paul's love for Clara gives him life and motion ("he raced her down the road to the green turf bridge. She could run well. The colour soon came, her throat was bare, her eyes shone. He loved her for being so luxuriously heavy, and yet so quick" [365]), and although their passion, too, brings life (they are swept up in a "tremendous living flood which carried them always" [354]), Clara presently seeks to get him (352), to "absorb" him (358). And Paul must shake her off: "He preferred to be alone. She made him feel imprisoned when she was there, as if he could not get a free deep breath, as if there were something on top of him. She felt his desire to be free of her" (359). So, like his father, he must escape the prison of suffocation. Should he fail to break free, he may become, like his father, "small and mean" (406).

There remains for Paul the problem of escaping from his mother. Although he has drawn the life warmth from her, he sees her as preventing his free development: "Sometimes he hated her, and pulled at her bondage. His life wanted to free itself of her. It was like a circle where life turned back on itself, and got no further. . . . He could not be free to go forward with his own life" (345). As *The Rainbow* develops the theme of escape from confining circles, so Lawrence here begins to introduce that theme of Emersonian expansion outward toward the infinite. Paul wants "maximum of being"; but as his mother dies, he is afflicted in much the same way as he was after making love to Miriam: "The realest thing was the thick darkness at night. That seemed to him whole and comprehensible and restful. . . . He wanted every thing to stand still, so that he could be with [his mother] again" (410). Motion and life fill him with "a flame of agony" (410). "He did not want to move." Again, when he meets Miriam, he sees that "a sort of stiffness, almost of woodenness, had come upon her," and he tells her that he "should die there [in Miriam's pocket] smothered" (416, 417). So, he is left, at the end, both craving and not craving death. But his final decision—to turn back to the "glowing town"—is the decision for life against death, and the imagery associated with the town suggests that it is the seat of life. Appropriately, in a novel that has everywhere dramatized the struggle of life against all that threatens to block and thwart human beings, the final word is "quickly."

The novel is not without its defects. Paul is so intensely alive, alert, observant, and quick, in a dozen different scenes, that one cannot help feeling uneasy about his neurotic behavior in the last chapters of the novel. Julian Moynahan's uneasiness about a conflict between a sort of Freudian determinism that is implicit in Paul's "drift toward death" and an "indeterminate" vitalism that permits Paul to turn back to the "glowing town" seems to me justified.[9] Stephen J. Miko's reply to Moynahan is that "the vital system is at bottom more fundamental than the pattern of fixation which Moynahan cogently spells out" (*Toward "Women in Love,"* 90); but this defense cannot stand up unless one can demonstrate that Paul's neurotic behavior arises through probability and necessity. But Paul's behavior does not seem inevitable. Lawrence does not convincingly establish that Paul's mother, who has disappeared from the novel during much of its second half, is the "one place in the world that stood solid and did not melt into unreality" (*SL*, 222). Trusting the tale and not the teller, one must conclude that Paul's psychic paralysis, even though thematically appropriate, is not adequately prepared for and is to a degree made implausible by the vivid representations of his vigorous life. Further, it is hard to accept that Gertrude's death would necessarily cause Paul's psychic injury because Lawrence does not build into the novel the sort of action that would lead conclusively to that result: the only adequate test of Paul's Oedipal problem would have been to confront him with a woman who, unlike Miriam and Clara, was well suited to him, thus showing that he could not love even the right woman.

Again, Lawrence's judgment of Morel—"He had denied the God in him"—understandably disturbs one critic.[10] This judgment is apparently contradicted by the observation that Mrs. Morel, "seeking to make him nobler than he could be, . . . destroyed him" (16). Here we confront one of the great problems that Lawrence had to solve in adjusting his psychology to his art. From the point of view of Lawrence the psychologist, Morel is innocent: he cannot be condemned for being what he is and what Gertrude and the mines have made him. From the point of view of the religious artist, Morel is guilty: like Siegmund in *The Trespasser,* Morel fails to strive beyond himself. But Lawrence cannot have it both ways. In a novel in which, as Stephen Miko notes, there is "curiously little moral judgment by the author" (*Toward "Women in Love,"* 62), the judgment of Morel arises from premises that lie outside the novel—the Nietzschean idea of the nobility of the higher man or the vitalist idea of aspiration and striving. The technical problem that Lawrence faces is that of grounding moral judgments in the innocence of life. Instead of imposing judgments, he has to make them arise from life itself, life as experienced by each individual. I shall examine his solution to this problem in *The Rainbow.*

Looking back over *Sons and Lovers,* one can see how richly it carries out the theme that Anais Nin calls central in Lawrence: the theme of "livingness." The achievement of "maximum of being" is possible only when the individual maintains his proud selfhood, asserting, "I am I." All connections with others lead to a cramping or contraction of the soul. Yet Lawrence knows that connection with other human beings, and with Being Itself, is essential to one's fullest development. The problem, the central problem in all of his work, is indeed to "connect" with other life (ultimately with the cosmos) and still to remain uncompromised in the depths of the soul. Paul Morel has a keen sense of the possibilities of life; he knows that he can do great things if he acts on his soul's wisdom. But Paul is Gertrude's son and, like Hamlet, is betrayed in his love for his mother. Like Hamlet, too, he sees that men everywhere are destroyed by their blind submission to society or to lovers who violate their souls. To fall in love—even to love one's neighbor—is to love one's enemy, who cripples and immobilizes the soul.

In *Sons and Lovers* Paul seeks "nourishment" in three women, and his spontaneous life is threatened by each.[11] The problem of loving and yet retaining one's individuality is not solved in this novel; Lawrence had to write six other novels to define to his own satisfaction the vital relationships between man and woman, man and man, and man and the cosmos that would ensure fullest connection while allowing fullest integrity. But in *Sons and Lovers*—this early definition of the central problem—Lawrence discovers the materials he needs in order to dramatize, with maximum apprehension and dread, the threat to the spontaneous life of the individual. In the context of ordinary life and of utter domesticity, in the mines that symbolize the industrial world and in middle-class respectability, he discovers the causes of the death of the soul.

In 1913 he was ready to write a novel in which his psychological realism would be joined to his religious vision of the way to a *Vita Nuova*. But to write his new novel, he needed a new style, a new form, and a completed vision of human fulfillment. In *Sons and Lovers* the rich sensuous surface of the prose tends to obscure the underlying processes of motivation and interaction. Lawrence wanted a new style that, while retaining the realistic details of daily intercourse, would lay bare the laws of unconscious psychic life acting beneath the surface. He had to "make the unconscious conscious." To do this, he needed not only external correlatives of psychic dualities, such as Hawthorne used, but also a new diction to present as directly as possible "the trembling and oscillating of the balance" of sympathetic and voluntary impulses. Scenic structure must be determined not by the conventions of realism but by the underlying laws of psychology. A character's behavior must not simply illustrate a psychological law; it must become the actualization of the law, at every moment a manifestation of the unconscious acting or reacting.

Sons and Lovers suggested a form for the new novel. With its depiction first of the father's failure, then of William's, and finally of Paul's struggle against failure, the novel suggested that in a family chronicle of several generations, one might trace the development of men in their relationships to women and to society, counterpointing the experience of each generation against that of the others. In each generation the soul would encounter the same problem and would embark on the same quest to come into being; but the experience of each generation would provide a commentary on the moral failures or achievements of the other generations. Moral evaluation would emerge clearly from the repeated comparisons and contrasts, and the counterpointing could define richly and subtly the moral and psychic deviations from the ideal of balance.

Perhaps Lawrence's greatest discovery at this time in his life was that he was a religious writer. Against the negativism and despair that he saw everywhere in modern writing, he felt he could write a great positive work—an affirmation not of his personal vision but of the great impersonal forces that swept through him. "One has to be so terribly religious, to be an artist,'' he declared (letter of 24 February 1913); and in ''Song of a Man Who Has Come Through,'' he recognized the difficulty of his new responsibility:

> If only I am sensitve, subtle, oh, delicate, a winged gift!
> If only, most lovely of all, I yield myself and am borrowed
> By the fine, fine wind that takes its course through the chaos of the world
> Like a fine, an exquisite chisel, a wedge-blade inserted;
> I only I am keen and hard like the sheer tip of a wedge
> Driven by invisible blows,
> The rock will split, we shall come at the wonder, we shall find the Hesperides. [*SP*, 74]

To create this new novel, he must take the path suggested by Nietzsche's Zarathustra: the new religion must affirm a new naturalism in life and in values. Thus a part of his religious purpose is the deepening and refining of his psychological realism, his making us aware, as he says, not of what we think we need but of what we really need.

But how is it possible to blend a naturalistic or scientific view of human behavior and a moral or religious view? Can ''innocent'' animals be condemned for their failures to achieve health and to build a new heaven and a new earth? And what is the *Vita Nuova*? Is it realizable in life? If so, how?

The difficulty of the questions suggests the difficulty of the artistic problems Lawrence confronted. Whatever we may think of the solutions of his ''philosophy,'' his solutions to the problems of his new art reveal the sensitivity and the chisel-hard power of intelligence that he knew he would need to ''come through.'' What is perhaps most remarkable in *The Rainbow* and in *Women in Love* is the daring and boldness of the form.

6

The Three Angels in *The Rainbow*

DHLDHLDHLDHLDHLDHLDHLDHLDHLDHLDHLDHLDHLDHLDHLDHLDHLDHLDHLDHLDHLDHLDHLDHLDHLDHLDHLDHLDHLDHLDHLDHLDHLDHLDHLDHLDHL

> *No, no, it is the three strange angels.*
> *Admit them, admit them.*
> —"Song of the Man Who Has Come Through"

Lawrence was never a timid artist, and when he began *The Wedding Ring*, which became *The Rainbow* and *Women in Love*, his daring was immense. His well known letter of 5 June 1914 to Edward Garnett about Marinetti and the futurists; his excited talk about the soul's "allotropic states" and the "*non-human* quality of life" (letter of 21 September 1914); his concomitant interest, as he wrote "Study of Thomas Hardy," in a theory of history and in "the vast, unexplored morality of life itself" (*Phoenix*, 419); his conviction, as he revised the novel, that "it's great—so new, so really a stratum deeper than I think anybody has ever gone, in a novel" (letter of 11 March 1913)—all this testifies to his conviction that he had "come through" in his efforts to construct an "answer to the *want* of today: to the real, deep want of the English people, not to just what they fancy they want" (letter of 1 February 1913). A new psychology and a new religion were to be blended in his vision of life; and he had found the technical means by which the blending might be effected. He had developed a vocabulary to define the nature of the unconscious motive forces within the psyche, as well as the laws governing their action. He had discovered, too, a form that would present the moral and religious journey of mankind in its quest for fulfillment, a form that would telescope, over three generations, the development of life from tribal unconsciousness to civilized consciousness and that would exhibit the difficulties at every stage of balancing the desire for independence and the desire for connection with others. The progress of the generations would be, moreover, a recapitulation of the progress of the individual: the ontogeny would recapitulate the phylogeny, and the record of mankind's growth—from childhood to adolescence to a dubious maturity—would be the record of each individual's moral and psychic experience. It is hardly surprising that Lawrence, seeing suddenly the beauty of his new project, was exhilarated. Scientific naturalism, religion, morality, history, sociology—all would be gathered up in this new novel; the method would be, as he said, "exhaustive" (letter of 29 January 1914). If he could only be "sensitive, subtle, oh, delicate," "a fine, an exquisite chisel," he might "find the Hesperides." I imagine him, in writing the novel, as opening the door, with passionate expectancy, to "the three strange angels"—let us call them the angels of religion, of science, and of mimetic art. But in admitting the three angels into his novel, he again posed difficult problems. For each angel had a different message to deliver, and the task Lawrence set for himself was to find a way to blend and harmonize the three voices. That blending, I think, is almost wholly successful. Critics are dissatisfied with the forcing of the ending, with the lapses of "psychological realism," or with Lawrence's preaching—his drawing upon resources "alien to the book," thus becoming a "propagandist" in the later part of the novel.[1] But much of the criticism issues from a failure to appreciate the uniqueness of the form Lawrence created. Before defining the nature of that form, I must examine the separate tasks of the three angels.

THE ANGEL OF RELIGION

The angel of religion seeks to convert the novel into a quest for the rainbow. This angel requires that all of experience, all of history, be viewed as a moral journey toward "maximum of being," from the dark to the light, from the Father to the Son, and then toward the reconciliation of the Holy Ghost—a journey toward the apocalyptic new heaven and new earth.[2] On this journey the pilgrims of the apocalypse encounter the demons and dragons that the devil of "halfness" puts in the way. The novel becomes a *Pilgrim's Progress*, enacting, as Frank Kermode and Mark Kinkead-Weekes point out,[3] the ages of Law and of Love, dramatizing the dangers and the temptations that threaten the sincere seeker, and holding out the promise of salvation in the rainbow.

Every stage of the journey is evaluated in relation to the moral evolution of mankind. The Old Testament world of the Father (i.e., of Tom Brangwen), of the undifferentiated tribal mass, which passively accepts the Law and the fixed form of sensual life, provides a fulfillment of sensual desire; but Tom remains inert, incapable of journeying into the beyond, into the light of the spirit.[4] The world of the Church also proves to be incomplete; fulfillment through blind faith in the creative mystery becomes impossible when skepticism and rationalism erode the Catholic solidarity. As for the modern world, in which mind and spirit (the Son) dominate, it too fails to achieve "maximum of being." Living only from the "upper centers," especially from the spiritual will, modern men and women create a world whose form is as fixed and static and limited as that of the ancient world. True balance and fulfillment is impossible in such a world; indeed, the denial of the blood drives men into perversity, sensationalism, and reduction—the madness of systematic bullying and ego competition. At the end of *The Rainbow* there remains only Ursula's vision of a new heaven and a new earth; but the world is the devil's, and mankind has, up to this point, failed in its quest.

As a religious allegorist, Lawrence, like Bunyan or Spenser, seeks to define both the evils confronted by mankind and the true path to salvation. Thus Lawrence is driven to create quasi-symbolic characters who would corrupt the true believer. These villains, whom Lawrence condemns sharply, are Miss Inger, Uncle Tom, and, to a lesser extent, Anton Skrebensky, all of whom represent the hideous domination of the spiritual will and the ugly failure to heed the promptings of the Holy Ghost. Miss Inger, perverse and willful, seeking only her own triumph, is a Duessa who would lead Ursula into the abyss of cold sensationalism and into the deeper abyss of machine- and Moloch-worship. For the sake of power, Uncle Tom, a nihilist and a cynic, accepts the machine and all the degradations that issue from the worship of the Lord of the Flies. Anton Skrebensky, the army engineer who serves the state and materialism, is a modern nullity, inert and undeveloped. Confronting these three representatives of the modern Age of Love, Ursula learns that the way of the spiritual will is a dead end. The angel of religion summons Ursula to search for one of the Sons of God, who worship the lord of the two ways, of darkness and of light. But Ursula will not meet one of the Sons of God until later, in Birkin of *Women in Love*.

The condemnation of the Age of Love is explicit and severe: Miss Inger, Uncle Tom, and Skrebensky anticipate the vile Loerke of *Women in Love*, who reduces life to pure mechanism, pure utility, pure willfulness; Lawrence approaches, in parts of *The Rainbow*, the bitterness and horror that inform the whole of that *Dies Irae* published in 1920. But Lawrence's moral judgments extend also to the Age of Law, in which men live in the drowse of the blood intimacy, in passive or "female" submission to the tribe, the undifferentiated mass. Tom Brangwen, challenged by a new world of subtle intellection, drinks himself into unconsciousness and burns out his soul. He fails to discover a meaningful life or meaningful work. All of his creative, purposive desires remain frustrated; so he dies in the dark waters of the unconscious, the waters from which he has never been able to emerge.

Lydia, too, remains unfulfilled in her soul: the man she yearns for would combine the sensuality of Tom and the intellectuality of her former husband, the Polish doctor and patriot.

In the second generation, Anna gives up her journey into the unknown and lapses into a continuous rapture of motherhood, like one of the fat cabbages that Lawrence condemns in "The Crown." Will Brangwen remains undeveloped and molelike until the extremes of perverse sensation seeking bring about "a passion of death." The plunge into sensation satisfies his craving for a sensual absolute, and he is partially liberated and enabled to turn to purposive work in the world of light. But Will, unlike Birkin, never challenges the form of modern life. Will's entrance into public life—teaching woodworking in Cossethay—is positive; but he never learns that the good man is a fighter, one who fights to break the old form of life.[5]

All of the characters therefore fail in their quest, and all are judged. Even Ursula is condemned at one point. Indeed, she condemns herself for her perverse desire to triumph over Skrebensky and for her destructive spiritual willfulness. The novel may be regarded as wholly formed by the angel of religion and as the inevitable product of Lawrence's conviction that "the essential function of art is moral" (*SCAL*, 180); the function of the novel is to lead "into new places the flow of our sympathetic consciousness" and to lead "our sympathy away in recoil from things gone dead" (*LCL*, 146).

THE ANGEL OF SCIENCE

Even readers like Leavis, however, who would stress the moral function of the art, recognize that much of the time Lawrence's characters are creatures driven by irresistible desires and compelled to act as they do: they are amoral, beyond good and evil. Most of the characters are seen, in the manner of Émile Zola or George Moore, in almost purely naturalistic terms. We are asked to view the characters' behavior from the perspective of the Angel of Science, Lawrence's "subjective science," which was deduced, as he tells us in *Fantasia*, from the novels and poems, from "pure passionate experience."

His scientific induction is strongly at work in *The Rainbow:* Lawrence is making a concerted effort to formulate the laws of psychic conflict, to determine the ways in which conflicting motive forces are manifested in normal human interaction. In scene after scene, we find more or less invariant patterns of psychic interaction in the allotropic behavior of particular people. Tom Brangwen, Will, and Skrebensky are all different; yet in their relationships with women they repeat the same patterns of psychic interaction. The same motivations and the same causes of failure are traced. So carefully are these patterns exhibited that *The Rainbow* might be taken as a primer of psychology, a psychology that postulates the desire to "come into being" as the deepest motive and that traces the action of this motive in the opposed love and power urges, both sensual and spiritual. The forms of psychic interaction are laid bare in three great phases of the individual's life: in courtship, in marriage or sexual love, and in subsequent efforts to transcend the limitations of love.

Courtship: The Impulse toward Unison versus the Impulse toward Individuation. In chapters 1 through 3 we saw that two great primal desires originate in man's nature. The first of these is the desire for unison or oneness with the infinite from which man derives, a desire manifested in man's relationship to woman, to humanity, and to the cosmos, or to "God." The self, split off from the whole, wants the joyous enlargement of self that occurs in the love relationship. The deep craving for union with the All is present not only in personal relationships but also in man's desire to "be unanimous with the whole of purposive mankind" (*R*, 235). This desire becomes man's "societal instinct," his "ultimate need and desire" to work with other men to "build a world . . . something wonderful" (*FU*, 18). As Lawrence said in a letter to Bertrand Russell on 15 July 1915, "The *most fundamental* passion in man [is] for Wholeness of Movement, Unanimity of Purpose, Oneness in Construction." Finally, that desire for "assimilatory unison" becomes a "God-passion," a desire for a "pure relationship" with the entire living cosmos, a desire to connect "religiously" with the inhuman world whose vibrations flow into man and are inseparable from his being.

Yet in seeking maximum of being in the All, the psyche fears that it will lose its own identity. Recoiling from sympathetic union, the psyche asserts, "I am I, I am not these others." A voluntary center is born, the center of assertive individualism. Herein lies the dilemma for the soul. The desire to remain separate and free conflicts with the desire to merge with the Other, to the point of self-obliteration.

Now it is impossible for the individual to remain isolated from the Whole. The isolated self is afflicted by a sense of insufficiency, meaninglessness, or emptiness. The psyche recognizes that it is "derivative," incomplete, or part of a greater reality. Hence the desire to connect with other beings or with Being itself cannot be denied. "Without God we are nothing." In the earliest stages of a relationship, the male seeks completion in woman, and she is identified as his gateway to the Absolute.

So Tom Brangwen, in the first generation, knowing that he is "only fragmentary, something incomplete and subject," and fearing that he must "remain as a nothingness" unless he connects with the "greater ordering," turns to Lydia Lensky, feeling that "with her, he would be real. . . . she would bring him completeness and perfection" (35). So much does she mean to him that he feels "reverence and fear of the unknown," which change "the nature of his desire into a sort of worship" (52); he wants to "give her all his love, all his passion, all his essential energy" (78). For she is "the symbol of that further life which comprised religion and love and morality" (13), the "embodiment of all the inarticulate, powerful religious impulse" (14).

At first "a daze had come over his mind, he had another centre of consciousness," and he submits to "that which was happening to him, letting go his will, suffering the loss of himself" (33–34). But this sympathetic impulse toward unison conflicts with his fear of losing himself. Afraid, he wishes "to escape her," and he feels a "fury . . . destructive," an impulse of "revolt" from her attraction. She, too, though stirred by "a quick, out-running impulse" and wanting "this new life from him," feels that "she must defend herself against it, for it was a destruction" (34–35): her independence is threatened. When Tom proposes, the scene becomes a series of attractions and withdrawals, a to-and-fro of sympathetic and voluntary impulses. He asks her to marry him, and she quivers, "feeling herself created, will-less, lapsing into him, into a common will with him" (40). She "flows" toward him, her eyes "newly-opened"; but it is "sheer bleached agony to him, to break away from himself." Presently he succumbs to "the fecund darkness," a "womb of darkness" in which he is "newly created." A few moments later, however, he feels "a certain negation of him" in her "tiredness," and she seems "to ignore him." He tries to make her his, but he is "afraid," and Lawrence observes, "again he had not got her." She turns away; then she returns to him and responds with passion. Then, because her passion comes "thundering at him till he could bear no more," "he drew away, white, unbreathing" (43). Shortly thereafter, "she was drifting away from him again," but she agrees to marry him, and the scene ends with his contemplating the moon—the female—running into the open, then plunging under cover of a cloud.

The structure of the flashback in chapter 2 is similar. Lydia, who lives in darkness and abstraction after the death of her first husband, is awakened by the light, the positive male creative force. The light rouses her to attention, but then she shrinks away again, "back into her darkness" (48). The morning, the light, beats in on her again until she, "resistant, . . . knew she was beaten, and from fear of darkness turned to fear of light" (49). She wants to be safe in "the old obliviousness, the cold darkness," and she "lapses into" her old isolation with "a will in her to save herself from living any more." But the sun beats in, and she begins to open up (50). Again, she lapses into "stupor and indifference"; again she opens and becomes "receptive to him" (51); then she closes "again, away from him, was sheathed over, impervious to him, oblivious"; but again she begins "to open towards him" (51). The oscillations proceed until she agrees at last to marry him.

In the second and third generation these oscillations are repeated, though with a significant difference. Sympathetic union is more difficult in the second generation. Yet Will, like Tom, is filled with a joyful sense of completion when he turns to the female. When Anna tells him " 'I love you, Will, I love you,' " he feels suddenly that "the veils had ripped and issued him naked into the endless space. . . . Whither, through this darkness of infinite space, was he walking blindly?" (115). Anna's "bright, transfigured face" is associated for him with "the Hidden Almighty" (125); she becomes "the essence of life" (125). And he, "ridden by the awful sense of his own limitation," feeling "uncompleted, as yet uncreated," "wanted her to come and liberate him into the whole" (176). Note that the cathedral in which he worships the absolute, the infinite, is female.

But in the remarkable sheaves-gathering scene, the sympathetic impulse conflicts with the voluntary urge to be separate, free, "unmixed" with another person. At the beginning of the scene, Lawrence tells us that Will and Anna were "separate, single" (117); but as they gather the sheaves, each working a separate row, they draw together: Will approaches Anna; then "she turned away toward the [female] moon"; then she returns again ("She was always first," Lawrence notes); but when Will again approaches, "she turned away." Again, she "walked toward him"; then "she broke away, and turned to the moon" (117–18); then, "he was drawing near, and she must turn again" (118). The oscillations proceed—a "moving to and fro in the moonlight"—until at length Will overtakes her and kisses her, whereupon he feels "possessed" of the "night" and trembles "with keen triumph" (119).

The sheaves-gathering scene presents a seesaw, a contest of wills: "His will drummed persistently, darkly, it drowned everything else" (119); and the moonlight to which Anna turns is symbolic of the virginal female, intact, complete, and separate. The contest of wills is a struggle for "triumph," and it ends with Anna's victory over Will: "He was hers. And he was very glad and afraid" (120). Once he commits himself utterly to her, however, she draws "away from his breast" (120), rather like the heroine of "The Horse Dealer's Daughter," who, having succeeded in getting the doctor to surrender entirely to her, withdraws in fear from her victory. Will Brangwen determines to marry Anna and, afraid that she will leave him, becomes "abstract, purely a fixed will," feeling that if he relaxes his will, "he must be destroyed" (123, 124). And during this courtship, Will's defeat is foreshadowed. Like Siegmund of *The Trespasser,* he is "consumed, till he existed only as an unconscious, dark transit of flame, deriving from her" (126).

In the third generation, the relationship of Ursula and Anton Skrebensky follows a similar to-and-fro but is even less sympathetic. Anton, who is less Victorian than Tom or Will, is not given to worship of the female; yet, like Tom and Will, he wants the woman to complete him. Early in his contact with Ursula we learn that Anton wished to "throw his detested carcase at her feet" (303), and later Lawrence tells us of Anton's "mad dependence on her": "He felt himself a mere attribute of her" (462). Only through Ursula can he come into being, escaping the nothingness and emptiness of himself, and so he confesses that "nothing else" but marriage means anything to him. Ursula is attracted to Anton as "one of the sons of God" (290); but as an independent modern woman, she is strongly inclined to assert her will over him. Their love-making becomes a game of provocation and challenge, "each playing with fire, not with love" (300). Ursula "must ever prove her power," and Anton, kissing her, "asserts his will over her" (300). So, Lawrence concludes: "It was a magnificent self-assertion on the part of both of them, he asserted himself before her, he felt himself infinitely male and infinitely irresistible, she asserted herself before him, she knew herself infinitely desirable, and hence infinitely strong. And after all, what could either of them get from such a passion but a sense of his or her own maximum self, in contradistinction to all the rest of life" (301). So their plunge into African sensationalism is foreshadowed. The sympathetic impulses in both of them are weak, as if the change of civilization from the torpor of the Marsh to modern industrial society has caused an overdevelopment of the will at the expense of the sympathetic centers.

Marriage or Sexual Union versus Failure (the Battle of the Wills). After a period of conflict between voluntary and sympathetic desires, the male and the female, drawn irresistibly into connection, join in sexual union. When sexual union is perfect, the old self is given up; it dies in the tomb and womb of the unconscious, and one experiences a miraculous rebirth. A profound wonder and joy and a deep creative, purposive desire are awakened in the male. This point in the relationship between man and woman is crucial. If the man acts upon his desire to make a new world, he may move forward into the unknown, seeking to fight for a new society that promotes life and also reflects the wonder of his love. If, however, he fails to strive for a new heaven and a new earth, or if in sexual union he has not given up the self but remains intact, unchanged, a separate ego perversely using sex for ego consolation or ego aggrandizement, then the union or marriage breaks down, and a conflict of wills between man and woman is inevitable.

The first and perhaps the most important cause of the conflict is that the male, in seeking union with a woman, is really seeking a mother to give him unstinted love and to console him in his weakness. In short, the male is still a child, incapable of acting independently and not even aware of the Holy Ghost. In mating, such a male is motivated chiefly by his fear of being alone, unimportant, "nothing" in himself. Incapable of achieving "being," he tries to make the woman his raison d'être. But meaning and purpose can never be found in another creature, only in the infinite, in God, or in the ultimate connectedness of all things.[6] The male's effort to make woman the be-all and end-all of existence satisfies neither him nor his woman. His deepest creative desires are frustrated, and because he puts the burden of life responsibility entirely upon the woman, she sees him as weak and childish, clinging to her as to a mother. Hence she rejects the man, and he, his ego insulted and betrayed ("I gave her my whole life, and she despises me"), retaliates in rage. The battle of wills commences. Carried to extremes it becomes reduction, or the desire to reduce the other person to inert matter. After the sympathetic connection between man and woman is broken, they become destructive. Hating the ego that defies them, they seek to destroy that antagonist. Love-making becomes ego assertion, or "conquest." The relationship of the lovers becomes that of the vampire to its victim or of the master to his slave. In its extreme forms, the lover becomes a sadist, a mad creature who, feeling himself to be helpless or impotent, seeks omnipotence—total control over another creature or over the whole of creation. Men would rather destroy the world than continue to live a meaningless life in which they feel "nullified."

Sometimes, if carried far enough, extremes of reduction may have a positive effect. Cruelty, perversity, sensationalism, or destruction may "unloose" or shatter the old self: corruption and death may breed new life; perversity may purge the soul. Having experienced the maximum of sensation, the soul may be ready for creative, not destructive, activity. On the other hand, extremes of reduction may issue, not in rebirth, but in death; the will to omnipotence may be carried to the point of absolute destruction of another person or of oneself. In each succeeding generation in *The Rainbow,* the couples move ever closer to the "passion of death," whose progress Lawrence traces so carefully in *Women in Love.*

In the first generation, as we have seen, Tom Brangwen, unable to develop as a purposive male, makes Lydia the be-all and end-all of his life. In his dependence on her, he feels he is not strong enough to conquer and become the master; he fears that she is "not really his, it was not a real marriage, this marriage between them. She might go away" (53, 55). He cannot share her "foreign life," and he feels that for her he is only "a peasant, a serf, . . . a shadow, a nothing" (57). His self-esteem wounded and his desire for fulfillment frustrated, he "stiffened with resistance" (57). The battle of wills commences. From the extreme of self-obliteration, he recoils to the extreme of voluntary resistance. When, once again, Lydia turns to him, he "burst into flame for her, and lost himself" (58). But so intense is his desire to possess her, to hold her sure and safe, so completely is his very being identified with her, that any sign of her indifference or self-sufficiency fills him with fear and rage. When she becomes pregnant, she is "not there for him"; he feels "deposed, cast out"; and his rage rises inevitably. Again and again the word *nothing* recurs as both male and female, seeking fulfillment from each other but unable to discover a meaning and purpose beyond themselves, feel the insignificance of their lives in the torpid Marsh. " 'To you I am nothing,' " Lydia says to Tom; " 'It is like cattle—or nothing.' " And he replies: " 'You make me feel as if *I* was nothing' " (89). It is not until Tom overcomes his "submission" to her and actively participates in sensual fulfillment that they experience a "transfiguration," and Tom travels "in her through the beyond" (91, 92).

The failure of a marriage unconnected with a higher purpose and goal is repeated in the second generation, but with a difference. For Will, Anna is the center of the great wheel of the universe. Ironically, she takes the place of the sun—the symbol of male creativity. She becomes "a more real day than the day could give" (144). But his sexual fulfillment awakens all his purposive impulses. When Anna decides to give a tea party, this return to the old world that has become unreal to him frustrates his religious desire. Like Tom, he plunges into anger because he does not possess her and into "shame at his own dependence on her" (147). She, on the other hand, resents his "futility" and his constant hovering about her in search of fulfillment.

For a time Will is compelled to "give everything to her, all his blood, his life, to the last dregs" (151); "there could be only acquiescence and submission" (153). But his dependency and submission breed anger.

Feeling her lack of respect for him, how she "jeered at his soul," he seeks to become "master-of-the-house," his will controlling hers (167, 170). Each feels "nothing" to the other; each resents the other's self-sufficiency and separateness. Yet each fears being alone (175), and Will's dependency breeds shame, rage, and frustration (179, 183, 184). From his positive sympathy with Anna, he reacts into a "negative" voluntary resistance, provoking in turn her hatred of him. The lovers become separate wills fighting for triumph. Will, hating Anna's self-sufficiency, wishes to destroy her (182). He seeks to sever himself altogether from her, and he is "born for a second time" as a "separate identity, he existed alone" (187). As a separate ego, he is driven into extremes of sensationalism and perversity, first seeking omnipotence in the triumph of his will (a "reducing force") over the girl from Nottingham, and then seeking with Anna a "passion of death," the perverse Absolute (234). "This supreme, immoral, Absolute Beauty, in the body of woman," in "pure darkness," this plunge into shame, carried to its final limits, liberates him. As noted in chapter 2, excess of activity in the mode of willful (or voluntary) sensuality awakens the desire for sympathetic activity in the spiritual mode. Will turns with interest to "public life," wants to "be unanimous with the whole of purposive mankind." As Lawrence summarizes, Will "had at length, from his profound sensual activity, developed a real purposive self" (235). But Will does not have a vision of a greater society, and he ends up in "redbrick suburbia," serving the old dead world which he had wanted, after his marital bliss, to make new.

In the third generation the failure of love is repeated in the relationship of Ursula and Anton Skrebensky, but the failure is different from those in the first two generations. The relationship between Ursula and Anton is, almost from the beginning, a battle of wills. We have seen in the sheaves-gathering scene that Will and Anna vie for triumph. In an almost identical scene under the moon, Ursula becomes the "quarry and hound" together (316). Anton takes her into his arms "as if into the sure, subtle power of his will"; then, as they dance, "his will and her will" are "locked in a trance of motion" (316). Like Helena in *The Trespasser*, Ursula, when the moon rises, offers herself to it for her "consummation," longing for "the coolness and entire liberty and brightness of the moon" (317), while Anton's will strains "with all its tension to encompass [her] and compel her" (318). But she is seized by a "sudden lust" to "tear him and make him into nothing" (319). And she succeeds, destroying "the core" of him (320). Months later, when their love-making resumes, they plunge into African sensationalism, the jungle of willful sensuality. That denial of the spiritual and of the sympathetic centers leads toward death. Anton, knowing that "she did not esteem him" and feeling shame at his dependence on her (462), weeps like a child when Ursula tells him she does not want to marry him. Like the other half-developed males of this novel, he blurts that he cares for "nothing else" but marriage; but if Ursula's "fear of herself" tempts her to marry him, she is driven, once again, to destroy him when they again make love under the moon. This third generation, acting entirely from the voluntary will, achieves no sympathetic union and no rebirth.

The Search for Other Centers of Living: Work, Children, the Spiritual. All of the males in *The Rainbow* realize dimly that it is impossible to make woman into the Absolute and that there is something shameful in their dependency on woman; they need something greater, the veritable Absolute, not solely the darkness of unconsciousness in which the Spirit is denied. Thus Tom Brangwen, feeling that Lydia is "cold" and "selfish, only caring about herself," reflects: "He had to go out, to find company, to give himself away there. For he had no other outlet, he could not work to give himself out, he had not the knowledge" (59). After the immersion in darkness, he is "elated" by the morning in which the male sun shines and the moon is "effaced on a blue sky" (68). "Then he worked and was happy," Lawrence notes, "and the zest of life was strong in him" (68). But Tom's physical work is meaningless to him; he feels himself "a prisoner . . . unadventurous" and wishes to "get out of this oppressive, shut-down, womanhaunt" (86, 87). The Marsh, that slough of the flesh, is "not enough" (88). So casting about for the fulfillment he seeks, he turns to his daughter. He "formed another centre of love in her child, Anna" (78); and for a time the child, seeking her own Absolute, rejoices in his "big, unlimited being" (64). But when Anna stiffens against him, he is filled with rage (73), and the relationship between father and child duplicates that between husband and wife. Tom's "joint activity" with Anna cannot possibly give him the support and solace he needs, and it is potentially dangerous to the child, who is not "set free" by her parents but for a time, like Hawthorne's Pearl, runs "hither and thither without relief" (68).

Presently Tom's old desire to experience, if only vicariously, the life of the spirit prompts him to make Anna into "a lady," and when he visits his brother's mistress, he feels an "almost reverential admiration" for this woman who reads. Despising his own "poor way of life," he wants to "clamber out" of the "mud" (86). But he cannot. His only fulfillment is to be found in his wife, mingling with her, "losing himself to find her, to find himself in her" (90). He is able to overcome his Victorian inhibitions; and in joyous sensual fulfillment, man and wife enter "another circle of existence," discover "a new world" (91). But the sensual fulfillment is not enough, and although Tom is proud of his marriage, he continues to yearn for "the further, the creative life" with Anna, "as if his hope had been in the girl" (125). He has "nothing to show, no work" in his life—no creative work; and like most men, he can only hope that his children will do what he has failed to do in his own life.

In the next generation, Will Brangwen has a more highly developed sense of purpose than Tom. Will's carving of the phoenix suggests his strong urge towards rebirth and a new life; after his marriage with Anna, he is transformed: "So suddenly, everything that has been before was shed away and gone" (141). So profoundly does love awaken his craving for the Absolute that now the world seems unreal: "pealed away into unreality, leaving here exposed the inside, the reality: One's own being, strange feelings and passions and yearnings and beliefs and aspirations, suddenly become present, revealed, the permanent bedrock, knitted one rock with the woman one loved." He feels that "the whole world could be divested of its garment, . . . and one could stand in a new world, a new earth, naked in a new, naked universe. It was too astounding and miraculous" (146). For him at this point "the old outward order was finished. The new order was begun to last for ever, the living life, palpitating from the gleaming core, to action" (147). But when he does not act upon this prompting to build a new heaven and a new earth, the marriage begins to break down. Then he turns, as Tom turned, to other centers of living.

The Church—which for him contains the All, in which are joined life and death, womb and tomb, light and darkness, spirit and flesh—gives Will his consummation. Yet Anna despises his mindless worship and destroys his passion for this dead symbol of the Absolute. The Cathedral becomes "dead matter" to him, though he still cherishes "the old, dear form of worship" and sometimes "lapses back [to the church] for his fulfillment." For a time, then, he remains passive, serving "the little matriarchy, nursing the child and helping with the housework, indifferent any more of his own dignity and importance" (205). But he cannot long endure this "cabbage" existence, and still "passionate for something," he turns for fulfillment to his daughter, Ursula, as Tom had turned to Anna. Compulsively, Will seeks Ursula out "in a darkness" until they become "in the thick darkness, married" (213–14). Ursula becomes the "light" to him, as Anna earlier had become the sun. His life is "based on her" (217). When, inevitably, Ursula relapses "on her own violent will into her own separate world of herself'' (221–22), the connection between father and child is broken, and the battle of wills begins again, as it had in his marriage with Anna: ''There was a curious fight between their two wills'' (222). Seeking the extreme of sensationalism, risking incest, Will begins to ''dare'' her to take violent risks with him. A ''curious taunting intimacy'' arises between them. When Ursula turns against him again, he searches for omnipotence through perversity. Then he is partially freed for purposive work.

In the third generation the search for other centers of living becomes most intense and adventurous. Ursula, after rejecting Christianity because she feels that the doctrine of love means the nullification of her pride and dignity, searches for one of ''the sons of God.'' Skrebensky proves hollow. His only center of living, beyond her, is the nation state, which he serves blindly; he finds his Absolute in the blind collective will. In himself, he is ''nothing,'' a man without a core. Ursula must seek elsewhere for religious purposiveness. She turns to Miss Inger, who argues plausibly that men ''have lost the capacity for doing. . . . They make everything fit into an old, inert idea'' and treat women as ''an instrument'' for this idea (342). But Miss Inger is a hideous creature of the will, one who worships ''the impure abstraction, the mechanisms of matter'' (349). Then Ursula turns to ''the man's world'' of work and tries teaching, only to discover that here, too, ''it was power, and power alone that mattered'' (377). Forced to bully others, she finds herself ''subjugate to a bad, destructive will'' (384). And she recoils from the system, as she has earlier recoiled from herself with a ''slow horror'' when she has been seized by the desire to triumph over Skrebensky. Then she turns back, half in desperation, to Skrebensky and to a sensual darkness in which she is ''shattered,'' ''all dark, will-less, having only the receptive will'' (446–47). But this desperate plunge into mindless sensation, which represents a rejection of society and the light, is also a plunge towards death: once again, she is prompted to destroy Skrebensky with her ''beaked harpy's kiss.'' Then, for a time, she is tempted to accept Skrebensky and her unborn child as ''enough.'' Finally, after climbing free of the horses' threat—a symbolic climbing—and after seeing that she has been ''trammelled and entangled'' in a dead world, she imagines a rebirth, a breaking free from the shell like a kernel ''thrusting forth the clear, powerful shoot'' (492). After a deep sleep, she begins to open like a flower to the new day; and the novel ends with her vision of a new world in which God is created in a social, political, and personal renaissance.

This brief summary of the laws of psychic interaction shows that Lawrence's ''subjective science'' was already highly developed in

1913 or 1914 when composition of *The Rainbow* began. If the novel is an allegory in the tradition of Bunyan or Spenser, it is even more impressively the culmination of nineteenth-century naturalism—of that effort to make literature scientific by explaining experience as exemplifying impersonal laws and by reducing human conduct to elemental motive forces or to material determinants.

How does Lawrence reconcile this scientific view of life with his religious view? How does he blend the voices of the angels of science and of religion? And how does he create, at the same time, a persuasive image of normal life? The angel of mimetic art has the difficult task of reconciling the claims of religion and of science while creating the illusion of reality and maximizing the emotional effects of the image of life.

THE ANGEL OF MIMETIC ART

Every character and every act must be seen from both the moral-allegorical and from the scientific point of view; yet the angel of mimetic art must avoid reducing characters either to mere allegorical counters or to simple electromagnetic forces. The characters must be real, their behavior convincingly normal. The mimetic artist must create an image of men and women like ourselves, whom we can care about. Three great problems must be solved: the problems of moral evaluation, of believability, and of sympathetic identification.

Consider first the problem of moral evaluation. The religious angel wishes to present characters in a moral framework, almost as allegorical counters, and to judge their conduct on the assumption that men, having free will, can choose the right path to the rainbow. The scientific angel wishes to present characters as impelled willy-nilly by dominant motive forces and by their temperamental make-up to act according to the strictest of laws. Can the artist have it both ways?—combine religion and scientific determinism? If Tom Brangwen is incapacitated from birth for the adventure into the unknown, how can he be condemned for failing to develop and grow? After all, Tom is very like an animal, destined from birth to illiteracy and life in the unconscious. We view him with the sort of sympathy, as well as detachment, that we might direct toward any suffering, bewildered, creature: because he is simply incapable of journeying toward the light, we pity his limitations and feel joy in his sensual fulfillment even as we might pity or take pleasure in the failures or triumphs of any honest animal. How then can he be condemned for his failures?

Lawrence's solution to this first problem is bold and simple. Tom Brangwen is not condemned; he condemns himself. "Oh, and he was shamed. He trampled himself to extinguish himself. . . . One was . . . never master of oneself" (124–25). In *The Rainbow* the deep shame that all the males feel because of their utter dependency on women, because of their failure to develop, and because of their recurrent regressions into childish irresponsibility (as in the extraordinary scene in which Lydia is in labor and Tom longs for the "irresponsibility and security" of his boyhood [75]) is a severe judgment on their lives.

In this way is Will Brangwen judged. Insofar as Will is blindly compelled to make first Anna and then Ursula the foundation of his being, he is not condemned: like Tom, he cannot help himself. Yet even though Will is driven by compulsion and is essentially "mole-like," Lawrence suggests that Will, more highly developed than Tom, might have tried to face Anna's destructive criticism forthrightly. Will knows in his soul "what a fool he was, and was flayed by the knowledge"; he also knows that in seeking to arrogate his authority over Anna, "he had gone on the wrong tack." It is wrong, he knows dimly, to make woman the center of his existence; in some way, he knows, he exists in eternity, not just in time. He is conscious of his sin against the Holy Ghost but is unable to overcome his compulsions until, through "reduction," he is partially liberated.

In the third generation, however, a significant change occurs. Protestant individualism leads to the triumph of reason: every man is free to be a priest or a sinner. Free will enters the novel, as skepticism, already gaining force during the second generation in Anna, awakens all men to the knowledge that God is dead and all is permitted, though nothing, as Nietzsche would have added, is authorized. Ursula throws off blind religious faith and, condemned to existential freedom, confronts a world of like-minded individuals, men and women free to do anything they want to do. The question now becomes: how is this freedom to be used? For religious ends or for self-aggrandizement? For life or for death?

Skrebensky is condemned because, with knowledge and choice open to him, he remains a part of the undifferentiated mass, serving the state. Ursula condemns herself, recoiling in horror when she imposes her egoistic will on Skrebensky and destroys him. Miss Inger and Uncle Tom are condemned because they are conscious of good and evil: they see the alternatives but choose to follow the way of Moloch. And the educational system is condemned because educators allow bullying and materialism to supplant genuine life development. The point is not simply that awareness entails responsibility for one's acts. More than this, the condemned characters always condemn themselves, recognize that their choices violate their deepest, most holy promptings. Ursula's self-condemnation is the most obvious illustration; but even Uncle Tom, Miss Inger, and Skrebensky are aware of how deeply they violate life:

> Her Uncle Tom and her mistress remained there among the horde, cynically reviling the monstrous state and adhering to it, like a man who reviles his mistress, yet who is in love with her. She [Ursula] knew her Uncle Tom perceived what was going on. But she knew moreover that in spite of his criticism and condemnation, he still wanted the great machine. His only happy moments, his only moments of pure freedom were when he was serving the machines. Then, and then only, when the machine caught him up, was he free from the hatred of himself, could he act wholly, without cynicism and unreality. [349]
>
> . . . .
>
> He too [Skrebensky] realised what England would be in a few hours' time—a blind, sordid, strenuous activity, all for nothing, fuming with dirty smoke and running trains and groping in the bowels of the earth, all for nothing. A ghastliness came over him. [465]
>
> . . . .
>
> He was always active, cheerful, gay, charming, trivial. Only he dreaded the darkness and silence of his own bedroom, when the darkness should challenge him upon his own soul. That he could not bear, as he could not bear to think of Ursula. He had no soul, no background. He never thought of Ursula, not once, he gave her no sign. She was the darkness, the challenge, the horror. He turned to immediate things. [481–82]

Self-condemned in the dark night of their souls, these characters obey the laws of psychic process even as they are subjected to a withering moral evaluation. Thus the scientific and the religious angels are admitted into the novel, and their antithetical demands are reconciled.

The problem of believability is more difficult to solve. The mimetic artist struggles to make human actions arise through probability and necessity, to make the image of life persuasively real and authentic; but the angels of science and religion are bent on forcing the novel into surrealistic shapes. The angel of religion wants people who are two-dimensional moral abstractions, like the characters in Hawthorne's *The Marble Faun;* the angel of science wants to reduce people to voluntaristic and sympathetic oscillations, to compulsion neuroses, to automatism. The problem for the angel of mimetic art is to rescue life from doctrine, to preserve the complex whole of personality, and to present the subtle reality of organic life, against the reductions of science and the moral simplifications of religion. The people must be individuals, not just symbols or universal forces. A very special effort must be made to establish the characters as normal human beings immersed in daily living.

Here Lawrence's ability to capture the richness of normal domestic life, to see his people always in the context of unvaryingly ordinary domesticity, is indispensable. Tom Brangwen may be the Unconscious, the Flesh, the Blood; the to-and-fro of his actions may be an oscillation of voluntary and sympathetic forces; but unlike Hawthorne's Hilda or Donatello, Tom has a rich life beyond allegory, beyond intellectual abstraction. He is a farmer who likes to drink with his friends at the (symbolic) Red Lion; his speech is unvaryingly commonplace, tinged with "country" ironies; his habits are as predictable as those of the sun to which he turns his face. He is solidly there as a farmer, as a part of the Marsh, as husband, and as father.

Again, Will Brangwen may have been conceived of as a creature of the molelike darkness, blindly seeking fulfillment in the cathedral; but Will has a garden, and he gets angry when Ursula tramples it; he has his wife's tea party to contend with; he has his little fling in Nottingham. Embedded firmly in the particulars of daily life—a life so ordinary that "Pass the butter" and "It's a lovely day" are characteristic speeches—Will is never dissolved in allegorical or psychological abstractions. Should any of his behavior seem abnormal, Lawrence is always quick to shift from the frenzies of Will's unconscious mind to an objective perspective that restores our sense of his normality. Thus, after the terrible "Anna Victrix" chapter, in which Will suffers unspeakable pain and humiliation, we see him as part of the gathering at Baron Skrebensky's and learn that "Will Brangwen, ruddy, bright, with long limbs and a small head, like some uncouth bird, was not changed in the least" (195). The passage underscores what is, I believe, a recurring experience in reading Lawrence: to realize with a shock that what Lawrence is always presenting, in language that captures the depth of unconscious experience, is life so commonplace that it would be dismissed by most writers as banal and undramatic: a young girl's first kiss or her infatuation with her boyfriend; a young couple's first discovery of the wonder of sex; a married couple's early misgivings—all so ordinary, yet so extraordinary, that Lawrence's fiction is truly, as Dr. Johnson might have said, a representation of "those passions and principles by which all minds are agitated." In *The Rainbow* there is nothing but normal sexual experience, normal living. This selection of materials from the most commonplace experiences of human beings is in large part what prevents the novel from becoming pure science or pure allegory.

Yet the handling of probabilities is never easy in this novel. The angel of science wants the characters to behave always according to the laws of psychic interaction. The battle of wills must always move toward reduction. Anna and Will *must* die of their perverse passion of death; and Will *must* be reborn, freed for work in the external world. Ursula *must* destroy Skrebensky, and later their following of the African way of pure mindless sensualism *must* issue in death of the soul. The mimetic artist must obviously take the greatest pains to make these extreme conclusions plausible. Does Lawrence succeed?

Most readers of *The Rainbow* do feel, from time to time, a certain forcing of the plot. Would Ursula really destroy Skrebensky with her "hard and fierce" kiss in the chapter entitled "First Love"? Is his annihilation inevitable? If we look carefully at the scene in which Anton is destroyed, we can see that Lawrence has provided entirely adequate causes for Anton's psychic death. In an earlier scene, in which Anton states that he will do whatever the state tells him to do, Ursula has told him bluntly that he isn't really "there," he is "nothing," a man without a core of belief, only a sodden acquiescence to the collective will. Thus, like Anna, she has undermined the only faith that her man has: she has already partially destroyed him. In addition, her virginal sense of her own power and of "the richness of her own life" prompts her to show him what a pitiful thing he is, to turn the tables on the male hunter: "A sudden lust seized her, to lay hold of him and tear him and make him into nothing." Finally, her youthful inability to understand the urgency of his sexual need, her indifference to his insistent physical demands, after she has roused him with her kiss, can only be interpreted as a devastating rebuff to his manhood, a kind of annihilation that many a young man has felt in such a situation. Anton has staked his entire manhood on his triumph over Ursula, but there wasn't any manhood there to stake!

The scene strikes me as plausible, then, even though it does not exhibit the sort of overwhelming inevitability that one sees in Will's attempts to "reduce" both the girl from Nottingham and Anna. Will always remains real to the reader, with the allegorical and scientific elements in his make-up dissolved into the persuasively rendered process of his development within normal surroundings. But Lawrence does not seem very interested in Skrebensky except as an allegorical figure—an army engineer who serves his country blindly and who fails to achieve "being." Skrebensky, more than any other character in *The Rainbow* (including Miss Inger or Uncle Tom), is a purely intellectual creation; and that he was willed onto the page is suggested by the fact that we know so little about his personal and domestic life. Lawrence had a clear idea of the man he wished to create; but the idea wasn't connected for Lawrence with the concrete particulars of life.

And yet—for there is always an "and yet" in discussing Lawrence—the psychology of Skrebensky's behavior is brilliant. The man who follows blindly the collective will of the nation, marching off to the Boer War mechanically, lacking belief in his "personal connection," and "dead" to his "own intrinsic life," has nothing to fall back upon, once the war is over, but "his five senses. They were to be gratified" (326). So his plunge into African sensuality—the way of death—is inevitable. Equally inevitable is his turning, in his weakness, to Ursula and to marriage as his sole salvation, his becoming "helpless, at her mercy" (443), and his pathetic weeping. By the same token, Ursula's destruction of him for a second time, with her "beaked harpy's kiss," is thoroughly prepared for. He stands for all that she resists and loathes in her soul—the hopelessness, the inertia, the terrible acceptance of a meaningless way of life (see especially 228–30). When she meets him again after the war, she knows "vaguely, in the first minute, that they were enemies come together in a truce" (442). The destructive frictional to-and-fro of their relationship can only lead to the climax of psychic death.

Lawrence's handling of the ending of the novel has been generally attacked. Is Ursula's vision of the rainbow really, as John Worthen argues, a vision "which grows out of the particular needs of the author" rather than out of the novel itself?[7] Is it really, as Leavis claims, "wholly unprepared and unsupported, defying the preceding pages"?[8] In truth, the vision of the rainbow—that is, of Wholeness, of the perfect joining of light and dark, male and female, spirit and flesh—has hovered over the novel from the beginning. It appears at the end of the first-generation section, when Tom and Lydia achieve sensual consummation and Anna is set free to play "between the pillar of fire and the pillar of cloud in confidence, having the assurance on her right hand and on her left. She was no longer called upon to uphold with her childish might the broken end of the arch. Her father and her mother now met to the span of the heavens" (92). It appears again at the end of the second-generation section, just prior to the shift to Ursula's life, when Anna, her child now born (but her husband defeated, "nullified"), strains to look at "something beyond":

> Anna loved the child very much, oh, very much. Yet still she was not quite fulfilled. She had a light expectant feeling, as of a door half opened. . . . She was straining her eyes to something beyond. And from her Pisgah mount, which she had attained, what could she see? A faint, gleaming horizon. a long way off, and a rainbow

> like an archway, a shadow-door with faintly coloured coping above it. Must she be moving thither? [192]

Finally the vision appears at the end of the third-generation episodes. Ursula, more highly developed than Anna, more spiritually determined to throw off "the old, hard barren form of bygone living," has much the same vision, but a vision clarified, richer, and more meaningful than Anna's because it seeks to embrace the entire social and political future. The vision, like the rainbow, is "arched in [men's] blood" and seeks always to "quiver in their spirit." The vision is eternal; and this novel, as John Worthen beautifully describes it, is "the timeless account of impulse and aspiration and fulfilment, always modified and always re-enacted by each succeeding generation."[9] The vision arises appropriately at the point when Ursula's child has been aborted and she is ready to resume a new way of life. The sudden brutal assault of the horses—those symbols of an oppressive brute sensual power, "never bursting free"—is connected with her pregnancy and with the threat to her further development: she has moved towards death in her following of the "African" way of pure sensation with Skrebensky. Now she must begin again. She turns to her vision of "the beyond"—to that which can free man from the tyranny of blind sensuality. She turns to the vision of Wholeness, and the eternal quest goes on.

It is apparent that Lawrence was in full control of his novel, including its conclusion. His control is particularly evident in his careful dramatization of the sufferings and joys of the characters while, at the same time, he stands aloof from them, regarding them with moral and scientific detachment in their struggles to achieve fulfillment and in their repeated failures. The distance had to be maintained; otherwise the scientific and religious character of the novel might be compromised; we might fail to see human experience with the proper ethical or scientific objectivity. But sympathetic identification with the characters is also necessary, for Lawrence wants us to feel the miracle of being alive and to understand life as it is lived, body and spirit fusing organically in the living moment. Hence Lawrence seeks, whenever possible, to see and experience everything from the point of view of each character, to imitate as accurately as possible each character's whole experience, conscious and unconscious, as the problem of finding fulfillment presents itself at successive stages of life. In short, Lawrence is determined to make his novel as dramatic as possible.

Lawrence would I think have liked Henry James's admonition "Dramatise! Dramatise!" as long as the "scenic method" did not blur our understanding of moral problems. Lawrence's novel is so thoroughly dramatized that even the passages which foreshorten, summarizing a character's experience and state of mind over several weeks or months (passages necessary and frequent in this three-generation novel), acquire the quality of felt life, partly because of the repetitive style, which imitates the pressure of a persistent desire, and partly because of the use of the Jamesian central consciousness (with the author looking over the character's shoulder and supplying information the character cannot supply). But Lawrence recognized that in order to harmonize the voices of the angels of science, religion, and mimetic art, point of view had to be flexible. To confine himself exclusively to the characters' points of view would be to present raw experience and raw feeling without understanding or evaluation. His problem then becomes that of simultaneously identifying with and critically appraising his people.

He has to have remarkable "negative capability":[10] he has to treat his protagonists' experience with the utmost sympathetic imagination and with the utmost respect, assuming that the frightened, desiring, bewildered animal is always innocent in the sense that his deep desires and fears are not subject to conscious control. Then, drawing back, Lawrence has to register the full moral significance of each act. Thus when Lawrence wishes to judge harshly, he has to abandon the character's point of view. Neither Miss Inger nor Uncle Tom, for example, can be seen from within; both must be seen almost entirely from Ursula's point of view; the absence of sympathetic identification makes possible the severity of the judgment. But Lawrence is generally reluctant to present people entirely from another's point of view. His usual procedure is to identify wholly with a character for a time, dramatizing the character's immediate experience, and then quickly to shift the point of view to another character or to the narrator so as to register the moral significance of the action. The following passage is typical:

> It was so unutterably still and perfect with promise, the golden-lighted, distinct land, that Ursula's soul rocked and wept. Suddenly he glanced at her. The tears were running over her cheeks, her mouth was working strangely.
>
> "What is the matter?" he said.
>
> After a moment's struggle with her voice,
>
> "It is so beautiful," she said, looking at the glowing beautiful land. It was so beautiful, so perfect, and so unsullied.
>
> He too realised what England would be in a few hours' time—a blind, sordid, strenuous activity, all for nothing, fuming with dirty smoke and running trains and groping in the bowels of the earth, all for nothing. A ghastliness came over him.

> He looked at Ursula. Her face was wet with tears, very bright, like a transfiguration in the refulgent light. Nor was his the hand to wipe away the burning, bright tears. He stood apart, overcome by a cruel ineffectuality.
>
> Gradually a great, helpless sorrow was rising in him. But as yet he was fighting it away, he was struggling for his own life. He became very quiet and unaware of the things about him, awaiting, as it were, her judgment on him.
>
> They returned to Nottingham, the time of her examination came. She must go to London. But she would not stay with him in an hotel. She would go to a quiet little pension near the British Museum.
>
> Those quiet residential squares of London made a great impression on her mind. They were very complete. Her mind seemed imprisoned in their quietness. Who was going to liberate her? [465–66]

Here Lawrence presents first Ursula's then Skrebensky's response to the beauty of the undefiled land. Ursula weeps for the hideous violation of the promise connected with the rainbow: a response commensurate with her passionate idealism, her search for one of the Sons of God. Skrebensky too is appalled in his soul as he considers the ghastly and pointless mutilation of beauty; but here the point of view shifts imperceptibly to that of the narrator, who delicately suggests both Skrebensky's incapacity for a deep sympathy and his moral inertia: "Nor was his the hand to wipe away the burning, bright tears. He stood apart, overcome by a cruel ineffectuality." Having registered his moral disapproval, Lawrence returns immediately, however, to Skrebensky's point of view, defining with sympathy the man's struggle "for his own life," yet again suggesting Skrebensky's failure to assume responsibility and his weak submission to the female's judgment.

Foreshortening, moving with the utmost rapidity, Lawrence next resumes the objective narrative—"They returned to Nottingham"—and immediately shifts to Ursula's anticipation of her examination in London. Almost without transition, following the motions of her mind rather than her physical journeying, Lawrence places Ursula in London and, again employing her point of view, presents not only a sympathetic dramatization of her central problem ("Who was going to liberate her?") but also, very delicately, a moral evaluation of the society in which men and women submit passively, in "quietness," to the dead form of life.

Thus on half a page Lawrence shifts from Ursula to Anton to the narrator to Anton to the narrator and Ursula. Everywhere Lawrence conveys the immediacy of felt life even as he continues to exhibit the laws of life (the continuing frictional to-and-fro of Ursula and Skrebensky); and everywhere he interjects the delicate moral discriminations reflecting his thoughtful analysis of basic psychological, ethical, and social problems.

Thus the voices of the three angels are blended, and the image of life is charged with dramatic tension. Everywhere our concern for the characters, our fear that they will fail to "come through," is maximized. Everywhere Lawrence multiplies the difficulties of achieving connection and of building a rainbow. His understanding of the extent and the danger of the forces that prevent us from achieving wholeness of self and a healthy relationship between the self and the world is so comprehensive that almost anything in experience may be used to dramatize the soul's dilemma. Difficulties from within (the duality within the psyche) are compounded by those from without (the mechanistic industrial system that violates organic life; the educational system; the dead forms of social intercourse; the dead habits). And everywhere Lawrence intensifies our concern and dread by multiplying ironic reversals. Seeking salvation, the lover weds himself to a betrayer. Or a parent becomes a lover of his child, and all the horrors of incest are suggested. Again and again the loved one, the center of one's life, becomes a harpy, a vulture, a vampire. Again and again people are driven toward compulsive cruelty and insane aggression. Again and again Lawrence provides vivid renderings of the anguish and frenzy of the soul as it is thwarted and driven blindly to find a frightening fulfillment or compensation. Fear and horror are intensified as we witness innocent creatures driven to extremes of perversity; and the horror is the greater because it is contrasted with stirring depictions of ecstasy and fulfillment. So precious is the goal, so powerful is the need for fulfillment, that any rupture of the connection, any break in the arch, acquires a singular dreadfulness. A slight jeering intonation stirs madness in the soul. The unique power of the "Anna Victrix" chapter—surely the best thing that Lawrence ever wrote!—derives largely from the terrifying momentum, the frightening compounding, of destructiveness. After the Edenic bliss in the marriage bed, the bed becomes a hearse; the bride becomes a demon; the groom is driven into a frenzy of retaliation. There is Gothic melodrama in this, but the dread and horror that arise from the inversion of all expectation and from the perversion of all innocent desire are the dread and horror of normal psychic experience. The laws of psychic interaction become the laws of ironic reversal, and Lawrence's analysis of the psyche becomes magnificent art.

Most remarkable is, as F. R. Leavis has suggested, Lawrence's ability to record with full intensity the actual experience of life and simultaneously to stand back as an impersonal observer, evaluating, analyzing causal relationships, and defining meanings with the utmost precision. There was always in Lawrence's work the danger that the allegorizing would get the upper hand and drive life from the novel, as when Lawrence invited Ciccio into *The Lost Girl* or Cipriano into *The Plumed Serpent*. In *The Rainbow* the three strange angels all sing out with strong voices in a miraculous harmony.

We need a name to suggest the uniqueness of the form Lawrence created. Recognizing that the book presents, from the perspective of "the vast, unexplored morality of life itself," the story of Western man's quest for fulfillment of all his deepest desires, we would approach adequate definition, I think, if we called the novel a psychological epic-romance, or perhaps a psychological mimetic allegory. The method is "exhaustive" because the book supplies the natural, cultural, and psychological framework within which the experience of every man and woman may be evaluated with a recognition of its moral significance in the timeless quest for balance and the fulfillment of man's deepest desires. If every effort must be made to maximize sympathy for the protagonists, one must never be allowed to identify with them completely: they must always be seen sharply as the fallible, passion-ridden creatures they are. The action must lay bare the causes of their suffering and their partial fulfillments and of their immorality and their goodness, from the point of view of "the vast, unexplored morality of life itself." The excellence of the novel arises largely from Lawrence's discovery of the mean between the particularization of experience in the interest of mimetic fidelity and the abstraction from experience of essential psychological patterns and of the moral principles inherent in each stage of the human struggle to achieve maximum of being.

7

The Laws of Action and Reaction in *Women in Love*

Women in Love, which Lawrence described as a sequel to *The Rainbow* (*CL*, 1:519), continues the timeless quest of men and women for fulfillment of their deepest needs and desires. As much of *The Rainbow*, particularly the Ursula-Skrebensky section, focuses on a voluntaristic reaction in sexual relationships and on the ensuing battle of wills, so *Women in Love*, with the war madness looming up behind its sometimes spectral images, focuses on the will to power in sexual relationships. Tighter in its construction than *The Rainbow*, it defines powerfully the hideous psychic and moral warping of the reaction away from "the love and benevolence ideal," and it examines the difficulties of "coming through" in a maddened world. The characters are far less ordinary than those of *The Rainbow:* Lawrence focuses on men and women who have swum furthest down the dark river of dissolution, and he draws, with a power reminiscent of Van Gogh's last paintings, the "accelarated grimace" of the age in which men seek fulfillment within the prison of the ego, insulated, separate, cut off from all organic relatedness in marriage, in comradeship, and in the natural world. What is so grotesque and horrible in this *Dies Irae* is the terrifying momentum of the compulsion to react. Far more savagely than in the later sections of *The Rainbow*, and with far deeper disgust, Lawrence exposes and evaluates the insanity of men and women seeking release from the ideal life they have forced themselves to live.

Several critics—Angelo P. Bertocci, F. R. Leavis, and Robert L. Chamberlain, among others[1]—have pointed out that the central choral passage of the novel is Birkin's reflection on the two ways of death—the Artic or spiritual way of ice abstraction and the African way of pure sensation and mindlessness. Another passage, perhaps more clearly indicative of Lawrence's central concern, is that in which Rupert Birkin, describing the conduct of Julius Halliday, defines the relationship in the modern world between the Artic and the African ways:

> "Of course," [Birkin] said, "Julius is somewhat insane. On the one hand he's had religious mania, and on the other, he is fascinated by obscenity. Either he's a pure servant, washing the feet of Christ, or else he is making obscene drawings of Jesus—action and reaction—and between the two, nothing. He is really insane. He wants a pure lily, another girl, with a Botticelli face, on the one hand, and on the other, he *must* have the Pussum, just to defile himself with her." [*WL*, 107]

This observation recalls the analysis of action and reaction already traced in Nietzsche (see chapter 2) and reminds one of the remark of Dostoevsky's antihero in *Notes from Underground:* "The more conscious I was of goodness and of all that was 'good and beautiful,' the more deeply I sank into my mire and the more ready I was to sink in it altogether."[2] This inversion suggests the major problem facing not only the characters in *Women in Love* but also the characters in all of Lawrence's mature fiction.

It is not simply the reaction from spirituality into "sensationalism" that Lawrence is talking about. In chapter 23 of *Women in Love* Birkin reflects that the pattern of action and reaction follows "a few great laws":

> He was not very much interested any more in personalities and in people—people were all different, but they were all enclosed in a definite limitation, he said; there were only about two great ideas, two great streams of activity, with various forms of reaction therefrom. The reactions were all varied in various people, but they followed a few great laws, and intrinsically there was no difference. They acted and reacted involuntarily according to a few great laws, and once the laws, the great principles, were known, people were no longer mystically interesting. They were all essentially alike, the differences were only variations on a theme. None of them transcended the given term. [348]

Birkin's words here are reminiscent of Lawrence's statement in the letter to Edward Garnett on 5 June 1914 that in *The Wedding Ring* he was dealing not with the "old stable ego" but with the allotropic states of the same basic carbon. Thus Birkin's words might seem to refer to the oscillation between extremes of spirituality and of sensuality, the "two great ideas, two great streams of activity." But it is clear from the first three chapters of this study and from *The Rainbow* that Lawrence had in mind a more basic kind of action and reaction. The oscillation between spirituality and sensual depravity is linked, as in the novels of Dostoevsky, with the action and reaction between the sympathetic and voluntary impulses. On the one hand, Dostoevsky's Underground Man or his Raskolnikov wants to be all-loving and compassionate, to bow down before suffering humanity in the spirit of Christian selflessness; on the other hand, he wants to have an independent will, to be absolutely free to do as he likes, heedless even of the laws of nature. So, as we have seen in *The Rainbow,* Lawrence's characters are torn between the desire to give themselves up sympathetically to other individuals or to humanity, and the opposing desire to hold themselves intact, single, separate, unmixed with others. The "two great streams of activity" that Birkin speaks of are not, then, simply spirituality and sensuality but love and power, which may be manifested either spiritually or sensually. As Rawdon Lilly says in *Aaron's Rod:*

> "I told you there were two great urges—two great life-urges, didn't I? There may be more. But it comes on me so strongly, now, that there are two: love, and power. And we've been trying to work ourselves, at least as individuals, from the love-urge exclusively, hating the power-urge, and repressing it." [345]

The love urge, as it is manifested in *Women in Love* and in *Aaron's Rod,* is the urge to surrender the self and to live wholly within the collective tribal life, accepting "the ideal of love, the ideal that it is better to give than to receive, the ideal of liberty [i.e., of democracy], the ideal of the brotherhood of man, the ideal of the sanctity of human life, the ideal of what we call goodness, charity, benevolence, public spiritedness, the ideal of sacrifice for a cause, the ideal of unity and unanimity—all the lot—all the whole beehive of ideals" (*AR*, 326). The power urge, in *Women in Love,* takes the form of a desire to control others, a sadistic desire for omnipotence and for ego aggrandizement.

The laws governing the conflict of love and power, later formulated explicitly in *Psychoanalysis and the Unconscious* and *Fantasia of the Unconscious,* obviously entered deeply into Lawrence's planning of the structure of *Women in Love.* Although several critics—most notably, perhaps, Peter Balbert and Howard M. Harper, Jr.[3]—have noted important linkages between Lawrence's theory of the unconscious and the psychodynamics of *The Rainbow* and *Women in Love,* the crucial importance of the laws of action and reaction as determinants of the plot complications of *Women in Love* has not been fully appreciated. Here I hope to show that these laws shape the entire novel. Chapters and episodes within chapters exhibit the to-and-fro of love and power. One witnesses a series of actions and reactions that define the nature of two radically different unions—Gudrun's and Gerald's union of death within "the motion of the will" (i.e., of power), and Ursula's and Birkin's union of life, a union in which love and power impulses are balanced and in which connection and separateness are achieved without the disastrous oscillations of domination and servitude or of spirituality and sensationalism. Minor characters also exhibit the pattern of action and reaction, and the novel may be seen as an effort to confront and answer the question, How can the opposing halves of the psyche be satisfied without our falling into the disastrous pattern of action and reaction "with nothing in between"?

To understand Lawrence's construction of the action, we must follow the to-and-fro of the contending impulses in the characters, both major and minor. But first it will be necessary to recall the discussion of action and reaction in the first two chapters. As we saw there, the idea of reaction is bound up with Lawrence's psychocosmology. In "Study of Thomas Hardy" Lawrence writes that "in the origin . . . the whole universe" must have been "one motionless homogeneity" but that there must have been "some *reaction*, infinitesimally faint, stirring somehow through the vast, homogeneous inertia" (*Phoenix*, 432; emphasis mine). This reaction—a voluntary impulse to split off from the homogeneous infinity—resulted in the ever-increasing differentiation of "orders and species." Reaction is thus a principle operating in nature—a will to differentiation, an electrical resistance to sympathetic union; and it is a principle of the unconscious mind, which finally is an expression of the natural forces of attraction and repulsion.

Since reaction is associated in Lawrence's thought with division or splitting off from the primal sympathetic unity, it is also associated with a destructive impulse—that is, an impulse to dismember the organic whole of life (that "sympathy of the whole" in which male and female are one) and to reduce life to individual particles or fragments. But the reaction to the whole may be either healthy or unhealthy: healthy insofar as it is a necessary and natural desire to achieve a noble integrity and individuality against the mindless homogeneity of nature or of society; unhealthy insofar as it may be the expression of a base egoistic desire for personal power and thus may lead to a sadistic self-assertion and the splitting of oneself off from the whole of being, which is our origin.

The law of action and reaction is basically simple, but to clarify Lawrence's thinking we may break it down into four parts.

1. Action and reaction are inherent in nature and in the constitution of the psyche—that is, they are manifestations of the rhythms of our natures. But any forcing of the psyche in one direction only is harmful. The forcing of life by the conscious will solely in a sympathetic direction breeds the unconscious reaction into *extremes* of voluntary

behavior. The forcing of life solely in a voluntary direction breeds a "reverse reaction" into extremes of sympathetic, or selfless and masochistic, behavior.

2. Reaction is always unhealthy when it is unchecked or unbalanced by action in the opposite direction. Unchecked, reaction moves toward psychic destruction. As Birkin reflects, "the climax of sensual reaction, once reached in any direction, is reached finally, there is no going on": that is, sensual reaction—or sensualism in the service of the voluntary impulse—cannot in itself lead to healthy development of the individual. A healthy development is possible only when the voluntary reaction is balanced by an impulse to act from the sympathetic center, the impulse to wed the self to others and to give up egotistical self-assertion. Reaction is healthy only when it is natural and "responsible"—that is, when it is carried out with full understanding of its role in accomplishing the dynamic balance of the whole psyche.

3. To react against a voluntary form of behavior is to imitate that behavior. Reacting against a militant society, we ourselves become militant. Reaction against a voluntary mode of behavior is healthy only when such reaction is joined to the unitive or creative impulses of the unconscious sympathetic center. Jesus, Zarathustra, or Don Ramón react against a bullying society which seeks to perpetuate a dead form of life, but these reactions are healthy because they are balanced by the deep sympathetic urge to unite with others in the creation of a new society.

4. Reaction in our time, within "the motion of the will," takes the form of oscillation in a struggle for power: a seesaw between masochism and sadism, subservience and pride, or self-abnegation and self-aggrandizement. No other relationship is possible within a struggle for power. Each party seeks triumph at the other's expense.

Close examination of *Women in Love* reveals how carefully these laws are worked into the action. The first and fourth laws are illustrated throughout the novel, not only in the relationship of Gudrun and Gerald but also in that of Birkin and Hermione and in that of Birkin and Ursula before these two are able to "die" as distinct egos and to become reborn in sympathetic connection with the Other.

At the outset Birkin's relationship with Hermione Roddice is, like that of Mr. and Mrs. Crich, one of "utter interdestruction." Birkin and Hermione have not entered into sympathetic connection. On the contrary, each remains a separate ego. Birkin is "by nature . . . separate": "there was a certain hostility, a hidden ultimate reserve in him, cold and inaccessible" (23); Hermione has sought to make herself "invulnerable; unassailable" (18). And their affair has become a battle for dominance, a battle that Hermione, with her superior will, has been winning. Birkin has been "subordinated," "neutralised" by her "demoniacal" possession (22, 24). But he is reacting to the spiritual, conscious "power and subservience" relationship that exists between them; he is trying to "break away from her finally, to be free" (18). He needs the life-giving renewal of connection in the unconscious, sensual, sympathetic mode.

The early chapters of the novel dramatize Birkin's voluntary "recoil" from a love that has threatened to destroy his individuality. He is driven into reaction against love not only of Hermione but also of all humanity. Yet persistence in separateness, in isolation from others, is intolerable. Somehow Birkin must find a sympathetic connection, one in which his "proud individual singleness" is not "forfeited." So he turns to Ursula.

The relationship between Birkin and Ursula is marked throughout by the ambivalence, the action and reaction, that issues inevitably from the conflict of sympathetic and voluntary centers. In the first chapter, when Ursula sees Birkin at the church, we learn that "something kept her from him, as well as attracted her to him" (22–23). In the third chapter, "Class-Room," she is again attracted and repelled. She joins Hermione in "jeering at him, jeering him into nothingness" (47); but if, with Hermione, Ursula is "hostile and resentful" when Birkin denounces the "self-righteous self-opinionated self-will" of men and women today, she is "fascinated" by Birkin's "physical attractiveness"; and when he leaves with Hermione, she weeps. In the development of Ursula's relationship with Birkin, the pattern will be repeated over and over. In her desire to preserve her selfhood inviolable, as the daughter of Artemis, and in her fear of being subjugated by the male, she will turn repeatedly to Hermione and Gudrun, those proponents of the will, for support; but when Ursula is impelled by her sympathetic inclination to give herself up to Birkin, she will also turn against Hermione and Gudrun. Indeed, the pattern is initiated in the very first chapter, where Ursula at first joins with Gudrun in laughing at the idea of marriage, then "wished to be alone, freed from the tightness, the enclosure of Gudrun's presence" (14).

In chapter 11, "An Island," the structure of attraction and repulsion, action and reaction, becomes a dominant principle of composition. The form of the lovers' interaction is suggested in *Fantasia*, where Lawrence states that even when the "circuit of vital sex magnetism" is growing more and more powerful, there is a "pulse and flow of attraction and recoil": "In wild free life, each touch brings about an intense recoil, and each recoil causes an intense sympathetic attraction. So goes on the strange battle of desire, until consummation is reached'' (*FU*, 186). Birkin and Ursula do not exist in ''wild free nature'': their conscious wills interfere with the natural rhythm of attraction and recoil. But their interaction does suggest a movement toward healthy union. When Ursula finds Birkin at work on a punt, she is sensually attracted: ''she did not want to go away'' (139). As they talk, she is simultaneously interested and tempted to jeer at him. When he says that humanity ''is a dead tree'' (thus repudiating the idea of sympathetic surrender to the tribe), she stiffens herself, becomes ''hostile''; they rouse each other ''to a fine passion of opposition,'' and Ursula is filled with ''a certain contempt and hatred for him.'' What is most threatening about Birkin is his resistance to her conscious female will to subjugate the male and make him hers: ''She wanted him to herself, she hated the *Salvator Mundi* touch'' (145). Yet Birkin seems to her ''quick and attractive,'' and Lawrence stresses ''the duality in feeling which he created in her'' (146). As the scene proceeds, Ursula wants Birkin to accept the *idea* of love; but when she insists upon love, he ''withdraws,'' sensing that ''love'' means destruction of his selfhood, surrender to the Magna Mater. She wants him to surrender, to become hers; at the same time she fears his ''control'' over her. The action and reaction have become a principle of scenic composition.

After this first all-but-open declaration of her love for Birkin, Ursula immediately recoils. In the next chapter, ''Carpeting,'' when Hermione asserts that '' 'the will can cure anything, and put anything right,' '' Ursula feels ''a curious thrill.'' In the ensuing conversation, Gerald argues that a woman is like a horse: '' 'Two wills act in opposition inside her. With one will, she wants to subject herself utterly. With the other she wants to bolt, and pitch her rider to perdition.' '' Ursula's response is to laugh: '' 'Then I'm a bolter' ''; and she is ''united in a sudden bond of deep affection and closeness'' with Hermione (159). Whereupon the reaction occurs once again. ''In spite of herself, Ursula felt herself recoiling from Hermione. It was all she could do to restrain the revulsion'' (160). So Ursula continues to oscillate, in league with Hermione but unable to ''bear her,'' drawn to Birkin but ''strictly hostile to him'' (161–62).

Birkin, analyzing the nature of the conflict within Ursula, denounces the ''dance of opposites'' which we have already noted in Halliday and Hermione. Love, for these people, is entirely a form of egoism. And this love process, always within the motion of the will, becomes an oscillation between domination and subservience. As Birkin says to Ursula:

> "I tell you, you want love to administer to your egoism, to subserve you. Love is a process of subservience with you—and with everybody. I hate it."
>
> "No," she cried, pressing back her head like a cobra, her eyes flashing. "It is a process of pride—I want to be proud—"
>
> "Proud and subservient, proud and subservient, I know you," he retorted dryly. "Proud and subservient, then subservient to the proud—I know you and your love. It is a tick-tack, tick-tack, a dance of opposites." [173]

Modern love is this action and reaction, with nothing in between. The ego's pride in domination is succeeded by self-abasement and degradation. Such oscillation is inevitable in a union that is a contest of egos competing for power and dominion over one another. Ursula, at this point, cannot free herself from the will to power. Indeed, she will subjugate herself to Birkin for the sake of power. She forces Birkin into "submission" by getting him to say "my love," a phrase that endorses her notion of love as possession or egoistic domination. Yet at the same time she feels the deep need to abandon her ego and to enter into a sympathetic connection with Birkin, not a subjugation but a "mystic conjunction" which would transform the anarchic "freedom" to exercise the will to power into a responsible freedom within a commitment.

That she will eventually accept Birkin's idea of the balance and equilibrium of male and female in conjunction is suggested by the symbolism of her lanterns in the next chapter, "Water-Party." In both of her lanterns are joined heaven and earth, the light and the dark, the male fire and the female water: " 'You've got the heavens above, and the waters under the earth,' " Birkin tells her; but the *Liebestod* that Birkin seeks—a love that will destroy the old self and create a new one—is not accomplished. On the contrary, he is "satisfied and shattered, fulfilled and destroyed," by his passionate embrace with Ursula. He has not found the peace that attends a passing away of the self; he has not really found the ultimately satisfying sympathetic union in which the self dies before undergoing rebirth. Nor has Ursula.

At this point in the action a significant change occurs—a change that has not, I believe, been noted by critics of Lawrence.[4] In parallel actions, in chapters 15 and 16, both Ursula and Birkin long for the death that will deliver them from the prison of the ego and the will. "Better a thousand times take one's chance with death," Birkin reflects, "than accept a life one did not want"; and Ursula thinks: "To die is also a joy, a joy of submitting to that which is greater than the known, namely, the pure unknown. That is a joy. But to live mechanised and cut off within the motions of the will, to live as an entity absolved from the unknown, that is shameful and ignominious.'' The full significance of their acceptance of death in the understanding is revealed in ''The Reality of Peace,'' in which, as I pointed out earlier, Lawrence argues that death and life, systole and diastole, move in the whole of creation and that man's acceptance of death gives him an intense life, life rooted in relationship to the entire universe. Surrendering himself to the current of life and death, man becomes ''a new being'': ''When we understand our extreme being in death, we have surpassed into a new being'' (676). To accept both the ''desire of life or desire of death, desire of putting together or desire of putting asunder'' (681) is to be ''saved from the vast and obscene self-conceit which is the ruling force of the world that envelops me'' (685). It is necessary to submit ''to the primal unknown out of which issues the all'' (695). And this is what Birkin and Ursula do when they accept death over the mechanical nullity within the motion of the will: they prepare themselves for a letting go of the ego and a ''glad refreshment'' in the inhuman life force.

Nevertheless, they have still a long way to go before they can meet ''in ultimate trust.'' When they next meet, Ursula is again ''separate'' from Birkin: ''he saw her revulsion.'' She hates him, seeing him as the enemy who defines her own nonexistence; and he hates her. It is not until Birkin contemplates the horrors of death through African sensualism and of death through Arctic knowledge that he overcomes his fear of marriage and proposes. Then Ursula again recoils ''upon herself'' and escapes from the ''danger'' he presents by becoming ''hard and self-completed, like a jewel,'' ''bright and invulnerable, quite free and happy, perfectly liberated in her self-possession'' (298). ''Perfectly stable in resistance,'' she turns to Gudrun for support, denouncing the male tyranny and asserting once again her own perfect independence. Yet this voluntary recoil can only breed emptiness, and once again Ursula feels ''a revulsion from Gudrun'' and withdraws. She continues, however, to want Birkin on her terms, as her man, accepting that ''she in return would be his humble slave—whether she wanted it or not'' (302). Thus the dance of opposites within ''the motion of the will,'' the assumption of a power relationship, continues.

Chapter 22, ''Woman to Woman,'' and chapter 23, ''Excurse,'' continue the pattern of action and reaction in the behavior of Birkin and Ursula. Ursula, still resisting the idea of submission to Birkin and fearing that he will only use her as ''his instrument,'' as other men have done (336), talks to Hermione, who attempts to strengthen Ursula's opposition by describing Birkin as unstable, swinging from an "*intensely* spiritual life" to "a fury of destruction": " 'He is never constant, always this awful, dreadful reaction' " (337). Hermione reflects: "It was all a foolish backward and forward, a violent oscillation that would at length be too violent for his coherency, and he would smash and be dead. There was no saving him. This violent and directionless reaction between animalism and spiritual truth would go on in him till he tore himself in two between the opposite directions" (339). It is an accurate description of the Birkin whom Hermione has known. And Ursula cannot yet see that Birkin has changed.

Thereafter Ursula, angry because she assumes Birkin is still attached to Hermione, tells him to " 'go where you belong.' " Whereupon Birkin accuses Ursula of obeying another law of action and reaction: " 'Ah, you fool!' " he cries, " 'with your "go where you belong." It's finished between Hermione and me. She means much more to *you*, if it comes to that, than she does to me. For you can only revolt in pure reaction from her—and to be her opposite is to be her counterpart' " (349). Reaction from Hermione, the woman of will, is another act of will (see law 3, p. 175). Ursula, furious, thereupon accuses Birkin of action and reaction: he wants "spiritual brides," but he goes to her "for daily use." He is a "purity-monger," but his "truth" and his "purity" stink. " 'What you are,' " she cries, " 'is a foul, deathly thing, obscene, that's what you are, obscene and perverse . . . death-eating' " (351). And the charge can scarcely be denied, for we know that Birkin "had taken her at the roots of her darkness and shame—like a demon, laughing over the fountain of mystic corruption" (348). Indeed, Birkin acknowledges to himself that "his spirituality was concomitant of a process of depravity, a sort of pleasure in self-destruction" (353); but if he knows that "the black river of corruption" rolls within him and that he, too, is prone to plunge into a dangerous perversity, his knowledge enables him to achieve a kind of balance, for knowing the worst about himself, he "had done" with it. Moreover, Lawrence suggests later that a certain perversity may be necessary to health in a world that refuses to accept corruption and death as part of life. What Ursula doesn't see, when she condemns Birkin's "death-eating," is that Birkin also hopes to achieve, through acceptance of corruption and through accepting her "at the quick death," a total abandonment of his old self and, ultimately, a rebirth and a new connection.

The rebirth of the lovers can occur, then, only when they accept death of the old self—the ego. At that point, Birkin becomes "one of the sons of God": it is now the inhuman in him, "the strange mystery of his life-motion," that Ursula discovers at the "darkest, deepest, strangest life-source of the human body, at the back and base of the loins''(359). Both lovers experience ''a perfect passing away'' and an ''accession into being.'' They are no longer cut off from organic life and ''absolved from the unknown'' (219). Their birth into being is made possible by their total giving up of their possessive human wills and their discovery of the life source beyond the ego: ''For she was to him what he was to her, the immemorial magnificence of mystic, palpable, real otherness'' (366). They fall into the profound darkness of the Source and Beginning of all things; they ''die'' as separate egos and are reborn, their death and rebirth replicating the God rhythm of the universe. As God is '' a flowing together and the flowing apart,'' so the lovers—darkness and light, female and male—flow together for a moment, then flow apart, each separate but each ''balanced in conjunction'' with the other.

The action and reaction are not finished, however. In the Tyrol, that symbol of cold spirituality, Birkin reacts into licentiousness, and Ursula reflects: ''Wasn't it rather horrible, a man who could be so soulful and spiritual, now to be so—she balked at her own thoughts and memories: then she added—so bestial? So bestial, they two!—so degraded? She winced. But after all, why not? She exulted as well. . . . She was free, when she knew everything, and no dark shameful things were denied her'' (470). Thus Lawrence suggests that reaction may be a condition of a healthy freedom: it may be necessary, in an atmosphere of life-denying spirituality, to plunge into the bestiality that makes one whole again. But here Lawrence is careful to stress that Birkin's initiation of the reaction is responsible: ''It was his responsibility, she would leave it to him'' (469). Unlike the creatures of the will, who plunge into anarchic licentiousness and sensationalism ''within the ego,'' seeking domination and triumph, Birkin and Ursula accept licentiousness as a part of life, an experience that makes them whole. With the knowledge of the experience, they ''have done'' with it; they are not compelled to swing compulsively and violently from action to reaction.

They break with the old world and begin their journey into the new. To remain in England, in a sordid *egoisme à deux*, with no object other than the collecting of possessions, is impossible. To remain in England, not creating a new life but only hostile to the old and unchanging mechanical way of life, is also impossible, for the law of action and reaction enters in here too. As Ursula says to Gudrun, '' 'I do think that one can't have anything new whilst one cares for the old—do you know what I mean?—even fighting the old is belonging to it' '' (499). To set one's will negatively against the old world is to become the counterpart of the creatures who live by the will. That kind of negation must be avoided. It is necessary to find "chinks" in the world where one can live outside of the motion of the will—those chinks that Lawrence was to search for over the rest of his life.

The pattern of action and reaction in the relationship of Birkin and Ursula is, to a degree, repeated in the relationship of Gerald and Gudrun. But there is, of course, a significant difference. Birkin and Ursula want a sympathetic connection, one in which the ego is given up and fulfillment is found in Being. Gudrun and Gerald, while seeking connection, are never capable of giving up their wills, and the pattern of action and reaction in their relationship is solely that of "pride and subservience" within the motion of the will. As Lawrence says in the final chapter of the novel: "It was this eternal see-saw, one destroyed that the other might exist, one ratified because the other was nulled" (507). And again: "The climax of sensual reaction, once reached in any direction, is reached finally, there is no going on. There is only repetition possible, or the going apart of the two protagonists, or the subjugating of the one will to the other, or death" (515). This last statement formulates the law that governs the interactions of Gerald and Gudrun.

Both of them want to be "high" (a word repeated throughout the novel). Gerald, like his father, accepts implicitly the spiritual ideals of charity and love of one's neighbor; Gerald is "subject to his necessity, in the last issue, for goodness, for righteousness, for oneness with the ultimate purpose" (516). Like his father, Gerald must try to force himself to live by a spiritual ideal, to love, to be "high" and "spiritual" and "uplifted." As a youth, "he wanted to be a pure Christian, one and equal with all men." His early acceptance of the ideal Christian life has its counterpart in his later acceptance of his role as "God of the Machine," for whom "man's will was the absolute, the only absolute" (255). Giving up his forced "Christian attitude of love and self-sacrifice," he decides that "position and authority were the right thing in the world, and it was useless to cant about it" (258). As his father tries to serve Christ, Gerald serves "the great productive machine," and his will as master of the machine is no less "spiritual" than the will of his father. Thus Lawrence defines the pattern of action and reaction in Gerald's life:

> For Gerald was in reaction against Charity; and yet he was dominated by it, it assumed supremacy in the inner life, and he could not confute it. So he was partly subject to that which his father stood for, but he was in reaction against it. Now he could not save himself. A certain pity and grief and tenderness for his father overcame him, in spite of the deeper, more sullen hostility. [249]

He acts and reacts, entirely within "the motion of the will." First love, then work, becomes the object of his life; but love and work are both expressions of the spiritual will to bully and force life. The intensity of this spiritual will is what drives Gerald into still other reactions—into his numerous affairs with women like Pussum, into a never-ending quest for ego fulfillment by dominating others. Like Halliday, he must "defile himself with the Pussum." But at the same time he wants to be "high": he does not like the fact that class barriers are breaking down (105); he protests that the African carving isn't "*high* art" (88); he is unwilling to recognize that a schoolteacher can be his "superior."

Gudrun, by the same token, affirms repeatedly that she is not "ordinary" (" 'We're not just the ordinary run,' " she says to Ursula); she "longs to be high-flown," "a swan among geese." She is drawn to Gerald because "he was the master." She thrills when "the master of them all pressed her to himself" (378) and compares herself arrogantly with the colliers' wives. Yet, as Birkin observes, her life "goes by contraries": " 'She's a bird of paradise. God knows what she's got to do with Beldover. It goes by contraries, like dreams' " (106). The "high-born lady" is in truth "rather dark than shady," as Ursula's song suggests (189). What draws Gudrun to Beldover, perhaps, is the "world of powerful, underworld men who spent most of their time in the darkness" (130). There is "a thick, hot attraction" in the colliery district; the colliers arouse "a strange, nostalgic ache of desire, something almost demoniacal, never to be fulfilled," for the colliers have "a secret sense of power, and of inexpressible destructiveness, and of fatal half-heartedness, a sort of rottenness in the will" (132–33). It is the counterpart of the power and will that she observes in Gerald when he forces the mare into "pure control" and "unutterable subordination" (128). Her attraction to Gerald is identical with Pussum's, for both women see Gerald as free, untameable, "unconditioned," a man who knows how to "manage" the savages in South America or the mare in England. Both Pussum and Gudrun want to know Gerald, to experience the "fearful source of power" arising from "the base of his spine" (81); they enter willingly into a relationship with him that they know subconsciously will become a violent battle for survival, a war for supremacy, in which one of the partners must be master and the other slave. What they seek is "the subtle thrills of extreme sensation in reduction. It was an unbroken will reacting against her [Gudrun's] unbroken will in a myriad subtle thrills of reduction, the last subtle activities of analysis and breaking down, carried out in the darkness of her, whilst the outside form, the individual, was utterly unchanged, even sentimental in its poses" (515). Love-making becomes, both for

Gerald and for Gudrun, sheer reaction of one will against another. The self remains single, separate, existing in a terrible isolation that is ultimately intolerable.

What is saddest and most dreadful about the relationship between Gerald and Gudrun is that each is so terribly cut off from everyone else and that each takes exactly the wrong steps to establish a connection. What they both need is to give up the ego, the old self, and to enter into a sympathetic connection with each other. Yet they can only be "balanced in separation" or "in opposition," unlike Birkin and Ursula, who are balanced in conjunction (201). As their battle of wills develops, both want, on occasion, to "let go." In the chapter "Water-Party," Gerald, in the boat with Gudrun, "lapsed out for the first time in his life, into the things about him. For he always kept such a keen attentiveness, concentrated and unyielding in himself. Now he had let go, imperceptibly he was melting into oneness with the whole. It was like pure, perfect sleep, his first great sleep of life. He had been so insistent, so guarded, all his life. But here was sleep, and peace, and perfect lapsing out" (202). Yet Gudrun, always desperately seeking support for her ego, is "uneasy . . . for some assurance," and she rouses him from this sleep, so that he becomes again "very keen and alert and single in himself, instrumental" (203–4). Frightened by his own insufficiency and isolation, Gerald knows that he must find "relief," perhaps in Birkin, perhaps in women (265). And in the "Gladiatorial" chapter, he does for a brief time enter into a rejuvenating connection with Birkin: the two men work "into a tighter closer oneness of struggle," and Gerald declares, " 'I feel better. It has certainly helped me' " (311). But the connection is broken, and after the death of his father, Gerald, threatened by "the great dark void which circled at the centre of his soul" (268), knows that "he must seek reinforcements. He did not believe in his own single self" (386). When he makes love to Gudrun, however, he does not achieve connection with her. He uses her for his "relief" and becomes like a child, "soothed and restored" by the "Mother and substance of all life" (394). But like the child, he cannot give; only take. His "worship" of the Mother as God, his "sleep of fecundity within the womb," is pure regression; and his "reduction back to infancy" is the reaction from the terrible overemphasis of the spiritual will. Gudrun, "destroyed into perfect consciousness," sees that he is "far off, in another world," and thinks in torment: "They would never be together. Ah, this awful, inhuman distance which would always be interposed between her and the other being!" (395). For she has not given herself up, and she can only envy and feel jealous hatred for Gerald, given peace in childlike unconsciousness.

As the relationship moves toward its catastrophic finish, Lawrence works extensively with the imagery of the prison. Seeking freedom and fulfillment, the lovers are trapped in the cage of egotism and will. Their freedom is a plunge into chaos and emptiness. Gudrun "felt as if she were caught at last by fate, imprisoned in some horrible and fatal trap" (372); Gerald's near rape of her makes her "subject" to him; and Gerald, too, "writhed under the imprisonment" (319). Their marriage, as Birkin points out, would condemn Gerald "to the mines of the underworld, living no life in the sun, but having a dreadful subterranean activity," yet Gerald "was willing to be sealed up thus in the underworld, . . . But he would not make any pure relationship with any other soul. He could not" (403).

Imprisoned within their own egos and their mutual hostility, the lovers seek freedom: "One must be free, above all, one must be free," Gudrun reflects (428); but this freedom is a denial of all "relationships in ultimate faith," an expression of a desire for absolute irresponsibility. Such "freedom," as Birkin says, shows a desire "for the constant going apart—this passion for putting asunder—everything—ourselves, reducing ourselves part from part—reacting in intimacy only for destruction,—using sex as a great reducing agent, reducing the two great elements of male and female from their highly complex unity—reducing the old ideas, going back to the savages for our sensations—always seeking to *lose* ourselves in some ultimate black sensation, mindless and infinite" (439–40).

In the Tyrol, the lovers are "shut up together" in a "cell of golden-coloured wood," both in "isolation" (456). And fearing destruction, each reacts against the other. Recoiling from Gerald, Gudrun seeks, in the terrible world of the snow, to pass into "the unfolded navel of eternal snow," to become "a oneness with all, . . . herself the eternal, infinite silence, the sleeping, timeless frozen centre of the All" (467). The desire to make herself absolute within the motions of her own will is further expressed in her attraction to Loerke, the man who believes only in "work" and the machine, the imposition of the abstract human will upon the earth. Unlike Gerald, Loerke is in *pure* reaction to the ideal. " 'He hates the ideal utterly,' " as Birkin says, " 'yet it still dominates him' " (488). Loerke's idea of art as pure form, without reference to life, reveals this inverted idealism: the reduction of the organic to pure instrumentality, to matter at the disposal of the human will. Thus Loerke leads mankind into "the sewers" of final reductionism and death (488). He and Gudrun, the two artists, substitute art, the assertion of the human will, for organic relatedness, "disintegrating the vital organic body of life" (515). Together they would become "the God of the show, working it all" (517). And here Lawrence, following closely Raskolnikov's dream in *Crime and Punishment*, predicts the horrible future that lies in store for humanity, a future in which the world is destroyed by competing creatures of the will, "white creatures" persisting in "ice cruelty" (517). As Svidrigailov's cold rationality and will drive him into extremes of perversion and then suicide, so, Lawrence shows, Gerald is destroyed. And Gudrun, tormented by "dead mechanical monotony and meaninglessness," hating a life that is a "terrible bondage of this tack-tack of time," hating Gerald's kisses, which are also the assertions of the mechanical will, and seeking, like Gerald, "rest, pure, deep, healing rest," chooses to accompany Loerke to Dresden, knowing that "death was inevitable, and *nothing* was possible but death." She prefers to live entirely within "illusion" and "possibility" (534) and rejects, to the end, all sympathetic connection with the great reality outside her ego and her will.

So much for the developing relationships of the two couples who move, contrapuntally, toward life and toward death. The minor characters exhibit the same patterns of action and reaction.

The Pussum, associated by Gerald with the carving of the African woman whose culture seeks to make sensation "final, supreme," is described several times as the victim and the slave. She is fascinated by Gerald's power, and when she submits to Gerald, Lawrence stresses that "his was the only will, she was the passive substance of his will" (89). She has the "inchoate look of a violated slave, whose fulfilment lies in further and further violation" (89). But her total violation and abasement are a part of the action and reaction of pride and subservience, for she, like Gudrun, also wants to be dominant. She is willing to become Gerald's "violated slave" because she wants power. Reacting against Halliday, who forced her to live with him when she did not want to, she now wants Halliday "completely in her power. . . . She had set her will on marrying Halliday" (91). Her subservience, then, is inseparable from her will to power. And when she encounters Gerald, she looks at him with "a look of a knowledge of evil, dark and indomitable" (76). Like Gudrun, Pussum wants to "know"; she wants "the secret of him," wants "her experience" of the man who has power. And when she determines to have him, she is "flushed as with battle" (83). She does not triumph over Gerald; on the contrary, his domination over her leaves her "mute and lifeless" (89); but of course she is not changed by the passion. From the beginning Lawrence stresses that she is "very still," and at the end of the "Totem" chapter she is "hard and established," her will intact and unchanged. Her violation and her triumph, her subservience and her pride, occur within the motion of a will that is fixed and unyielding in its lust for power.

The relationship between Mr. and Mrs. Crich follows a similar pattern. Mr. Crich fixes his will upon the ideal of love and charity: "With unbroken will" he forces himself to love and pity his wife, even when her bad temper provokes his hostility. And Mrs. Crich is forced into "subjugation"; she is a "prisoner" within "the cage" of his spiritual will. But she recoils, setting her will against his and, in reaction, becoming "like a hawk in a cage," "consumed in a fierce tension of opposition, like the negative pole of a magnet" (248, 247). It is she, Lawrence suggests, not the cancer, that destroys Mr. Crich. And here again Lawrence stresses that in the battle of wills each partner remains essentially unchanged, passively accepting the willful mode of our age. Mrs. Crich is in "isolation" and has "no connection with the world" (247); Mr. Crich is dying "with all his ideas and interpretations intact" (248). Fixed within the motion of the will, they can only destroy each other; no connection is possible.

The children, too, react. Gerald, as we have seen, "was in reaction against Charity"; as a child, he was "destructive." "He rebelled against all authority. Life was a condition of savage freedom" (252). The reaction toward "a sort of savagedom" is the counterpart of the assertion of the spiritual will. But action is followed by reaction. Reacting against the freedom of the Bohemians, he "wanted to go back to the dullest conservatism, to the most stupid of conventional people. He wanted to revert to the strictest Toryism" (252). Then he seeks to assert his will over matter and over other human beings by becoming the god of the machine, in a reaction that is, as Lawrence emphasizes, the counterpart of his father's will.

Diana's reaction is shown in chapter 14, when she drowns in the darkness of Willey Water—the waters of the will—with her "arms tight round the neck of the young man, choking him" (215). Her name relates her to the "sisters of Artemis," the independent and willful Gudrun and Ursula.

Winifred, too, is in reaction to the love and charity ideal that her father tries to impose (the father senses that he has "some responsibility of love, of Charity, upon his heart"). But to react is to become, once again, the counterpart, and Winifred's will is as fixed as her father's. Indeed, she, like Loerke, is in pure reaction against love and charity. She lives "quite single and by herself, deriving from nobody"

(250–51). She is "cut off from all purposes of continuity," a creature "who could never suffer, because she never formed vital connections, she who could lose the dearest things of her life and be just the same the next day, the whole memory dropped out, as if deliberately, she whose will was so strangely and easily free, anarchistic, almost nihilistic, who like a soulless bird flits on its own will, without attachment or responsibility beyond the moment, who in her every motion snapped the threads of serious relationship with blithe, free hands, really nihilistic" (251). She has all the traits of the modern world in its blind destructive momentum of the will; and so it is not surprising that Gudrun feels "some mysterious connection" with the child. Teacher and pupil meet, Lawrence tells us, "in a kind of make-belief world" (267), the world from which all vital connections with reality have been excluded. It is the artist's world, the pure embodiment of the will. As Winifred likes people to "make life a game for her," so Gudrun, in her last appearance in the novel, joins with Loerke in "enjoying a pure game" (534). What is attractive about art is that it permits perfect control by the human will.

The other minor characters—Sir Joshua Malleson and the crowd at Breadalby—are all intensely spiritual and intensely destructive. Their talk is "like a rattle of small artillery" (94), an emanation of a "ruthless mental pressure, this powerful, consuming, destructive mentality" (102). And it is "curiously anarchistic" (102), for it is an expression of a divisive rivalry and willfulness. In the prison of the dead society, in the static world of the spiritual will, the spiritual people are "saurian" and belong to "the primeval world" (114). Thus again Lawrence underscores the failure to move beyond the blind pattern of action and reaction. We know how Lawrence viewed Bertrand Russell, the pacifist, as the superwarrior, having only a lust to destroy. The mental pressure of Breadalby issues inevitably in the destructive reaction—typified by Hermione's effort to find her "voluptuous ecstasy" in the destruction of Birkin. Will reacts against will, ego against ego; and the world is a hellish prison which can be broken open only when men achieve connection beyond the human will and the human ego.

Lawrence's disgust in *Women in Love* was the product of a number of his experiences in the years that preceded his final draft of the novel. His intense interest in the action and reaction "within the motion of the will" arose in part from his reading of Dostoevsky, in part from his contact with the Cambridge homosexuals and with Russell and Lady Ottoline, in part from the war (the spectacle of civilized nations plunging into barbarism), and in part from his acute awareness of the tendency toward action and reaction in his own behavior. From his reading of Dostoevsky's *The Idiot*, Lawrence concluded that Dostoevsky's profession of "love, all love" was linked to hatred and wilfulness: "His nose is sharp with hate, his running is shadowy and rat-like, he is a will fixed and gripped like a trap" (letter of 24 March 1915). After meeting John Maynard Keynes at Cambridge—a meeting that Lawrence described as "one of the crises of my life"—he concluded that Keynes, like David Garnett and, Francis Birrell, and others of the Cambridge circle, was a "beetle" and that the "inward corruption" of these rationalists and cynics was horrible (*CL*, 332). His intense hatred of the homosexuals might have been the expression of "panic and hysteria at any intimacy with homosexuals,"[5] but it was also, no doubt, the result of his conviction that the intense intellectuality of the group was really a lust to dominate, of a piece with Russell's desire to be "lustful and cruel" while speaking "words of goodness" (*CL*, 367). Lawrence saw, too, that to react against the hostility of the "established world" was to become the counterpart of that world. In a letter to Russell he wrote: "You can't imagine how it wears on one, having at every moment to resist this established world, and to know its unconscious hostility. For I am hostile, hostile, hostile to all that is, in our public and national life. I want to destroy it" (*CL*, 336). Again, he wrote: "Soon we in England shall go fully mad, with hate. I too hate the Germans so much, I could kill every one of them" (*CL*, 340). As Paul Delany has pointed out, Lawrence was actually diagnosing his own problem when he attacked Lady Ottoline and Russell: "After lecturing Ottoline on her over-developed will, for example, he had admitted 'I'm too much like this myself.' He made a similar avowal to Russell, though not until two months after the original attack: 'After all, my quarreling with you was largely a quarreling with something in *myself*, something I was struggling away from in myself' " (*D. H. Lawrence's Nightmare*, 146). Drawn sympathetically to others, having what Russell called a "fund of gentleness and universal love," Lawrence recoiled from the bullying he saw about him, as others recoiled from him for the same reason. Moreover, his intense self-consciousness drove him repeatedly to seek pure unconsciousness, pure sleep, rest, delivery from self. It is hardly surprising that he came to reflect on the laws of action and reaction or that he made these laws determine the form of *Women in Love*. His experience had demonstrated to him that the giving of oneself too sympathetically to others was followed inevitably by the recoil into self-assertion. It had also demonstrated that to react against the will of another person was to become equally competitive, seeking the same power and triumph of the will. Again, he had seen that in the lives of modern men and women, the action and reaction between "work" and "love" occur solely within the will and that the action and reaction between spirituality and bestiality also occur solely within the will. The chief problem for modern men and women was to give up the egoistic will, to enter into a pure connection with others based upon trust instead of fear. But such a connection could not mean a merging with others, which would only contravene what he calls, in *Studies in Classic American Literature*, the first law of organic life—that one is single and separate. Unlike Dostoevsky, who resolves the action and reaction between self-assertion and selfless Christian love by putting his thumb into the scale, thus forcing his hero Raskolnikov to accept selfless love, Lawrence insists upon a right balance of the voluntary and sympathetic urges within the soul. But Lawrence, like Dostoevsky, saw that violent action and reaction constitute a law of the unregenerate men of our time. Forcing themselves by an effort of the will to live by the ideals of love, equality, and self-sacrifice, they react with a savagery commensurate with the intensity of their idealism.

At the beginning of this chapter, I suggested a comparison of *Women in Love* to the last paintings of Van Gogh. Picasso's *Guernica* is another possible analogy. There is a nightmarish atmosphere in this novel; dread and horror mingle with disgust as the reader witnesses the perversion of all healthy human relationships and purposes. The sober joy of Birkin's and Ursula's "coming through" in such a world is intensified by the contrast with the degeneration of Gerald and Gudrun; but at the end, Birkin and Ursula alone exhibit health in this diseased world, and there are no other signs of renewal.

Much of the power of the plot derives from the hourglass form (Birkin moves from illness to health; Gerald from apparent health to illness) and from the ironic reversals that exhibit the law of action and reaction. Hermione, seeking angelic sweetness and light, plunges into diabolically destructive hatred. There is a peculiar horror in her rigid, "static," "drugged," or "tranced" condition as she struggles to maintain control; and the intensity of her suffering and strain as she forces herself to play the role of the pure spirit builds toward her blind reaction and her nervous breakdown. Gudrun, too, seeking to be free and "high," is drawn to a sordid destruction. Lawrence builds the dread with finely imagined foreshadowings: her goading of the cattle, the rabbit scene, and her attraction to the submarine world in which Gerald swims and to the underworld of the miners. Similarly, warnings and ironic reversals mark Gerald's plunge toward destruction: his murder of his brother; his brutal forcing of the mare, as well as of Pussum and Gudrun; and his compulsive work to reorganize the mines. These decent, well-meaning people become monsters or compulsive automatons, like Faulkner's Joe Christmas; and organic life is everywhere reduced to inorganic mechanism.

The depiction of horror might have become melodramatic, and the characters unreal. Yet we never see them only as illustrations. Judiciously shifting the point of view, Lawrence enables us from time to time to enter sympathetically into the feelings of Hermione, Gudrun, and Gerald, to feel their fears and desires as experienced in immediacy; then he draws back to observe them as frightening monomaniacs or compulsives. Scenes of normal social intercourse prevent the Gothic horror from subverting the sense of reality, and in fact Lawrence characteristically blends normality and abnormality in each chapter. The contrast intensifies the horror of the abnormal and of the dangers lurking beneath the surface of daily life.

The imagery and symbolism build the dread. As the action unfolds, the pattern of corruption and dissolution expands, and each image acquires, incrementally, a deeper significance. In the "Crême de Menthe" chapter, for example, Lawrence picks up the imagery of demonism earlier introduced; but here he suggests a plunge into hell and a terrible entrapment, after the relative calm and the open rural atmosphere of the first five chapters. Images of corruption combine with images of fixity, stillness, and paralysis (earlier introduced in connection with Hermione), and Lawrence suggests an entire world drugged or imprisoned or submerged in the heavy liquor of narcissistic sensualism. There is a phantasmagoric effect in this, as Lawrence introduces a "host" of "lost souls"; and Lawrence's cinematic shifts from prison to prison—from Halliday's flat in chapter 7, to Breadalby in chapter 8, to the mining district in chapter 9—suggest a nightmarish flux of events passing without coherence or intelligibility. The inhabitants of this world are like the crowds in Eliot's *The Waste Land*: Pussum, Halliday, Hermione, Sir Joshua, Miss Bradley, and the little Contessa are all like prisoners, "static," mechanical, and associated with beetles, lizards, rats, or other creatures that live in corruption and fail "creatively to change and develop" (545).

Yet the many characters are not just demonic types, but individuals; and their speech, while continually suggesting their moral and psychological bankruptcy, as do the speeches in *The Waste Land*, is realistic:

> "There is a most beautiful thing in my book," suddenly piped the little Italian woman. "It says the man came to the door and threw his eyes down the street."

> There was a general laugh in the company. Miss Bradley went and looked over the shoulder of the Contessa.
>
> "See!" said the Contessa.
>
> "Bazarov came to the door and threw his eyes hurriedly down the street," she read.
>
> Again there was a loud laugh, the most startling of which was the Baronet's, which rattled out like a clatter of falling stones. [97]

Even Loerke is convincing, shaking his flask and saying, " 'All gone!' " then rattling a box and telling Gerald, " 'Biscuits there are still' " (537). Yet he is "allegorically" impressive as the demonic will to power.

The novel would be stronger if Lawrence had worked more carefully with the last stages of the Birkin/Ursula relationship. The frictional to-and-fro of these lovers is perhaps unnecessarily drawn out, because Lawrence needed to keep them present to us as his attention shifted to the last stages of the Gerald/Gudrun relationship. Also, Lawrence ignored the difficulties of Birkin's giving up his job and leaving England. Birkin's relationship to the economic and social system might have been presented in such a way as to heighten our sense of the difficulty of making the break and might have expanded our awareness of the life-denying forces that must be overcome. But Birkin seems to be unconnected with this society, and his rootlessness makes him a special case. He would be a more persuasive hero if seen confronting the difficulties that most men would confront who decide to break with an established way of life.

Several critics have noted, too, that Lawrence needed to deal more directly with Birkin's relationship to Gerald. Lawrence's difficulties in handling Birkin arise, apparently, because he was working too close to the bone.

Yet Lawrence's control and detachment are impressive. So intense was his personal horror and revulsion during the war that *Women in Love* (completed in 1917) might have become a diatribe. Lawrence successfully grounds his attack in particulars, and the nightmare of the modern world is seen philosophically as a manifestation of his laws of psychology and of the moral premises implicit in his idea of health. Presenting conduct that exemplifies "a few great laws" and retaining his essential detachment, Lawrence remains, at the same time, alert and observant. The variety and quickness of life are caught in the formal pattern of the plot.

8

Psychology and Art After the Nightmare

DHLDHLDHLDHLDHLDHLDHLDHLDHLDHLDHLDHLDHLDHLDHLDHLDHLDHLDHLDHLDHLDHLDHLDHLDHLDHLDHLDHLDHLDHLDHLDHLDHLDHLDHLDHLDHLDHLDHLDHLDHLDHL

In *Women in Love* Lawrence presented for the first time a fulfilling relationship between male and female. His depiction of that fulfillment was made possible partly because he had found with Frieda a love relationship corresponding to the one he deemed necessary for psychic health. But the task of depicting fulfillment in a man-to-man relationship, a *Blutbrüderschaft,* was more difficult, for Lawrence had little in his own experience to provide the realistic bases for such a fulfillment. He had not found with Middleton Murry the comradeship he wanted; and "Rananim" lay in ashes, destroyed by the fires of the world war and by Lawrence's bitter attacks on those who he felt had betrayed him.

As the war drew to an end, he continued to search for the man-to-man relationship he had determined was essential to full psychic and moral health. In the novels that followed—*Aaron's Rod* and *Kangaroo*—he records, with fidelity to his own experience and to his laws of psychology, the quest of a man for that male relatedness that might provide the basis for creation of a new, sane society. These novels are records of an inconclusive search. Now, as earlier, he continues to work with the laws of action and reaction. But because he has not found the companions or the society he was seeking, the psychological realist inevitably comes into conflict with the artist-prophet. The religious artist wants a heroic soul, a greater man; the psychologist, aware of inner weakness, indecision, and continual vacillation, can find little in life to correspond to his vision of the greater man and of his comrade-disciples building the sane society. To find the male relationships and the healthy society he seeks, Lawrence needs either to discover a different tradition and a different "spirit of place" or to turn to myth and allegory for the correlatives of his Utopia. He seems not to grasp that truth until later, when he finds in the Indian psyche in America the materials he needs to create his picture of fulfillment in the religion of "the two ways." In *Aaron's Rod* and *Kangaroo* he continues to search for the rainbow within the limitations of his own experience and within the limitations of the realistic novel. These limitations severely hamper his effort to create, in plot and characterization, persuasive imaginative demonstrations of his moral and religious convictions.

LAWRENCE'S LETTER TO HIMSELF: *AARON'S ROD*

The implied thesis of *Aaron's Rod* is that the only solution for Aaron lies in asserting the male will to power and in submitting to the heroic soul in a greater man. But the action of this novel does not demonstrate that marriage and the "life-centrality" of woman are inevitably the wrong choice for Aaron, or for any man. It does not persuade us that love, equality, and socialism are inevitably the wrong way—the way of "halfness"—or that Rawdon Lilly holds out the only solution to Aaron's problems. It does not show persuasively that Lilly's way of "power" will yield fulfillment; still less that Lilly could lead the children of Israel to the Promised Land. Lawrence has created a heroic soul who does little but pontificate and who appears only intermittently in the action. And Aaron does little more than oscillate between love and power; he is so static, so uncommunicative, and so taciturn that it is always difficult to see why others find him charming or wish to continue associating with him. Lawrence's "default of imagination," as F. R. Leavis calls it,[1] is so severe that it can only be explained by "an inherent tendency of the special circumstances of Lawrence's life to affect his perception of the problems in ways he is not sufficiently aware of" (Leavis, *D. H. Lawrence,* 50).

But the question then arises: does the novel fail as art because Lawrence was unable to free himself from his personal problems or because he was unwilling to? Or: was he both unable and unwilling to free himself?

If he was unable to free himself, the novel becomes the product of neurosis or obsession, and Lawrence must be seen, as indeed several critics have seen him, as a neurotic Oedipus or as a schizoid or as a paranoid who cannot see his compulsions for what they are. If, on the other hand, Lawrence was able but unwilling to free himself from his personal problems, then the novel acquires a different character: it becomes, as Leavis suggests, a "kind of 'letter' " written by Lawrence to himself, a novel in which "self-testing or self-exploration" plays a major role "in the creative impulsion" (*D. H. Lawrence: Novelist,* 37, 32). It becomes Lawrence's effort to contemplate honestly his existential situation, leaving out none of the personal facts essential to the authenticity of the self-examination. This view suggests a different kind of art from what we expect; it suggests that Lawrence was not the helpless victim of his obsessions but rather a writer whose probity rules out make-believe as a tool of his art.

The third possibility—that Lawrence both could not and would not free himself from his personal problems as he wrote the novel—is on the whole, I think, correct. It seems fair to say that Lawrence, even if he had wanted to, could not have freed himself from the consciousness of the rebuffs, the humiliations, and the persecutions he had suffered during the war.[2] But the curious form of the novel suggests that he did not want to free himself from that consciousness, that in fact he was determined to contemplate his existential situation in all truthfulness, without distortion. It is the novel as Lawrence's letter to himself that I examine here.

Aaron's Rod is the record of an inner struggle translated into fiction: an effort to contemplate the terrible dilemma of a man who has virtually reached dead end. The novel permits Lawrence to register again and again the brutal shocks to his pride and to his confidence in his beliefs and his choice of life. Like the anxiety dream, it dredges up materials so injurious to Lawrence's psyche that they threaten its stability. Reviewing the past over and over, it raises all the objections to the decisions made by the protagonists who are surrogates of the writer—all the misgivings and doubts about these decisions. It reviews the mistakes that have led him to his present straits; and it helps him to find a bedrock of self-validation, an irrefutable answer to his opponents and to his self-doubts.

Such a novel, refusing to distort the writer's existential situation, cannot be a conventional novel of art, in which a central conflict is developed through probability and necessity to its implied resolution. Rather, it is a novel of the soul's irresolution and uncertainty. The novel, like Aaron's flute, must speak a sound "entirely unaesthetic" (271), the sound of the soul in doubt of itself as it blindly gropes to understand and come to terms with its actual condition and as it desperately tries to overcome weakness and to "come into being." The *sine qua non* of such a letter to oneself is ruthless honesty. Lawrence must not lie about anything essential in his existence; he must not "invent." His position—as Lawrence defines it very carefully in chapter 21—is perfectly existential: he must follow Husserl in going "back to the things," back to his own choices in concrete situations and to the intentionality of his own consciousness. Nothing essential may be falsified. He cannot, for example, introduce quasi-mythological creatures, such as Ciccio in *The Lost Girl* or Cipriano in *The Plumed Serpent*, who hold out the promise of a new life. Recalcitrant existential reality is the subject. The vision of a harmonious life in the rainbow gives way to experiential truth.

To understand what Leavis calls the "creative impulsion to *Aaron's Rod*," we must try to reconstruct the state of Lawrence's mind as he wrote the novel. He was thirty-three when he began to write it and facing a crisis peculiar to that age: "I am a man now," Aaron says, "not an adolescent." The youthful enthusiasm that impelled him to cry out, "Life can be quite godlike—God be thanked, I have proved it," had been supplanted by the dismay, the rage, the hatred that boiled in him after the suppression of *The Rainbow,* the eviction from Cornwall, the humiliation of the medical examinations, and the quarrels with his friends. He was poor, although he had expected to make two thousand pounds a year. The infinite possibilities of life had ended in a marriage indistinguishable from the *egoisme à deux* he condemned in *Women in Love* and condemns again in *Aaron's Rod*. As for his "philosophy," a part of which was burned along with other papers before he left Cornwall, there was, I think, a shift in his new emphasis on power—a shift that reflects a deepening fear of "nullification." (I shall say more about this later.) Even more significant is the doubt, voiced by Aaron, that Lilly is "something special." Has Lilly been indulging himself, wallowing in words, and escaping from reality, like "a man who drops into a pub for a drink, to liven himself up a bit?" (121). By the same token, if Lawrence imagined himself to be a genuine leader, a Jesus or a Zarathustra, the reality was his obscurity, his poverty, his failure to create Rananim, his flight. The blue ball of his mask had been smashed to bits.

The puritanical Lawrence, always prone to feel guilt and shame, heaps up accusations against himself during this dark night of his soul. Hearing the Judas voices of betrayal and perhaps most insistently the whisper of self-betrayal—"You've only been kidding yourself"—he cross-examines himself to lay bare only those facts in his life that cannot be challenged: Not the rainbow, not Rananim, but proof, in his actual living, that he is justified in his beliefs. What he has to fall back on, with all illusions stripped away, is only the demonstration of an equanimity in his soul.

To a degree, Lawrence still clings to the canons of conventional art. He wants to bring about Aaron's transformation and acceptance of Lilly's views and authority. But Lawrence refuses in the end to put his thumb onto the scales to bring about a change unwarranted by the facts of his own life. Nor does he try to demonstrate that Lilly has triumphantly mastered the problems of his life. On the contrary, Lilly is forced to accept that most limited of solutions—"quietness" of soul—for only his own soul is amenable to his power.

The very helplessness of Lilly underscores the honesty of the novel. The religious Lawrence might have wished to make Lilly successful, masterful, and utterly persuasive, like Don Ramón in *The Plumed Serpent;* the naturalistic Lawrence refuses to accept a neat solution. The facts testifying to the "success" of Lilly's life are so meager that we may say that the naturalistic Lawrence assumes almost total control of the novel.

Fidelity to psychic and material fact is further exhibited in Lawrence's handling of Aaron. Aaron's conduct, from beginning to end, exhibits the oscillation between sympathetic and voluntary impulses that the naturalistic Lawrence sees as the predictable pattern of the weak men of our time. One should recall here that while Lawrence was finishing up *Aaron's Rod,* he was also writing *Psychoanalysis and the Unconscious.* Aaron's "love" impulse is countered by his "power" impulse. He withdraws from others, then is drawn to others: he recoils; he is attracted. His behavior is precisely what we would predict on the assumption that the unconscious mind is structured as Lawrence says it is. Although Aaron changes during the course of the action, he never "arrives"; he simply oscillates. And these oscillations in Aaron's conduct are exactly those which biographers have noted in Lawrence's own life.

Everyone is familiar with Lawrence's "unhappy faculty of attracting people greatly by his charm and then wantonly repelling or even insulting them into dislike and resentment."[3] As already seen, Lawrence himself took note of these violent swings in *Women in Love,* where Hermione says of Birkin: " 'That which he affirms and loves one day—a little later he turns on it in a fury of destruction. He is never constant, always this awful, dreadful reaction.' " In *Aaron's Rod,* the scientific Lawrence contemplates the action and reaction of Aaron, "with nothing in between"—that state of moral bankruptcy described in *Women in Love.* Aaron's swings between love and power and his inconclusive search for a more stable life are unmistakably Lawrencian.

Reading *Aaron's Rod* as Lawrence's "letter to himself," one may conclude, then, that F. R. Leavis's description of Aaron as the man "Lawrence might very well have been if he had married in his own class and things had gone more ordinarily" (*D. H. Lawrence: Novelist,* 40) is too cautious. Aaron is the man Lawrence actually was—was, that is, if viewed with unchecked doubt. Aaron is the weak Lawrence, impractical, immature, clinging to others, afraid to make a clean break with women, and using his talent (his flute) only to make "bread and butter." The "Judas" voices that whisper so insistently in this novel jeer that Aaron/Lawrence is a pathetic escapist, fleeing to Italy without purpose, without any raison d'être. Lilly, then, is the strong Lawrence, unshakeable, impervious to petty attacks, a heroic figure who possesses his soul in quietude, superior to other men because he realizes the divine power in life. But even Lilly, the strong Lawrence, is very vulnerable, having only his own quietness to offer as evidence that he is not a sententious fraud. He has no persuasive reply to the Judases who deride him for his pretensions. Refusing to yield to Woman or to the State or to the Love-and-Equality-Ideal, Lilly can only affirm, " 'I am I, and only I am I, and I am only I,' " and this is " 'my last blessedness' " (289). But it is his only blessedness, and this novel, in its utter honesty, offers nothing more in his defense than this stubborn conviction and pride.

Viewing the novel as Lawrence's letter to himself, as his effort to come to terms with his existential situation and to assert his faith in himself in the face of destructive criticism, we can see why the novel came to have the strange structure that it has.

As the war drew to a close, Lawrence had to confront four great problems in his search for a fulfilling life in a world hostile or indifferent to his views: the problems of marriage, of his relationship to others, of poverty, and of self-doubt. The four problems are ultimately one problem, to be sure, and discussion of any one of them in isolation from the others is artificial. Yet this classification calls attention to the brooding, obsessive character of Lawrence's letter to himself—to his habit of dredging up, in chapter after chapter, and in different contexts, the same materials—the threats and insults to the psyche that could never be forgotten.

The novel begins with the problem of marriage. The breaking of the blue ball, in the first chapter, is symbolically the breaking of Aaron's "mask," his false self, that pliable, acquiescent self which submits to the "life-centrality" of woman and exists only to serve her. The parallel between Aaron's view of his wife and Lawrence's view of Frieda is unmistakable; Lawrence's letter to Katherine Mansfield in November 1918 has often been quoted:

> At certain periods the man has a desire and a tendency to return into [unto?] the woman, make her his goal and end, find his justification in her. In this way he casts himself as it were into her womb, and she, the Magna Mater, receives him with gratification. . . . I have done it, and now struggle all my might to get out. In a way, Frieda is the devouring mother. It is awfully hard, once the

> sex relation has gone this way, to recover. If we don't recover, we die. [*CL*, 565]

In chapter 13, "Wie Es Ihnen Gefaellt," Aaron's meditation on the causes of the deep division and strife in his marital life recalls with unmistakable vividness the relationship between Frieda and Lawrence:

> After their most tremendous and, it seemed to her, heaven-rending passion—yea, when for her every veil seemed rent and a terrible and sacred creative darkness covered the earth—then—after all this wonder and miracle—in crept a poisonous grey snake of disillusionment, a poisonous grey snake of disillusionment that bit her to madness, so that she really was a mad woman, demented.
>
> Why? Why? He never gave himself. He never came to her, *really*. He withheld himself. . . . He withheld the central core of himself, like the devil and hell-fiend he was.
>
> . . . .
>
> She drove him mad too: mad, so that he beat her: mad so that he longed to kill her. [194–95]

With his characteristic honesty, Lawrence examines the deep tensions in this marriage and, far more concretely than in *Women in Love*, confronts the problem of the "life-centrality" of woman, the belief that woman "was the centre of creation, the man was but an adjunct. She, as woman, and particularly as mother, was the first great source of life and being, and also of culture. The man was but the instrument and the finisher. She was the source and the substance" (192).

One sees now why the novel must begin at night and continue "in darkness." The darkness is not only the dark night of the soul but also, as in all of Lawrence's works, the flesh, the female origin, the beginning. The darkness represents not only the domination of Woman as source and substance but also the nullification of the male as the separate being, the spirit, who "pivoted on the fact of his isolate self-responsibility, aloneness" (197). The female source seeks to eradicate all individuality, to compel the male to lose himself and to merge with her in a darkness of automatic service of the procreative instinct. In these early chapters and throughout the book, Aaron is afraid of "drowning," of "giving in," of "dissolution of self."

Yet Aaron's decision to leave his wife is just the beginning of Lawrence's debate. Aaron leaves his wife, but Lilly loves Tanny and affirms that marriage can be fulfilling, not destructive. Which of the two, Aaron or Lilly, is right? Lilly says that he and Tanny can be "together and apart at the same time, and free of each other, and eternally inseparable"; he argues that one can "flower" through connection with the female, through "a lot of sensual fulfillment." In short, Lilly affirms an idea central to Lawrence's view of life: it is through sensual fulfillment that the male is renewed, transformed, and given the strength to venture into the unknown to fulfill the creative, religious promptings of his soul. But the idea is not dramatized in the action. Lilly says that he's "got a *bit* of the real quietness" inside him, and that assertion is born out by his poise throughout the novel. Nevertheless, his relationship with Tanny seems to be anything but satisfactory. In chapter 9 Lilly reflects that Tanny " 'does nothing really but resist me: my authority, or my influence, or just *me*. At the bottom of her heart she just blindly and persistently opposes me' " (119). Indeed, the action reveals her opposition very vividly: Tanny sides with Lilly's opponent, Jim Bricknell, the "Judas" who punches Lilly and then professes his deep attachment to him; Tanny jeers at Lilly, saying that he has to "have a woman always there, to hold *your* hand" (101); laughing "riskily," Tanny says that she thinks a "Japanese lover would be marvellous"—with perhaps an implied jab at Lilly's sexual deficiencies. And Tanny's "slimy creepy personal intimacy" with Jim Bricknell is loathesome to Lilly. So in truth Lilly's relationship to Tanny would appear to be not very different from Aaron's relationship to his own wife. And one must note that Lilly's claim that he and Tanny have established the fulfilling relationship of togetherness-cum-separateness is made in conditional clauses: Lilly says, " 'And *if* Tanny possesses her own soul in patience and peace as well—and *if* in this we understand each other at last—then there we are, together and apart at the same time' " (128; emphasis mine). Since we have already learned that Tanny really only opposes Lilly, the argument looks feeble. Neither Aaron nor Lilly solves the marital problem; Lawrence, in his honesty as he writes this letter to himself, can only yearn for a satisfactory relationship.

Does the letter permit him to raise the question of whether he should break with Frieda? Their ferocious quarrels must have led him to raise the question seriously. Then there was Frieda's attachment to her children: are they the spoiled brats who vie nastily for superiority in the first chapter of the novel? Obviously Lawrence resented Frieda's failure to give herself without any reservations to him. Yet he still clung to her, fearing isolation more than he feared the strife of marriage. With a kind of icy rage the novel examines that clinging—examines, especially, the weakness of the male who *cannot* free himself from woman. But where would Lawrence have been without Frieda, without any woman? The novel raises these questions, for which there are never any clear answers.

Aaron's relationship to his wife is paralleled by his relationship to a society that accepts the "life-centrality" of woman. Just as those parts of the novel dealing with the marital problem warn Aaron against submitting to his wife, so the chapters dealing with society warn him against surrendering to a world hostile to his deepest convictions. In chapter 2 Aaron, having left his wife, goes to a pub called the Royal Oak. The men he meets there all believe in equality and in money. The lascivious landlady (whose "great fierce warmth" "enveloped [Aaron] particularly") asserts what Aaron's wife and indeed what almost everyone else believes—that men are selfish; they never think of the children but only of politics and themselves. Aaron is tempted to yield, as he has yielded so often in the past—to the whiskey, to the woman, and to this warm camaraderie and egalitarianism: "He *wanted* to let himself go, to feel rosy and loving and all that. But at the very thought, the black dog showed its teeth."

Thus the rhythm of the action is established: Aaron oscillates continually between the pole of sympathetic identification with the Whole—that is, the female undifferentiated mass and the collective will of a society that subscribes to equality, brotherhood, and love—and the pole of voluntary reaction: the assertion of his individuality and self-responsibility. Again and again he is tempted to yield to "the human good," or the collective will, which is identical with the female will; but behind the "good intentions" he sees clearly the "secret lustful inclinations to destroy the man in a man" (34). At the end of chapter 2 he stands, like Dante, "in the middle of the dark road," and the question he confronts is whether to return home or to go off on his own.

The question is repeated in a different way in chapter 3. Having rejected association with the working men whom, he said, " 'I love so much' " (Aldington, *Portrait*, 75), Lawrence turns here against the upper middle classes, the "nice" people who have invited him into their homes and have befriended him. Should he continue his association with them? As he has contemplated the moral bankruptcy of the workers, he now looks icily at the "beastly" bourgeois, and his depiction of their lives may be regarded both as an effort to deny any claims these people may have on his soul and as a justification for his turning upon them. The intensity of his indignation is commensurate with the disillusionment of a man who has " '*believed* so in everything—society, love, friends' " (Aldington, *Portrait*, 199). After his eviction from Cornwall and his departure from England, Lawrence turns on them all, on all of the English people and on most of his friends, whom he curses as a canaille who have joined collectively to destroy him and to destroy the world.

How can one justify the severance of all connection with people who are fundamentally decent, "nice," considerate, gracious, sympathetic, and well mannered? Chapters 2 and 3 provide adequate reasons. The novel acquires something of the quality of *The Waste Land*. " 'Isn't there something we could do to while the time away?' " asks Jim Bricknell. The pit bank is on fire; the darkness smells of sulphur. It is as if Aaron's journey will carry him straight to the terrible city of Dis. Jim Bricknell looks "satyr-like" with his reddish moustache. Julia Bricknell looks "like a witch." Josephine Ford's licking of her lips "with the rapid tip of her tongue" suggests "a snake's flicker" (38–39). The talk centers on beer, cigarettes, and adultery: it is all reminiscent of the second part of *The Waste Land*—first the pub; then the neurotic rich woman. The hollowness of these hollow men, "distracted from distraction by distraction," is sharply suggested: after the candles are lighted on the Christmas tree, " 'We ought to do a ritual dance! We ought to worship the tree,' sang Julia, in her high voice." These people, to Aaron, are "all illusory" (45). Yet he yields to their importunities and "negatively allowed himself to be led off" (47), whereupon he is treated by them as a wonderful curiosity and is interrogated. Only Josephine Ford seems to respond to him with real sympathy; but his refusal to return to his wife causes her to break into tears. " 'You're wrong!' " she cries. " 'You're wrong!' " In the morning Aaron leaves the house. Yet here, too, his decision is not firm; later he will allow himself again to be drawn into this company and into an affair with Julia.

The dangers of giving himself up are sharply defined. As we learn in chapters 5 and 6, all of these people are preoccupied, even obsessed, with love. All seek to find in adultery (e.g., in Julia's affair with Cyril Scott and in Robert's possible affair with Josephine) a reason for living. Jim Bricknell, the most hollow of them all, is also the most dogmatic proponent of their destructive gospel. Neurotically afraid that he is "losing life," starving, slowly dying, he repeatedly affirms that "Love is life," that God is love, that Christ's love and "sacrificing one's self to love" are the greatest joy. But his endless pursuit of Eros cannot fill the void in his life, and like the characters in *The Waste Land*, he wanders in circles, seeking a fulfillment.

Lawrence, in these chapters, is still working with the idea of the insentient herd, which he found in Nietzsche and developed four years earlier in "Study of Thomas Hardy" and "The Crown." There is an important difference, however, which reflects Lawrence's state of mind at the time: What Lawrence condemns now most vehemently is not so much the egoistic search for triumph or conquest as it is the nullification of self in this modern world that lives by the belief in love, self-sacrifice, and equality. The "nightmare and nullity" of "the swarm" during the war—when all men were "absent—asleep—or drugged—inert—dream-logged" (144), all men were "false," were Judases betraying themselves—is what continues to possess Jim Bricknell and all of the others. Because the deep desire to be utterly oneself has been frustrated, they all seek the sensationalism and reduction that Lawrence sees as the inevitable consequence of the failure of men to develop and to break the dead form of the era. Thus all of these people hanker for an explosion, for a revolution. Josephine Ford, who is more honest than any of the others, wants to say *Merde!* to society (61). " 'My, wouldn't I love it,' " she says of the coalminers, " 'if they'd make a bloody revolution!' " Indeed, she doesn't believe " 'in revolutions that aren't bloody.' " In fact she says: " 'I wouldn't mind getting killed. I'd love it, in a real fight.' " And Lawrence defines the connection between the Love ideal and the impending violence when Lilly writes on the mantelpiece the slogans for the age:

WHEN YOU LOVE, YOUR SOUL BREATHES IN—
WHEN YOUR SOUL BREATHES OUT, IT'S A BLOODY REVOLUTION. [79]

The overemphasis on love leads inevitably to the voluntary reaction—the desire to pull down society, to smash the system.

That overemphasis also breeds illness. Jim Bricknell is slowly losing his life because he has accepted the love ideal as the answer. In a parallel action, Aaron very nearly loses his life when, surrendering himself to Josephine, he breaks down: " 'I gave in,' " Aaron says to Lilly. " 'I gave in to her, else I should ha' been all right' " (110). It is the same illness that afflicts Rupert Birkin in *Women in Love* as a result of his submission to Hermione Roddice. The parallels in Lawrence's life were Middleton Murry's illness (and Lawrence's nursing of Murry back to health) and probably Lawrence's own illness during the war, which he could trace to his surrender in childhood to his mother and perhaps to his surrender in marriage to Frieda in 1914.

Aaron, like Lawrence during the war, goes "dead" in his soul: " 'I'm nothing but a piece of carrion' " (115). Impoverished, persecuted by the police, humiliated by the army medical inspector, Lawrence must have felt it necessary to "stiffen his backbone," as Lilly advises Aaron, and to "get hold of himself." But how? The facts of Lawrence's life testified to the failure of a foolish idealist whose belief in the rainbow was vain. As Lawrence ruefully admitted in *Studies in Classic American Literature,* he was, perhaps, like Melville, "at the core, a mystic and an idealist" (152). Against this admission he had to reiterate that his resistance to the mob was not folly, that to follow them would have meant self-destruction as well as mass destruction. So Lawrence reviews the horrors of that engulfing swarm of men in Herbertson's descriptions of his war experiences and in Lilly's attack on the world that subscribes to "the ideal of sacrifice for a cause, the ideal of unity and unanimity—all the lot—all the whole beehive of ideals." And Lawrence predicts another explosion. As Julia wants a bloody revolution, so, in the second part of the novel, the Marchesa says that the harmony of an orchestra " 'makes me blind with hate or I don't know what. But I want to throw bombs' " (269). The mob that Aaron encounters in Italy, with its "demon-like fixed purpose and sharp will," is prophetic of the Fascist hordes that, like the rest of the modern world, will do anything to sweep away the inner nullity.

Lawrence's depictions of the hollowness and the moral bankruptcy of both the workers and the affluent classes in the society that is committed to the ideal life thus even the score with those who have persecuted him and driven him into seclusion. But he had more than his eviction from Cornwall to remember.

His brooding on poverty, especially on the contrast between Aaron's and Lilly's poverty and the wealth of others, is obsessive. To understand the "creative impulsion" behind the scenes contrasting poverty and wealth, we have to remember Lawrence's youthful hopes—his delight when he dined with gentlemen, his confidence that he would make a potful of money in London, his obvious elation as he approached the realization of his mother's dream that he would get ahead in the world. The dream had smashed; but when a King's scholarship winner is still poor at thirty-three, the folly of his position cannot be ignored. The coal-miner's son, who strove *consciously* to be indifferent to money, said poignantly, just before his death: " 'I shan't die . . . a rich man now . . . perhaps it's just as well, it might have done something to me' " (*Not I, But the Wind . . .*, 290–91).

One must note that Lawrence represents Aaron as being impressed by the money, the luxury, the hot water, and the Turkish towels of the Frankses. Aaron, like the other guests, defers to the money. When Lady Franks asserts that *Ivan* is " 'such fine music,' " Aaron first protests that *Ivan* is artificial; but when Lady Franks insists that he is wrong, he defers "to her opinion: that is, to her money" (165). The folly of Aaron's and Lilly's position is also underscored by Sir William Franks, thrice decorated for his war work and regarded as one of the "valuable men" whom the nation "knows how to distinguish" (169). This frail old man, who believes " 'in a little hard cash, and in my own ability to earn a little hard cash' "—in " 'Providence, plus a banking account' "—points out, a bit smugly, that Lilly's belief in " 'casting his bread upon the waters' "—that is, Lilly's refusal to write " 'with any eye to the market' "—is " '*tempting* providence' " and is putting Lilly in " 'a state of jeopardy' " (173). " 'His whole existence, and that of his wife, is completely precarious' " (173). When, taking Lilly's side, Aaron says that he believes " 'in chance,' " Sir William responds that the belief is " 'unwarrantable' " but at least " 'more logical' " than Lilly's faith in " 'the Invisible' " (174). Thereafter Aaron is challenged by the young Major, who asks: " 'Isn't it pretty selfish, to marry a woman and then expect her to live on very little indeed, and that always precarious, just because you happen to believe in Providence or in Chance: which I think worse. What I don't see is where others come in. What would the world be like if everybody lived that way?' " (175). " 'Pure selfishness,' " the Major says, echoing all the women in the novel who have accused men of being selfish.

Lawrence, the child of a mother who "never dreamed a dream that wasn't well-off" (*Phoenix*, 822), must have felt the charge keenly. He accepted money from the rich, but his desire to be self-sufficient was intensely middle class. Nomadic during the war, he could not afford a decent home. He had proclaimed defiantly that a woman in love with her man would sleep on a board, but Frieda longed for a permanent home. He had to keep affirming that he had made the right decision, no matter how silly his decision might look to the successful people.

It must have been difficult for him to accept his position. Hadn't he taken for granted that his obvious superiority to other men would be rewarded handsomely? And did he really despise money? Aaron raises the question, "Did he scorn fortunes and fortune-making?" And he answers: "Not he, otherwise whence this homage for the old man [Sir William Franks] with much money. Aaron, like everybody else, was rather paralysed by a million sterling, personified in one old man. Paralysed, fascinated, overcome. All those three. Only having no final control over his own make-up, he could not drive himself into the money-making or even the money-having habit" (187). So Lawrence condemns Aaron's "shoe-licking" (205) and seeks to persuade himself that he doesn't really care about money. Yet his poverty cannot be forgotten. In chapter 15, when Aaron sets out for Florence with Angus and Francis, who travel first class, Aaron must travel third class: "They had the inestimable cash advantage—and they were going to keep it. They knew it was nothing more than an artificial cash superiority. But they gripped it all the more intensely. They were the upper middle classes. They were Eton and Oxford" (236). Moreover, like the rest of the upper middle class, Angus and Francis eventually turn on Aaron and snub him: "They were afraid of finding the new man an incubus. They wanted to wash their hands of him" (246). Thus Lawrence strikes again at the beastly bourgeois by exposing their lack of manhood, their moral bankruptcy, their snobbishness, and their cruelty. In Florence, Aaron looks scathingly at the English homosexuals, the old maids who, as Argyle says, are impotent and "can't do it" (258). " 'Go before they have time to do the dirty on you,' " Argyle counsels Aaron; " 'If they think you want anything from them, they'll treat you like a dog, like a dog' " (260). Later, when Aaron's *wallet* is stolen, he reviews the danger of any association with others: " 'I gave myself away: and there was someone ready to snatch what I gave. I gave myself away. It is my own fault. I should have been on my guard. I should be always on my guard: always, always.'. . . Never again. Never expose yourself again. Never again absolute trust" (274–75). The obsessive brooding, the circling back and back on the injustice, proceeds, says Lawrence, "not in his mind but in his soul, his active, living soul," and "thus thinking, . . . he gathered his equanimity once more, and accepted the fact" (275). It is, in miniature, a statement of what occurs throughout the novel: prolonged repetition of the injuries, and then the effort, through repetition, to gather "his equanimity once more."

The problems of marriage, of his relationship to society, and of poverty all converge in the most disturbing problem of all: self-doubt. The doubt is particularly evident in the scene in which Aaron confronts and challenges Lilly. Aaron's assault on Lilly's confidence is devastating: The charges pierce every chink in the armor: (1) Lilly is an escapist, running away to Malta; (2) Lilly is always "grinding [himself] against something inside" him, always "chafing," never "free" or "content"; (3) most dreadful of all, Lilly "won't change" himself; (4) and, after all, Lilly isn't "something special"; he's "no more than a man who drops into a pub for a drink, to liven himself up a bit," as Aaron had done earlier! " 'Only you give it a lot of names,' " says Aaron, " 'and make out as if you were looking for the philosopher's stone, or something like that. When you're only killing time like the rest of folks, before time kills you' " (127).

And what can Lilly reply? The charges come so near to the whole truth that they can hardly be answered. Can Lilly maintain that he is "something special" when all the evidence points to his isolation, his lack of influence on others? Could Lawrence be sure that the rainbow he had sought wasn't a pipe dream? Meantime Lawrence had soured his life with his bitterness. And his life had not changed at all. He was still just writing books; he was different from Aaron or Jim Bricknell only in his having "a bigger choice of words."

Lilly admits the truth of Aaron's accusations but points out, in an argument that follows Birkin's, in *Women in Love,* that one can possess one's own soul "in patience and in peace" and that he is learning to do this. The defense is rather feeble—and a bit sad, if we think of what it meant in Lawrence's life. Lilly says that all he asks is to possess his own soul "in isolation—and, at the same time, to be perfectly *with* someone else." It is as if Lawrence has given up his ambition to change the world. What he can achieve, he recognizes, is far less than what he has hoped to achieve; but it *is* concrete, a positive achievement that cannot be denied. Lawrence holds on to this as his final argument against the mockers. But he continues to yearn for a society in which men have not been subjugated by the love ideal. Reading Frobenius, Lilly thinks of "these old Africans! And Atlantis! Strange, strange wisdom of the Kabyles" (135).

The same doubts are encountered by Aaron. In chapter 13, Aaron again asks whether he has really been the "special kind" of man he thought himself to be, or whether he had not simply escaped from responsibility:

> Ach, the horror of responsibility! He had all his life slept and shelved the burden. And he wanted to go on sleeping. It was so hateful to have to get a new grip on his own bowels, a new hard recklessness into his heart, a new and responsible consciousness into his mind and soul. He felt some finger prodding, prodding, prodding him awake out of the sleep of pathos and tragedy and spasmodic passion, and he wriggled, unwilling, oh, most unwilling to undertake the new business.
>
> In fact he ran away again. [183]

Aaron runs away to Italy, precisely as Lawrence had done. And essentially unchanged, Aaron continues to play his flute, as Lawrence continued to write for his bread and butter, without committing himself to any action in the world of affairs. By the same token, Lilly can defend himself only by saying that he has achieved, alone and with Tanny, something positive. He can point to no positive action in the world of men except for his writing; and like most literary men, he is open to the charge of daydreaming, fantasizing, or escaping.

I pointed out earlier that the breaking of the blue ball is symbolic of the smashing of the false self. The imagery of smash-up of the personality is recurrent in this novel. Aaron, having flown "loose in a recoil" from his wife, "swung wildly about from place to place, as if he were broken" (196). The parallel in Lawrence's life is the admission that he was dead during the war, a corpse. "His mask, his idea of himself dropped and was broken to bits. There he sat now maskless and invisible. That was how he strictly felt: invisible and undefined, rather like Wells' *Invisible Man*.'' He is invisible because he feels helpless and impotent, threatened everywhere with engulfment, afflicted by that ''ontological insecurity'' to which Marguerite Beede Howe has called attention. The mood of defiance, of an almost desperate self-defense, is so strong in this chapter that Lawrence is led to defy even the reader, in that lapse of taste to which so many critics have called attention: ''Don't grumble at me then, gentle reader, and swear at me that this damned fellow wasn't half clever enough to think all these smart things, and realise all these fine-drawn-out subtleties. You are quite right, he wasn't, yet it all resolved itself in him as I say, and it is for you to prove that it didn't'' (199).

Aaron turns to Lilly for peace; or rather he turns to the lily, which is ''life-rooted, life-central. She *cannot* worry. She is life itself, a little, delicate fountain playing creatively, for as long or as short a time as may be, and unable to be anxious'' (201). It is enough to be alive, like the lily, to be part of the life process (here one may recall that Lawrence's consumption had flared up during the war). It is not necessary that one ''succeed.'' If a man is rooted in life rather than in society, he need not be anxious about his failures in society, his poverty, his marital struggles.

But how is the actual conduct of life changed? Lawrence wanted Aaron to ''come to life.'' In sending Aaron to Italy, Lawrence wanted to bring about the metamorphosis of Aaron's soul and its phoenixlike resurrection from death. But the effecting of the resurrection is half-hearted, almost perfunctory. In Florence, in the Piazza della Signoria, contemplating the statues—''the great, naked men in the rain''—Aaron reflects on the ''fearlessness'' of the men who had made these statues: ''But men! Men! A town of men, in spite of everything. The one manly quality, undying, acrid fearlessness'' (254). And we are told that ''Aaron felt a new self, a new life-urge rising inside himself. Florence seemed to start a new man in him'' (254). Later, when the Marchesa responds to him in a ''mood of faith and at last peace, life-trust,'' his desire returns: ''the powerful male passion, arrogant, royal, Jove's thunderbolt'' returns—''Aaron's black rod of power, blossoming again with red Florentine lilies and fierce thorns. . . . He had got it back, the male godliness, the male godhead'' (301). The emotion is forced; the passage reads like a parody of the passion in Lawrence's earlier novels. But Lawrence must find some way to bring about Aaron's rejuvenation, and he works here mechanically with his old idea that sexual fulfillment in a mood of ''life-trust'' releases the male to do creative, purposive work. Thus the love-making is followed by Aaron's writing of the letter to himself, which Lawrence compares to the novel itself. In his letter, Aaron affirms that he does not believe in harmony and people loving one another: "I believe in the fight and nothing else." This, for all its vagueness, is at least positive. Although, as Lawrence observes, Aaron's repudiation of love issues from "the dryness of his withered mind," Aaron affirms Lawrence's now grim belief that life is a fight, bitter and unending, and that there is no peace short of the grave—one can only strive for a measure of equanimity as one fights.

Aaron's realization that "in the world there was nothing left to choose" but Lilly is, in effect, Lawrence's avowal that there is nothing left to hold onto but his purposive, creative self, in the face of the evidence that the "public" Lawrence is a failure. To hold on to that self required courage. The proof of his "success" lay in his actual living: his ability to live life without chafing. To do that, he had to discipline himself to wait patiently for other men to join him voluntarily in a common effort to affirm the "dark, living, fructifying power" of life that seeks to displace "the old leaves" and to give birth to the new (345–46). As he wrote in his essay "Life," published in February 1918, "I must have patience in my soul to stand and wait" (*Phoenix*, 697). If he could not get other men to accept his views, he could, at least, "redeem the time" through the discipline of living.

Unfortunately, however, Lawrence does not use, in *Aaron's Rod*, the evidence of his own very real achievement in living. Not many months after he was evicted from Cornwall and after he underwent a humiliating medical examination by jeering, gibing examiners in October of 1918, Katherine Mansfield reports that Lawrence was "just his old, merry, rich self, laughing, describing things, giving you pictures, full of enthusiasm and joy in a future where we become all 'vagabonds'—we simply did not talk about people. We kept to things like nuts and cowslips and fires in woods and his black self *was* not. Oh, there is something so lovable about him and his eagerness, his passionate eagerness for life—that is what one loves so" (Aldington, *Portrait*, 205). Then there is Lawrence's description, after a severe illness in the winter of 1918/19, of the tracks of wild creatures in the snow (ibid., 207). And there is his praise of spring after winter in his essay "Whistling of Birds," published in April 1919: "And what we are, and what, it seems, we have always been, is this quickening lovely silver plasm of pure creativity. All the mortification and tearing, ah yes, it was upon us, . . . But it was never really our innermost self. Within, we are always apart, we were this, this limpid fountain of silver, then quiescent, rising and breaking now into the flowering" (*Phoenix*, 5). If Lilly had exhibited this "flowering," one might have seen why, after all, it was necessary for Aaron to turn to "the greater man." But as Lawrence wrote this letter to himself, his obsessive brooding on the wounds of the war years made it impossible for him to summon up his old joy. What was most real in his soul was the insult to his pride and confidence; his self-doubt dispelled joy and quick responsiveness to the world.

KANGAROO

Even if *Aaron's Rod* is read as Lawrence's letter to himself, it is a failure as art because it raises conventional expectations that it fails to gratify. Lawrence's fidelity to his own experience prevents him from inventing a plot that can demonstrate persuasively the premises of the novel. The problem in *Kangaroo* is similar. Again Lawrence is too close to his personal problems to convert them into satisfactory art; again he pours out his gospel of power, of "integral manhood," and of the "God passion" as the Way and the Truth that must balance the overemphasized love impulse and social movements based on the love impulse. Again his didacticism is vehement but inadequately supported.

Because Lawrence is driven by his religious zeal to keep hammering away at his "philosophy," his readers may tend to ignore, however, the degree of detachment he achieved in *Kangaroo*—a detachment issuing from his inveterate desire to see life naturalistically: that is, to recognize actual psychic process and to lay bare the to-and-fro of unconscious motive forces in experience. His detachment, which manifests itself on one level, as F. R. Leavis has pointed out (*D. H. Lawrence,* 54), in the "complexity of attitude" and in "the subtlety and variety of the tone," is shown also in his continuing interest in the laws of action and reaction that he had begun to formulate as early as 1914 (see chap. 5 supra). *Kangaroo,* written in June and July of 1922, follows *Fantasia of the Unconscious;* Lawrence is continuing his efforts to abstract the laws of psychic behavior from his own "passional experience." The behavior of the hero, Richard Lovat Somers, perfectly exemplifies these laws. The weaknesses of the novel arise not only because Lawrence is compulsively didactic or too close to his materials but also because he is in this novel, as in *Aaron's Rod,* unwilling to falsify for his artistic purposes the experiential realities he has discovered when viewing life through the lens of his psychology. In the struggle between the psychologist and the artist in Lawrence, the psychologist often prevails. Lawrence would not violate psychological truths for the sake of making a novel of "art"—a novel, that is, in which motivations and attitudes that might work against maximum emotional intensity are necessarily discarded.

Lawrence's complex problem in *Kangaroo*—the problem of creating a moving image of life without falsifying the complexities of experience—is revealed strikingly in his handling of the hero. If the reader is to be persuaded by Somers's doctrine and moved by his plight, Lawrence, as a conventional artist, must make Somers into a brave life voyager who earns our sympathy by fighting for his beliefs and by resisting the pressures of the mob and of those political reformers who would build a new society upon the love impulse instead of on Somers's "integral manhood" and the "God passion." But Somers is not very heroic: far less so, in fact, than the novel would require him to be if we are to be persuaded that he's right. In truth, he does very little except talk and agonize; indeed, at times others see him—and he sees himself—as a "fool" and a "child," a "detestable little brat," so weak and unstable that he falls again and again into the "ointment" of love and then scrambles out, unable to commit himself to any active political or social movement even though he makes so much of his "responsibility" and "manhood." Thus Jack's and Kangaroo's and Harriet's disgust with him are, on one level, justified; and Somers has reason to be sickened by himself. In the end, after being "nosy" and "interfering," after dallying with political and social realities, he takes flight to America; and the novel groans under the weight of all his spewed-out emotional and philosophical eruptions. One of Lawrence's chief problems is that of presenting the full weakness of Somers without altogether sacrificing our sympathy for him.

The refusal to make Somers into a hero directs our attention to Lawrence's detachment and to his scientific interest in Somers's responses to an Australia that both attracts and threatens his soul. Somers's behavior, from Lawrence's perspective as psychologist, illustrates universal laws of action and reaction. What happens to Somers happens in one way or another to all men. The action of the novel traces his rise of hope and his attraction to a political movement, then his intense revulsion from politics and his removal of himself from the "bother" and "caring" of social action—not quite to a state of indifference but to one of isolation and quiet determination to fight on for the things he believes in. Somers, intelligent and well meaning but in many ways foolish and ineffectual, moves toward a sympathetic connection with the political activist Kangaroo (Ben Cooley), considers also a collaboration with the Communist Willie Struthers, and then, because this acquiescence to a collective sympathetic impulse violates his soul's deepest promptings, reacts into repudiation and disgust. He can find no equilibrium in his own soul; he swings from sympathy to repudiation because he fails to find a way in which his "God passion," together with his belief in "civilised consciousness," can be adapted to the world of practical politics. However penetrating Somers's evaluation of his problem may be, he fails in the conduct of life. Lawrence contemplates with mixed irony and sympathy Somers's gropings for a social and political solution that he can accept in his deepest self. Somers's vacillations, his to-and-fro between commitment and repudiation, constitute a record of the normal experience of intelligent people in an age of unbelief: Somers is like us; and the novel, in its exposure of human weaknesses and inconsistencies, may be seen as a naturalistic depiction of a man who is not, as Harriet says, "master of himself."

The note of objectivity is struck at the very beginning of the novel, where Lawrence contemplates the Somerses, as they arrive in Sydney, from the point of view of a group of Australian workers. To the workers the Somerses look "different from other people"; in this land where the proletariat are the authority and there are no class distinctions, the workers regard them with amusement and puzzlement. Somers, with his "Englishman's hatred of anarchy, and an Englishman's instinct for authority," immediately recoils from this new democratic land, whose threat is described later as that of the "aboriginal *sympathetic* apathy." The threat is emphasized in Somers's early encounter, in the bush, with the spirit of the place, which makes his hair "stir with terror" and which "might have reached a long black arm and gripped him" (9). Recoiling, longing for Europe, Somers does not wish to be drawn in by neighbors—by Jack and Vicky Callcott—or by the "irresponsible freedom" of Australia, which he sees as "formlessness and chaos" (22, 21). The "promiscuous mixing in" with others, the putting of oneself "aside" in the sympathetic unison of neighbors, is anathema to him.

But in chapter 2, "Neighbours," a swing from repudiation to attraction begins—a swing, in the language of *Fantasia*, from a voluntary to a sympathetic impulse. Somers, we learn, has "in a very high degree . . . the power of intuitive communication with others," and "much as he wanted to be alone, to stand clear from the weary business of unanimity with everybody, he had never chosen really to suspend this power of intuitive response" (32): "He could not withhold his soul from responding to [Jack]" (32). As Jack aggressively insists that Somers is his "mate" and "one of us," Somers, even though he feels alone, vibrates "helplessly in some sort of troubled response" (42–43). The oscillation between love and power, between sympathetic and voluntary impulses, begins. Somers is not in full control of himself but is, rather, in the grip of natural law, helplessly vibrating toward others and unable to "suspend this power of intuitive response''—unable, in Lawrencian language, to act in accordance with the promptings of the Holy Ghost.

From this point on, we follow Somers's prolonged ambivalence. ''Waves of friendliness,'' ''yearning and amicable advance'' are in the atmosphere (46), and it is as if ''one blood ran warm and rich between'' Somers and Jack (49). When Jack asks whether he can't trust Somers with ''everything,'' Somers replies ''Yes.'' Nevertheless, Somers's misgivings about Jack's ''breezy intimacy'' keep popping up, and Somers feels a sudden ''revulsion from all this neighbouring.'' As Lawrence explains: ''It was usually the same. He started by holding himself aloof, then gradually he let himself get mixed in, and then he had revulsions'' (61).

These early scenes are done with a fine mimetic fidelity; and Somers is like any intelligent, sensitive person in a new land. His fears do not necessarily exhibit the insecurities that psychoanalytic critics find in Lawrence.[4] Experience here, as in most of Lawrence's fiction, is normal, even commonplace, and the attractions and revulsions are what one might predict of any Englishman (or any intellectual) being introduced into a thoroughly democratized society.

The insistence on the normality, the dailiness, of Somers's experience continues into the next chapters, where Lawrence traces both Somers's revulsion from '' 'treacly democratic Australia' '' (62) and his desire (the desire of an isloated man) to '' 'move with men and get men to move with me before I die' '' (64). Harriet warns him that he will be nipped '' 'in the bud again' ''; she finds his desire for comradeship silly and pathetic (65). Jaz also warns that Australians will '' 'drag [Somers] down to their level, and make what use they can of him' '' (69). But when the Somerses are installed in Coo-ee, Harriet is overjoyed, and the house, together with the ''unspeakable beauty'' of the mornings and the ''wonder'' of the sky, bring them closer to Australia, closer to identification with the land.

Lawrence beautifully makes the ''picture'' element in *Kangaroo* work with ''scene'' to dramatize the psychic ambivalence of Richard Somers. ''Picture'' takes on a dual function: on the one hand, the beauty of the Australian landscape constitutes a sympathetic attraction—it brings Somers closer to Australia; on the other, the inhuman landscape is an escape from the pressures of Australian democratic society, from the all-too-human world. Turning away, in a voluntary motion of rejection, from the narrowness, the abstractions, and the bullying of the human world, Somers seeks out the richness, the largeness, and the restorative sense of something far more deeply interfused in the natural world. And in this, he is contrasted with the

Australians, who are oblivious of this richness. Jack, for example, is unaware of "the gull that had curved across the sky" (54); and Kangaroo "saw nothing: he might as well have been blind" (115). Australians, says Somers, "care about nothing at all, neither in earth below or heaven above" (59). But Somers is responsive to the realities outside their mental world—to a child's uniqueness (56), to Harriet's real beauty (62), to the "strange, as it were, *invisible* beauty of Australia" (73), to the "fascinating detail" (84), to the bird that likes to be talked to (!), and, above all, to the sea, the symbol of the nonhuman world on one level, of the unconscious mind on another, of the primal female source of life on still another, and most importantly, of his own "inward soul, his own unconscious faith, over which his will had no exercise" (155). Whenever Somers is in danger of losing his inward soul through sympathetic contact with others (and he is continually endangered throughout much of the novel), it is the sea that calls him back to himself.

In the early stages of the novel, however, so intense is Somers's desire to move with other men that he is determined, despite the fact that "his heart refused to respond" to Jack's ideas of purely political power, "to go forward in this matter with Jack" (93). But this consciously willed decision to move in sympathy with the Diggers is not in harmony with Somers's deep unconscious desire for balance. His desire for collective action is not balanced by the voluntary impulse to act as an individual or by the "God passion," which checks the egotism of the human will. Although, in his quarrel with Harriet, Somers persuades himself that he is justified in moving into impersonal male activity, he senses that he is cutting himself off from connection with the female (95). On a symbolic level, he is turning to the "fire" of the conscious male spirit and is denying the sea, the unconscious source. That act of cutting himself off from the female, Lawrence makes clear later, is linked to a cutting of himself off from God, for "a man must strive onward, but from the root of marriage, marriage with God, with wife, with mankind" (165).

A more conventional novelist, having brought Somers to the point of determining to "go forward in this matter with Jack," would have chosen an obvious plot development. Somers would commit himself wholly to the Diggers, would earn our sympathy by the earnestness and intensity of his work with them, and then, with a resounding crash, would be brought to disillusionment and a poignant departure from Australia. Such a plot (similar to that of James in *The Princess Casamassima*, in which the hero, Hyacinth Robinson, is, like Somers, deeply divided, both a plebeian and a gentleman) is what the novel, considered as art, would require if we are to feel maximum sympathy for the hero. But Lawrence's procedure is different, chiefly because the psychologist in Lawrence saw that the oscillation between sympathetic and voluntary impulses in Somers could not be suspended. A Don Ramón could behave with such single-minded purposefulness; but Somers is less heroic—he continues to vacillate. If he defends the need for moving into impersonal male activity, he has to admit the truth of many of Harriet's objections ("'You've always said you despise politics, and yet here you are'") and to realize that his debate with Harriet has "ended in a draw" (96, 98). If he feels "mistrust and reluctancy," he also feels "the thrill of desire," the joy of becoming "mates with Jack in this cause. Life and death mates" (102). Yet again, he realizes that "in his innermost soul he had never wanted" a "blood brother," had not wanted a "mate" and "equality" but rather "the mystery of lordship."

When he meets Kangaroo, Somers's sympathetic impulse again surges up. "'Why, the man is like a god, I love him,' he said to his astonished self" (112). He is tempted to cuddle "cosily, like a child, on [Kangaroo's] breast" (117). But after Kangaroo launches into a Zarathustrian peroration, denouncing the "white ants," extolling "the fire of sympathy," and declaring his love for all "fiery, living hearts" (120), Somers again reacts. He is "filled with fury. As for loving mankind, or having a fire of love in his heart, it was all rot. He felt almost fierily cold. He liked the sea, the pale sea of green glass that fell in such cold foam" (123). So he turns from the fire of Kangaroo's conscious or spiritual will to the water of the unconscious: he wishes to swim "in the watery twilight before sympathy was created to clog us" (124). The law of the action and reaction between sympathetic and voluntary impulses continues to determine his conduct.

But Lawrence's psychological realism here comes into conflict with his lingering allegiance to conventional novelistic form. The chapters "Kangaroo" and "The Battle of Tongues," even though vigorously written, strike a false note. They are instances of those failures in Lawrence's work to which R. E. Pritchard has called attention, failures that occur when Lawrence "disregards the adjustment of the symbolic with the realistic levels of writing, or when he has committed some 'passionate exclusion,' where personal fantasy or compensation have distorted or narrowed the complexity of life."[5]

What goes wrong is that Lawrence ignores the probabilities in the situation and writes what would be regarded, from the point of view of conventional art, as a "big scene," the scene to which Somers's earlier encounters with Jack and Jaz have been building. It must be a dramatic encounter for Somers, who wants so deeply to find a true leader; it must be important for Ben Cooley too, because Somers is a prize catch, a man to whom Cooley avers, "'I loved you before I saw you.'" Recognizing the importance of the scene, Lawrence obviously felt that he had to heighten the drama of the encounter, had to suggest that two real leaders, two titans, are confronting each other. Yet we already know that Somers oscillates between sympathy and antipathy. The probabilities are that Somers can't commit himself; and despite Kangaroo's avowal that "I loved you before I saw you," it is hard to believe that Somers's commitment to the Diggers would mean much to the Australian politician. Lawrence has not prepared us for Kangaroo's avowals. Lacking adequate grounds for such a scene, Lawrence substitutes melodrama and symbolism for authentically felt life. The forcing is revealed in the trite diction: "Somers thrilled to [Kangaroo's voice] as he had never thrilled" (112); Kangaroo shakes Somers "till his head nearly fell off" (131); "But Richard sat cold and withheld, and Kangaroo had not the power to touch him" (135); "'My soul cries for you. And you hurt me with the demon that is in you'"; "Richard became very pale" (136).

We may grant that, in Somers's first encounter with Kangaroo, the artificial language suggests the imbalance of Somers's sudden swing to sympathetic identification with Kangaroo: Kangaroo's "warm wise heart" is "too much for [Somers]," and he "thrills" to a man who becomes a father figure, a man who calls Somers "boy." But even that justification vanishes in the "Battle of Tongues" chapter, where symbolism and fustian are substituted for genuine interaction. Kangaroo becomes the "thunder-god" whose "fire is love," while Somers becomes a "damp spirit" (131). Then Somers sees that the "passionate thunder-god" is in fact cold and static," "working everything from the spirit, the head," and argues, "in a somnambulist voice," that it is "'time for the spirit to leave us'" (135). The symbolism is thematically impeccable, sometimes even powerful. After Somers's second meeting with Kangaroo, Somers turns back to the water and thinks of the gannet that plunges symbolically "into the sea" and then flashes "back . . . into the air and white space" (137). The gannet's possession of two worlds is a perfect correlative of Somers's desire to wed the spirit and the flesh, fire and water, the conscious and the unconscious. But while Lawrence discovers in nature this fine correlative of the wholeness that Somers seeks, the image remains to be translated into social action, and Somers's poetic alternative would scarcely interest Kangaroo or any other political activist. Even if one grants that Kangaroo might take Somers seriously, the great dramatic encounter of the two men involves a shift from the mimetic fidelity of the early chapters to the "heroic," the elevated, and the melodramatic. Not even Lawrence's virtuosity can disguise the artificiality resulting from that shift to conventional heroic drama.

After Somers's early meetings with Kangaroo, Lawrence returns to the psychological and mimetic ordinariness of the early chapters. Somers's oscillations continue. At first he finds confirmation for his rejection of the love ideal. When Vicky Callcott shows that she is attracted to him, Somers reflects that what he feels is "not love—just weapon-like desire"; there is the Bacchic reality beyond love. But after he has gone swimming and has made love to Harriet—after that renewal of self in the female sea and the woman—he feels "cool and refreshed and detached" (147) and, ironically strengthened by the female, is ready again for conscious male activity. He reflects that perhaps he is only a Pommy (an immigrant) and a fool who has prejudged Australians from his old-world point of view. He feels that, having rejected Kangaroo, he is at "the end of his own tether" (149), and in a spirit of sang-froid, Somers writes to Kangaroo, saying that he can accept and serve the courage and the *virtus* in the latter. While Somers thus subscribes to male "power," he also invites Jack and Victoria to visit him and Harriet. Then, disgusted by a packet of letters from Europe, he decides that he has been wrong to abuse Australia and to carp at Kangaroo and Jack (153). Does he subscribe then to "power" or to "love"? The turmoil of his inner debate drives him down to the sea "to get away from himself" and to seek, in "the sea of his inward soul," momentary peace and the remembrance of the rainbow, the symbol of the correspondence between the universe and the innermost self (156). But he still longs for men who are "*fit* to follow Kangaroo" (159) and, after talking to Jaz, agrees to broach to Kangaroo Jaz's idea of using the Reds to make the revolution to smash the social and industrial world.

His to-and-fros bring down Harriet's wrath: " 'You and revolutions! You're not big enough, not grateful enough to do anything real' " (163); and at this point Lawrence makes clear that Somers has made a cardinal error. Insisting upon abstraction, he has broken "that inner vital connection which is the mystery of marriage": "Now in this revolution stunt, and his insistence on 'male' activity, Somers had upturned the root flow, and Harriet was a devil to him—quite rightly—for he knew that inside himself he was devilish. She tried to keep her kindness and happiness. But no, it was false when the inner connection was betrayed" (165). Somers, by forcing himself into a sympathetic connection with other males, has become "devilish": " 'I felt fairly beatific last evening—I felt I could swim Australia into a future, and that Jaz was wonderful, and I was a sort of central angel. So now I must admit I am flabbergasted at finding my devil coiled up exultant like a black cat in my belly this morning, purring all the more loudly because of my "goodness" of last evening, and lashing his tail so venemously' " (166). He has become like one of the dormant volcanoes of Australia: his suppressed voluntary impulse now threatens to erupt in rage and repudiation. Like Halliday of *Women in Love,* he appears to be a pathetic flux of a man, all "action and reaction—with nothing in between." The analysis of his quarrels with Harriet culminates in his realization that he has failed to open the door of his soul to the dark gods; he has instead sought to act egoistically, as if his conscious will were absolute:

> He did not yet submit to the fact which he *half* knew: that before mankind would accept any man for a king, and before Harriet would ever accept him, Richard Lovat, as a lord and master, he, this self-same Richard who was so strong on kingship, must open the doors of his soul and let in a dark Lord and Master for himself, the dark god he had sensed outside the door. Let him once truly submit to the dark majesty . . . : and the rest would happen. [178]

Because he has failed to accept the divine will to create a new life, a torpor invades his spirit. Like Carlyle's Teufelsdröck, Somers finds himself falling into the center of indifference, the "twilight indifference of the fern world" (181). He is in danger of becoming like Jack, whom he sees as one of "the living instruments of fate," with a "slowly disintegrating" psyche (182, 183): the "aboriginal *sympathetic* apathy was upon [Jack], he was like some creature that has lost its soul, and simply stares" (184). But the apathy of allowing fate to control one's life, of not asserting one's individual creative purpose against the aboriginal sympathetic apathy, fills Somers again with disgust. He plunges into the most prolonged reaction of the entire book: an "inversion which had brought up all that corrosive and bitter fire from the bowels of his unconsciousness"; and it is the same eruption of rage as will occur in all men: "One thing he realised, however: that if the fire had suddenly erupted in his own belly, it would erupt one day in the bellies of all men. Because there it had accumulated, like a great horrible lava-pool, deep in the unconscious bowels of all men" (266). His revulsion to Jack deepens and extends to all of the Diggers, who, he concludes, "gave only their allegiance and their spirit of sympathy" out of a desire for excitement (188).

At this point—when Somers repudiates the Diggers—what lines of action remained open to Lawrence? Three would seem possible: (1)

Somers's flight from all political involvement (a "solution" extremely dangerous because Somers might seem to be a contemptible and self-absorbed escapist); (2) his acceptance of some political movement other than the Diggers' (but could he accept any of the existing political solutions?); or (3) his development of his own theocracy. The last alternative, given Somers's irresolute and impractical cast of mind, is not possible in Australia: it would not become possible until Lawrence could create a world, like that of *The Plumed Serpent*, from which the utilitarian, Benthamite consciousness would be virtually excluded. For the second alternative, there remained the Communists; and in chapter 11 Lawrence does present, half dutifully, the alternative of Willie Struthers. Fearful, perhaps, of making Somers entirely negative, Lawrence tries, once again, to exhibit Somers's good intentions and hopes. Meeting Struthers in Canberra Hall, Somers is again sympathetically "drawn towards a strange sweetness—perhaps poisonous. Yet it touched Richard on one of his quivering strings—the latent power that is in man to-day, to love his near mate with a passionate, absolutely trusting love" (200). We learn that Somers "was moved" and that "his heart was big within him, swollen in his breast. Because in truth he did love the working people . . . . he did also believe, in a way, that they were capable of building up this great Church of Christ" (204). But the language denoting his sympathetic attraction to Struthers is almost as mechanical as that describing his pull toward Kangaroo; and while such language may suggest, once again, the artificiality of Somers's sympathetic response, communism is hardly considered as a serious option. The scene is short, only nine pages, half of which are devoted to an essay on the abortiveness of "human love without the God-passion" (202). Communism, then, is given the scantest of hearings; and Somers, who is suspicious of Struthers from the start, is glad to flee Canberra Hall and to drive round the Botanical Gardens. In the second part of this chapter, Somers sees Kangaroo once more and also flees from him, seeing him as "a great Thing, a horror" (214). The conflict is over. What remains to be done with Somers? Only flight from the political world?

The end of chapter 11 prepares us for an explosion: "Dark streets, dark, streaming people. And fear. One could feel such fear, in Australia" (215). A conventional novelist doubtless would have involved Somers in the catastrophe; Somers's sympathy with Jaz, whom both Kangaroo and Jack regard with deep suspicion, might have provided the means to effect such an involvement. But Lawrence chooses not to implicate Somers in the "row in town," during which Kangaroo is shot. And before proceeding to that row, he turns to "The

Nightmare,'' Somers's remembrance of his persecution during World War I. That long flashback, even though prepared for obliquely in earlier parts of the novel and even though consistent with Lawrence's focus on Somers's conflicting motivations, would seem, to the conventional novelist, an artistic mistake. It diverts attention from Somers's struggle to work out a solution to his problem within the established probabilities of the action and upsets the ''logical'' plot development, which would place the hero at the center of the climactic scene. But we can see why Lawrence includes the flashback. The great problem Lawrence faces, after Somers has rejected both Kangaroo and Struthers, is to justify Somers's repudiation of the love ideal and of political ''solutions.'' Lacking that justification, the reader would find it difficult to regard Somers with any sympathy at all. Somers might well appear to be a self-absorbed, contemptible political teaser, offering himself and then withdrawing himself and wallowing in his own feelings, always in danger of becoming merely the ''detestable little brat.'' Lawrence has to build sympathy for this hero, whose actions and reactions are traced so pitilessly.

His decision to use the materials of ''The Nightmare'' was therefore necessary. It was also, I think, psychologically brilliant. As he traces Somers's rage against the system that destroys ''the integral soul,'' Lawrence establishes an essential link with the rage that the Diggers and the Communists feel—the rage that culminates in the violence in Sydney. As Somers lets loose his ''hell-rage,'' his lava fire, against ''democratic society, the mob,'' he sees that all men will react into ''revenge on all that the old ideal is and stands for. Revenge on the whole system'' (270). Explicitly, Lawrence defines the psychological law: ''The revenge is inevitable enough, for each denial of the spontaneous dark soul creates the reflex of its own revenge'' (272). Whenever men force themselves to act only in one mode, the mode of sympathetic unison, the reaction occurs. Somers's desire to be ''embalmed in balm''—the balm of humanity—brings about ''the inevitable recoil'' of volcanic rage and destructiveness or of withdrawal into ''the central self, the isolate, absolute self'' (286). The Australians recoil into destructiveness. But Somers, mocking himself for being a fool, ''a preacher and a blatherer,'' ''nosy'' and ''interfering,'' reaches a kind of detachment. He has passed beyond sympathy and knows that he must follow, not Kangaroo's conscious will, but the unconscious impulse to achieve male mastery, ''the communion in power'' (289).

His prediction that men will seek revenge on all that is ideal is borne out in chapter 15, where ''Jack Slaps Back,'' warning Somers uglily to keep quiet about the Diggers, and then in chapter 16, where, after a preliminary essay on mob psychology, there occurs the inevitable "vengeance against the dominant consciousness of the day" (307). What Lawrence had said in *Fantasia* he here repeats: "Insist on one direction overmuch, derange the circuit, and you have a terrible débâcle" (309). The Australians may appear to be friendly and harmless, but when Willie Struther's speech is interrupted by the count-down of the Diggers, Somers sees the "blood-murder passion" of the mob with its "many different centres" (321). And Jack's "exultant satisfaction" in killing underscores the horror of blind action and reaction: " 'Cripes, there *nothing* bucks you up sometimes like killing a man—*nothing*. You feel a perfect *angel* after it.' " " 'Jack was a killer in the name of Love,' " Somers observes, thus confirming his diagnosis of the dangers of excess in one direction (335). Fully conscious of those dangers, he refuses to let the dying Kangaroo bully him into admitting that he loves. After his inner eruption and after the great outward eruption, he returns to the sea, "his great solace," seeking to be alone, removing himself from the "soulful world where love is and the burden of bothering" (340). Thus he repeats the psychic journey he had taken earlier: from caring to revulsion to complete removal from the social world.

His retreat from the social and political world might be seen as pathetic or contemptible. Attempting to reveal that Somers's decision is positive, Lawrence does as much to exhibit the wisdom of Somers's choice as can be done through an interior monologue. The "great, healing darkness" that takes the place of love in Somers and gives him "the dark, unexplained blood-tenderness that is deeper than love, but so much more obscure, impersonal, and the brave, silent blood-pride, knowing his own separateness, and the sword-strength of his derivation from the dark God" (334)—this is presented with the immediacy of pure intuition, almost of sensation, in exact and persuasive language; and it is coupled with precise observations of the sea, with the "black, skulking fin of a shark," the "wonder" of "five big dark dolphins," and the "sly exultance" of the gannetts.

But Somers's consciousness of the dark god is hardly enough to cancel out the often disgusting welter of his emotions. Nor can one quite be convinced that Somers is "almost blinded with stress and grief and bewilderment" when he sees the dying Kangaroo. Lawrence tries to heighten sympathy for Somers when he has Harriet tell Jaz that "Kangaroo went awfully deep with him, and now he's heart-broken, and that's why he's rushing to America" (357). But when we remember that Somers saw Kangaroo as a "Thing, a horror," and that Somers never committed himself to the man, the truth is less beautifully sad.

Lawrence's tracings of Somers's to-and-fro do not permit us to credit Harriet's observations.

Yet one does credit Somers's integrity. Despite his rejection of all political solutions, Somers continues bravely to hold on to his faith in the dark gods. Although he does not make a choice in the political or social world, he does maintain in consciousness the sense of balance, of a reconciliation of contraries that he has been unable to carry into action. There is something positive in his holding onto his convictions.

In the last scenes, even though his inability to act continues, his moral awareness is consolidated. As his "caring," his involvement in the human problem, is "broken inside him" (349), his love for Australia awakens. The land, he sees, pulls "social mankind back to its elements" and reduces men to "the profound Australian indifference, which still is not really apathy" (353). There is a value in this disintegration of the communal life. European ideals and work, he realizes, have been superimposed upon the land, but the land remains still new, a "call" waiting for an "answerer." So he is tempted to remain. But he realizes that he cannot " 'give in' " to this land, which, like a female, would " 'lure me quite away from myself' " (355). Though he has rejected the "machine civilisation" and the "ideal civilisation," still he will not "give up the flag of our real civilised consciousness" (356). The wisdom of his refusal to surrender to the female call of the land is confirmed by the cyclone, which reveals the reaction in nature from the Australian freedom and indifference: "The freedom, like everything else, had two sides to it. Sometimes a heavy, reptile-hostility came off the sombre land, something gruesome and infinitely repulsive" (358). Somers argues: " 'You can't have this freedom absolved from control. It can't be done. There is no stability. There will come a reaction and a devastation. Inevitable. You must have deep control from within . . . . must be under the hand of the Lord' " (359). The sea lashes up "female and vindictive" (361), and Somers sees that the male, or the voluntary impulse, is needed to balance and check the reaction. In his full awareness of the contradictions in man's being, he reposes at last on his faith in reconciling those contradictions.

The novel might have been a moving depiction of an idealist's commitment to a cause, of his disillusionment, and of his subsequent efforts to pull himself together and continue to fight for the highest good. Lawrence half wanted to write such a novel: beginning with a central conflict that raises the conventional question, Will the hero, as he turns from one alternative to another, find a way of life in harmony with his deepest convictions?, Lawrence prepared us for a conventional denouement. But Lawrence's desire, as psychologist, to exhibit the remorseless truth about human actions and reactions led him to disappoint our expectations. John Worthen defends Lawrence's "experimental art" in *Kangaroo:* "It is . . . very odd to find critics still objecting to a novel written in 1922 because it lacks a strong 'consecutive thread,' and because its apparent digressions are as important as its central narrative. No one says such things about a novel like *Ulysses*."[6] But this defense ignores the fact that *Kangaroo,* unlike *Ulysses,* is written in such a way as to arouse conventional expectations. Lawrence could not reconcile the demands of conventional art and those of psychology. The Richard Lovat Somers that Lawrence presents is as weak and inconsistent, and as detestable in some ways, as most sensitive men know themselves to be when they look honestly and searchingly into their hearts, those crooked hearts with which, as W. H. Auden wrote, we love our crooked neighbors.

9

From Reaction to Sympathy: *The Plumed Serpent* and *Lady Chatterley's Lover*

Lawrence could not continue to work within the confines of his own experience if he was to create a novel to dramatize the social and religious fulfillment that Richard Somers seeks in *Kangaroo*. By 1923 it must have become clear to Lawrence that to paint his picture of the healthy society, he must draw upon poetic resources such as Nietzsche had employed in creating *Thus Spake Zarathustra*. Atmosphere, incantation, and symbolic landscape must be summoned to aid him: his new novel would contain lyrics arising from the spirit of place and from moral and religious reflection and affirmation. Yet Lawrence could never completely abandon his psychological realism. Kate Leslie's skepticism checks the hypnotic trance. Kate's revulsions and attractions engage Lawrence's interest, as psychologist, in the question of whether a white woman can surrender herself to the mysteries of Quetzalcoatl. Given the enormity of what the European consciousness must give up to return to a healthy relatedness to other men and to the cosmos, what transformations must occur in the psyche before Kate can surrender to Cipriano! Yet Lawrence manages Kate's transformation with skill and almost persuades the reader that her surrender is the only alternative to the world of the machine and of conscious bullying. *The Plumed Serpent* is a flawed novel: the heroic figures are too wooden to compel full credibility, and the alternative of Christianity is insufficiently tested by the dramatic conflict. Nevertheless, the feat of imagining a new religion in such richness and of justifying that religion against Christianity is considerable. The completeness of Lawrence's vision testifies to a lifetime's concentration on the psychological and moral problems of the modern era; and the novel is singular as a Utopia written by a psychologist with a keen grasp of human needs in our time.

There is nothing new in the psychology that Lawrence brings to his last novels. But viewing *The Plumed Serpent* in relation to the two novels that preceded it, we notice a shift in the emphasis of Lawrence's psychology, a shift of real importance for our understanding of the total meaning of the novel. Criticism has attended carefully to Lawrence's moral, political, and religious ideas, which are viewed either as frightening or as healthy for modern man. But Lawrence's ideas in *The Plumed Serpent* are inseparable from his emphasis on man's "unborn needs" (*WL*, x); ideas are born in the passional interchanges and reactions of life and reflect the deepest desires and fears of the psyche. Their "validity" is measured by their correspondence to psychic need. The questions are: What *are* man's deepest needs at this time? And how can they be satisfied?

The great shift of emphasis in Lawrence's thinking about psychology, as well as in his thinking about himself, during the years between *Kangaroo* and the composition of *The Plumed Serpent* arose, I think, from Lawrence's growing awareness that his reaction against "the love ideal" had brought him dangerously close to pure negativism. In reacting against Christianity, socialism, and "brotherhood," he had virtually driven the sympathetic impulse out of his own soul. It was necessary for him to right the balance—to establish a healthier relatedness to other men, a relatedness such as he had imagined during the war years, a *Blutbrüderschaft*, a unison of mates in the building of "Rananim." Consider the contrast between Richard Lovat Somers's flight from Australia in *Kangaroo* and Kate Leslie's gradual overcoming of her antagonism to Mexico in *The Plumed Serpent*.

The spirit of place in Australia—the spirit that causes Richard Somers's hair to "stir with terror"—is defined as that of "aboriginal *sympathetic* apathy" (K, 184). As we have seen, that continent is one on which European consciousness is threatened, all individuality is lost, and a person is reduced to "the profound Australian indifference." Somers realizes that he cannot " 'give in' " to this continent, for it is like a female that will " 'lure me quite away from myself' " (K, 355). Affirming that he will not " 'give up the flag of our real civilised consciousness,' " he reacts against the sympathetic spirit of the place; he turns away in a voluntary motion of rejection.

In *The Plumed Serpent* Kate Leslie also feels threatened by the spirit of place. The spirit of Mexico is a spirit of negation, resistance, opposition; not the sympathetic, but the voluntary, spirit, "this terrible, natural *will* which seemed to beat its wings in the very air of the American continent" (423). Kate Leslie fears that her white woman's spirit will be engulfed by the reptilian negation and destructiveness of these men who " 'have no centre, no real *I*' " (40). Kate, like Richard Somers, wishes to flee from a place that threatens her European consciousness. But while Somers's reaction is endorsed, Kate's is not. Kate needs to become more sympathetic: in the language of *Fantasia* she is, like Mexico itself, too "voluntary," too resistant to others; she needs to discover a balance. And the balance can be discovered only by learning to give up her will, only by opening herself to the tiny flame of sympathy that flows to her from men like Cipriano and Don Ramón.

In dramatizing Kate's isolation, her independence, and her repudiation of the down-dragging spirit of death in modern Mexico, I suspect that Lawrence was indirectly dramatizing his own predicament. In *Journey with Genius* Witter Bynner tells how Lawrence launched endless diatribes against the human race and seemed to be motivated solely by hatred and jealousy. Although Bynner's testimony is probably slanted, the tendency toward wholesale repudiation is exactly what Lawrence had diagnosed in his portrait of Richard Somers. Toward the end of *Kangaroo*, Somers realizes that he must move beyond hatred to return to "the central self, the isolate, absolute self" (286).

But that central self is both voluntary and sympathetic, both spiritual and sensual; Somers repeatedly departs from himself because he denies his connection "with God, with wife, with mankind" (165). Cutting himself off from Harriet, Somers cuts himself off, too, from God.

It is for Kate to rediscover the connection, the essential relatedness to the male, to the cosmos, and to God. But both Cipriano and Don Ramón must also fight against the tendency to act in a purely voluntary or negative resistance to the world. In his treatment of all three major characters, Lawrence dramatizes the struggle toward sympathetic connection.

Cipriano is not a purely unconscious Indian. Although he is identified with Pan at one point, he is "half a priest and half a soldier" (*PS*, 74), one part of him wishing to join Ramón in a religious effort, the other part wishing to crush the world with his own power. Thus the love impulse and the power impulse contend within him, and the division is symbolized by the conjunction of water and fire, or the unconscious sympathetic impulse toward peace and the voluntary impulse toward male destructiveness. As Cipriano says to Kate:

> "Each man has two spirits in him. The one is like the early morning in the time of rain, very quiet, and sweet, moist, no?—with the mocking-bird singing, and birds flying about, very fresh. And the other is like the dry season, the steady, strong hot light of the day, which seems as if it will never change. . . . In the first time, you can feel the flowers on their stem, the stem very strong and full of sap, no?—and the flower opening on top like a face that

> has the perfume of desire. And a woman might be like that.—But this passes, and the sun begins to shine very strong, very hot, no? And the flowers crumple up, and the breast of a man becomes like a steel mirror. And he is all darkness inside, coiling and uncoiling like a snake. . . . And then women don't exist for a man." [204–5]

Water and fire, the bird and the serpent, the female and the male: Lawrence's two lower centers, the sympathetic and the voluntary, are here defined; and the sympathetic is identified with the female, the voluntary with the male. Lawrence is working with what Jungians call the balance of *anima* and *animus*, a balance that neither Kate nor Cipriano achieves until they become lovers. Cipriano the fighter must, like Kate, yield to his sympathetic impulse. He must give himself up, as must Kate, to the unconscious source, must "die" as an independent ego, acting from the voluntary spirit, and experience rebirth as a new soul.

His development corresponds to that of the divided Kate. Uncertain, he is "always testing Ramón, to see if he could change him"; and although he can sink down toward the darkness of total submission to the dark gods, he is unable to surrender himself completely (210–11). " 'We have to shut our eyes and sink down,' " Ramón tells him, " 'sink away from the surface, away, like shadows, down to the bottom. Like the pearl divers. But you keep bobbing up like a cork' " (211). (Kate, too, must learn to shut her eyes—" 'the itching, prurient, *knowing*, imagining eye' " which is " 'my curse of curses, the curse of Eve' " [203].) Unable to surrender himself to God, Cipriano remains restless, his manhood " 'like a devil inside me' " (211). He wants to be " 'a serpent, and be big enough to wrap one's folds round the globe of the world, and crush it like that egg' " (211). But Ramón points out that such an assertion of the power impulse would only cause them to " 'go howling down the empty passages of darkness' " in a reversion to the savage, the mindless impulse of destruction. Cipriano must check the evil destructive impulse within himself by submitting to a greater power.

The learning does not take place until after his marriage to Kate, when Ramón tells Cipriano, " 'It is time you let General Viedma be swallowed up in the red Huitzilopochtli' " (402). Cipriano, uncertain about what such "swallowing up" might mean, must be initiated into perfect darkness. So Ramón covers Cipriano's eyes, his heart, his navel, and his loins, until Cipriano attains to perfect darkness and the disintegration of himself. When Ramón asks him, " 'Who lives?' " Cipriano's reply is " 'Who—!' " (404). He passes into "perfect unconsciousness . . . within the womb of undisturbed creation" (404). And having died as General Viedma, he is reborn, enabled to tell Kate that he belongs " 'there, where I went, . . . where there is no beyond, and the darkness sinks into the water, and waking and sleeping are one thing' " (405–6). It is like the sexual act, he tells Kate, " 'only further.' " Having utterly surrendered to the reality behind the dream, he is now the living god. And as he was "swallowed up," so Kate must learn to be "swallowed up" (406).

Don Ramón, like Cipriano, must also struggle against his impulse to react into pure opposition to a world of bullies. When Kate turns to Doña Carlota in opposition to male "vanity" and in hatred of the men who would force her to give up her own will, Don Ramón must make a special effort to drive out the anger and opposition that rise up in him. Furious because of the women's opposition, Ramón employs the discipline of Yoga to drive out his destructive rage and to break "the cords of the world": "He lifted his breast again in the black, mindless prayer, his eyes went dark, and the sense of opposition left him" (187). He must lose consciousness altogether, covering his eyes in order that he may return to the source that is below the Heraclitean to-and-fro of opposites, below the to-and-fro of love and power. In his subsequent sermon, which treats of the dream, or maya, of the world and of the reality beneath the dream (the great I AM), he alludes to this release from the warring contraries of strife and love:

> Deep in the moistures of peace,
> And far down the muzzle of the fight
> You shall find me, who am neither increase
> Nor destruction, different quite.
>
> I am far beyond
> The horizons of love and strife.
> Like a star, like a pond
> That washes the lords of life. [196]

Quetzalcoatl lies below all psychic division, below the love impulse, which is associated with "moisture," and below the voluntary or destructive impulse associated with fire. Again, in chapter 13, "The First Rain," Ramón must fight against his rage—rage "against Carlota, against Cipriano, against his own people, against all mankind, till he was filled with rage like the devil" (211). The passage is reminiscent of Richard Somers's volcanic eruption of hellfire, his lava rage; and again Ramón must pray until "his mind dissolved away in the greater, dark mind" (212). Still later, in chapter 17, "Fourth Hymn and the Bishop," he struggles once more against his disgust for the world and his dislike of Kate, "with this centre of sheer repudiation deep in the middle of her, the will to explode the world'' (278). Again he reflects that he must pass beyond love and strife, beyond liking and disliking:

> But to find the way, far, far along, to the bright Quick of all things, this is difficult, and required all a man's strength and courage, for himself. If he breaks a trail alone, it is terrible. But if every hand pulls at him, to stay him in the human places; if the *hands of love* drag at his entrails and the *hands of hate* seize him by the hair, it becomes almost impossible. [278–79; emphasis mine]

He explodes in ''sudden volcanic violence'' in hatred of men who are only ''monkeys,'' but his anger is sublimated in his writing of the fourth hymn, in which Quetzalcoatl calls upon the forces of the cosmos to destroy ''the living dead'' in order to accomplish the death that must precede rebirth.

Kate's metamorphosis follows the oscillating course that for a decade Lawrence had seen as inevitable in the person unable to achieve balance through submission to the dark gods. At the beginning of the novel she is almost entirely negative. She flees from any connection with the democratic mob, seeks isolation, and is relieved to ''get away'' not only from the ''beastly'' arena but also from Cipriano, who has ''that heavy, black Mexican fatality about him, that put a burden on her'' (22). She respects the archaeologist Mrs. Norris for ''her isolation and her dauntlessness'' (32). Rejecting both Americans, such as Judge and Mrs. Burlap, Owen Rhys, and Villiers, and Mexicans, she also rejects both Americanism and Bolshevism (44). The latter, with its abstraction from life, is, she says, ''a misdemeanour'' to ''anyone with the spark of human balance'' (54). Yet she herself, like the Mexicans, has no hope and no real balance, and on her fortieth birthday the life before her seems ''black, black and empty'' (52).

But in these early chapters she experiences, almost unconsciously, the first stirrings of a sympathetic impulse. After the ''ghastly'' tea party, we learn that ''stronger than her fear [of the Mexicans] was a certain sympathy with these dark-faced silent men. . . . Anyhow they had blood in their veins: they were columns of dark blood'' (48). When she meets the young socialist Garcia, her response changes from irritation to a restrained sympathy, for she sees that he is not simply full of hatred for the capitalists but that ''the two moods, of natural, soft, sensuous flow, and of heavy resentment and hate, alternated inside him like shadow and shine on a cloudy day'' (58). Thus there are faint indications of the sympathetic flow in these resistant Mexicans; and although Kate continues to desire to ''escape into her true loneliness'' (62), she is drawn to Cipriano and to Don Ramón, who she feels are men—"men face to face not with death and self-sacrifice, but with the life-issue" (70). And Cipriano is attracted to her in "a dark, fiery cloud of passionate male tenderness" (75). (The watery cloud is "female," sympathetic; the fire is male.)

The unfolding relationship between her and Cipriano, as well as the one between her and Don Ramón, follows the paradigm of the sexual relationship that Lawrence had established in his earlier novels. Kate is much like Ursula Brangwen, for Kate desires "the free, soaring sense of liberty" and is "strong in the pride of her own—her very own *will*" (77, 79). She resists Don Ramón's assertion that freedom in "free Mexico" is only a bullying of the will. Nevertheless, like Ursula, Kate is attracted to "the strange soft flame of life" in the Mexicans; and preferring Don Ramón to "the sterility of nothingness," she finds "her blood flowing softly sunwise" in response to "the sunwise sympathy" (113, 114). Thus she is drawn to the burning fire of the male soul, and joining in the great dance in the plaza, she discovers her "greater womanhood" (144). " 'Dancing round the drum' " is not " 'reverting to the savage,' " she sees, for Don Ramón's return to " 'the old rhythm' " is " 'conscious, carefully chosen,' " and Ramón will not " 'let slip the control' " over the unconscious energies of Pan (149–50). Her recognition of this "control" is the counterpart of Ursula's recognition, in the Tryol, after she and Birkin have engaged in "bestial" sexual acts, that Birkin is nevertheless "self-responsible."

Yet Kate continues to fear that her free spirit will be broken by Mexico (148), and as Ursula turns to Hermione Roddice to support her in her opposition to Birkin, Kate turns to Doña Carlota. Opposing male vanity and hating Don Ramón even though she thinks him "wonderful" (181), Kate oscillates. Doubtful and "unwilling" when Cipriano and Ramón urge her to join them, she nevertheless saves Ramón's life in "The Attack on Jamiltepec" and prays that Ramón will not die. After the horror of the bloodshed, she plunges for a time into indifference, her soul and spirit gone. But then her soul revives like a flame, and she knows that it is Ramón who has kindled it. She has been "dipped in death" but has been reborn, "new and vulnerable" (343). Thus she has undergone the death process—death of the old self—that Lawrence viewed as essential to any psychic renewal; and she turns to Cipriano, viewing him as her "demon lover" with "the undying Pan face" (342, 341). Her pride dissolves, and her will leaves her (349, 351); she melts in the fire of the blood, that fire of which Cipriano is "master" (351).

Thus her transformation appears to be complete. Indeed, her giving up of her self-will has caused almost irreparable violence to the probabilities established in the first half of the novel. When Kate says to herself, " 'My demon lover!' " and when she becomes childlike and passive, hiding her face and averting her eyes, mesmerism is substituted for persuasively felt and imagined life. For more than fifty pages "tapestry-work" supplants vital human interaction; Lawrence subjects the reader to pure symbolism, pure didacticism.

It is not until chapter 22, "The Living Huitzilopochtli," that Lawrence returns to the psychological probity of the first part of the novel. When Cipriano declares that he is " 'more than just a man,' " Kate insists that she is not the mere victim in the primitive rites of these men but has a " 'life of her own' "; reacting, she is "in love again with her old self, and hostile to the new thing" (407). While she remains "spellbound" by Ramón and Cipriano, she opposes the will of these men and wants to affirm "the little star of her own single self" (425). Although she has been "dipped in death," she cannot accept the death of self; she sees Teresa, Ramón's bride, as a foolish slave to the pasha.

Yet Kate's reaction is mixed, as before, with her sympathetic impulse. Cipriano, she sees, is not a *will* in his relationship to her, but a *wish*. He wishes to unite himself to her, and in this he becomes childlike and virginal; he is not like the white lover who seeks "her ends," but rather is a man who seeks, in the lanuage of the earlier chapter, his "greater manhood" together with Kate's "greater womanhood." The relationship between them, for Cipriano, is more than love; as Teresa says of her relationship to Don Ramón, " 'It is not simply love. . . . I might have loved more than one man: many men are lovable. But Ramón—My soul is with Ramón!' " (447). When Kate answers that it is " 'better for one to live one's own life,' " Teresa points out that " 'you can no more keep your own soul inside you for yourself, without its dying, than you can keep the seed of your womb. Until a man gives you his seed, the seed of your womb is nothing. And the man's seed is nothing to him' " (448–49). Thus she repeats what Don Ramón had said earlier, that " 'one alone cannot have a soul' " and that the soul is made by a man and woman together (425). So, by degrees, Kate is led to see that wholeness of being and greater selfhood are possible only when men and women meet, not as individuals in a personal relationship, but in "the abiding place" that must never be betrayed—in a commitment beyond the self, in a relatedness to the whole, which makes new life possible:

> Yet Kate herself had convinced herself of one thing finally: that the clue to all living and to all moving-on into new living lay in the vivid blood-relation between man and woman. A man and a woman in this togetherness were the clue to all present living and future possibility. Out of this clue of togetherness between a man

> and a woman, the whole of the new life arose. It was the quick of the whole. [436]

Finally recognizing this need for togetherness, Kate is quick to add, however: "The togetherness needed a balance. Surely it needed a balance!" (436). It is precisely this balance that Lawrence suggests is necessary to the white consciousness. Kate, surrendering herself to Cipriano, may become, for a time, "like Teresa" (465); she may feel a new pride by relinquishing her will, by giving up her old "pride"; and she may recognize that her submission to Cipriano is "positive" (462, 465). But she is finally unlike Teresa; as the latter says: " 'You are a soldier among women, fighting all the time. . . . I am not such. But some women must be soldiers in their spirit, and they need soldier husbands. That is why you are Malintzi, and your dress is green. You would always fight. You would fight with yourself, if you were alone in the world' " (476). In the end, then, Kate decides that she must have both submission to the dark man, the blood, the Pan spirit, and a measure of her own independence:

> "Without Cipriano to touch me and limit me and submerge my will, I shall become a horrible, elderly female. I ought to *want* to be limited. I ought to be *glad* if a man will limit me with a strong will and a warm touch. Because what I call my greatness, and the vastness of the Lord behind me, lets me fall through a hollow floor of nothingness, once there is no man's hand there, to hold me warm and limited. Ah yes! Rather than become elderly and a bit grisly, I will make my submission; as far as I need, and no further." [482]

She refuses to accept total submergence of herself, and Lawrence apparently views her course as the only possible one open to the white woman with her spiritual consciousness. Kate does not accept fully the idea that individuality is not in the self but rather in relatedness to God. She appears to be clinging still to her old dead self. In that clinging to selfhood, she fails fully to grasp Ramón's repudiation of "individuality"—a view nowhere more clearly defined than in *The Plumed Serpent.*

Now individuality, Lawrence had contended in "Study of Thomas Hardy," is the product of spiritual development: the more spiritual a man is, the more is he an individual. At the same time, however, Lawrence had asserted over and over that the soul, or integral spirit, is finally "derivative." As Cipriano says to his men: " 'You are not of yourselves. Of yourselves you are nothing' " (401). The individual, as Kate reflects—though it is "hard to have to reflect this"—is "an illusion"; and as Lawrence comments in a choral passage: "The individual, like the perfect being, does not and cannot exist, in the vivid world. We are all fragments. And at the best, halves. The only whole thing is the Morning Star. Which can only rise between two: or between many'' (426). Again, as Ramón believes: ''Not in the blood nor in the spirit lay his individuality and his supremacy, his godhead. But in a star within him, . . . which unites the vast universal blood with the universal breath of the spirit, and shines between them both'' (458).

Individuality consists in a relationship between flesh and spirit—in other words, in identification with God, who is defined as the relationship of Origin and End. The idea is not new in Lawrence, but this fresh emphasis on the illusoriness of individuality underscores Lawrence's own movement from voluntary repudiation to sympathetic connection. Individuality is achieved only in connection with others or with ''the other.'' In underscoring the importance of sympathetic connection in *The Plumed Serpent*, Lawrence is already turning to the theme of his last novel, *Lady Chatterley's Lover*—the theme of tenderness. Cipriano is drawn to Kate with ''passionate male tenderness'' (75). Ramón, Teresa insists, ''gives himself back to me far more gently than I give myself to him. Because a man like that is more gentle than a woman'' (476). The boatman on the lake testifies to ''the strange and mysterious gentleness between a scylla and a charybdis of violence'' (101); Kate feels ''a frail, pure sympathy . . . between herself and the boatman'' (101). What Kate encounters in Mexico is ''a certain sensitive tenderness of the heavy blood'' (53) and ''the sunwise sympathy of unknown people'' stealing into her (114); and she is touched by ''a strange fire of compassion'' and by ''tenderness,'' as well as by revulsion (82). But as tenderness arises, as a sympathetic connection is made, Kate's European ''individuality'' is lost, and she meets Cipriano in ''the abiding place,'' in God, where she loses her self and finds her soul. Lawrence says: ''If we would meet in the quick, we must give up the assembled self, the daily I, and putting off ourselves one after the other, meet unconscious in the Morning Star. Body, soul and spirit can be transfigured into the Morning Star'' (277).

The Christian paradoxes are thus emphasized: to lose oneself is to find one's self; to die is to live. To give up the self is to find the soul. To give up one's individuality is to find one's greater individuality in relatedness to the cosmos and to God: it is to realize that one's purpose is to act in accordance with the unconscious will of the cosmos, that destructive will to destroy the outworn, the dead, in order that the new may be born, and that creative will which prompts man to build a new heaven and a new earth.

The finding of one's greater selfhood means release from the ego's assertiveness and desire for triumph (or death) through a frictional violence; and it is equated with the discovery of tenderness in the Godhead. In Lawrence, as in Blake, hell is reserved for the self-righteous—the Doña Carlotas, the priests and the Knights of Cortez, the socialists, the capitalists. Escaping the temptation of their will to power, Ramón calls upon Mexicans to be tolerant, to accept all religions, to " 'lay forcible hands on nothing' " (396).

Where, then, is the Lawrence who celebrates horror, irrationalism, pure savagery?

Students of Lawrence have recently been more charitable in their assessment of *The Plumed Serpent* than were the earlier critics, such as Bertrand Russell, W. H. Auden, F. R. Leavis, Eliseo Vivas, and Mary Freeman, who denounced the book for its "fascism," its Aztec savagery, its recommendation of oblivion as the final solution of the woman's problem, and a host of other crimes against Reason and Love.[1] The mythic structure of the plot has been recognized by such critics as Jascha Kessler, James C. Cowan, and L. D. Clark;[2] and Lawrence's mysticism is no longer dismissed automatically as pure irrationalism. Unfortunately, however, psychoanalysis often has the last word. Even Robert Langbaum, who analyzes the problem of identity in Lawrence with intelligence and sensitivity, concludes that

> "The Princess," *The Plumed Serpent*, "The Woman Who Rode Away" move in one direction, the direction leading to oblivion, by which sophisticated moderns seek relief from the self-consciousness that produces sexual inadequacy. These are "sick" works, in which Lawrence writes out of the very real sickness in himself and his generation; of the three, "The Woman Who Rode Away" is the masterpiece because the most imaginatively complete rendition of the regressive death-wish aborted in the other two. . . .
>
> *The Plumed Serpent* is a glittering fabrication, very intelligent and carefully wrought. It is by Lawrence's own criteria a bad novel, because Lawrence does not really believe in his own fabrication; the personal relationships do not ring true, the affirmations are a willed, abstract attempt to spin out of Lawrence's genuine experience of right relationships a religion, culture, society that would make such relationships generally available.[3]

With Langbaum's judgment of the artificiality of the personal relationships and the "willed, abstract" nature of the book I entirely agree. Once again, Lawrence's religious vision is not translated into persuasive action. Lawrence frees himself from the confinement of his own experience, but he is still too much the psychological realist to use the conventions of myth freely, and his heroic "greater men" are often wooden and unbelievable. "The Woman Who Rode Away" is, as Langbaum observes, more successful because it suspends our disbelief in the woman's desire to be sacrificed.

But the charge that *The Plumed Serpent* expresses a "regressive death-wish," a charge often made by Lawrence's critics, is reductive; it ignores Lawrence's subtle handling of the psychological and moral problems presented to Kate in Mexico. In accepting submission to Cipriano and hence to the "nuclear fire" at the center of Ramón's theocracy, Kate is not seeking oblivion but rather that form of creative destruction well known to the religious: the death of the old self, or the ego, and the acquisition of a greater self, a soul.

In her tenacious clinging to her old self and to her old freedom and will throughout half of the novel, Kate has refused to join positively in the religious effort to build a new world. She has refused to accept that the daily self is an illusion and that man exists only in relation to the deity. But her disconnected, egoistic life is a dead end, a horror. She is as negative in her own way as are the Mexicans, whose negative, destructive spirit she recoils from in the early chapters. The only fitting epitaph for this wasteland of the secular world in which man and woman, each in his own private cell, cannot give, sympathize, or control, is the Sybil's whimper: "I want to die." The only path to renewal is to die as the old self.

Such death is hardly regression. When Langbaum, like so many other critics, argues that Lawrence finds his gods at the ultimate "point of regression," he ignores the important role of the Holy Ghost in Lawrencian thought. The unconscious is the source, to be sure; from it we derive. But the unguided or uncontrolled unconscious has produced "the old, evil forms of consciousness" as well as new, creative forms. Kate reflects: " 'I don't believe the old Pan can wrench us back into the old, evil forms of consciousness, *unless we wish it*. I do believe there is a greater power, which will give us the greater strength, *while we keep the faith in it, and the spark of contact*' " (150; emphasis mine). There is a creative power in nature that can prevent regression into the old, evil forms of life; but that force, she sees, must be guided by "controlling leaders."

Kate's surrender to Cipriano is not, then, a seeking of oblivion but a seeking of new life and a necessity—it is the only possible way to give up the ego and the madness of secularism and to move toward life. Her love for Cipriano is thus more than love: they meet in "the abiding place"—in the source from which they derive—in a religious surrender to the will of a god who sometimes produces evil but may produce new life when his destructive/creative energies are understood, when men realize that it is evil to seek to preserve a way of life which they no longer accept in their hearts and which is actually leading them into destruction. Before a new and healthy life can emerge, the sickness of the past must be cast off. The modern cult of the ego is a part of the sickness. Kate's movement from egoistic negation into sympathetic union in creation of a new world testifies, not to Lawrence's sickness, but to his continued refusal to accept the norms of a sick society as *his* norms.

LADY CHATTERLEY'S LOVER

That sympathetic drawing-together and tenderness are also the theme of Lawrence's last novel, *Lady Chatterley's Lover.* In a horrifyingly unreal and tyrannical world, Connie's and Mellors's love acquires an unparalleled beauty and significance. Lawrence's "imagination of disaster" creates a world so much like Orwell's *1984* that all objections to the novel tend to collapse under the force of its message: tenderness is all that remains. Yet Lawrence does not give up on social solutions: Mellors knows that he must fight "the electric thing." If the fight seems foredoomed, he and Connie "redeem the time" by reposing on the great source that urges them into the maximum of being through love.

Mark Spilka's eloquent interpretation and defense of the novel seem to me entirely persuasive.[4] Critics have complained that Clifford and Mellors are "caricatures" (see, for example, H. M. Daleski, Marguerite Beede Howe, or Julian Moynahan); that the love-making is "narcissistic" or concerned (Lawrencian doctrine to the contrary notwithstanding) with "sensations" and "thrills" (Diana Trilling, Aidan Burns); and that the simple opposition of "the mechanical principal" to "the organic and paradisal" is so crude as to suggest "the art of the cartoon strip" (Colin Clarke).[5] But such criticism tends to ignore the carefully sustained tone of the novel, a tone arising, like that of Hemingway's *A Farewell to Arms,* from the sense of the terrible psychic wound inflicted by the World War and the near impossibility of "coming through" in a world in which "money, and the machine, and the insentient ideal monkeyishness of the world" act in concert against tenderness and organic life. The novel begins on a note of desperation: "The cataclysm has happened . . . . We've got to live." And Lawrence builds the sense of desperation in a manner akin to that of Hemingway in *A Farewell to Arms:* key words are introduced, then repeated to intensify the overwhelming pressure of a single unvarying state of existence. In chapter 1, as Lawrence summarizes the state of mind before and during the war, the words "talking" and "ridiculous" are repeated; in chapter 2, as he describes Wragby and Tevershall village, "black," "ugly," "mechanical," and "void" are reiterated. The repetitions build the desire for a shift to a different quality of experience, and the desire mounts as Lawrence creates a whole society that exhibits the cold hard ideal monkeyishness of the world: not just Clifford but also Michaelis, Tommy Dukes, Lady Bennerly (Connie's aunt), the Winterslows, the Strangeways, Mr. Winters, Mrs. Flint, Hilda, Duncan Forbes, and all of the townsfolk, whose attitudes are vividly represented in Mrs. Bolton's reports. So insistent is the sameness, so unrelenting the mechanical repetitions, and so sharp the note of "spite and envy" beneath the surface of conversation that Connie has good reason to fear "nothingness."

Sometimes Lawrence forces his characters to become mouthpieces of his ideas and impoverishes felt life by hammering away at his theme. But Lawrence was at his best when he wrote of *his* England, as Henry James was best writing about *his* Americans. If Lawrence's bitterness and disgust are intense, his response to life is marked by an unfailing curiosity and accuracy of observation:

> Sobs, snuffles, a fist taken from a blubbered face, and a black shrewd eye cast for a second on the sixpence. Then more sobs, but subduing. "There, tell me what's the matter, tell me!" said Connie, putting the coin into the child's chubby hand, which closed over it.
>
> "It's the . . . it's the . . . pussy!" Shudders of subsiding sobs. [73–74]

The child, whom Mellors has denounced as a "false little bitch," is drawn with a fine objectivity; her reality is vividly established in a few strokes, while Connie's conventional sweetness and sympathy are exposed as another instance of the forced ideal consciousness that Mellors despises. The scene is typical in its vividness, accuracy, and power.

Refusing to sentimentalize, Lawrence evokes a keen sense of the loss of old England. Against the ugliness of Wragby he sets "the spirit of the wood." When Connie, escaping the mental pressure of the human world, comes upon the hens, "fluffed so wonderfully on the eggs, . . . warm with their hot, brooding female bodies"; when she holds the chick "on its impossible little stalks of legs, its atom of balancing life trembling through its almost weightless feet into Connie's hands"; when she exclaims, " 'So adorable! So cheeky!' "—and then begins to cry "blindly," (137–38); it is hard to imagine a scene more poignantly expressive of the violation of life that she has suffered and the depth of her need for renewal. The strong contrast between "the mechanical principle" and "the organic and paradisal" is as expressive as Hemingway's contrast, in *A Farewell to Arms*, between the hopeless and dirty world of the war and the purity and joy that Frederic Henry and Catherine Barnes find in Switzerland.

It is not only the opposition from without that confronts Connie and Mellors; a number of inner difficulties also threaten their personal connectedness. The class barrier is always there, as are the fear of nonconformity, the reluctance to "get involved," the misunderstandings that spring from distrust and, especially, from self-will. Connie, who, like Kate Leslie or Ursula Brangwen, "breathes in" art and "ideal politics" in her youth, finds it nearly impossible to give up her old self. As psychologist, Lawrence follows objectively the to-and-fro between her sympathetic impulse and her egoistic will:

> Cold and derisive her queer female mind stood apart, and though she lay perfectly still, her impulse was to heave her loins, and throw the man out, escape his ugly grip, and the butting overriding of his absurd haunches. . . .
>
> And yet when he had finished, soon over, and lay very still, receding into silence, and a strange, motionless distance, far, farther than the horizon of her awareness, her heart began to weep. She could feel him ebbing away. . . .
>
> And in real grief, tormented by her own double consciousness and reaction, she began to weep.
>
> . . . .
>
> "I . . . I can't love you," she sobbed, suddenly feeling her heart breaking.
>
> "Canna ter? Well, dunna fret! There's no law says as tha's got to. Ta'e it for what it is."
>
> . . . .
>
> "Dunna fret thysen about lovin' me. Tha'lt niver force thysen to it. There's sure to be a bad nut in a basketful. Tha mun ta'e th' rough wi' th' smooth."
>
> He took his hand away from her breast, not touching her. And now she was untouched she took an almost perverse satisfaction in it. She hated the dialect: the *thee* and the *tha* and the *thysen*. He could get up if he liked, and stand there above her buttoning down those absurd corduroy breeches, straight in front of her. After all, Michaelis had had the decency to turn away. This man was so assured of himself he didn't know what a clown other people found him, a half-bred fellow.
>
> Yet as he was drawing away, to rise silently and leave her, she clung to him in terror.

> "Don't! Don't go! Don't leave me!". . . It was from herself she wanted to be saved, from her own inward anger and resistance. Yet how powerful was that inward resistance that possessed her! [204–5]

It is the same sort of action and reaction we have seen in Ursula and Birkin; but the intensity is much greater here than in *Women in Love*. Connie's fears go deeper than Ursula's; she has more to lose than Ursula has; and, because we are aware of her desperation and of Mellors's warmth, she has more to gain. When she does finally yield herself entirely, it is her courage, no less than her new-found warmth, that underscores the preciousness of her achievement.

Mellors, too, has many resistances to overcome; he must fight not only against his suspicion of Connie and his fear of again getting involved with a woman but also against Clifford, Hilda, and even Duncan Forbes, whose art Mellors despises. At the end, Mellors is developing his ideas for a new society, determined that his life, after its prolonged isolation, must have meaning. He is contrasted with the joy hogs sprawling on the beach in Venice, and his responsibility is set against the attitude of the "conservative-anarchist" Clifford, who assumes no responsibility for the industrial horror that men like him have created. It is Mellors's metamorphosis in this novel—from a man holding onto solitude as his "only and last freedom in life" to a man beginning to fight actively against "the sparkling electric Thing outside there"—that is ignored when a critic like Wayne C. Booth tells us that it is impossible to take seriously Mellors's belief that the world will "come all right" if there is more "warm-hearted fucking."[6] Through sympathetic connection—through tenderness—Mellors is reborn as an individual wishing to fight "side by side" with other men. And Connie supports him in his stubborn determination.

As Lawrence creates this persuasively real world and builds his action toward its inevitable conclusion, he creates a plot that verges on allegory. The damsel, imprisoned by the ogre, drugged by the poisoned apple of knowledge, is awakened by the prince who emerges from the green world. The ogre is robbed of his prize. That allegory of the awakening to life, which Lawrence introduced tentatively in his portrayal of Clara Dawes in *Sons and Lover* and continued in *The Rainbow, The Lost Girl, Women in Love, The Plumed Serpent,* and *The Virgin and the Gipsy,* is presented here with perfect psychological realism. Lawrence normalizes, at last, his mystical vision. The mystical "flowing together" into oneness becomes tenderness of contact. Acceptance of desire and natural fulfillment constitutes a precious release from the intolerable isolation, loneliness, and abstraction of

modern life. Connie and Mellors "flow together" not mystically but humanly; yet Lawrence also suggests that they are instruments of the great impersonal will of nature, objectified in John Thomas and Lady Jane. Their union gives them peace; and "flowing apart," they are ready to fight for a new way of life. In union and separation, in sexual intercourse and in chastity, the rhythms of nature are manifested. At the end, Mellors realizes that his chastity, after the period of warm-hearted fucking, gives him peace in his soul: "Now is the time to be chaste, it is so good to be chaste, like a river of cool water in my soul. I love the chastity now that it flows between us. It is like fresh water and rain" (355). Fire and water, summer and winter, love and power, surrender and fighting—these are the vital oppositions, originating in the primal unknown and objectified in the psyche, that must be held in balance, in a natural rhythm, if men and women are to move out of the dead world and into the new.

Thus once again Lawrence's psychology blends with his religious vision in a realistic image of life. The voices of his three angels—scientific, didactic, and mimetic—have never before been so well blended. What is unique in *Lady Chatterley's Lover* is the humanity of the characters. Even Clifford, so far from being a caricature, is humanly plausible.[7] The sharp contrast between his external control and his inner disintegration is presented with sufficient sympathy to dispel the grotesquery of a Dickensian caricature:

> But he had been so much hurt that something inside him had perished, some of his feelings had gone. There was a blank of insentience. [10]
>
> "Does it matter very much? . . . It's what endures through one's life that matters; . . . It's the living together from day to day, not the sleeping together once or twice. You and I are married, no matter what happens to us. . . . You and I are interwoven in a marriage." [56–57]
>
> But his dread was the nights when he could not sleep. Then it was awful indeed, when annihilation pressed in on him on every side. Then it was ghastly, to exist without having any life: lifeless, in the night, to exist. [167]

Objectively Lawrence presents Clifford's state of mind before his injury: his uneasiness joined to a modern sense of absurdity. Seeing the world as ridiculous, he fears above all being ridiculous himself:

> Clifford only smiled a little uneasily. Everything was ridiculous, quite true. But when it came too close and oneself became ridiculous too . . . ?

> Clifford felt his father was a hopeless anachronism. But wherein was he himself any further ahead, except in a wincing sense of the ridiculousness of everything, and the paramount ridiculousness of his own position? [16–17]

It is impossible not to recognize, and vaguely to sympathize with, his problem: he suffers the skepticism and disillusionment of intelligent men in our time. Yet he is a monster: a unique horror is created as we witness the ugliness of his fixed will, which masquerades as control and graciousness, and his plunge into abstraction and intoxication in his resort to the wireless, to gambling, and to the madness of running the mines.

In handling Clifford's relationship with Mrs. Bolton, Lawrence again examines the symbiosis of pride and subservience that he had explored in *Women in Love*. Clifford enjoys educating Mrs. Bolton because "it gave him a sense of power" (93). And she, to get Clifford in her power, "put herself absolutely at his service, for him to use as he liked" (93). Her subservience eventually gives her complete control over him, and he, "letting go all his manhood," submits to her as Magna Mater. The master becomes child and slave; yet this regressive submission ironically gives him "a certain remarkable inhuman force" in business (273). Infantilism and pride go hand in hand, both expressions of the egoistic will to omnipotence. Yet one never feels that Clifford or Mrs. Bolton is forced to obey the Lawrencian laws of action and reaction. Clifford's infantilism is entirely plausible. He remains himself. Even his revenge on Connie and Mellors is appropriately genteel.

The characterization of Mellors is equally strong. He is like many tough-minded men of integrity and ability who cannot flourish in a society that they despise in their hearts. His marriage has failed; his career is dead; he is physically frail. Yet he remains capable and stubbornly courageous, retaining his dignity even in his subservient position. "Odd" but convincingly normal, he is more interesting humanly than any other of Lawrence's heroes, with the possible exception of Paul Morel. By comparison, Somers, Birkin, and Cipriano strike one as abnormal, even slightly unsavory, because they lack Mellors's sturdy common sense and tenderness. And Connie is sensitive, normal, and considerate, but spunky too, created with a sympathetic touch that one does not feel in Lawrence's creation of Ursula or Kate Leslie. The "philosophical" Lawrence, contemplator of the inhuman forces in experience, is here so responsive to the human problems of his hero and heroine that it is difficult to enter into the spirit of any criticism that condemns Mellors as a "caricature" and the novel as a mechanical expression of what Lawrence had done spontaneously in his earlier work. Grounded in particulars that are presented with a fine mimetic fidelity, *Lady Chatterley's Lover* is incomparable in its dynamic power as a serious image of life that moves through pity and fear to a sober joy, and as a didactic work demonstrating the horror of materialism-mechanism-idealism and the beauty of sympathetic connection, organic vitality, and acceptance of the rhythms of nature.

10

The Psychologist as Psychologist

Always this same morbid interest in other people and their doings, their privacies, their dirty linen. Always this air of alertness for personal happenings, personalities, personalities, personalities. Always this subtle criticism and appraisal of other people, this analysis of other people's motives. If anatomy presupposes a corpse, then psychology presupposes a world of corpses. Personalities, which means personal criticism and analysis, presupposes a whole world-laboratory of human psyches waiting to be vivisected. If you cut a thing up, of course it will smell. Hence, nothing raises such an infernal stink, at last, as human psychology.

—"St. Mawr"

A religious attitude is an element in psychic life whose importance can hardly be overrated.

—C. G. Jung

It is easy to understand Lawrence's disgust with that "infernal stink" of human psychology. A fine psychologist himself, he would cut up corpses when he wanted to. What distinguishes him from most psychologists, however, is an awareness that man is not just a personality, not just human, but an objectification of the inhuman forces that work through all of nature and, as such, a living mystery, a soul that inhales the rest of the universe and exhales the universe transformed. He is an individual, to be sure; but, individuality is finally an illusion, and the psychologists who stress self-realization are prone to omit that profound relatedness in which man resides.

If we are to understand the reach and subtlety of Lawrence's thinking, then, as well as the limitations of his insights, we need to bring his psychology into comparison not only with psychologies that stress man's instinctive and unconscious motivations or the processes of socialization that form his social consciousness but also with those that stress a religious dimension in human experience. Lawrence himself explicitly endorsed this dimension when he said in 1925, speaking of Hindu thought, "That seems to me the true psychology, how shallow and groping it makes Western psychology seem."[1] Jung comes to mind at once. The affinities of his thought to Lawrence's have been noted by several critics. Also striking are certain parallels in Lawrence's thinking to that of Erich Fromm, who has sought to combine an existential-biological view with a sociological and a religious perspective. My purpose is not simply to examine parallels, however. The question is whether Lawrence makes a genuine contribution to psychological theory. It will be helpful to begin by considering Lawrence's comment on the "infernal stink" of human psychology.

Lawrence questions whether the psyche and its life can be divorced from its deep relationships with society, nature, and the infinite. A psychology that isolates "self" from the historical and social matrix in which "selfhood" arises, or from the biological sources of motivation, is hopelessly subjective. Ego psychologies tend to assume that the individual is independent, the potential master of his fate, and are thus prone to ignore both the social-historical conditioning and the biological "programming" that become a part of human "second nature," if not of "primal nature." The tendency to abstract the self from its social reality is, as Herbert Marcuse and Russell Jacoby have pointed out, both a regression to a pre-Freudian psychology and an illustration of the process of "reification," which is peculiar to bourgeois society with its emphasis on the "free individual" and his "free enterprise."[2] The tendency to abstract the individual from his biological inheritance—to consider him as a rational psyche capable of modifying his innate drives—suggests a similar regression.

Yet a behaviorism that reduces man to his instinctual drives ignores subjectivity altogether and explains all human activity as deriving from primordial impulses or conditioned reflexes. Such a psychology abstracts human behavior from historical and cultural patterns and denies the vitalist idea of purposiveness and striving, as well as the existential idea of action grounded in "the human condition." It may thus fail to take into account the extent to which human behavior is modified by social relations or by existential awareness.

The great danger, therefore, is always that psychology will perpetuate a myth of isolation, abstracting from the totality of detail only those facts relevant to the "self" or relevant to physiology and ignoring, in its explanations of conduct, facts derived from economics, sociology, religion, philosophy, and other disciplines.

A usual objection to Lawrence's psychology, as to Freud's, is that it ignores social and cultural determinants and is narrowly fixed on genetic causes. Even the most careful of critics tend to oversimplify Lawrence's psychology. Philip Rieff, for example, speaks of Lawrence's "advocacy of the impulsive Unconscious,"[3] forgetting the important qualification of the Holy Ghost's insistence on balance. "It was futile, if not dangerous," Rieff writes, "for Lawrence to insist as he did that men ought not arbitrate their passions, primarily through their analytic intelligences, or even postpone them" (210–11). In the same vein, Aidan Burns warns against Lawrence's putative jettisoning of reason and judgment: "When the faculty of judgment is jettisoned it is impossible to tell super-reason from sub-reason or super-sense from nonsense" (*Nature and Culture*, 10–11). Such a view ignores Lawrence's important idea that nature itself seeks a balance and that the Holy Ghost, voice of the whole self (upper centers included), counsels balance.

Again Rieff, like many other critics, regards Lawrence as a proponent of "the irrational power of love" (212), but this half-truth does the greatest violence to Lawrence's thought. He was not the Priest of Love but the Priest of Love and Power; nor does he recommend, as Rieff claims, "a condition of innocence, a return to that naïveté which can persist beyond the oceanic feelings of identity known at times to mystics and perhaps (Lawrence thought) to life in the womb" (218). Rieff's cardinal error is that he thinks of the Holy Ghost as the "power of love" (229).

Similarly, Elizabeth Brody Tenenbaum, in *The Problematic Self*, argues that "Lawrentian doctrine forbids any attempt to resist a natural impulse."[4] She argues that Lawrence contradicts himself, for on the one hand he says, "I shall never know wherein lies my integrity, my individuality, my me," and on the other he "stresses the importance of trying to understand one's own nature" (73). But there is no contradiction: Lawrence is simply arguing that one must understand oneself as part of the Unknowable Reality. Such understanding permits one to be oneself—that is, to be a spark of the great process, a creature whose "individuality" is finally illusory. Again, Tenenbaum argues that Lawrence contradicts himself when he says that the desire for masculine independence and achievement does not square with his notion that man's primary goal is communal and that in realizing such a goal "we forfeit the individual" (107). Here she fails to make a basic distinction between egoistic and nonegoistic independence. The sort of independence that Lawrence advocates is resistance to false communal organization and a refusal to identify with any community fixed in a life-denying way of life.

Yet again, Eugene Goodheart, in a standard attack, argues that Lawrence accepted the way of immanence and denied the reality of the self as a finite historical being.[5] The Marxist critic Scott Sanders makes a similar charge, condemning Lawrence not, however, for accepting the way of immanence but for his subjectivism.[6] In condemning the individual who denies "the God within him," Lawrence, says Sanders, divorces that individual from the objective conditions that determine his social being. Still another critic, representative of recent psychoanalytic interpreters of Lawrence, views Lawrence as emphasizing identity and ontological insecurity, as if Lawrence's psychology were exclusively an ego psychology stressing a Laingian fear of engulfment by external forces and as if Lawrence's analysis of man's biological inheritance were beside the point.[7] Lawrence himself is explained, accordingly, as an ontologically insecure person or, as Delavenay holds, an escapist, a regressive or narcissistic personality seeking return to the womb.

The differences in these criticisms suggest that we have not seen Lawrence's psychology whole. Modern subjectivism in psychology either lauds the subjectivist emphases in Lawrence or condemns him because he was a reductionist, tracing all human behavior to electromagnetic oscillations. Marxist objectivism not only condemns Lawrence because he ignores the social relations that determine human action but also sees his emphasis on God as another reification of bourgeois thought.

This either/or thinking distorts his subtle psychology. In truth, Lawrence sees that man is a biological creature, a social creature, *and* "an individual," while adding that individuality is finally an illusion and that "self" cannot be divorced from the infinite. But how, then, shall we characterize Lawrence's psychology? "Religious behaviorism"—T. S. Eliot's phrase—is not accurate because behaviorism eschews normative standards and is indifferent to free will and responsibility: it is finally a form of mechanistic materialism that Lawrence condemns as inapplicable to organic life. "Mystical materialism"—Aldous Huxley's phrase—also seems to ignore the role of the Holy Ghost. On the other hand, Lawrence is not an existential psychologist; for although he stresses human freedom and responsibility, he does not locate these in a conscious self that seeks to create its essence. Existentialism denies biology, or the unconscious. May's idea of a conscious ego exerting its will and controlling man's destiny Lawrence would have rejected altogether as being another form of "working ourselves from the head."[8] Lawrence would have been appalled, too, by Viktor E. Frankl's logotherapy, which proclaims that the ego is "the boss, who chooses the best 'forces' [from the id] for its purposes"—that it is "the personal center and spiritual core around which are grouped the peripheral layers of psychological 'creaturality' and of instinctuality, the id."[9] Freedom and responsibility, in Lawrence, derive not from such an imperial ego but from an innate purposiveness in highly developed individuals. Choice is both conscious and unconscious, and the religious chooser is not an ego; instead, he is a spokesman for "a greater power" that seeks natural balance, not egoistic control.

In truth, Lawrence's psychology illustrates the prevailing tension in psychology itself—the tension between Freudian instinctualism and neo-Freudian revisionism, which argues that the "total personality," largely shaped by culture and interpersonal relationships, is capable of optimal development or realization of its potentialities. On the one hand, Lawrence accepts that the roots of the psyche are the great creative and destructive energies of nature; and although Lawrence denies that he is a determinist, he sees man as the manifestation of these energies. Thus he holds to "hormic" psychology. On the other hand, Lawrence insists that there is an integral self—the Holy Ghost—whose action is not determined purely by instinct or by the introjected repression of the conservative psyche but also by a free will which is the voice of the whole self, a creative or religious power found in higher man. The Holy Ghost can guide man to a wise balance against the one-sidedness of cultural conditioning or repression.

Freudians would say that Lawrence cannot have it both ways: a psyche cannot be determined phylogenetically and ontogenetically and also be autonomous. Lawrence, however, does not claim that all men are capable of autonomous behavior; on the contrary, he maintains that only the superior man has such ability. Autonomy is a function of an extraordinary religious creativity, of highly developed sympathetic and power instincts, together with highly developed intuitive powers.

This view of the psyche can scarcely be dismissed as romantic irrationalism or simple mysticism. But to grasp its strengths and limitations, we need to compare it with a number of other psychologies that have won widespread acceptance.

FREUD

Lawrence's quarrel with Freud, as well as the congruencies between Freudian and Lawrencian ideas, has been examined by a number of scholars, notably Frederick J. Hoffman, Philip Rieff, and James C. Cowan; but it will be helpful to review the parallels and disagreements in their theories in the light of the first three chapters.

Lawrence's sympathetic impulse has obvious affinities to Freud's Eros instinct, which is not, as Lawrence mistakenly thought, exclusively sexual but seeks "to combine organic substances into ever larger units and to preserve them thus—in short, to bind together.''[10] As Lawrence argued that man's deepest desire is for unanimity with the whole of purposive mankind, so Freud contended that ''culture obeys an inner erotic impulse which bids it bind mankind into a closely knit mass.''[11] Another interesting correspondence between Freudian and Lawrencian ideas has been noted by James C. Cowan, who has shown that Lawrence's conception of the four centers of the unconscious is paralleled by Freud's idea of oral, anal, and phallic stages in sexual development (*D. H. Lawrence's American Journey*, 17–19). Again, Lawrence's idea of the desire for death perhaps corresponds roughly to the Freudian death instinct; and a remote kinship exists between Lawrence's idea that life always seeks a balance of sympathetic and voluntary impulses and Freud's ''principle of conservation,'' the idea that life strives for equilibrium and that both Eros and Thanatos are manifestations of a deep resistance to extremes of tension.

Yet Lawrence would have disagreed with the Freudian conservation principle. For Lawrence, life does not seek equilibrium through return to a prior state of being, a return to the womb or the tomb. The seeking of equilibrium in Lawrence is always a vital striving for balance and maximum of being. Freudian critics claim that what Lawrence sought was precisely the bliss of Nirvana in the womb/tomb of the female, who is an embodiment of Eros and Thanatos; Lawrence recognized that desire in himself, but he fought against it, insisting that the healthy power impulse counters the desire for a regressive submission. To Daniel Weiss, that counterassertion is evidence of an anti-oedipal reaction;[12] for Lawrence, such a reaction is a striving for balance.

Lawrence's picture of the repressive forces in modern civilization is as bold and sensitive as Freud's. Lawrence certainly shared Freud's view that ''the more a man checks his aggressive tendencies toward others the more tyrannical, that is aggressive, he becomes in his ego-ideal'';[13] ''every impulse of aggression which we omit to gratify is taken over by the super-ego and goes to heighten its aggressiveness (against the ego).''[14] Repressed aggression returns in the form of the capitalistic domination and exploitation of the environment; it also returns in the self-destructive personality of a Gerald Crich who, unable to love, pursues his own death. Thus the progress of civilization, which is progress in repression, leads inevitably, Lawrence contended, to ever-more-violent reactions into sadism and tyranny. ''Bullying'' becomes a way of life. In the reaction from the repressiveness of the love and benevolence ideal, the psyche strikes out blindly and viciously, seeking the unique modern anarchy of sensationalism and reductionism. The overemphasis of modern civilization on the ideology of the common welfare, equality, and unanimity produces the inevitable release of the destructive impulse.

Like Freud, Lawrence did not call for abandonment of the self to the instincts. Lawrence saw that the instincts, left to themselves, lead to the death process of "African" sensation, a pit from which Western man struggled to emerge. In *Kangaroo* Lawrence argues strongly that the instincts, if not controlled, will bring on catastrophic eruptions in society. Anarchic reaction against the repressive love ideal must be countered by an assertion of power, by the control and mastery of genuine leaders. Thus Lawrence, like Freud, accepts the necessity of "repression."

There is a difference, however. While insisting on male control of the irrational hard impulse, Lawrence does not accept the inevitability of a reality principle that necessitates harsh repression or sublimation of the Eros instinct. Rather, Lawrence seeks a healthy society in which the instincts may be controlled without destructive repression. Like Herbert Marcuse, Lawrence calls for an end to the repressive ethics of production and for a reduction of the chief form of repression in industrial civilization: work. As long as most of their time is spent on alienated labor, men cannot achieve fullness of being. It is necessary, therefore, to shift from an ethic of production, with its emphasis on consumption, accumulation, and "comforts," to an ethic of sufficiency, akin to Thoreau's at Walden Pond. Instead of domination and exploitation of nature, Lawrence wants a return to a sense of unity with the living cosmos—a sense of "creative receptivity."

But it is not a simple return to nature he calls for. The Holy Ghost, a moral arbitrator, must operate in any transformation of society. Thus punishment is needed. But Lawrence calls for "swift passional justice" rather than for prolonged "rehabilitation," that dehumanizing consequence of humanitarian sympathy. The flogging of a disobedient sailor is, Lawrence argues, healthier than rehabilitation and reform. The anger of the authority figure is released, not repressed; the punished person, his crime paid for, is released to live as a human being. With this, compare the anger in a respectable citizenry who resent the "coddled" criminal, and the resentment of the prisoner, whose prolonged debasement and dehumanization unfits him for a return to sanity and fosters his desire for retaliation.

Thus, in part, Lawrence accepts the Freudian idea that repression is needed for the continuance of civilization. (In this, he is opposed to the views of Wilhelm Reich, whose affinities to Lawrence have been traced by David Boadella in *The Spiral Flame*.) Yet Lawrence disagrees with Freud on the nature of the unconscious and on the goals of psychoanalysis. While there is a rough parallel between Lawrence's sympathetic/voluntary impulses and Freud's Eros/Deros instincts, the striking difference is that Freud relegates religion to an illusion or a "substitute gratification" and does not seem to recognize the inherent desire for purposive activity. Thus Lawrence regards Freud's psychology as mechanical and limited. Because it postulates, Lawrence believes, only a single cause—namely, sex—it arrives at absurd conclusions. Incest-craving, Lawrence argues, is abnormal, not normal—the result of "getting sex in the head"—and Freud's view of infantile sexuality is false: children, says Lawrence, have very little sex consciousness. Lawrence also rejects Freud's view of the dream.

Some of these charges are based on a superficial reading of Freud. Yet today several of Lawrence's criticisms appear to be sound. Recent findings of human ethology suggest that activities regarded by psychoanalysis as sexual are "behavior-patterns of parental care in the service of group cohesion." In his *Love and Hate: The Natural History of Behavior Patterns,* Irenäus Eibl-Eibesfeldt writes:

> Many behavior patterns that are regarded as typically sexual, such as kissing and caressing, are actually in origin actions of parental care. We remind the reader of this because Sigmund Freud, in a strikingly topsy-turvy interpretation, once observed that a mother would certainly be shocked if she realized how she was lavishing sexual behavior patterns on her child. In this case Freud had got things reversed. A mother looks after her children with the actions of parental care; these she also uses to woo her husband.[15]

Yet again, Eibl-Eibesfeldt points out that so-called regressive behavior, such as "infantile appeals," are part of "the normal behavioral repertoire of animals" and of man:

> People who need help or who wish, as in courtship, to elicit affectionate behavior relapse quite involuntarily into the role of a small child. Regression of this kind is not at all pathological, a fact that should be emphasized, for in the writings of psychoanalysts the impression is often created that this is an abnormal phenomenon. This is true only in the case of people who cannot find their way out of this role. [152]

Lawrence's objections to Freud's eroticizing of the unconscious thus receive support from ethology's claim that man's genetic inheritance issues in two twin drives: for social bonding (not necessarily erotic in origin; originating in parental care) and for aggression. "Both aggressive and altruistic behavior are preprogrammed by phylogenetic adaptations and . . . are therefore preordained norms for our ethical behavior'' (*Love and Hate,* 5). In short, the sympathetic and the voluntary impulses are, as Lawrence believed, innate.

Lawrence's contention that man's deepest desire is for purposive activity (rather than for pleasure) is also confirmed by evidence from ''purposive behaviorism.'' T. S. Eliot's description of Lawrence as a ''religious behaviorist'' was witty, but a link between behaviorism and religion is not as preposterous as Eliot thought it was. Edward Chace Tolman, in his *Purposive Behavior in Animals and Men* (1949),[16] showed conclusively that behavior is inherently purposive. It cannot be reduced to stimulus and response; rather, it possesses a totalizing or ''molar'' character that is associated with Gestalt psychology. There are ''immanent determinants'' of response, and these have to do not only with organic capacities but also with goals, expectations, and readinesses. In short, all gestalts have a purposive structure. In the most highly developed men, Lawrence concluded, that purposive structure assumes a religious character.

Lawrence's view of the dream is also subtler than Freud's idea of wish fulfillment, later modified, to be sure, by the conception of the anxiety dream. For Lawrence there are two kinds of dreams: body dreams and soul dreams. In arguing that the body dream telegraphs distress to the mind, Lawrence suggests Piaget's theory that the dream is an effort of the unconscious mind to cope with a problem, as when a person, having visited a dentist who has left a piece of dental wool between two molars, dreams of seaweed between two boulders. The unconscious mind, unable to objectify, struggles for cognition. The soul dream may arise from repression, as in a dream that apparently indicates a desire for incest; but what the dream represents, Lawrence argues, is what the soul fears, not what it desires: ''The dream-conclusion is almost invariably the *reverse* of the soul's desire, in any distress dream'' (*FU,* 169). Here Lawrence's theory is similar to Freud's idea of the anxiety dream and suggests also Jung's belief that the dream has a compensating function—namely, to warn the total psyche against an imbalance in its activity. The ''distress-dream'' in Lawrence tells the psyche that there is blockage of its life flow and that something must be done to achieve balance. A dream of wild horses tells the dreamer that his wild, sensual life has been arrested. Such a dream is the mechanical product of a ''conservative psyche,'' unable to objectify the real problem and therefore presenting images or symbols terrifying to the waking self.

Most important, however, is Lawrence's attack on the implicit ''idealism'' of psychoanalysis. Seeking to help the patient to function better, psychoanalysis attempts to strengthen the ego: ''Where id is, there shall ego be.'' In this effort, psychoanalysis shows no awareness of the evil inherent in such strengthening, evil so powerfully exhibited by Dostoevsky. Indirectly, and against its own diagnosis of the evil inherent in a repressive society, psychoanalysis reflects the bourgeois assumptions that perpetuate evil. As Philip Rieff says,

> Freud had plunged furthest into an analysis of the old therapeutic potential for a purpose that to Lawrence seems sacrilegious: to surround this potential with more powerfully rational controls, distributed, like oil derricks, along the superficies of life. It is this rationalist ambition to strengthen the machinery of control that Lawrence opposes. [*Triumph of the Therapeutic,* 195]

JUNG

The analytic psychology of Jung, because of its strong religious emphasis, might seem, at first blush, to be closer to Lawrence's psychology than was Freud's. In reaction to modern rationalism, both Jung and Lawrence call for a new balance, a compensating emphasis on feeling; and both view the unconscious as being inherently compensatory. As Jung says in *Modern Man in Search of a Soul:* ''The psyche is a self-regulating system that maintains itself in equilibrium as the body does. Every process that goes too far immediately and inevitably calls forth compensations, and without these there would be neither a normal metabolism nor a normal psyche.''[17] Healthy balance is the balance of feeling and intellect, female and male, Eros and Logos. In Jung, as in Lawrence, the mother archetype ''refers to the place of origin, to nature, to that which passively creates, hence to substance and matter, to materiality, the womb, the vegetative functions. It also means the unconscious, our natural and instinctive life, the physiological realm, the body in which we dwell or are contained'' (*Collected Works* [hereafter *CW*], 16:158). The male archetype, on the other hand, refers to the spirit, to logic, and to conscious, rational control. Healthy individuation requires discovery of ''a new centre of equilibrium,'' which is the Unconscious Source—that is, Energy or God; and for Jung, as for Lawrence, it is as if the ego orbits around that center (*CW*, 16:49). In this process of change and revitalization, there is inherent, moreover, ''a peculiar purposefulness.'' Those who assimilate the shadow side of the psyche, and thus move towards integration, no longer put ''the personal ego'' in the center of their lives, for the ego, ''with its futile willing and striving,'' is ''inadequate.'' Rather, they are sustained and guided by the archetypes cast up from the great ''ocean'' of the Unconscious (*CW*, 16:49, 11:345). Hence, ''a religious attitude is an element whose importance as a psychic function can hardly be overrated'' (*CW*, 16:46). According to Jung, the myths of primitive cultures cannot be dismissed as mere superstition, for the archetypes—those a priori forms of psychic life—exhibit our deepest desires and fears; they reflect the creative and destructive Source from which we derive.

These parallels are impressive. Yet there are sharp differences. Lawrence was perhaps influenced by Trigant Burrow, who regarded Jung's analytical psychology as ''impersonal and unhistorical'' and as failing to recognize ''a true biological science.''[18] Lawrence found Jung ''very interesting'' but added, ''in his own sort of fat muddled mystical way'' (letter of 23 September 1926). A major disagreement is that Lawrence views the unconscious as individual, not as collective. In this respect, Lawrence is closer to Freud, who always stresses individual development, even though he contemplates inherited or archaic dispositions of the psyche, as in the idea of ''the return of the repressed.'' A second disagreement has to do with the nature of the compensatory needs in the modern age. Both Jung and Lawrence see modern man as being too rational, too conscious. But Jung's cure—to activate the archetypes of the female—conflicts with Lawrence's contention that the need of our time is to assert the male power impulse against the collective sympathetic female impulse, which has caused mankind to react into compensatory sadism and war.

Both men have been accused of trusting in the Irrational, of elevating the Unconscious to a religious principle. In reply to this charge, Jung maintains that a Heraclitean principle of *enantiodromia* obtains in the psyche, so that ''the destructive powers [are] converted into healing forces'' (*CW*, 11:345). Evil turns to good, and ''the warring halves of the personality'' are reunited. Lawrence views reaction as a possible way to rebirth and health, but he also sees that uncontrolled reaction may well culminate in destruction and death. Jung's view of *enantiodromia* is sanguine by comparison. The ''acceptance of the shadow-side of human nature'' seems to result in a repression of the shadow-side: ''It was to arm himself against [the] threat [of irrational natural forces] and to heal the damage done, that [man] developed religious and magical practices'' (*CW*, 11:344). Christianity and Buddhism come to the rescue: guidance comes from God, or from the Collective Unconscious. But, in practice, such guidance amounts to the repression of natural desire. It is not surprising, then, that Lawrence spoke of the ''fat muddled mystical way'' of Jung! Lawrence's religion of ''the two ways'' attempts to avoid the repression of established religions. Don Ramón's cure for the diseased, self-conscious men of our time employs what Lawrence called "physical and passional meeting, as there used to be in the old dances and rituals" (*Letters*, 671).

TRIGANT BURROW

Lawrence's keen understanding of psychology is also evident in his response to Trigant Burrow, a psychoanalyst who rejected most of Freud's assumptions. Eugene W. Dawson, in a comprehensive study of the congruencies between Lawrence's "pollyanalytics" and Burrow's phylobiological psychology, stresses Lawrence's sympathy with Burrow's position and interest in Burrovian group therapy. The deepest agreement of the two lies in their recognition that egoistic individualism is a severance from organic "primary identification." According to Burrow, "the primary phase of consciousness" is that of identification with the mother. It is not "competitive and contentious," does not seek satisfaction "either in domination and aggression or in abject subordination and sentimental dependency."[19] There is thus a "primal awareness of phylic unity or oneness within the species." But this preconscious state of primary identification is broken down by the systematic inculcation of the idea of a false or separative self, which Burrow calls the I-persona. The child learns to conform to ideas and ideals of "self" which are set up by parents, teachers, and the whole of society. Thus ideal images are substituted for actual experiences, and the primal mood of unity or oneness is broken down. The preconscious flow towards others is destroyed, and the destroyer is society, with its emphasis on ownership, property, getting, the right and the wrong way, saving face, and so forth—in sum, "the egocentric absolute of the individual," as Lawrence characterizes it in his review of Burrow's *The Social Basis of Consciousness.*

Neurosis, in phylobiology, is thus "heightened subjectivity"—the intensification of the egocentric self and its fixation at the egocentric level. The repressed content of the psyche is the I-persona: "The separative or the personal *is* unconsciousness." Our individualism is not natural; it has been artificially induced by society. Conflict within the psyche arises between the primal phyletic or visceral self, which seeks unity, and the I-persona, which seeks self-aggrandizement.

Burrow seems entirely right to Lawrence insofar as phylobiology explains the inability of modern men to overcome their egotism. And Burrow's contention that life "traces its source to a homogeneous matrix that is organically confluent and unitary" (*Social Basis,* 157) is in accord with Lawrence's idea that the solar plexus seeks "the old oneness." But Burrow's contention that life at the preconscious levels is cooperative or unitive does not account for phylobiological aggression. Lawrence spotted this apparent omission. In a letter to Burrow, after agreeing that his "primeval societal instinct" has been frustrated because of "the individualist illusion," Lawrence adds: "Of course, men will *never* agree—can't—in their '*subjective sense perception.*' Subjective sense perceptions are individualistic *ab ovo.* But do tell them to try!" (*Letters,* 693). In another letter he reminds Burrow: "There will *never* be a millenium. There will *never* be a 'true societal flow'—all things are relative. Men were never, in the past, fully societal—and they never will be in the future" (*Letters,* 695). What Burrow ignores is the voluntary center of resistance to "true societal flow." His Christian bias is reflected in what to Lawrence seems the sentimentalism of his plea "To understand all is to forgive all." Burrow must have seemed a bit like Swedenborg in phylobiological clothing. His assumption of "primal identification" harkens back to the myth of the Noble Savage. Lawrence, who has been accused of resurrecting the same myth, holds that aggression is as much a part of our phylobiological inheritance as is love. Lawrence would agree that a psychology which explains aggression as a socially induced pattern of behavior is accurate to a point: the horrors of sadomasochism in Lawrence's fiction *do* arise from the ideal consciousness. But Lawrence contends that the unconscious striving for identity entails sundering as well as union.

EGO PSYCHOLOGIES; THE FRANKFURT SCHOOL

Lawrence thus shows a limited sympathy for the views of Freud, Jung, and Burrow, if only because all three stress the importance of the unconscious. Lawrence's view of post-Freudian revisionists who have constructed an ego psychology would be far harsher. It is their interest in "personalities"—instead of in the infinite or the biological—that prompted his outburst against the "stink" of psychology.

Lawrence would probably have liked some of Alfred Adler's ideas. Adler rejects determinism; he stresses the creative power of the individual in his striving for a final goal; and in his later work (*Social Interest: A Challenge to Mankind* [London: Faber, 1938]) he argues that an innate *Gemeinschaftgefühl,* or social feeling, can be fostered if society can learn not to impose self-boundedness on the child (in this, Adler's thought is close to Burrow's). But the Adlerian "aggressive drive," "masculine protest," and the striving for superiority would be for Lawrence a plain indication of pathological reaction, such as that of Clifford Chatterley. When Adler says that aggression is a "great upward drive" that causes culture and progress,[20] Lawrence's rejoinder would probably be that such culture is bullying, a perversion of the natural voluntary impulse. The striving to realize a self-ideal is simply egotism, and the idea of inferiority is a product of a monstrous competitive society.

In short, Adler's psychology, even though it begins with the innate aggressive drive, seems to deny the unconscious. As Russell Jacoby has pointed out, "The drift of Adler's concern . . . was essentiality confined to a *conscious* dimension: first organ inferiority-compensation, degradation-sensitivity, and, later, inferiority-masculine protest" (*Social Amnesia*, 21). Such a psychology virtually eliminates repression and libido, and culminates in the therapeutic interest which Adler expresses in *Understanding Human Nature:* the interest in teaching the individual "to recognize his own mistakes, and finally . . . how he may effect a harmonious adjustment to communal life." This emphasis on the ego's power to control life prompted Freud, the determinist, to condemn Adler's "whole doctrine" as "reactionary and retrograde" (quoted in *Social Amnesia*, 24).

From Lawrence's perspective, Adler's ideas of self, self-assertion, and sociability testify to a collective insanity created by the combined forces of capitalism, the Protestant work ethic, and liberalism. The ego is regarded as the whole self; the "will to power" is not the unconscious will but the petty egoistic will of the bourgeois or of the subjugated proletariat. Of the deeper, religious will to power that Lawrence postulated—a creative will which is essentially disinterested—Adler seems oblivious.

Adler's psychology might be a psychology of the Kwakiutl Indians, whose normal madness Ruth Benedict has so vividly described in her *Patterns of Culture*. It is certainly a psychology that explains the "nightmare" of the First World War, in which Lawrence saw "the crowd of assertive egos" moving collectively toward the horror that Lawrence called "the consummation of reduction" (*Phoenix II*, 391, 394). As an explanation of the madness that has become normal, then, Adler's psychology might stand; failure to acknowledge the great forces of the unconscious leads inevitably, Lawrence would say, to a psychology of madmen.

Adler's psychology was just the beginning of the entire neo-psychoanalytic school that was to place the stress on self, self-image, identity, personality, self-actualization, self-fulfillment, and self-help. "Conformist psychologies," Jacoby calls them, "regression to a pre-Freudian position, where one knows nothing of the unconscious, repression, and sexuality, but only of surface motives, interests, and desires" (*Social Amnesia*, 53). In effect, he adds, they help to "keep bourgeois society on its tracks" (51). Karen Horney, Erich Fromm,

Harry Stack Sullivan, Heinz Hartmann, Gordon Allport, Rollo May, Abraham Maslow, Viktor E. Frankl, R. D. Laing, Erik Erikson, David Cooper—they are all, Jacoby argues, conformist psychologists. The titles of some of their books suggest their limitations: *Ego Psychology and the Problem of Adaptation* (Hartmann); *Personality and Social Encounter* (Allport); *Psychotherapy and Existentialism* (Frankl); *The Art of Loving* (Fromm). All such psychologists, according to Jacoby, assume what remains to be proved: an autonomous individual capable of directing his own destiny and able to transcend the repressive effects of the superego and the deep conflicts arising from social relations.

Lawrence could have endorsed much of what Jacoby says against conformist psychologies. Yet it is doubtful that Lawrence could have accepted the conclusions of the Frankfurt School, which Jacoby extolls because of its sane explorations of the relationships between psychoanalysis and dialectical materialism. Jacoby's heroes are Wilhelm Reich, Otto Fenichel, Theodor Adorno, and Herbert Marcuse, all of whom hold onto Freud's basic insights, preserving "both individual-instinctual and social components without reducing one to the other." Fenichel's work, for example, "illustrates critical theory's loyalty to the tension within psychoanalysis. . . . Against interpretations that conceived of capitalism as derived from individual instincts, Fenichel stressed its social and extra-individual factors; against analyses that abstracted capitalism from the instinctual dynamic, Fenichel recalled its instinctual roots [i.e., the erogenous pleasure in collection]" (*Social Amnesia,* 95). But while Lawrence might have endorsed such a correction of conformist ego psychologies (i.e., the wedding of psychoanalysis and Marxism which reveals the emptiness of existential talk about a timeless "Man" and a timeless "human condition"), Lawrence could scarcely have supported a school of psychoanalysis that explains religious phenomena in terms of "sublimation" or "superstructure." Fenichel views an idealistic tendency in human beings as arising from biological needs conditioned by social determinants. In Lawrence that tendency is assigned to "conservative psyche" or to the upper centers, while the deep source of purposiveness is biological and is not conditioned by society. In short, Lawrence assumes that man is innately religious, though his deepest religious impulses are normally smothered by conservative psyche or by the socially enforced persistence in the exclusively sympathetic mode.

Analysis of Lawrence's psychology in relation to psychoanalysis and to post-Freudian "subjectivism" returns us to the earlier comment about the prevailing tension in psychology today: the tension between a biologism built on the foundations of natural science in the nineteenth century—Darwin's theory of evolution, Ernst Haeckel's principles of biogenetics, the theories of the preservation of energy and homeostasis—and the reaction to reductionism manifested in vitalism, creative evolution, Gestalt psychology, and, more recently, existentialism. Lawrence's psychology, rejecting Freudian or Marxist determinism but at the same time accepting the idea of dark gods (unconscious impulses of love and power) that are much like inhuman natural forces such as electricity, illustrates that tension. It also manifests the existentialist thought that Lawrence found in Dostoevsky and Nietzsche. In his recognition that man feels cut off from his primal unity with nature, Lawrence picks up Nietzsche's idea of a new and frightening situation in which "all is permitted" and man, alone and "unsponsored," is free to choose his path toward salvation or destruction. As T. H. Adamowski has noted, Lawrence's emphasis on man's existential situation and his effort to "come into being" suggests an affinity to the thought of Jean-Paul Sartre, who has sought to ground his psychology in ontological problems.[21] Rollo May, Erwin Straus, and Erich Fromm have followed a similar line of thought.

ERICH FROMM

Erich Fromm's psychology, like Lawrence's, illustrates the tension between "biologism" and the new subjectivism based on existential awareness. Clinging to Freudian and Marxist determinism, yet strongly influenced by his recognition of man's existential situation and of the ethical and religious elements in human behavior, Fromm often seems to think along Lawrencian lines. Indeed, the parallels between his and Lawrence's thinking are so striking that their psychologies mutually illuminate each other. And this is so, I think, because man's existential situation is, for both, an important starting point of their analyses. Both, drawing on a variety of disciplines—philosophy, anthropology, history, sociology, and religion—develop their psychologies by meditating on man's "religious" response to his existential situation. To understand Lawrence's contribution to psychology, one must follow the contours of this thought—without obscuring the significant differences between Fromm and Lawrence.

Fromm, who has been accused of "undervaluing biology,"[22] seems unaware of "the sacred mysteries" that Lawrence celebrates. Although Fromm called himself an "atheistic mystic" and found insights for his psychology in Martin Buber, Meister Eckhart, the Muslin poet Jalal uddin Rumi, Paul Tillich, and Zen Buddhism, his religious thought remains tied to a conception of a rational self that Lawrence would have distrusted, just as Fromm, who rejected Jung's elevation of the unconscious "to a religious phenomenon," might have distrusted Lawrence's "Jungian" emphases. Once these important differences have been noted, however, their thinking on three major points shows impressive congruence.

Beginning with similar conceptions of the existential situation, of human nature, and of the needs that must be satisfied if man is to be sane, both men arrive at similar conclusions about (1) the duality within the psyche—the split between the need for relatedness and the need for identity—and the psychic problem created by the historical emergence of human individuality; (2) the failure of Western culture to foster healthy development of the individual's sense of real identity as well as of genuine relatedness; and (3) the causes of illness as related, particularly, to the failure to find adequate satisfactions for man's intrinsic needs.

1. *Duality within the Psyche and the Development of Western Man.* For Fromm the starting point of psychology is an analysis of the human condition: as he states in *The Sane Society,* "the most powerful forces motivating man's behavior stem from the condition of his existence, the 'human situation.' "[23] That situation is one of self-division caused by man's emergence from a state of oneness with nature into a state of individuality and separateness. In the historical development of the race, man at some point became aware of himself and of his separateness from the rest of nature. Pointing to Bachofen's theory of the matriarchal society, Fromm argues that attachment to the mother figure in early societies gave men a positive sense of the affirmation of life, but "*by being bound to nature, to blood and soil, man is blocked from developing his individuality and his reason*" (*SS,* 45). "The member of a primitive clan might express his sense of identity in the formula 'I am we'; he cannot yet conceive of himself as an 'individual,' existing apart from his group" (*SS,* 61). In passing, one might note that, for Fromm as for Lawrence, woman is closer to nature than man: she is charged with the task of nursing and taking care of children. Man, "because he is less rooted in nature, . . . is forced to develop his reason, to build up a man-made world of ideas, principles and man-made things which replace nature as a ground of existence and security" (*SS,* 46). With the breakdown of the feudal system, however, man's "sense of identity was shaken and the acute question 'who am I?' arose" (*SS,* 61). Thereafter "the development of Western culture went in the direction of creating the basis for the full experience of individuality," and "the positive aspect of the paternal principle asserted itself in the renaissance of rational thought and individualism" (*SS,* 62, 56).

Man, as the product of evolution, is thus divided. Reason, self-awareness, and imagination have "thrown [him] out of the original oneness with nature," and he "cannot return to where he came from" (SS, 27). Yet he remains a "part of nature, subject to her physical laws and unable to change them" (*MFH*, 49). The development of consciousness and self-awareness means that man has given up "a situation which was definite, as definite as the instincts," for "a situation which is indefinite, uncertain and open" (SS, 25). Hence he is torn by conflicting tendencies: "We are never free from two conflicting tendencies: one to emerge from the womb, from the animal form of existence into a more human existence, from bondage to freedom; another, to return to the womb, to nature, to certainty and security" (SS, 27). Reason and imagination have made man "aware of his aloneness and separateness; of his powerlessness and ignorance; of the accidentalness of his birth and of his death" (SS, 30). But so frightening is this existential fact of "aloneness and separateness" that it breeds an "imperative need" for relatedness to others and to the rest of nature:

> He could not face this state of being for a second if he could not find new ties with his fellow man which replace the old ones, regulated by instinct. Even if all his physiological needs were satisfied, he would experience his state of aloneness and individuation as a prison from which he had to break out in order to retain his sanity. . . . The necessity to unite with other living beings, to be related to them, is an imperative need on the fulfillment of which man's sanity depends. This need is behind . . . all passions which are called love in the broadest sense of the word. [SS, 30]

Love is "the overcoming of human separateness, . . . the fulfillment of the longing for union" (*AL*, 33). And beyond the specific biological need for "union between the masculine and feminine poles" (*AL*, 33) there is the need to discover a unity beyond man himself to give completeness in the process of living. Therefore, "all men are 'idealists,'" all are religious animals; hence the human "devotion to an aim, or an idea, or a power transcending man such as God" (*MFH*, 58, 55).

But if the need for unity is intense, the contrary need for "identity" is of an equal intensity: "Because [man] has lost the original unity with nature, has to make decisions, is aware of himself and of his neighbor as different persons, he must be able to sense himself as the subject of his actions. As with the need for relatedness, rootedness, and transcendence, this need for a sense of identity is so vital and imperative that man could not remain sane if he did not find some way of satisfying it'' (*SS*, 60–61). It is ''the paradox of human existence,'' Fromm says, ''that man must simultaneously seek for closeness and for independence; for oneness with others and at the same time for the preservation of his uniqueness and particularity'' (*MFH*, 102–3). This idea has also been developed extensively by Erwin W. Straus in his essay ''Psychiatry and Philosophy.'' Straus argues that the fact that all

> sensory experience is embedded within the person's primal relation to the world, stresses the reality that *I am and have a body* which asserts itself by resisting gravity. Through my living body I become present and here, as opposed to some place else. When the healthy self acts, he asserts the heft and strength in his being within and against the world. Bound to the world, I am yet separate from it, for without separation-in-relation I would have no mobility, i.e., I could not ex-ist and I would not have consciousness. Primary separation is paired with primary solidarity.[24]

Thus there is an ''amphiboly of contact and distance'' (39)—both a movement toward contact and a resistance to that identification which would mean a loss of self.

But most men, according to Fromm, have been unable to find an adequate response to the paradoxical need for closeness *and* independence. Fromm points out that ''by making the individual free politically and economically, by teaching him to think for himself and freeing him from an authoritarian pressure, [liberal Western culture] hoped to enable him to feel 'I' in the sense that he was the center and active subject of his powers and experienced himself as such. But only a minority achieved the new experience of 'I.' For the majority, . . . many substitutes for a truly individual sense of identity were sought for, and found. Nation, religion, class and occupation serve to furnish a sense of identity'' (*SS*, 62). But as Fromm shows in *Escape from Freedom*, ''a new herd identity,'' which rests on ''belonging to the crowd,'' has provided only the illusion of individuality: ''People are willing to risk their lives, to give up their love, to surrender their freedom, to sacrifice their own thoughts, for the sake of being one of the herd, of conforming, and thus of acquiring a sense of identity, even though it is an illusory one'' (*SS*, 63).

In contrast with those who seek identity in herd conformity, Fromm places ''the mature and productive individual.'' The ''productive'' individual realizes ''the potentialities characteristic of him, the use of his *powers*'' (*MFH*, 94). Like Lawrence, Fromm distinguishes between the unhealthy *Wille zur Macht*, or ''power over,'' and the healthy ''power to'': that is, the power to reason, to love, and to imagine. Among Fromm's many illustrations of the productive character is

Nietzsche's "strong" individual, who has "'true kindness, nobility, greatness of soul, which does not give in order to take'" (*MFH*, 130). Commenting on Nietzsche's *Zarathustra,* Fromm writes: "Love is a phenomenon of abundance; its premise is the strength of the individual who can give. Love is affirmation and productiveness, 'It seeketh to create what is loved!'" (*MFH*, 131).

We have, then, according to Fromm, two contrary needs: the need for relatedness, unity, and fusion and the need for identity, individuality, and separateness. Denial of either of these needs brings insanity. For Fromm there is only one course if we would remain sane: a relationship to others in which the love impulse toward unity and the power impulse toward individuality are satisfied. As he says in *The Sane Society:* "There is only one passion which satisfies man's need to unite himself with the world, and to acquire at the same time a sense of integrity and individuality, and this is *love. Love is union* with somebody, or something, outside oneself, *under the condition of retaining the separateness and integrity of one's own self*" (*SS*, 31). It should not be, however, an egotism *à deux*—"two people who identify themselves with each other, and who solve the problem of separateness by enlarging the single individual into two. They have the experience of overcoming aloneness, yet, since they are separated from the rest of mankind, they remain separated from each other and alienated from themselves; their experience of union is an illusion" (*AL*, 55). To overcome separateness, the individual, beginning with a healthy self-love or natural self-affirmation, should move, as in Plato, from love of another individual to love of others and to love of the Good, or of God.

Fromm's description of the conflict between love and power and his prescription for satisfying these needs are obviously in harmony with Lawrence's thinking about man's inner division, about the need to achieve "integral selfhood" and the need for that satisfying love which Birkin, in *Women in Love,* defines as that of two individuals who are, like stars, "separate but in conjunction."

Their analyses of mankind's development from matriarchal to patriarchal societies are also similar. Fromm's analysis of the individual's submergence in matriarchal society is matched by Lawrence's conception that "previous to 2000 B.C. . . . the self had not really become aware of itself, it had not separated itself off, the spirit was not yet born, so there was no internal conflict" (*Phoenix*, 769). In "Study of Thomas Hardy" Lawrence traces the development of mankind from the female society of the Old Testament, the society of Law—a Monism of darkness and the unconscious in which the supremacy of the flesh and the senses is affirmed and the individual is one with the tribe—to the epoch of Love, which is characterized by a contrary Monism, that of the Spirit, of consciousness, of differentiation and individuation against the homogeneous mass of men. The female principle is succeeded by the male, the darkness by light. Hebrew society affirmed: "'All that exists is Me. We are all one family, out of one God, having one being.'" But Jesus affirms the Spirit, which asserts: "Ye must be born again." Man is born again "unto knowledge of his own separate existence, as in Woman he is conscious of his own incorporate existence. Man must be born unto knowledge of his own distinct identity, as in woman he was born to knowledge of his identification with the Whole. Man must be born to the knowledge, that in the whole being he is nothing, as he was born to know that in the whole being he was all" (*Phoenix*, 453). Breaking away from the tribe, man, as exemplified by Jesus or Shelley, is "a thought-adventurer" (*Phoenix II*, 616); "the male exists in doing, the female in being" (*Phoenix*, 481); but man's outward motion into "the unknown" rests upon the axle of Nature, the female. The whole development from man's passive rootedness in nature and in the tribe to his assertion of his separate individuality is traced in *The Rainbow*, where the worlds of the Marsh and of the Cathedral are shattered by the incursions of reason and spirit.

In Lawrence's novels, there is always the tendency to return to the Magna Mater—that is, to lapse into unconsciousness and utter darkness. At the same time there is the insistent urge to move forward into "the unknown" and "the beyond." There is also, as in Fromm, the imperative need to escape from one's solitary existence by wedding oneself to the Whole. Blindly, unconsciously, man craves "assimilatory unison," identification of the self and the All; as Lawrence says in his essay "Aristocracy":

> . . . *living* and having *being* means the relatedness between me and all things. In so far as I am I, a being who is proud and in place, I have a connection with my circumambient universe, and I know my place. . . .
>
> [Man's] life consists in a relation with all things: stone, earth, trees, flowers, water, insects, fishes, birds, creatures, sun, rainbow, children, women, other men. But his greatest and final relation is with the sun, the sun of suns: and with the night, which is moon and dark and stars. In the last great connections, he lifts his body speechless to the sun, and, the same body, but so different, to the moon and the stars, and the spaces between the stars.

> In his ultimate and surpassing relation, man is given only to that which he can never describe or account for; the sun, as it is alive, and the living night. [*Phoenix II*, 481–82]

In ". . . Love Was Once a Little Boy," he defines this sympathetic relatedness to the rest of the cosmos as the great "love-urge": "Love is a relationship between things that live, holding them together in a sort of unison. There are other vital relationships. But love is this special one. In every living thing there is the desire, for love, or for the relationship of unison with the rest of things" (*Phoenix II*, 444). In "The Crown" he argues that it is precisely the relationship of unison, the making of oneness out of multiplicity, that creates God, without whom "we are nothing." And in *Studies in Classic American Literature*, Lawrence defines the psychic duality that informs his fiction as the two great laws of organic life:

> The central law of all organic life is that each organism is intrinsically isolate and single in itself. . . .
>
> But the secondary law of all organic life is that each organism only lives through contact with other matter, assimilation, and contact with other life, which means assimilation of new vibrations, non-material. Each individual organism is vivified by intimate contact with fellow organisms: up to a certain point. [*SCAL*, 71]

Assimilation must stop at the point at which the selfhood of the individual is threatened. The relationship of the self to the Other must be one of sympathetic relatedness, not of fusion.

2. *The Attack on Western Culture.* Because Lawrence and Fromm agree that modern society has violated the individual's integrity, they both attack that superstructure of capitalistic society which Fromm, with his Marxist leanings, sees as making men want to act in the ways they are forced to act. As Lawrence bitterly attacks the worship of the bitch goddess of success and the idea of equality, in whose name integral selfhood has been obliterated, so Fromm attacks the view that "the aim of life" is a man's "fulfillment of his duty to work, or his success. Money, prestige, and power have become his incentives and ends. He acts under the illusion that his actions benefit his self-interest, though he actually serves everything else *but* the interests of his real self" (*MFH*, 28). For Fromm,

> the word *equality* has also changed its meaning. The idea that all men are created equal implied that all men have the same fundamental right to be considered as ends in themselves and not as means. Today, equality has become equivalent to *inter-*

> *changeability*, and is the very negation of individuality. Equality, instead of being the condition for the development of each man's peculiarity, means the extinction of individuality, the "selflessness" characteristic of the marketing orientation. [*MFH*, 81]

As Lawrence sees that "the social consciousness" and the idea of selflessness have undermined man's "proud noble selfhood" (*Phoenix*, 761–64), so Fromm, defining "the social character" formed by advanced capitalism as the "marketing" character, points to the loss in our time of the "sense of dignity which is so characteristic of man even in most primitive cultures" (SS, 143) and attacks psychologists like H. S. Sullivan, who make a virtue of "the selflessness of modern man." As Lawrence attacks herd conformity, the blind will of the mob that turns against all individualism, so Fromm attacks the herd conformity of "men who co-operate smoothly" and are "willing to be commanded, to do what is expected, to fit into the social machine without friction" (SS, 110), men who are "*imprisoned in* [a superficial] *brotherhood*" (SS, 162). As Lawrence attacks the "Joy-Hogs" who seek in "sensationalism" a cure for their inner emptiness, so Fromm castigates the society in which "having fun" is the aim of life and "The Principle of Nonfrustration" rules our conduct (SS, 164; also 134, 139). As Lawrence sees that modern man worships hideous idols (the Nation, Success, the Machine) and attempts to find in idolatrous love a counterpart to God, so Fromm identifies the great idolatries of our time: the worship of another person as God in what is called "love" (SS, 123), the worship of the state, of money, of the machine, and of efficiency: "Our gods are the machine, and the idea of efficiency" (SS, 175). As Lawrence contends that abstraction governs modern thinking and cuts men off from relatedness to the physical world ("The amazing move into abstraction on the part of the whole of humanity—the film, the radio, the gramophone" [*Phoenix II*, 590]), so Fromm points out that the "abstractification" and the "routinization" of life under capitalism have erased "concreteness and uniqueness"; there is a "lacking sense of reality," a loss of awareness of "fundamental facts of [man's] existence" (SS, 114, 170–71, 144). As Lawrence recognizes that work is the counterpart of love in modern life—that is, an effort to lose the self in some ideal—so Fromm sees that work, in capitalistic society, has become "an answer to man's sense of aloneness and isolation" (SS, 179). Finally, as Lawrence sees that modern man's soul has gone dead from his cooperation with a society that frustrates his deep desires, so Fromm argues that in the twentieth century, "*man is dead*" (SS, 360) and points to the guilt that men feel because they have failed to use their productive powers (SS, 205). These parallels in the thinking of the two men are the consequence of their shared premise: that society in our time prevents the full development of relatedness or union and "integral selfhood."

3. *The Causes of Illness.* In a sick society the needs for relatedness and integral selfhood are inevitably gratified in unsatisfactory or disastrous ways. Seeking love, the modern man without a self looks for fulfillment in what Fromm calls "symbiotic relatedness" and what Lawrence calls the relationship of "pride and subservience." Fromm describes symbiotic relatedness as being manifested in two "non-productive" character orientations—the receptive and the exploitative:

> Man can attempt to become one with the world by *submission* to a person, to a group, to an institution, to God. . . . Another possibility of overcoming separateness lies in the opposite direction: man can try to unite himself with the world by having *power* over it, . . . The common element in both submission and domination is the symbiotic nature of relatedness. Both persons involved have lost their integrity and freedom; . . . and furthermore [are] constantly threatened by the conscious or unconscious hostility which is bound to arise from the symbiotic relationship. The realization of the submissive (masochistic) or the domineering (sadistic) passion never leads to satisfaction. . . . [B]ecause no amount of submission, or domination (or possession, or fame) is enough to give a sense of identity and union, more and more of it is sought. The ultimate result of these passions is defeat. [SS, 30–31]

In *The Art of Loving* Fromm points out that symbiotic union "has its biological pattern in the relationship between the pregnant mother and the fetus" (19) and that the masochist inflates the power of the one to whom he submits: "He is everything, I am nothing, except inasmuch as I am part of him" (*AL*, 19). The sadist, like the masochist, feels that "the source of all good is outside, . . . that one cannot produce anything oneself" (*MFH*, 71). Sadism is equally the expression of an impotent self seeking security and compensation through "complete domination over a powerless person."

According to David Schecter, Fromm brought "a new depth of understanding of authoritarianism, sadomasochism, and symbiotic relatedness into focus when these latter three concepts were viewed as being thoroughly interwoven one with the other."[25] Schecter points out that René Spitz, John Bowlby, and Margaret Mahler have confirmed, by direct observation of infants, Fromm's claim that "man's fear of separateness" is "an even more primary source of motivation in his interpersonal behavior" than the Oedipus and castration complexes. Schecter concludes:

> *The relative freedom to oscillate between symbiotic and individuated forms of relatedness cannot be over-stressed in importance at any stage of development. . . .* The freedom of oscillation—within realistic bounds—affords the possibility of a natural rather than a forced equilibrium to be reached by the ego in the polarity of its strivings toward fusion on the one hand and individuation and separateness on the other. . . . Only after a self has an *individuated center* can it voluntarily give up its boundaries (as in the orgiastic love or mystical experience) without loss of integrity. [''Of Human Bonds,'' 92–93]

In his analysis of ''the pathology of love'' in Western society, Fromm stresses the failure of modern men and women to emerge ''from a pattern of infantile relatedness'' (*AL*, 94). Men in particular seek in all women a substitute for the mother: ''They want mother's protection, love, warmth, care, and admiration: they want mother's unconditioned love. . . . Anything short of the attitude of a loving mother toward a charming child is taken as proof of a lack of love'' (*AL*, 95–96). In more severe pathology a desire to return to the womb arises, usually ''in relation to mothers who relate themselves to their children in [a] swallowing-destroying way'' (*AL*, 97). (Several of Lawrence's critics have also stressed this pathological desire in his fiction and its origin in Lawrence's relation to his own mother.) Finally, Fromm emphasizes the effects of such idolatrous love:

> If a person has not reached the level where he has a sense of identity, of I-ness, rooted in the productive unfolding of his own powers, he tends to ''idolize'' the loved person. He is alienated from his own powers and projects them into the loved person, who is worshipped as the summum bonum, the bearer of all love, all light, all bliss. In this process he deprives himself of all sense of strength, loses himself in the loved one instead of finding himself. Since usually no person can, in the long run, live up to the expectation of her (or his) idolatrous worshiper, disappointment is bound to occur, and as a remedy a new idol is sought for, sometimes in an unending circle. [*AL*, 99–100]

This might be taken as a succinct summary of the male's problem in Lawrence's *The Rainbow*. In all three generations, the male, incomplete in himself, turns to the woman as his raison d'être. In every case the male, frustrated by his wife's or lover's indifference, turns upon her, fights a battle for supremacy, and finally turns to his children or to other women for fulfillment.

Lawrence's analysis of the symbiotic relationship in that ''union in antagonism'' of Gerald and Gudrun in *Women in Love* or in the symbiotic relationship of Clifford Chatterley and Mrs. Bolton is, if anything, more searching than Fromm's.

In his analysis of symbiotic relatedness, Lawrence sees sadomasochism as originating not only in man's unconscious desires but also in the egotism that prevents man from entering into relationships "in ultimate trust." In a healthy person, he makes clear, the sympathetic desire to surrender the self is balanced by the voluntary desire to preserve one's separate identity. But in a capitalistic society, the conscious ego, being overdeveloped, abnormally stimulates the cravings for self-surrender or for self-assertion. The ego, seeking to substitute itself for God, demands omnipotence either in abject surrender to power or in the sadistic assertion of power. The ultimate realization of its craving to be Absolute is a death wish: the wish to reduce the entire world to inorganic matter. The Freudian conservation principle operates in this pathology of Western civilization. The desire to destroy all other egos (or the whole world, which resists the egoistic will) is coupled with the desire to return to the womb, "to reduce and resolve back all the complexity of . . . consciousness, to the rudimentary condition of childhood" (*Phoenix II*, 395).

Love, then, takes the form of egoistic triumph or conquest and a childlike surrender, though the ego of the person who surrenders will eventually react and seek power. In the symbiotic oscillation of "pride and subservience," Lawrence's lost souls seek their fulfillment in egoistic possession of each other or in masochistic submission to a god or goddess. The counterpart is found in capitalist domination and submission to an authoritarian master. When Gerald Crich introduces a rational system to increase production and "all the control was taken out of the hands of the miners," the miners

> submitted to it all. . . . Gerald was their high priest. . . . The men were satisfied to belong to the great and wonderful machine, even whilst it destroyed them. . . . They were exalted by belonging to this great and superhuman system which was beyond feeling or reason, something really godlike. . . . It was the first great step in undoing, the first great phase of chaos, the substitution of the mechanical principle for the organic. [*WL*, 263]

Although the workers submit to this system, they are resentful: "The driving force *underneath* our society remains the same: recoil, revulsion, hate" (*Phoenix II*, 591). The great insight Lawrence has hit upon is that a masochistic surrender breeds a reaction into sadism, into maximum ego assertion, into bullying, coercion of others, and cruelty. Also, men who seek to re-create in their marriages the relationship they enjoyed with their mothers react from idolatry into rage, hostility, and counterattack.

Lawrence's heroines, too, oscillate between sympathetic and voluntary poles. In a competitive society, the female ego has also become overdeveloped. Thus women have become masculine, seeking triumph and fearing male domination. They cannot surrender to the male because surrender means destruction of their egos.

In dramatizing woman's submission to the strong male, Lawrence has been widely condemned for denying woman's integrity as an individual. His professions to the contrary are dismissed as constituting a conscious denial of what is latent in his dramatic situations. Moreover, Lawrence's insistence on the subordination of women is interpreted, with some justification, as an indication of his own insecurity, his need for total support to sustain his precarious sense of identity. According to Robert Daniels,[26] who has examined Lawrence's *Women in Love* from the perspective of Heinz Kohut's psychology of the self, Rupert Birkin "cannot tolerate any sign of individuality" in Ursula. The fragmented Birkin depends heavily on others for sustenance, wants a "mirroring" of his "grandiose self," and is "a narcissistic personality" who requires a "symbiotic tranquility" and does not recognize Ursula's individuality but, on the contrary, wants her destruction. Seen from this perspective, Lawrence's idea of dying and rebirth is an effort to escape the struggle and tension of dealing with individual differences.

This analysis of Birkin's motives—repeated in various ways by Marguerite Beede Howe, Gavriel Ben-Ephraim, Charles Rossman, and others—ignores, however, the social dimension of Lawrence's thinking. The reconciliation of differences between Birkin and Ursula—a cheerful modern "compromise"—would destroy everything Birkin stands for. It would be reconciliation within a bad society that both Birkin and Ursula hate in their souls. To reconcile oneself to the status quo is, in effect, to seek a mind cure rather than the reconstruction of the world. A recognition of Ursula's point of view would bring Birkin to the sort of compromise with bourgeois values—particularly with possessiveness—that Lawrence condemns in Forster's *Howards End*.

The argument that Lawrence condemns women to subservience simply ignores the social and religious character of Lawrence's thought. The feminist movement addresses itself to the problem of emancipation within the destructive society. To call for equal rights is to call indirectly, and contrary to what many feminists say they want, for equal aggressiveness. Almost invariably Lawrence's sympathetic heroines—Ursula, Kate, Connie, Alvina Houghton—are presented initially as thoroughly modern independent women who, like Hermione Roddice, are "cocksure" (*Phoenix II*, 553). They seek to [illegible] from the spiritual will and are crippled psychically, as are Lawrence's males, by the fixation of their wills on possessive love and their own freedom. Every increase of freedom, however, only increases their insecurity, their sense of being victims of the general alienation that pervades bourgeois society. They can achieve completeness, then, only when they surrender their wills to the sensual purposive male. But in such surrender they are not used. On the contrary, they discover their greater womanhood as participants in the mysteries of life and death rather than as competitors for success, for possessions, and for power.

Lawrence, like Jung and Fromm, believed that woman is biologically destined for motherhood and submission to the virile male, whose biological role is doing (a sort of territorial imperative) rather than being. If we deny that woman is biologically programed to submit herself to the male and family, we side with "culture" as against "instinct." Whatever our conclusion, we must note that it is the ego-dominated symbiotic relationship of sadomasochism that Lawrence's women escape when they choose submission to one of "the sons of God." There is an impersonality in such a relationship, as Lawrence insisted. Both male and female are joined, finally, in an acceptance of the sacred mysteries in which they participate. Ideas of domination and servitude are irrelevant in this context. It is pertinent to add that Lawrence favors a matriarchy "to give woman her full independence, and with it, the full responsibility of her independence" (*Phoenix II*, 552).

The chief danger, for women as well as for men, is blind reaction against one another instead of a healthy reaction against "the dead form of our era." Lawrence's analysis of this latter reaction brings us to another striking parallel between Lawrence and Fromm. In *The Sane Society* Fromm points out that "whole nations, or social groups within them, can be subjugated and exploited for a long time, but *they react*" (18–19). Like Lawrence, Fromm believes that if man "lives under conditions which are contrary to his nature and to the basic requirements for human growth and sanity, he cannot help reacting; he must either deteriorate and perish, or bring about conditions which are more in accordance with his needs" (*SS*, 19). One such reaction is found in the "unselfish" person, who "lives only for others"; such "neurotic unselfishness is pervaded by hostility toward life" and hides an intense self-centeredness" (*AL*, 61–62). Another form of reaction is "destructiveness" (Lawrence's "reduction"): "*If I cannot create life, I can destroy it. . . .* In the act of destruction, man sets himself above life; he transcends himself as a creature'' (*SS*, 37). Like Malraux's Kyo in *Man's Fate* or like Jack in *Kangaroo*, man can become a god through killing. Or he can seek, in what Lawrence calls ''sensationalism,'' a cure for his inner emptiness. Much of *The Sane Society* is an analysis of the forms of reaction of alienated men to a world in which they feel themselves to be powerless, manipulated, and lacking a sense of self; and Fromm is convinced that ''they will destroy their world and themselves because they cannot stand any longer the boredom of a meaningless life'' (*SS*, 360). Man ''can protect himself from the consequences of his own madness only by creating a sane society which conforms with the needs of man, needs which are rooted in the very conditions of his existence'' (*SS*, 362).

The affinities in the thinking of Lawrence and Fromm issues, then, from their basic agreement on the needs of man and on the assumption of a definable ''human nature.'' For both, symbiotic relatedness and reaction become the inevitable consequences of the frustrations of these deep needs. In addition, both emphasize the importance of religious and ethical attitudes in psychic health.

Fromm, who has been accused of being a preacher, sees man as a religious animal, being driven by his existential situation to seek unity with others and with the cosmos. Though Fromm rejects ''a theistic concept'' (*AL*, 72), he is aware of the limitations of Aristotelian logic and its contrast with Eastern ''paradoxical logic.'' In *The Art of Loving* Fromm points out: ''In Taoist thinking, just as in Indian and Socratic thinking, the highest step to which thought can lead is to know that we do not know. . . . The ultimate reality, the ultimate One cannot be caught in words or in thoughts'' (*AL*, 75). In the search for unity behind manifoldness, Vedantic thinkers see thought as ''only a more subtle horizon of ignorance, in fact the most subtle of all the deluding device of maya'' (*AL*, 76). God, then, cannot be thought; He can only be experienced. Fromm quotes Meister Eckhart: ''God and I: we are one. By knowing God I take him into myself.'' At ''a mature stage'' of human development, Fromm argues, God ''ceases to be an outside power''; man incorporates ''the principles of love and justice into himself,'' becomes ''one with God,'' and speaks of God ''only in a poetic, symbolic sense'' (*AL*, 80–81).

This version of a mature religious orientation calls to mind Lawrence's idea that ''a man, if he win to a sheer fusion in himself of all the manifold creation, a pure relation, a sheer gleam of oneness out of manyness, then this man is God created where before God was uncreated'' (*Phoenix II*, 412). But Lawrence is talking about the union of flesh and spirit, of darkness and light, the experience of being one with the infinite, not simply about incorporating the principles of love and justice. He is talking about the death of the ego in the infinite, not about the strengthening of the conscious self through satisfaction of the need for relatedness. When Lawrence speaks of man's being reborn to "the knowledge that in the whole being he is nothing, as he was born to the knowledge that in the whole being he is all," he is speaking of a mystical insight that eludes Fromm. Fromm deals with man as a rational and spiritual being; from a Lawrencian point of view, Fromm shows little appreciation of "the dark gods" and of "the flowing together and the flowing apart" of the flesh (the unconscious) and the spirit (consciousness).

In Lawrence, man is one manifestation of the creative forces that inform nature:

> I am not a windmill. I am not even an ego. I am a man.
>
> I am myself, and I remain myself only by grace of the powers that enter me, from the unseen, and make me forever newly myself.
>
> And I am myself, also, by the grace of the desire that flows from me and consummates me with the other unknown, the invisible, tangible creation.
>
> The powers that enter me fluctuate and ebb. And the desire that goes forth from me waxes and wanes. Sometimes it is weak, and I am almost isolated. Sometimes it is strong, and I am almost carried away. [*Phoenix II*, 457]

This insight is akin to Wordsworth's idea of "something far more deeply interfused" and his faith that nature, acting in man, builds up his soul, restores his mind, becomes the guardian of his moral being. From nature he takes; to nature he gives. The reciprocity is continuous. No man is cut off from the influx of the infinite unless he acts only as a conscious ego, fixing his will only upon his human good. In Lawrence the good arises from the inhuman; the dark gods give us our aspirations and desires, our sense of beauty and wonder, and the urge toward the maximum of being, toward love and power. Fromm concentrates exclusively on the human world of desire and gratification. Lawrence's view is suggested by Paul Tillich, who asked, in reviewing *The Sane Society*, "whether man's power of love and reason is *his* in an ultimate sense." In the last analysis, Fromm's secular humanism cannot approach the ennobling power of Lawrence's belief that man is nothing in the whole being and man is all in the whole being.

Yet this comparison of Lawrence's psychology to Fromm's suggests the extent to which Lawrence's philosophical awareness of man's existential situation influenced his reasoning, as well as his awareness of historical and social determinants of human behavior. Lawrence's resolution of the problems arising from man's paradoxical situation—his rootedness in nature and his consciousness that separates him from nature—is entirely different from Fromm's. In calling for "Humanistic Communitarian Socialism" and for mastery of "the art of loving," Fromm exhibits, from a Lawrencian point of view, that vicious habit of "working ourselves" from the ideal consciousness; in effect, Fromm reverts to a pre-Freudian position. Lawrence sturdily resists all such idealization and rationalism. But to see Lawrence in relation to Fromm is to realize how much of modern existential psychology Lawrence anticipated. Lawrence's singular contribution to psychology is his grounding of a psychology of being in deep biological drives to which existential psychologists generally give only lip service. In his analysis of the relationship of self and other and the striving to achieve the maximum of being, Lawrence does not reject the principles of the conservation of energy and homeostasis that underlie Freudian psychology; but he reinterprets these principles as expressions of a vital striving for being instead of a striving for pleasure or the reduction of tension. Dostoevsky and Nietzsche were his precursors, along with Shaw, Bergson, Edward Carpenter, and other vitalists. Rooted in nineteenth-century biologism, Lawrence's psychology is as current as Laing's or Erikson's; and it is far more subtle than many suppose, for, like Fromm's, it uses history, sociology, and religion to interpret psychic phenomena.

It is time to return to those critics who have charged that Lawrence's thought is irrational, dangerous, incoherent, or immoral.

Among critics who have examined Lawrence's thought carefully over the past several decades, one of the most intelligent is Eugene Goodheart. He has read carefully, appreciates the complexity of Lawrence's thinking, and states well what a score of critics have contended. His attacks on Lawrence therefore deserve careful examination.

Consider, first, his attack on Lawrence's idea that one should act on one's "deepest impulse":

> [Lawrence's] vision of life finally should not be taken as a guide to conduct, the hortatory, preacherish manner of much of his work notwithstanding. The urging to follow "one's deepest impulse" is either nonsensical or dangerous, for given the human condition impulsiveness would sooner issue in horror than in vitality. Only those in a state of grace can be trusted to follow their deepest impulses.[27]

There are at least two replies that can be made to this objection. The first reply would be to agree with Goodheart, though for Goodheart's phrase "a state of grace" Lawrence would wish to substitute "those with heroic souls" or "those who have come into being." Lawrence's Birkin counsels that you should act spontaneously on your impulses "provided you're fit for it." Two questions then arise: first, what kind of men are able to act on their deepest impulses? and second, what are the deepest impulses?

The answers to both questions return to Lawrence's central idea of flowing together and flowing apart. The kind of men who are able to act on their deepest impulses are those who are "born again" after giving up their egos in sexual union. They have come into being, "new and eager to start again," ready to build a new heaven and a new earth. Unlike the "cabbages" who remain fixed in their one will, these heroic souls, in becoming utterly themselves, are urged to gratify their deepest impulses—that is, to satisfy the "inherent passion . . . to produce, to create, to be as God" (*Phoenix*, 429).

As we have seen, the deepest impulses are love and power—the love that unites one to others and to the cosmos, the power that resists assimilation and seeks to destroy dead forms of life and to build a new world. Only men who act upon these two deepest impulses come into being and flower like the poppy; the others remain part of "a great not-being," "the living dead," inert, static, and accepting the fixed form of life (*Phoenix*, 432).

Accordingly there is no danger in what Kingsley Widmer calls the "impious, irrational, immoral, and really impossible Lawrencean imperative: 'I shall accept all my desires, and repudiate none.' " Man's deepest desire is religious—the passion to become "a perfect self" through purposive activity, both sympathetic and voluntary. If allowed to act, this passion exerts the severest discipline. As George Bernard Shaw once remarked, "Your passions, if you really and honestly let them all loose impartially, will discipline you with a severity which your conventional friends, abandoning themselves to the mechanical routine of fashion, could not stand for a day."[28] "If 'the heart of man is deceitful above all things, and desperately wicked,' then, truly, the man who allows himself to be guided by his passions must needs be a scoundrel; . . . But how if the youth thrown helpless on his passions found that honesty, that self-respect, that hatred of cruelty and injustice, that the desire for soundness and health and efficiency, were master passions: nay, that their excess is so dangerous to youth that it is part of the wisdom of age to say to the young: 'Be not righteous overmuch: why shouldst thou destroy thyself?' " (*Sanity of Art*, 42–43). Lawrence, like Shaw, accepted the vitalists' idea that one's deepest passion is to be purposive, to strive for perfection of being. Hence,

> The profoundest of all sensualities
> is the sense of truth
> and the next deepest sensual experience
> is the sense of justice. [*SP*, 116]

Most men, however, do not let loose all of their passions impartially, including the passion to be perfect. Hence, most are consumed by that *ressentiment* which Nietzsche saw at the root of the ideal life, in Christianity, socialism, and the life of reason. Hatred and blind destruction are the consequences of their failure to break free from the tribal collective will and to act on their passions for both union and creative power.

Goodheart finds a contradiction, however, in Lawrence's calling for "a mystic identification with the divine energy in the universe"; Lawrence is really calling, Goodheart argues, for "the annihilation of individuality," and "loses the imagination of the self as finite, vital substance" (*Utopian Vision*, 35–36). Moreover, in seeking a "fusion or a reconciliation" of flesh and spirit, Lawrence "ignores his own insistence . . . that the two modes of being are radically and fiercely irreconcilable" (95). Goodheart quotes Lawrence's statement that

> the consummation of man is two-fold, in the Self and in Selflessness. . . .
>
> But he must never confuse them. They are eternally separate. The lion shall never lie down with the lamb. The lion shall eternally devour the lamb, the lamb shall eternally be devoured. [*TI*, 46, quoted in *Utopian Vision*, 95]

Goodheart then comments:

> If, as Lawrence feels, self and selflessness, lion and lamb, law and love, are each "a great half-truth" about life, "the only thing you can do is to have a little Ghost inside you which sees both ways [*MM*, 46]." But the capacity to see both ways is not the same as reconciliation, for "one man can belong to one great way of consciousness only [ibid.]." The unmistakable implication of Lawrence's somewhat elliptical expression is that a man may have the power to make a choice, and if the choice is made under the aegis of "the little Ghost," he will choose the way through which the greatest life is manifesting itself at the particular moment. "The little Ghost" in Lawrence chose the way of the body: the way of the law, of immanence. [*Utopian Vision*, 95–96]

Goodheart overlooks, however, the fact that Lawrence always assumes, in his discussions of Self and Selflessness, the rhythm of the life process, the to-and-fro, the pulse of "mystic identification" followed by the pulse of utter individuation. Making his connection with the whole of being, a man is born as a new self; by "dipping into" the whole of being continually,[29] a man is reminded that neither his ego's will nor the collective will of other egos is the will of life. His individuality is not annihilated but strengthened: reborn, he is able to break free of the collective will and to act in unison with the will of Life. If the individual chooses to surrender to the "divine will" as manifested in "a greater man," he remains responsible.

Goodheart is right to point out that acceptance of the will of life entails the acceptance of ferocity and terror. But Lawrence does not celebrate nature "in its aspect of fierceness and terror" (*Utopian Vision*, 71). He recognizes the existence of the tiger: like Blake, he insists that any whole view of man must take into account the aggressive and destructive tendencies in human nature and must accept death as a part of life. But Lawrence was as fearful of blind instinct as he was of the unregenerate spiritual will. Blind instinct, as seen in the West African tribe that produced the beetle-faced statue of a woman in *Women in Love*, leads to death; when Lawrence says that we must know if only to learn not to know, he is not calling for a surrender to blind instinct (which is simply automatism, not acting from the deepest will) but rather for a subtler kind of intelligence: an awareness of our true promptings which will enable us to balance our sympathetic and voluntary promptings. The Holy Ghost sees that both blind instinct (the African way) and spirituality (the Nordic way) lead to death. The Ghost, a balancing will, checks extremes of law or love, instinct or reason, Eros or Thanatos, blood consciousness or mind consciousness, and so can lead us to new ways of living—of sympathetic connection together with utter individuation, of the flowing together and the flowing apart.

Goodheart's criticism of Lawrence appears to be based on the assumption that only an ego armed with knowledge and acting with conscious motive can behave morally, choosing good over evil. Lawrence disagrees, arguing that mind is an instrument devised by life to carry out its purposes. With Nietzsche, Lawrence holds that "the body is a great reason" and that "an instrument of your body is also your little reason, my brother, which you call 'spirit'—a little instrument and toy of your great reason" (*Zarathustra*, 146). This is not to say that the mind is powerless. The mind, in becoming *aware* of unconscious impulses, can be used by the ego to interfere unhealthily with our promptings or by the Holy Ghost to check healthily a prompting towards excess. But our deepest knowledge is premental, the mind is merely instrumental, and ''knowing'' is ''the slow death of being'' (*SCAL*, 121). This argument, discounted by many of Lawrence's critics, is based upon a careful analysis of ''conscious motive'' and knowledge, an analysis that draws heavily upon the insights of Schopenhauer, Nietzsche, Bergson, and, perhaps, Hegel and William James.

There are two great objections to the ego's attempt to guide and control the process of living by establishing ideal goals. The first is that any ideal goal, such as love or equality or brotherhood, is incapable of embodying the whole will of man or of the life source. As Hegel sees that any predication we make of the Divine Will is necessarily partial, expressing only one of the attributes of the Whole, never the totality, so Lawrence sees that formulating ideal goals violates the reality of being: the finite mind can never speak of the infinite without creating ''a myth of isolation,'' to use Whitehead's phrase. Hence, if human beings are to live in unison with the life force, they must transcend human dialectic and identify the soul with the Divine Will, not with some human predication of the Divine Will. Lawrence argues that only the unconscious mind is in touch with the will of the great Source. As Schopenhauer sees that the will to live is the *Ding an sich*, whereas ideas provide only representations of a phenomenal world, so Lawrence accepts that only if man acts from his deepest desire can he trust the human will to coincide with the Divine Will.

The second objection to ''conscious motive'' as a guide to the conduct of life is that an ego establishing goals is always motivated, Lawrence believes, by a base will to power. The ego desires to control life, instead of allowing life to control man; it seeks to force organic life, which is process and change, to act always in the ideal direction; and it suppresses any organic promptings that arise in opposition. Such a will becomes tyrannical. Acting from ''conscious motive,'' man does violence not only to himself but also to others. When Gerald Crich forces the mare to stand before the train, or when he forces the coal miners to submit to the ''ethics of production,'' he is seeking to control life, to become the omnipotent ''God of the machine.'' He uses the mind and the conscious will to bully and to conquer life instead of to assist life in achieving its purposes.

Lawrence acknowledges, of course, that man is not a purely unconscious creature. In the essay ''On Human Destiny,'' he writes:

> Man *can't* live by instinct, because he's got a mind. . . . Man has a mind and ideas, so it is just puerile to sigh for innocence and naïve spontaneity. Man is never spontaneous. Even children aren't spontaneous, not at all. . . .
>
> Since man ate the apple and became endowed with mind, or mental consciousness, the human emotions are like a wedded wife; lacking a husband she is only a partial thing. The emotions cannot be ''free.'' [*Phoenix II*, 624]

Man is the supremely conscious being. His consciousness has evolved as an instrument in life's striving to free itself from blind instinct. As Lawrence says in ''Study of Thomas Hardy,'' man, although moving ''in the channels long since built,'' ''the fixed channels and courses of life,'' finds these ''old, fixed courses'' to be a prison and therefore desires ''to be free to be himself'' (*Phoenix*, 424–25). Man, unlike any purely unconscious creature, is not exclusively driven by the ''necessity for self-preservation''; he strives to be free of ''mechanical movement'' and work, strives to be utterly himself, not the mere victim of necessity. And in this striving he seeks ''the extension of human consciousness'' (431); indeed, ''it seems as if the great aim and purpose in human life were to bring all life into the human consciousness'' (430–31). Here, however, Lawrence is quick to point out that consciousness is not ''an aim in itself.'' Consciousness is the ''manifestation of individuality'': the more conscious a man is, the more he is ''singled out into utter individuality'' (431–32). In short, without consciousness it would be impossible for man to be ''utterly himself.''

But consciousness interferes with ''the progress of life'' whenever the mind is used to make life submit to the human ego, to take a direction humanly determined. This is why Lawrence puts so much stress on the ''inhuman'' in life and why he argues that the proper use of the mind is finally to check the mind—to check ''conscious motive'' and to make the conscious choice of an unconscious way of living, or the conscious decision to live only in accordance with the creative promptings of the life force and in harmony with the organic processes of life. As Lawrence says in *Fantasia of the Unconscious:* ''The supreme lesson of human consciousness is to learn how *not* to know. That is, how not to interfere . . . how to live dynamically, from the great Source, and not statically, like machines driven by ideas and principles from the head, or automatically, from one fixed desire'' (98).

But how is it possible to live ''devoid of knowledge and conscious motive''? What does it mean to make the decision ''not to know''? We may easily infer, from Lawrence's writings, his answers to these questions.

To decide not to know is, first, to reject all ideas as *goals*, since ideas are only partial definitions of the Divine Will and are but the expressions of the power-craving ego. We must recognize that we cannot "have things our own way" (*SCAL*, 26), that it is folly to seek to become God. Man must act in harmony with the will of the Source, inexpressible in ideal terms. Not that one should reject ideas, but only ideas as goals. Ideas are born in the passional impulses of life. They arise, says Lawrence, in "interchanges" and in "volitions"—in the great love and power centers. Their value is that they enable us to objectify and fix human desire at a given moment in history, in response to unique historical events. But to accept an idea as a goal is to force life always in the direction determined by the past—by a dead self in a dead world.

Second, "not knowing" means accepting change as a law of life. There "is no eternal system, there is no rock of eternal truth" (*Phoenix II*, 413). God may be revealed, but the revelation "vanishes as the rainbow," and when God reappears, He is "different"—He is "always different." If we would act in harmony with the divine energy, we must recognize, then, that evil is the "desire for constancy, for fixity in the temporal world," is "the denial of the absolute good, the revocation of the Kingdom of Heaven" (414). Now man's soul, or what Ursula in *Women in Love* calls "the integral spirit," always prompts him toward healthy change, toward "transmutation" in accordance with the flux of reality. And "transmutation" will occur inevitably, Ursula recognizes, "unless I set my will, unless I absolve myself from the rhythms of life, fix myself and remain static, cut off from living, absolved within my own will." Man will develop, will move toward maximum of being, as long as he allows the deepest will to speak in his life: "Not I, but the wind." But he can do this only if he "does not know"—only, that is, when he does what he *really* wants, what the deepest impulses within him want, and not what is ideally prescribed as the aim of life. "Knowing" cannot direct his living because knowing is always at odds with life, always works against the "transmutation" that life unconsciously brings to pass.

Third, "not knowing" means substituting "intuition" for conscious, abstractive knowledge. Like Bergson, Lawrence sees the abstractive intellect as fixing ideas and falsely imposing them, in all situations and at all times, upon organic reality, which is always movement and change. But ideas can never do justice to the uniqueness and the flow of concrete reality; they only reduce organic uniqueness, interconnectedness, and temporal flow to abstractions, to elements already known and common to many individual things. They freeze what Wallace

Stevens calls "the fluent mundo" and obliterate uniqueness. Hence we can never mentally "know" reality. Accurate knowledge of reality is possible only when, as in Bergson, one employs a kind of "intuition," which is "instinct refined," a capacity to enter into another being and to feel its reality as a thrusting forward of being from the past into the present. Lawrence calls this intuitive knowledge "blood consciousness," and he affirms that the blood "is always wiser than the mind" because the blood responds directly to an immediate and concrete reality whereas the mind does not. In advocating a "religion of the blood," Lawrence calls for a finer, more delicate "knowledge," not the belated knowledge of the abstractive intellect but the immediate knowledge of the whole being. The knowledge of the blood is a kind of vibratory response, intelligent beyond mental intelligence, because it contains elements of sympathetic understanding or of sympathetic imagination and because it is not abstracted from concrete reality.

Conscious knowledge is of a world that no longer exists, a dead world. That is why conscious knowledge is always a "death-process": it has nothing to do with being. To know, mentally, is to destroy life. To know intuitively or through "the blood" is to make a vital connection with reality.

But what about the charge that Lawrence is committed "to sensationalism—that is, to disintegrative sex and the machine-principle"? What about the Lawrence who affirms reductive violence as "a principle built in to the nature of things just as certainly as creativeness and fecundity"?[30] In Lawrence's talk about "the flowing together and the flowing apart," where is the acknowledgment that "integrative tenderness and disintegrative violence can not only live together but imply each other," the acknowledgment of "the will to ecstasy in destruction," and the will to be master of life? (*River of Dissolution*, 139, 144–45).

Lawrence's reply to these charges would be to make a very simple distinction. There are an unhealthy and a healthy way to seek destruction and death. In unhealthy sensationalism and reduction, the ego, seeking fulfillment in sadomasochism, is incapable of freeing itself for new life; neither sadism nor masochism can satisfy the deep cravings for a pure relationship and for utter selfhood. The healthy way is to accept destructiveness and death "in the understanding," as one of our human desires, and thus to purge oneself of the smug egoistic assumption that one is "above" the horrors of sadism or masochism. As Lawrence argues in "The Reality of Peace," one must accept that "the serpent of abhorrence nests in [one's] very heart," but this acceptance may "drain the swampy place" so that the serpent "will evaporate as his condition evaporates'' (*Phoenix*, 678). Even if the serpent does not evaporate, however, the healthy man recognizes that his desire for death is ''single'' and must be balanced by the desire for life. By refusing to separate his passion for death from his passion for life and creation, the healthy person guards against the insane monomania of his destructive desire. The destructive impulse is kept ''in proportion'' and is, indeed, ''subordinate'' to the desire for life, though ''not subjected'' (*Phoenix*, 679–80). The balancing of the two desires prevents the compulsive plunge into a frenzy of destruction and death.

In the unhealthy way, the ego compulsively pursues sensation and liberation until the soul recoils in horror from the destruction it has done. In the healthy way, man is checked at the outset by the understanding that the desire for death, in the service of the ego, is dangerous; and one is liberated by the acceptance of the desire for death as a part of one's whole nature. '' 'I only want to *know* what we are,' '' says Rupert Birkin in acknowledging that he, too, is part of the dark river of dissolution. Similarly, in the introduction to the Maurice Magnus *Memoirs*, which Colin Clarke quotes in support of his attack, Lawrence asserts:

> Humanity can only finally conquer by realizing. It is human destiny, since Man fell into consciousness and self-consciousness, that we can only go forward step by step through realization, full, bitter, conscious realization. . . . And we've got to know humanity's criminal tendency, . . . Knowledge, true knowledge is like vaccination.
>
> And so it is with war. . . . We all fell . . . . We fell into hideous depravity of hating the human soul. [*Phoenix II*, 358]

Clarke argues: ''In *Women in Love* the impulse to 'realize,' or undergo the death-process, contends throughout with the desire to avoid realization. Or, to make the same point rather differently, a yearning to be born again—or to *avoid* the death-process—contends with a conviction that it is not possible to be born again, that 'the life that belongs to death' is the only life humanity will ever know; inescapably this is 'our kind of life' '' (135). But Clarke misses Lawrence's essential point: there is no choice between being born again and the death process. One can be reborn only after dying. Lawrence never wishes to avoid the death process. In ''The Reality of Peace'' he condemns those who avoid the knowledge of death. Both Birkin and Ursula accept the death process, but healthily. They ''die'' and are reborn, by the healthy flowing together into death and the healthy flowing apart into individuality. By accepting that death process and rebirth, they avoid the death process of the dead society with its fixed form of life. Others, like

Gerald and Gudrun, remain fixed and separate egos, driven to continue the war of ego against ego, to continue destruction and death. So the World War was continued. But if humanity would accept that it is part of death as it is part of life, such knowledge would "vaccinate" men against their "criminal tendency"—that is, the tendency to continue as egos instead of relinquishing the will by the life-giving act of flowing together.

The fullest depiction of what it means practically to accept death as part of life is seen, as Clarke says, in *Women in Love*. But Lawrence carefully defines the healthy way of accepting one's death impulse along with one's life impulse. After Birkin and Ursula have passed away and become reborn in their love, they go with Gerald and Gudrun to the Tyrol. There, in the ice and snow—which are symbolic of the virulent northern way of consciousness, spirituality, and the spiritual will—Birkin finds it necessary to react into licentiousness. He indulges his desire for perversity, and the couple become "bestial," "degraded." But there is a difference between Ursula's freedom and Gudrun's. Gudrun's freedom is irresponsible, associated with the chaos and anarchy in the souls of the licentious who seek maximum assertion of the ego in their perversity. Ursula, before giving way to Birkin's perversity, has seen that "he was self-responsible." Twice the word "responsible" is repeated: "His licentiousness was repulsively attractive. But he was self-responsible, she would see what it was" (*WL*, 470). "He knew all the time what he was doing, she could see it in his smiling, concentrated eyes. It was his responsibility, she would leave it to him" (469). Birkin knows what his desire means for the soul; knows that the desire for perversity and corruption is, in the environment of the hostile spiritual will, necessary to "restore the balance." The lovers are not always able to give themselves up to the inhuman in the self-rejuvenating and self-transforming act of love. But they can welcome "sensationalism" and "corruption" (anal sex) with the realization that such activities, if not carried too far, can lead to health. It is the Holy Ghost, finally, that checks the impulse toward destruction and reminds us never to carry any of our promptings to excess. Neither the sympathetic desire for unison nor the voluntary desire for separateness must be carried too far. The balance must be maintained. The flowing together must be succeeded by the flowing apart, and the flowing apart by the flowing together. The only evil is fixity. That tremendous insight is what gives us health; it justifies Leavis's and Spilka's claims for Lawrence's extraordinary intelligence and healthiness.

It is time for criticism to rediscover the healthy and the detached D. H. Lawrence. Lawrence's desire to be "comprehensive in a detached way" is not, as Philip Heseltine thought,[31] a weakness of his art but is, on the contrary, the source of much of Lawrence's power not only as an artist but also as a psychologist and as a religious thinker. What is remarkable is that while defining his laws of psychology and articulating his religious vision, Lawrence still manages to capture the authentic felt life of individual experience.

Lawrence's vision is indeed "metaphysical" and "utopian." But it has acquired a growing significance in "a tragic age," when men and women are keenly aware of the need for psychic and social renewal. The sources of renewal, as Lawrence views them, are not so mystical as they have sometimes been taken to be. Most men and women have experienced the tremendous awakening, through love, to the vision of a new heaven and a new earth, have "died" at least once in their lives and have been reborn to the knowledge that "in the whole being we are nothing as we were born to the knowledge that in the whole being we are all." One thinks of Gandhi's remark: "I am nothing. It is what I serve that counts." The individual who can speak in this way is the brave man who, as Lawrence said, will fight for "a new conception of life and God" (*Phoenix II*, 629). In such a person, the flowing together and the flowing apart are continuous; and at rare moments he is freed from the to-and-fro of love and power and is balanced in orbit between the infinites of the darkness and the light.

Notes

CHAPTER 1
Lawrence's Psychology, I: Materialism

1. Marguerite Beede Howe, *The Art of the Self in D. H. Lawrence* (Athens: Ohio University Press, 1977). For "ontological insecurity" see also David J. Kleinbard, "Laing, Lawrence, and the Maternal Cannibal," *Psychoanalytic Review* 58, no. 1 (Spring 1971): 5–13.

2. Gavriel Ben-Ephraim, *The Moon's Dominion: Narrative Dichotomy and Female Dominance in Lawrence's Earlier Novels* (London and Toronto: Associated University Presses, 1981), pp. 22–23.

3. Ann Englander, "D. H. Lawrence: Technique as Evasion" (Ph.D. diss., Northwestern University, 1966).

4. Colin Clarke, *River of Dissolution: D. H. Lawrence & English Romanticism* (London: Routledge & Kegan Paul, 1969), p. 147.

5. Émile Delavenay, *D. H. Lawrence, the Man and His Work: The Formative Years: 1885–1919*, tr. Katharine M. Delavenay (Carbondale: Southern Illinois University Press, 1972).

6. Yudhishtar, *Conflict in the Novels of D. H. Lawrence* (Edinburgh: Oliver & Boyd, 1969).

7. The phrase is Charles Lamb's, quoted in Lionel Trilling, "Freud and Literature," in *Critical Theory since Plato*, ed. Hazard Adams (New York: Harcourt Brace Jovanovich, Inc., 1971), p. 953.

8. Edward Glover, *Freud or Jung?* (Cleveland and New York: World Publishing Co., Meridian Books, 1964), p. 14.

9. *The Letters of D. H. Lawrence*, ed. Aldous Huxley (New York: Viking Press, 1932), p. xx; T. S. Eliot, quoted in Martin Jarrett-Kerr, *D. H. Lawrence and Human Existence* (London: Rockliff, 1951), p. 97.

10. Lawrence's affinity to Gestalt psychology has been noted by James C. Cowan, *D. H. Lawrence's American Journey: A Study in Literature and Myth* (Cleveland and London: Press of Case Western Reserve University, 1970); also by Mary Freeman, *D. H. Lawrence: A Basic Study of His Ideas* (Gainesville:

University of Florida Press, 1955). Among scholars who have stressed "identity" and existential psychology in Lawrence, see Marguerite Beede Howe, *The Art of the Self;* Gavriel Ben-Ephraim, *The Moon's Dominion;* Robert Langbaum, *The Mysteries of Identity: A Theme in Modern Literature* (New York: Oxford University Press, 1977), pp. 251–353; John Durham, "D. H. Lawrence: Outline for a Psychology of Being" (Ph.D. diss., Occidental College, 1966); Martin Jarrett-Kerr, *D. H. Lawrence and Human Existence;* and T. H. Adamowski, "*The Rainbow* and 'Otherness,'" *D. H. Lawrence Review* (hereafter cited as *DHLR*) 7 (Spring 1974): 58–77.

11. Frieda Lawrence, "*Not I, But the Wind* . . ." (New York: Viking Press, 1934), p. 200.

12. For abbreviations of the titles of Lawrence's works, see List of Abbreviations.

13. Delavenay, *D. H. Lawrence*, p. 73.

14. Ibid., pp. 72, 51, 48.

15. Ibid., p. 48.

16. L. S. Hearnshaw, "Psychology," in *The Twentieth-Century Mind: History, Ideas and Literature in Britain*, ed. C. B. Cox and A. E. Dyson (London and New York: Oxford University Press, 1972), 1:225, 227–28.

17. Herbert Spencer, *First Principles* (New York: De Witt Revolving Fund, 1958), p. 279.

18. Ernst Haeckel, *The Riddle of the Universe at the Close of the Nineteenth Century*, tr. Joseph McCabe (New York and London: Harper & Brothers, 1900), pp. 218–19.

19. Gerald E. Myers, "Introduction: The Intellectual Context," in William James, *The Principles of Psychology* (Cambridge, Mass., and London: Harvard University Press, 1981), 1:xvi.

20. William James, *Psychology* (Greenwich, Conn.: Fawcett Publications, Inc., 1963), p. 6.

21. Quoted in Gerald E. Myers, "Introduction," pp. xxxvii–xxxviii.

22. James, *Psychology*, p. 4.

23. Ibid., p. 333.

24. Richard J. Kuczkowski, "Lawrence's 'Esoteric' Psychology: 'Psychoanalysis and the Unconscious' and 'Fantasia of the Unconscious'" (Ph.D. diss., Columbia University, 1973), p. 182.

25. Myers, "Introduction," p. xvi.

26. John Adams, *The Herbartian Psychology Applied to Education* (Boston: D. C. Heath & Co., 1898), pp. 18, 37.

CHAPTER 2
Lawrence's Psychology, II: Schopenhauer and Nietzsche

1. Émile Delavenay, *D. H. Lawrence, the Man and His Work: The Formative Years: 1885–1919*, tr. Katharine M. Delavenay (Carbondale: Southern Illinois University Press, 1972), p. 64.

2. Arthur Schopenhauer, *The Will to Live: Selected Writings of Arthur Schopenhauer*, ed. Richard Taylor (New York: Frederick Ungar Publishing Co., 1967), p. 152. Hereafter page references to this edition will be included in the text.

3. Alan R. Zoll, "Vitalism and the Metaphysics of Love: D. H. Lawrence and Schopenhauer," *DHLR* 11 (Spring 1978): 19.

4. Mitzi M. Brunsdale, *The German Effect on D. H. Lawrence and His Works, 1885–1912* (Berne: Peter Lang, 1978).

5. See also Eleanor H. Green, "Schopenhauer and D. H. Lawrence on Sex and Love," *DHLR* 8, no. 3 (Fall 1975): 335–38.

6. Kenneth Rexroth, in his "Introduction" to *D. H. Lawrence: Selected Poems* (New York: Viking Press, 1959), p. 10, points out that "the dream" is seen emerging from "the reality" in the early poems.

7. *The Trespasser* (London: William Heinemann Ltd., 1955).

8. *Phoenix: The Posthumous Papers of D. H. Lawrence*, ed. Edward D. McDonald (New York: Viking Press, 1968; first published in 1936), p. 415. Hereafter citations to this edition are included in the text.

9. The source of this idea might have been Schopenhauer (see next note); it might also have been Ernst Haeckel in *The Riddle of the Universe*.

10. *The World as Will and Idea*, tr. R. B. Haldane and J. Kemp, 3 vols. (London: Trübner, 1883–86), 1:193–94.

11. See especially Armin Arnold, *D. H. Lawrence and German Literature, with Two Hitherto Unknown Essays by D. H. Lawrence* (Montreal: Mansfield Book Mart, Heinemann, 1963); Brunsdale, *German Effect;* John B. Humma, "D. H. Lawrence as Friedrich Nietzsche," *Philological Quarterly* 53, no 1 (January 1974); and the many references to Nietzsche in Delavenay, *D. H. Lawrence, the Man and His Work*.

12. This and all subsequent references to Nietzsche are found in *The Portable Nietzsche*, ed. Walter Kaufmann (New York: Viking Press, 1954). The phrase is Kaufmann's, p. 489.

13. Humma, "D. H. Lawrence as Friedrich Nietzsche," p. 111.

CHAPTER 3
Lawrence's Psychology, III: Theory of the Unconscious

1. William York Tindall, *D. H. Lawrence & Susan His Cow* (New York: Columbia University Press, 1939), pp. 150 ff.

2. Richard J. Kuczkowski, "D. H. Lawrence's 'Esoteric Psychology': 'Psychoanalysis and the Unconscious' and 'Fantasia of the Unconscious' " (Ph.D. diss., Columbia University, 1973), pp. 6–55, 154–78.

3. Ibid., p. 37.

4. Both Tindall and Kuczkowski reach this conclusion. Kuczkowski finds a "number of echoes" of Jung's book in Lawrence's work: see p. 120n. It is interesting to note, in this connection, a similarity between Lawrence's anatomical terminology and that of Jung's student Erich Neumann. In *Depth Psychology and a New Ethic* (tr. Eugene Rolfe [London: Hodder & Stoughton Ltd., 1969]), p. 72, Neumann writes: "The continuing identity of man's primary reactions, as these are revealed in the instincts and archetypes, is a correlate to the structure of his psycho-physical system, with its tension between the opposing poles of the autonomic [i.e., sympathetic] and cerebrospinal nervous system, the belly-soul and the head-soul."

5. See Evelyn J. Hinz, "The Beginning and the End: D. H. Lawrence's *Psychoanalysis* and *Fantasia*," *Dalhousie Review* 52 (Summer 1972): 251–65.

6. Neumann, *Depth Psychology and a New Ethic*, p. 67.

7. This "egoless ego" is perhaps to be distinguished from the deep self which Lawrence refers to in his letter of 5 June 1914 as "another ego." By

"another ego" Lawrence apparently meant the unconscious self. The Holy Ghost is the voice of the whole self.

8. Paul Tillich, *The Courage to Be* (New Haven, Conn., and London: Yale University Press, 1952), p. 51.

CHAPTER 4
Problems of the Artist-Psychologist

1. Robert H. MacDonald, " 'The Two Principles': A Theory of the Sexual and Psychological Symbolism of D. H. Lawrence's Later Fiction," *DHLR* 11 (Summer 1978): 152.

2. Jacques Berthoud, " 'The Rainbow' as Experimental Novel," in *D. H. Lawrence: A Critical Study of the Major Novels and Other Writings*, ed. A. H. Gomme (Sussex, Eng.: Harvester Press; New York: Barnes & Noble, 1978).

3. Roger Sale, "Narrative Technique in *The Rainbow*," *Modern Fiction Studies* 5, no. 1 (1959/60): 28–38.

CHAPTER 5
Psychology and Art in the Early Novels

1. Samuel A. Eisenstein, *Boarding the Ship of Death: D. H. Lawrence's Quester Heroes* (The Hague: Mouton & Co., 1974), p. 41.

2. John E. Stoll, *The Novels of D. H. Lawrence: A Search for Integration* (Columbia: University of Missouri Press, 1971), pp. 45–46. See also Marguerite Beede Howe, *The Art of the Self in D. H. Lawrence* (Athens: Ohio University Press, 1977), pp. 15 ff.; and Ernest W. Tedlock, Jr., *D. H. Lawrence, Artist and Rebel: A Study of Lawrence's Fiction* (Albuquerque: University of New Mexico Press, 1963), pp. 51–52.

3. John Worthen, *D. H. Lawrence and the Idea of the Novel* (London: Macmillan Press Ltd., 1979), p. 23. A number of critics have concluded that Lawrence was writing to impress; but his own statement about the novel—"I give myself away so much, and write what is my most palpitant, sensitive self, that I loathe the book because it will betray me to a parcel of fools" (quoted in Worthen, p. 25)—underscores what most readers of Lawrence value so highly in him: his effort to be ruthlessly honest in presenting his personal experience. Graham Hough's contention, in *The Dark Sun: A Study of D. H. Lawrence* (New York: Macmillan Co., 1957), p. 34, that *The Trespasser* "had no very deep roots in Lawrence's experience" would seem to be mistaken.

4. Eleanor H. Green, in her "Schopenhauer and D. H. Lawrence on Sex and Love," *DHLR* 8 (Fall 1975), argues that Schopenhauer "sums up the theme of both *Tristan and Isolde* and *The Trespasser* in his essay on 'The Metaphysics of Love' "; but she points out that Lawrence does not accept Schopenhauer's "pessimistic outlook on life" (pp. 337–38).

5. R. E. Pritchard, *D. H. Lawrence: Body of Darkness* (Pittsburgh: University of Pittsburgh Press, 1971), p. 29.

6. Richard Swigg, *Lawrence, Hardy, and American Literature* (London and New York: Oxford University Press, 1972), p. 46.

7. Stephen J. Miko, *Toward "Women in Love": The Emergence of a Lawrentian Aesthetic* (New Haven, Conn., and London: Yale University Press, 1971), p. 86.

8. Howe, *Art of the Self*, p. 14.

9. Julian Moynahan, *The Deed of Life: The Novels and Tales of D. H. Lawrence* (Princeton, N.J.: Princeton University Press, 1963).

10. See, for example, Scott Sanders, *D. H. Lawrence: The World of the Five Major Novels* (New York: Viking Press, 1973), p. 38.

11. According to Mark Spilka (*The Love Ethic of D. H. Lawrence* [Bloomington: Indiana University Press, 1957], p. 61), *Sons and Lovers* is an exploration of "destructive or counterfeit loves"—"oedipal, spiritual, and 'unbalanced possessive.'"

CHAPTER 6
The Three Angels in *The Rainbow*

1. See, for example, John Worthen, *D. H. Lawrence and the Idea of the Novel* (London: Macmillan Press Ltd., 1979), pp. 69–82. In these early paragraphs I am much indebted to Worthen for his fine account of Lawrence's development of *The Rainbow*.

2. The views of the angel of religion are everywhere implicit in the novel; they are stated explicitly in "Study of Thomas Hardy" and "The Crown" and in many other essays by Lawrence.

3. Frank Kermode, *D. H. Lawrence* (New York: Viking Press, 1973); Mark Kinkead-Weekes, "Introduction," *Twentieth Century Interpretations of "The Rainbow": A Collection of Critical Essays* (Englewood Cliffs, N.J.: Prentice-Hall, Inc., 1971), pp. 4–6. Kinkead-Weekes describes *The Rainbow* as "a kind of Bible, recalling its readers to a religious vision of the world" (p. 6).

4. Nietzsche, in *The Birth of Tragedy*, speaks of the individual's sinking back into the original oneness of nature in Dionysian revels. Lawrence may have had Nietzsche in mind when he formulated, in "Study of Thomas Hardy," his ideas about the historical development of mankind. Émile Delavenay, in his *D. H. Lawrence, the Man and His Work: The Formative Years: 1885–1919*, tr. Katharine M. Delavenay (Carbondale: Southern Illinois University Press, 1972), p. 311, points out that Lawrence's ideas of moral evolution were influenced by Houston Chamberlain.

5. See Lawrence's remark in *Studies in Classic American Literature* (Harmondsworth, Eng.: Penguin Books, 1977), p. 148: "There is no paradise. Fight and laugh and feel bitter and feel bliss: and fight again. Fight, fight. That is life." Compare Cipriano's assertion in *The Plumed Serpent*: "We are men! We are fighters!"

6. In "The Crown" (*Phoenix II*, p. 410) Lawrence defines "God" as "the utter relation between the two eternities [the beginning and the end, the dark and the light, the flesh and the spirit, matter and life], He is in the flowing together and the flowing apart."

7. Worthen, *D. H. Lawrence*, p. 79.

8. F. R. Leavis, *D. H. Lawrence: Novelist* (New York: Simon & Schuster, 1955), p. 142.

9. Worthen, *D. H. Lawrence*, p. 64.

10. Aldous Huxley's comment on Lawrence's negative capability is the best of many written by Lawrence's friends: "He seemed to know, by personal experience, what it was like to be a tree or a daisy or a breaking wave or even the mysterious moon itself. He could get inside the skin of an animal and tell you in the most convincing detail how it felt and how, dimly, inhumanly, it

thought'' (*The Letters of D. H. Lawrence* [New York: Viking Press, 1932], pp. xxx–xxxi).

CHAPTER 7
The Laws of Action and Reaction in *Women in Love*

1. Angelo P. Bertocci, ''Symbolism in *Women in Love*,'' in *A D. H. Lawrence Miscellany*, ed. Harry T. Moore (Carbondale; Southern Illinois University Press, 1959), pp. 83 ff.; F. R. Leavis, *D. H. Lawrence: Novelist* (New York: Simon & Schuster, 1955), p. 168; Robert L. Chamberlain, ''Pussum, Minette, and the Africo-Nordic Symbol in Lawrence's *Women in Love*,'' *PMLA* 78, no. 4, pt. 1 (September 1963): 407–16.

2. Fyodor Dostoevsky, ''Notes from Underground,'' in *Classics of Modern Fiction*, ed. Irving Howe (New York: Harcourt Brace Jovanovich, Inc., 1972), pp. 16–17. Lawrence was well aware of his indebtedness to Dostoevsky, and Lawrence's theory of the unconscious, emphasizing the conflict between sympathetic and voluntary urges, might be read as pure Dostoevskyan psychology. In a letter to John Middleton Murry and Katherine Mansfield, Lawrence provides the following ''notes'' on Dostoevsky: ''1. He has a fixed will, a mania to be infinite, to be God. 2. Within this will, his activity is twofold: (a) To be selfless, a pure Christian, to live in the outer whole, the social whole, the selfless whole, the universal consciousness. (b) To be a pure, absolute self, all-devouring and all-consuming. That is the main statement about him'' (*Letters*, pp. 329–30).

3. Howard M. Harper, Jr., ''*Fantasia* and the Psychodynamics of *Women in Love*,'' in *The Classic British Novel*, ed. Howard M. Harper, Jr., and Charles Edge (Athens: University of Georgia Press, 1972), pp. 202–19; Peter Balbert, *D. H. Lawrence and the Psychology of Rhythm: The Meaning of Form in ''The Rainbow''* (The Hague and Paris: Mouton, 1974). A number of critics, following F. R. Leavis, have pointed out the relationship between idealism (and will) and destructiveness in *Women in Love*. A number of others, like H. M. Daleski, Colin Clarke, George H. Ford, Mark Kinkead-Weekes, and Kingsley Widmer, have examined carefully Lawrence's subtle thinking about the stream of dissolution and the stream of creation—that is, the importance of perversity or corruption as a means to destroy the old fixed ego and to make rebirth possible.

4. Stephen J. Miko, in *Toward Women in Love*, pp. 215–89, quotes from ''The Reality of Peace'' to show that the novel ''was in large part written to gain an understanding of death in order that life might move beyond it'' (215).

5. Paul Delany, *D. H. Lawrence's Nightmare: The Writer and His Circle in the Years of the Great War* (New York: Basic Books, Inc., 1978), p. 88.

CHAPTER 8
Psychology and Art after the Nightmare

1. F. R. Leavis, *D. H. Lawrence: Novelist* (New York: Simon & Schuster, 1955), p.40.

2. I have not come across any critic who views the novel in detail as Lawrence's ''letter to himself,'' but a number of critics have called attention to the relationship between the novel and Lawrence's own life. Representative of their comments are the remarks of Paul G. Baker, in his ''Profile of an Anti-Hero: Aaron Sisson Reconsidered,'' *DHLR* 10 (1977): 182–92, and of Alastair

Niven, in his *D. H. Lawrence: The Novels* (London: Cambridge University Press, 1978). Baker points out (p. 192) that "the restless compulsion to flight of [Lawrence's] strange new anti-hero is a reflection of Lawrence's own febrile inertia during the unsettled months of the *dopoguerra* when withdrawal alone seemed, paradoxically, to be the inevitable but frustrating means of self-preservation." Niven says that "the novel's intrinsic interest surely lies in its implicit commentary upon the Lawrence of 1917–21, bored with fiction, doubtful about his marriage, uncertain where to live, and wholly out of tune with the chaos of attitudes he encountered both in England and abroad" (p. 138). Émile Delavenay, in his *D. H. Lawrence, the Man and His Work: The Formative Years: 1885–1919* (Carbondale: Southern Illinois University Press, 1972), p. 447, says that the novel provides an "absolutely true and often singularly indiscreet picture of Lawrence's immediate circle in the autumn of 1917"—that is, the circle that appears in the early section of the novel. Delavenay also observes the parallels between Aaron/Lottie and Lawrence/Frieda and between Lilly/Tanny and Lawrence/Frieda (p. 448).

Perhaps the best psychoanalytic treatment of *Aaron's Rod* is that by Marguerite Beede Howe, *The Art of the Self in D. H. Lawrence* (Athens: Ohio University Press, 1977). Howe views the novel as an expression of Lawrence's "ontological insecurity" and points out that the novel is "uncomfortably close to the realm of writing as psychotherapy" (p. 80). The novel reflects Lawrence's fear of "invasion and death," she says; and the self, as Lawrence views it, is "shored up against the onslaught of woman love by self-aggrandizement, which takes the form of male-glorification, for the self is now seen as male" (p. 89). Aaron, to make himself whole, needs Lilly, his alter ego: Aaron is reborn "of man who is imitating woman" (p. 92); and "the novel is a fantasy in which men undo the power of women." This interpretation is fascinating and, within Howe's psychoanalytic perspective, generally acceptable. My objection to Howe's interpretation is that, in defining Lawrence's ontological insecurity, Howe tends to ignore the specific problems that Lawrence was confronting; and she tends to overemphasize Lilly's "self-aggrandizement" and his success. Lilly, she says, is "Lawrence the successful litterateur." If Lawrence's intention, conscious or unconscious, was to glorify the male, he found pitifully inadequate means to do so! M h as I am impressed by Howe's study, I cannot accept her conclusion that Lawrence was as insecure, or as "schizoid," as she finds him to be.

3. Richard Aldington, *D. H. Lawrence: Portrait of a Genius But—* (London: William Heinemann, 1950), p. 170.

4. See, for example, Howe, *Art of the Self*, especially p. 104.

5. R. E. Pritchard, *D. H. Lawrence: Body of Darkness* (Pittsburgh: University of Pittsburgh Press, 1971), p. 208.

6. John Worthen, *D. H. Lawrence and the Idea of the Novel* (London: Macmillan Press Ltd., 1979), pp. 136–51.

CHAPTER 9
From Reaction to Sympathy: *The Plumed Serpent* and *Lady Chatterley's Lover*

1. Bertrand Russell, *The Autobiography of Bertrand Russell: 1914–1944* (Boston: Little, Brown & Co., 1968), pp. 13–14; W. H. Auden, in *Critics on D. H. Lawrence*, ed. W. T. Andrews (Coral Gables, Fla.: University of Miami

Press, 1971), p. 50; Frank Waters, "Quetzalcoatl versus D. H. Lawrence's *Plumed Serpent*," *Western American Literature* 3, no. 2 (Summer 1968): 109; F. R. Leavis, *D. H. Lawrence: Novelist* (New York: Simon & Schuster, 1955), p. 21; Eliseo Vivas, *D. H. Lawrence: The Failure and the Triumph of Art* (London: George Allen & Unwin Ltd., 1961); Mary Freeman, *D. H. Lawrence: A Basic Study of His Ideas* (Gainesville: University of Florida Press, 1955).

2. Jascha Kessler, "'Descent in Darkness': The Myth of *The Plumed Serpent*," in *A D. H. Lawrence Miscellany*, ed. Harry T. Moore (Carbondale: Southern Illinois University Press, 1959); James C. Cowan, *D. H. Lawrence's American Journey: A Study in Literature and Myth* (Cleveland and London: Press of Case Western Reserve University, 1970), pp. 99–121; L. D. Clark, *Dark Night of the Body: D. H. Lawrence's "Plumed Serpent"* (Austin: University of Texas Press, 1964), passim.

3. Robert Langbaum, *The Mysteries of Identity: A Theme in Modern Literature* (New York: Oxford University Press, 1977), pp. 288–89.

4. Mark Spilka, *The Love Ethic of D. H. Lawrence* (Bloomington: Indiana University Press, 1955).

5. H. M. Daleski, *The Forked Flame: A Study of D. H. Lawrence* (Evanston, Ill.: Northwestern University Press, 1965); Marguerite Beede Howe, *The Art of the Self in D. H. Lawrence* (Athens: Ohio University Press, 1977); David Cavitch, *D. H. Lawrence and the New World* (New York and London: Oxford University Press, 1969), p. 200; Diana Trilling, "A Letter of Introduction," in *The Selected Letters of D. H. Lawrence* (New York: Farrar, Straus & Cudahy, Inc., 1958), p. xxvii; Colin Clarke, *River of Dissolution: D. H. Lawrence & English Romanticism* (London: Routledge & Kegan Paul, 1969), pp. 138, 143.

6. Wayne C. Booth, *The Rhetoric of Fiction* (Chicago: University of Chicago Press, 1961), p. 80.

7. Julian Moynahan, in *The Deed of Life: The Novels and Tales of D. H. Lawrence* (Princeton, N.J.: Princeton University Press, 1963), p. 155, sees Clifford as a man who, "because he is only half human, is not human at all." But Moynahan's comparison of Lawrence's people to the "incredibly energetic yet two-dimensional characters one finds in Dickens and in the novels of Smollett and Fielding" (p. 151) seems to me misleading: it ignores Lawrence's intuitive powers.

CHAPTER 10
The Psychologist as Psychologist

1. Quoted in Chaman Nahal, *D. H. Lawrence: An Eastern View* (New York: A. S. Barnes & Co., 1971), p. 20.

2. Herbert Marcuse, *Eros and Civilization: A Philosophical Inquiry into Freud* (Boston: Beacon Press, 1955), pp. 238–74; Russell Jacoby, *Social Amnesia: A Critique of Conformist Psychology from Adler to Laing* (Boston: Beacon Press, 1975), passim.

3. Philip Rieff, *The Triumph of the Therapeutic: Uses of Faith after Freud* (New York: Harper & Row, 1966), p. 208.

4. Elizabeth Brody Tenenbaum, *The Problematic Self: Approaches to Identity in Stendhal, D. H. Lawrence, and Malraux* (Cambridge, Mass., and London: Harvard University Press, 1977), p. 72.

5. Eugene Goodheart, *The Utopian Vision of D. H. Lawrence* (Chicago: University of Chicago Press, 1963), pp. 35–36.

6. Scott Sanders, *D. H. Lawrence: The World of the Five Major Novels* (New York: Viking Press, 1973), p. 38.

7. Marguerite Beede Howe, *The Art of the Self in D. H. Lawrence* (Athens: Ohio University Press, 1977), passim.

8. Rollo May, *Man's Search for Himself* (New York: New American Library, Signet Book, 1967), p. 100.

9. Viktor E. Frankl, *The Doctor and the Soul: An Introduction to Logotherapy*, tr. Richard and Clara Winston (New York: Alfred A. Knopf, 1957), pp. 100, 184.

10. Sigmund Freud, *An Outline of Psycho-analysis*, in *The Standard Edition of the Complete Psychological Works of Sigmund Freud*, tr. and ed. James Strachey (London: Hogarth Press, 1955), 23:148.

11. Freud, *Civilization and Its Discontents*, in *The Standard Edition*, 21:122.

12. Daniel A. Weiss, *Oedipus in Nottingham: D. H. Lawrence* (Seattle: University of Washington Press, 1962).

13. Freud, *The Ego and the Id*, tr. Joan Riviere (London: Hogarth Press, 1947), p. 79.

14. Freud, *Civilization and Its Discontents*, 21:129.

15. Irenäus Eibl-Eibesfeldt, *Love and Hate: The Natural History of Behavior Patterns*, tr. Geoffrey Strachan (New York: Schocken Books, 1974), p. 151.

16. Edward Chace Tolman, *Purposive Behavior in Animals and Men* (Berkeley and Los Angeles: University of California Press, 1949).

17. C. G. Jung, *The Collected Works of C. G. Jung*, 2d ed. (New York: Bollingen Foundation, 1966), 16:153.

18. Quoted in Eugene W. Dawson, "D. H. Lawrence and Trigant Burrow: Pollyanalytics and Phylobiology, An Interpretive Analysis" (Ph.D. diss., University of Washington, 1963), p. 18.

19. Trigant Burrow, *The Biology of Human Conflict*, quoted by Dawson, "D. H. Lawrence and Trigant Burrow," p. 46.

20. Alfred Adler, "Individual Psychology," in *Psychologies of 1930*, ed. Carl Murchison (Worcester, Mass.: Clark University Press, 1930), p. 398.

21. For an analysis of Lawrence's affinities to existential psychology see John Durham, "D. H. Lawrence: Outline for a Psychology of Being" (Ph.D. diss., Occidental College, 1967).

22. See Don Hausdorff's study *Erich Fromm* (New York: Twayne Publishers, 1972), p. 16; also Herbert Marcuse, *Eros and Civilization*, pp. 241–74.

23. Erich Fromm, *The Sane Society* (New York: Rinehart & Co., Inc., 1955), p. 28; hereafter abbreviated in the text as SS. Fromm frequently repeats himself, and for the purposes of this book I have found it sufficient to present his views as formulated in *The Sane Society*; *Man for Himself: An Inquiry into the Psychology of Ethics* (New York: Holt, Rinehart & Winston, 1947), hereafter abbreviated *MFH*; and *The Art of Loving* (London: George Allen & Unwin Ltd., 1957), hereafter abbreviated *AL*. *Escape from Freedom* (New York: Farrar & Rinehart, 1941), *Psychoanalysis and Religion* (New Haven, Conn.: Yale University Press, 1950) and a number of Fromm's writings during the sixties do not modify his essential position.

24. Erwin W. Straus, Maurice Natanson, and Henri Ey, *Psychiatry and Philosophy* (New York and Berlin: Springer-Verlag, 1969), p. 38.

25. David E. Schecter, "Of Human Bonds and Bondage," in *In the Name of Life: Essays in Honor of Erich Fromm*, ed. Bernard Landis and Edward S. Tauber (New York: Holt, Rinehart & Winston, 1975), p. 85.

26. Robert Daniels, "An Analysis of D. H. Lawrence's *Women in Love* from the Perspective of Heinz Kohut's Psychology of the Self" (unpublished undergraduate essay, University of Tennessee).

27. Goodheart, *Utopian Vision*, p. 169.

28. Kingsley Widmer, *The Art of Perversity: D. H. Lawrence's Shorter Fictions* (Seattle: University of Washington Press, 1962), p. 219. Lawrence's view of Shaw was sometimes very positive. In a letter of 31 December 1908 Lawrence wrote: "Do not think because I rave at Bernard Shaw I don't like him." In a letter of 27 March 1912 Lawrence wrote that he found *Man and Superman* to be "very good" (1:103, 377, of Cambridge edition of *Letters*). George B. Shaw, *The Sanity of Art: An Exposure of the Current Nonsense about Artists Being Degenerate* (London: New Age Press, 1908), p. 45.

29. See Lawrence's poem "Shadows" (*Collected Poems*, 726): "And if tonight my soul may find her peace / in sleep, and sink in good oblivion / and in the morning wake like a new-opened flower / then I have been dipped again in God, and new-created."

30. Colin Clarke, *River of Dissolution: D. H. Lawrence & English Romanticism* (London: Routledge & Kegan Paul, 1969), pp. 147, 139.

31. Heseltine is quoted in Richard Aldington, *D. H. Lawrence: Portrait of a Genius But—* (London: Heinemann, 1950), p. 178.

Bibliography

Adamowski, T. H. "Character and Consciousness: D. H. Lawrence, Wilhelm Reich, and Jean Paul Sartre." *University of Toronto Quarterly* 43 (1974): 311–34.

———. "*The Rainbow* and 'Otherness.'" *D. H. Lawrence Review* (hereafter cited as *DHLR*) 7, no. 1 (Spring 1974): 58–77.

Adams, John. *The Herbartian Psychology Applied to Education*. Boston: D. C. Heath & Co., 1898.

Adler, Alfred. "Individual Psychology." In *Psychologies of 1930*, edited by Carl Murchison. Worcester, Mass.: Clark University Press, 1930.

———. *The Practice and Theory of Individual Psychology*. Translated by P. Radin. New York: Harcourt, Brace & Co., 1927.

———. *Social Interest: A Challenge to Mankind*. Translated by John Linton and Richard Vaughan. London: Faber, 1938.

Aldington, Richard. *D. H. Lawrence: Portrait of a Genius But—*. London: William Heinemann, 1950.

Alldritt, Keith. *The Visual Imagination of D. H. Lawrence*. London: Edward Arnold, 1971.

Allport, Gordon. *Becoming: Basic Considerations for a Psychology of Personality*. New Haven, Conn.: Yale University Press, 1955.

Andrews, W. T., ed. *Critics on D. H. Lawrence*. Coral Gables, Fla.: University of Miami Press, 1971.

Arnold, Armin. *D. H. Lawrence and German Literature, with Two Hitherto Unknown Essays by D. H. Lawrence*. Montreal: Mansfield Book Mart, H. Heinemann, 1963.

Baker, Paul G. "Profile of an Anti-Hero: Aaron Sisson Reconsidered." *DHLR* 10 (1974): 182–92.

Balbert, Peter. *D. H. Lawrence and the Psychology of Rhythm: The Meaning of Form in "The Rainbow."* The Hague and Paris: Mouton, 1974.

Barber, David S. "Community in *Women in Love*." *Novel* 5 (Fall 1971): 32–41.

Beal, Anthony. *D. H. Lawrence*. New York and Edinburgh: Oliver & Boyd, 1961.

BIBLIOGRAPHY

Ben-Ephraim, Gavriel. *The Moon's Dominion: Narrative Dichotomy and Female Dominance in Lawrence's Earlier Novels*. London and Toronto: Associated University Presses, 1981.

Boadella, David. *The Spiral Flame: A Study of the Meaning of D. H. Lawrence*. Nottingham: Ritter Press, 1956.

Booth, Wayne C. *The Rhetoric of Fiction*. Chicago: University of Chicago Press, 1961.

Brunsdale, Mitzi M. *The German Effect on D. H. Lawrence and His Works, 1885–1912*. Berne: Peter Lang, 1978.

Burns, Aidan. *Nature and Culture in D. H. Lawrence*. Totowa, N.J.: Barnes & Noble Books, 1980.

Burns, Robert. "The Novel as a Metaphysical Statement: Lawrence's *The Rainbow*." *Southern Review* (Australia) 4 (1970): 139–60.

Burrow, Trigant. *The Social Basis of Consciousness: A Study in Organic Psychology Based upon a Synthetic and Societal Concept of the Neuroses*. New York: Harcourt, Brace & Co., 1927.

Cavitch, David. *D. H. Lawrence and the New World*. New York and London: Oxford University Press, 1969.

Chamberlain, Robert L. "Pussum, Minette, and the Africo-Nordic Symbol in Lawrence's *Women in Love*." *PMLA* 78, no. 4, pt. 1 (September 1963): 407–16.

Chambers, Jessie (pseud., E. T.). *D. H. Lawrence: A Personal Record*. 2d ed. Edited by J. D. Chambers. London: Frank Cass & Co., 1965.

Clark, L. D. *Dark Night of the Body: D. H. Lawrence's "Plumed Serpent."* Austin: University of Texas Press, 1964.

Clarke, Colin. *River of Dissolution: D. H. Lawrence & English Romanticism*. London: Routlege & Kegan Paul, 1969.

Corke, Helen. *In Our Infancy: An Autobiography*. Cambridge, Eng., and New York: Cambridge University Press, 1975.

Cowan, James C. *D. H. Lawrence's American Journey: A Study in Literature and Myth*. Cleveland and London: Press of Case Western Reserve University, 1970.

Cox, C. B., and Dyson, A. E., eds. *The Twentieth-Century Mind: History, Ideas and Literature in Britain*. Vol. 1: *1900–1918*. London, Oxford, New York: Oxford University Press, 1972.

Daleski, Herman M. *The Forked Flame: A Study of D. H. Lawrence*. Evanston, Ill.: Northwestern University Press, 1965.

Dawson, Eugene W. "D. H. Lawrence and Trigant Burrow: Pollyanalytics and Phylobiology, An Interpretive Analysis." Ph.D. diss., University of Washington, 1963.

Delany, Paul. *D. H. Lawrence's Nightmare: The Writer and His Circle in the Years of the Great War*. New York: Basic Books, Inc., 1978.

Delavenay, Émile. *D. H. Lawrence, the Man and His Work: The Formative Years: 1885–1919*. Translated by Katharine M. Delavenay. Carbondale: Southern Illinois University Press, 1972.

———. *D. H. Lawrence and Edward Carpenter: A Study in Edwardian Transition*. New York: Taplinger Publishing Co., 1971.

Dostoevsky, Fyodor. "Notes from Underground." In *Classics of Modern Fiction*, edited by Irving Howe. New York: Harcourt Brace Jovanovich, Inc., 1972.

Durham, John. "D. H. Lawrence: Outline for a Psychology of Being." Ph.D. diss., Occidental College, 1967.
Eibl-Eibesfeldt, Irenäus. *Love and Hate: The Natural History of Behavior Patterns*. Translated by Geoffrey Strachan. New York: Schocken Books, 1974.
Eisenstein, Samuel A. *Boarding the Ship of Death: D. H. Lawrence's Quester Heroes*. The Hague: Mouton & Co., 1974.
Engelberg, Edward. "Escape from the Circles of Experience: D. H. Lawrence's *The Rainbow* as a Modern *Bildungsroman*." *PMLA* 78, no. 1 (March 1963): 103–13.
Englander, Ann. "D. H. Lawrence: Technique as Evasion." Ph.D. diss., Northwestern University, 1966.
Erikson, Erik. *Childhood and Society*. New York: W. W. Norton & Co., 1950.
Farr, Judith, comp. *Twentieth Century Interpretations of "Sons and Lovers": A Collection of Critical Essays*. Englewood Cliffs, N.J.: Prentice-Hall, 1970.
Ford, George H. *Double Measure: A Study of the Novels and Stories of D. H. Lawrence*. Reprint of 1965 edition. New York: W. W. Norton & Co., 1969.
Frankl, Viktor E. *The Doctor and the Soul: An Introduction to Logotherapy*. Translated by Richard and Clara Winston. New York: Alfred A. Knopf, 1957.
Freeman, Mary. *D. H. Lawrence: A Basic Study of His Ideas*. Gainesville: University of Florida Press, 1955.
Freud, Sigmund. *The Ego and the Id*. Translated by Joan Riviere. London: Hogarth Press, 1947.
———. *The Standard Edition of the Complete Psychological Works of Sigmund Freud*. Translated and edited by James Strachey. Vol. 12. London: Hogarth Press, 1958.
Fromm, Erich. *The Art of Loving*. London: George Allen & Unwin Ltd., 1957.
———. *Escape from Freedom*. New York: Farrar & Rinehart, 1941.
———. *Man for Himself: An Inquiry into the Psychology of Ethics*. New York: Holt, Rinehart & Winston, 1947.
———. *Psychoanalysis and Religion*. New Haven, Conn.: Yale University Press, 1950.
———. *The Sane Society*. New York: Rinehart & Co., Inc., 1955.
Glover, Edward. *Freud or Jung?* Cleveland and New York: World Publishing Co., Meridian Books, 1964.
Gomme, A. H., ed. *D. H. Lawrence: A Critical Study of the Major Novels and Other Writings*. Sussex, Eng.: Harvester Press; New York: Barnes & Noble, 1978.
Goodheart, Eugene. *The Utopian Vision of D. H. Lawrence*. Chicago: University of Chicago Press, 1963.
Green, Eleanor H. "Schopenhauer and D. H. Lawrence on Sex and Love." *DHLR* 8, no. 3 (Fall 1975): 329–45.
Gregory, Horace. *Pilgrim of the Apocalypse: A Critical Study of D. H. Lawrence*. New York: Viking Press, 1933.
Gurko, Leo. "*The Trespasser*: D. H. Lawrence's Neglected Novel." *College English* 24, no. 1 (October 1962): 29–35.
Gutierrez, Donald. *Lapsing Out: Embodiments of Death and Rebirth in the Last Writings of D. H. Lawrence*. Rutherford, N.J.: Fairleigh Dickinson University Press, 1980.

Haeckel, Ernst. *The Riddle of the Universe at the Close of the Nineteenth Century*. Translated by Joseph McCabe. New York and London: Harper & Brothers, 1900.

Hamalian, Leo, comp. *D. H. Lawrence: A Collection of Criticism*. New York: McGraw-Hill Book Co., 1973.

Harper, Howard M., Jr. "*Fantasia* and the Psychodynamics of *Women in Love*." In *The Classic British Novel*, edited by Howard M. Harper, Jr., and Charles Edge. Athens: University of Georgia Press, 1972.

Hausdorff, Don. *Erich Fromm*. New York: Twayne Publishers, 1972.

Heilman, Robert B. "Nomads, Monads, and the Mystique of the Soma." *Sewanee Review* 68, no. 4 (Autumn 1960): 635–59.

Hinz, Evelyn J. "The Beginning and the End: D. H. Lawrence's *Psychoanalysis and Fantasia*." *Dalhousie Review* 52 (Summer 1972): 251–65.

Hochman, Baruch. *Another Ego: The Changing View of Self and Society in the Work of D. H. Lawrence*. Columbia: University of South Carolina Press, 1970.

Hoffman, Frederick J. *Freudianism and the Literary Mind*. Reprint of 1945 edition. New York: Grove Press, 1959.

Hough, Graham. *The Dark Sun: A Study of D. H. Lawrence*. New York: Macmillan Co., 1957.

Howe, Marguerite Beede. *The Art of the Self in D. H. Lawrence*. Athens: Ohio University Press, 1977.

Humma, John B. "D. H. Lawrence as Friedrich Nietzsche." *Philological Quarterly* 53, no. 1 (January 1974): 110–20.

Jacobi, Jolande. *The Psychology of Jung*. Translated by K. W. Bash. Revised edition. New Haven, Conn.: Yale University Press, 1951.

Jacoby, Russell. *Social Amnesia: A Critique of Conformist Psychology from Adler to Laing*. Boston: Beacon Press, 1975.

James, William. *The Principles of Psychology*. Cambridge, Mass., and London: Harvard University Press, 1981.

———. *Psychology*. Greenwich, Conn.: Fawcett Publications, Inc., 1963.

Jarrett-Kerr, Martin [Father William Tiverton, pseud.]. *D. H. Lawrence and Human Existence*. London: Rockliff, 1951.

Jung, Carl Gustav. *The Collected Works of C. G. Jung*. 2d ed., vols. 11 and 16. New York: Bollingen Foundation, 1966.

———. *Modern Man in Search of a Soul*. Translated by W. S. Dell and Cary F. Baynes. New York: Harcourt, Brace & Co., 1933.

———. *Psychology of the Unconscious: A Study of the Transformations and Symbolism of the Libido; A Contribution to the History of the Evolution of Thought*. New York: Dodd, Mead, 1916.

Keith, W. J. "D. H. Lawrence's *The White Peacock*: An Essay in Criticism." *University of Toronto Quarterly* 37, no. 3 (April 1968): 230–47.

Kermode, Frank. *D. H. Lawrence*. New York: Viking Press, 1973.

Kleinbard, David J. "D. H. Lawrence and Ontological Insecurity." *PMLA* 89, no. 1 (January 1974): 154–63.

———. "Laing, Lawrence, and the Maternal Cannibal." *Psychoanalytic Review* 58, no. 1 (Spring 1971): 5–13.

Köhler, Wolfgang. *Gestalt Psychology*. New York: H. Liveright, 1929.

Kuczkowski, Richard J. "Lawrence's 'Esoteric' Psychology: 'Psychoanalysis and the Unconscious' and 'Fantasia of the Unconscious.'" Ph.D. diss., Columbia University, 1973.

Laing, R. D. *The Divided Self: An Existential Study in Sanity and Madness.* Harmondsworth, Eng.: Penguin Books, 1965.

Lainoff, Seymour. "*The Rainbow:* The Shaping of Modern Man." *Modern Fiction Studies* 1, no. 4 (November 1955): 23–27.

Langbaum, Robert. *The Mysteries of Identity: A Theme in Modern Literature.* New York: Oxford University Press, 1977.

Lawrence, D. H. *Aaron's Rod.* First published in 1922. Harmondsworth, Eng.: Penguin Books, 1950.

———. *Apocalypse.* Introduction by Richard Aldington. First published in 1931. New York: Viking Press, Compass Books, 1966.

———. *The Collected Letters of D. H. Lawrence.* Edited by Harry T. Moore. 2 vols. New York: Viking Press, 1962.

———. *The Complete Poems of D. H. Lawrence.* Edited by Vivian de Sola Pinto and Warren Roberts. 2 vols. New York: Viking Press, 1964.

———. *The Complete Short Stories.* 3 vols. Harmondsworth, Eng.: Penguin Books Ltd., 1980.

———. *Etruscan Places.* First published in 1932. In "*Mornings in Mexico*" *and* "*Etruscan Places.*" London: William Heinemann Ltd., 1956.

———. *Fantasia of the Unconscious.* First published in 1922. In "*Fantasia of the Unconscious*" *and* "*Psychoanalysis and the Unconscious.*" Introduction by Philip Rieff. Harmondsworth, Eng.: Penguin Books Ltd., 1977.

———. *The First Lady Chatterley.* First published in 1944. Harmondsworth, Eng.: Penguin Books, 1969.

———. *Kangaroo.* First published in 1923. New York: Viking Compass, 1976.

———. *Lady Chatterley's Lover.* First published in 1928. New York: Grove Press, Inc., 1957.

———. *The Letters of D. H. Lawrence.* Edited by Aldous Huxley. New York: Viking Press, 1932.

———. *The Lost Girl.* First published in 1920. Harmondsworth, Eng.: Penguin Books, 1950.

———. *Mornings in Mexico.* First published in 1927. In "*Mornings in Mexico*" *and* "*Etruscan Places.*" London: William Heinemann Ltd., 1956.

———. *Movements in European History.* First published in 1921. Oxford: Oxford University Press, 1925.

———. *Phoenix: The Posthumous Papers of D. H. Lawrence.* Edited by Edward D. McDonald. First published in 1936. New York: Viking Press, 1968.

———. *Phoenix II: Uncollected, Unpublished, and Other Prose Works by D. H. Lawrence.* Edited by Warren Roberts and Harry T. Moore. London: William Heinemann, 1968.

———. *The Plumed Serpent.* First published in 1926. New York: Vintage Books, Inc., 1951.

———. *Psychoanalysis and the Unconscious.* First published in 1921. In "*Fantasia of the Unconscious*" *and* "*Psychoanalysis and the Unconscious.*" Introduction by Philip Rieff. Harmondsworth, Eng.: Penguin Books Ltd., 1977.

———. *The Rainbow.* First published in 1915. Harmondsworth, Eng.: Penguin Books, 1976.

———. *Sea and Sardinia.* First published in 1921. Harmondsworth, Eng.: Penguin Books, 1944.

———. *Sons and Lovers.* First published in 1913. Harmondsworth, Eng.: Penguin Books, 1979.

———. *Studies in Classic American Literature.* First published in 1923. Harmondsworth, Eng.: Penguin Books, 1977.

———. *The Symbolic Meaning: The Uncollected Versions of "Studies in Classic American Literature."* Edited by Armin Arnold. New York: Viking Press, 1961.

———. *Three Plays.* Introduction by Raymond Williams. Harmondsworth, Eng.: Penguin Books, 1969.

———. *The Trespasser.* First published in 1912. London: William Heinemann, 1955.

———. *Twilight in Italy.* First published in 1916. In *D. H. Lawrence and Italy: "Twilight in Italy," "Sea and Sardinia," "Etruscan Places."* New York: Viking Press, 1972.

———. *The White Peacock.* First published in 1911. London: William Heinemann Ltd., 1955.

———. *Women in Love.* First published in 1912. New York: Random House, Modern Library, 1950.

Lawrence, Frieda. *The Memoirs and Correspondence.* Edited by E. W. Tedlock, Jr. London: William Heinemann, 1961.

———. *"Not I, But the Wind . . . ."* New York: Viking Press, 1934.

Leavis, F. R. *D. H. Lawrence: Novelist.* New York: Simon & Schuster, 1955.

Lesser, Simon O. *Fiction and the Unconscious.* New York: Vintage Books, 1957.

MacDonald, Robert H. "'The Two Principles': A Theory of the Sexual and Psychological Symbolism of D. H. Lawrence's Later Fiction." *DHLR* 11 (Summer 1978): 132–55.

Marcel, Gabriel. *Being and Having.* Translated by A. and C. Black. London: Collins, 1954. (The Fontana Library: Theology and Philosophy.)

Marcuse, Herbert. *Eros and Civilization: A Philosophical Inquiry into Freud.* Boston: Beacon Press, 1955.

May, Rollo, ed. *Existential Psychology.* 2d edition. New York: Random House, 1969.

———. *Love and Will.* New York: Dell, Laurel Books, 1974.

———. *Man's Search for Himself.* New York: New American Library, Signet Book, 1967.

Miko, Stephen J. *Toward "Women in Love": The Emergence of a Lawrentian Aesthetic.* New Haven, Conn., and London: Yale University Press, 1971.

———, ed. *Twentieth Century Interpretations of "Women in Love": A Collection of Critical Essays.* Englewood Cliffs, N.J.: Prentice-Hall, Spectrum, 1969.

Moore, Harry T., ed. *A D. H. Lawrence Miscellany.* Carbondale: Southern Illinois University Press, 1959.

———. *The Intelligent Heart: The Story of D. H. Lawrence.* New York: Farrar, Straus & Young, 1954.

Mortland, Donald E. "The Conclusion of *Sons and Lovers*: A Reconsideration." *Studies in the Novel* 3, no. 3 (Fall 1971): 305–15.

Moynahan, Julian. *The Deed of Life: The Novels and Tales of D. H. Lawrence.* Princeton, N.J.: Princeton University Press, 1963.

Murry, J. M. *D. H. Lawrence: Son of Woman.* First published in 1931. London: Jonathan Cape, 1954.

Myers, Gerald E. "Introduction: The Intellectual Context." In William James, *The Principles of Psychology.* Cambridge, Mass., and London: Harvard University Press, 1981.

Nahal, Chaman. *D. H. Lawrence: An Eastern View*. New York: A. S. Barnes & Co., 1971.

Nehls, Edward, ed. *D. H. Lawrence: A Composite Biography*. 3 vols. Madison: University of Wisconsin Press, 1957–59.

Neumann, Erich. *Depth Psychology and a New Ethic*. Translated by Eugene Rolfe. London: Hodder & Stoughton Ltd., 1969.

———. *The Great Mother: An Analysis of an Archetype*. London: Routledge & Kegan Paul, 1955.

Nietzsche, Friedrich. *The Portable Nietzsche*. Edited by Walter Kaufmann. New York: Viking Press, 1954.

Nin, Anais. *D. H. Lawrence: An Unprofessional Study*. Denver, Colo.: Swallow Press, 1946.

Niven, Alastair. *D. H. Lawrence: The Novels*. London: Cambridge University Press, 1978.

Pritchard, R. E. *D. H. Lawrence: Body of Darkness*. Pittsburgh: University of Pittsburgh Press, 1971.

Reeves, Clement. *The Psychology of Rollo May*. San Francisco; Washington, D.C.; London: Jossey-Bass Publishers, 1977.

Rexroth, Kenneth. "Introduction." In D. H. Lawrence, *Selected Poems*. New York: Viking Press, 1959.

Rieff, Philip. *The Triumph of the Therapeutic: Uses of Faith after Freud*. New York: Harper & Row, 1966.

Ross, Charles L. "The Composition of *Women in Love*: A History, 1913–1919." *DHLR* 8, no. 2 (Summer 1975): 198–212.

Rossman, Charles. " 'You Are the Call and I Am the Answer': D. H. Lawrence and Women." *DHLR* 8, no. 3 (Fall 1975): 255–328.

Russell, Bertrand. *The Autobiography of Bertrand Russell: 1914–1944*. Boston: Little, Brown & Co., 1968.

Sagar, Keith M. *The Art of D. H. Lawrence*. Cambridge: Cambridge University Press, 1965.

Sale, Roger. "The Narrative Technique of *The Rainbow*." *Modern Fiction Studies* 5, no 1 (Spring 1959): 29–38.

Salgādo, Gāmini, ed. *D. H. Lawrence: "Sons and Lovers"; A Casebook*. London: Macmillan & Co., 1969.

Sanders, Scott. *D. H. Lawrence: The World of the Five Major Novels*. New York: Viking Press, 1973.

Schecter, David E. "Of Human Bonds and Bondage." In *In the Name of Life: Essays in Honor of Erich Fromm*, edited by Bernard Landis and Edward S. Tauber, pp. 84–99. New York: Holt, Rinehart & Winston, 1971.

Schneider, Daniel J. "The Symbolism of the Soul: D. H. Lawrence and Some Others." *DHLR* 7, no. 2 (Summer 1974): 107–26.

Scholes, Robert, and Kellogg, Robert. *The Nature of Narrative*. Oxford: Oxford University Press, 1966.

Schopenhauer, Arthur. *The Will to Live: Selected Writings of Arthur Schopenhauer*, edited by Richard Taylor. New York: Frederick Ungar Publishing Co., 1967.

———. *The World as Will and Idea*. Translated by R. B. Haldane and J. Kemp. 3 vols. London: Trübner, 1883–86.

Shaw, George B. *The Sanity of Art: An Exposure of the Current Nonsense about Artists Being Degenerate*. London: New Age Press, 1908.

Spencer, Herbert. *First Principles.* New York: De Witt Revolving Fund, 1958.
———. *The Principles of Psychology.* New York: D. Appleton & Co., 1877.
Spender, Stephen, ed. *D. H. Lawrence: Novelist, Poet, Prophet.* London: Weidenfeld & Nicolson, 1973.
Spilka, Mark. "Lawrence's Quarrel with Tenderness." *Critical Quarterly* 9, no. 4 (Winter 1967): 363–77.
———. *The Love Ethic of D. H. Lawrence.* Bloomington: Indiana University Press, 1955.
Squires, Michael. "Lawrence's *The White Peacock:* A Mutation of Pastoral." *Texas Studies in Literature and Language* 12, no. 2 (Summer 1970): 263–83.
Stanford, Raney. "Thomas Hardy and Lawrence's *The White Peacock.*" *Modern Fiction Studies* 5, no. 1 (Spring 1959): 19–28.
Stoll, John E. *The Novels of D. H. Lawrence: A Search for Integration.* Columbia: University of Missouri Press, 1971.
Straus, Erwin W.; Natanson, Maurice; and Ey, Henri. *Psychiatry and Philosophy.* New York and Berlin: Springer-Verlag, 1969.
Sullivan, H. S. *The Interpersonal Theory of Psychiatry.* Edited by Helen Swick Perry and Mary Ladd Gawel. New York: W. W. Norton, 1953.
Swigg, Richard. *Lawrence, Hardy, and American Literature.* New York and London: Oxford University Press, 1972.
Tedlock, Ernest W., Jr. *D. H. Lawrence, Artist and Rebel: A Study of Lawrence's Fiction.* Albuquerque: University of New Mexico Press, 1963.
———, ed. *D. H. Lawrence and "Sons and Lovers": Sources and Criticism.* New York: New York University Press, 1965.
Tenenbaum, Elizabeth Brody. *The Problematic Self: Approaches to Identity in Stendhal, D. H. Lawrence and Malraux.* Cambridge, Mass., and London: Harvard University Press, 1977.
Tillich, Paul. *The Courage to Be.* New Haven, Conn., and London: Yale University Press, 1952.
Tindall, William York. *D. H. Lawrence & Susan His Cow.* New York: Columbia University Press, 1939.
Tolman, Edward Chace. *Purposive Behavior in Animals and Men.* Berkeley and Los Angeles: University of California Press, 1949.
Trilling, Diana. "A Letter of Introduction." In *The Selected Letters of D. H. Lawrence,* edited by Diana Trilling. New York: Farrar, Straus & Cudahy, Inc., 1958.
Trilling, Lionel. "Freud and Literature." In *Critical Theory since Plato,* compiled by Hazard Adams. New York: Harcourt Brace Jovanovich, Inc., 1971.
Vivas, Eliseo. *D. H. Lawrence: The Failure and the Triumph of Art.* Bloomington: Indiana University Press, 1961.
Waters, Frank. "Quetzalcoatl versus D. H. Lawrence's *Plumed Serpent.*" *Western American Literature* 3, no. 2 (Summer 1968): 103–13.
Weiss, Daniel A. *Oedipus in Nottingham: D. H. Lawrence.* Seattle: University of Washington Press, 1962.
West, Anthony. *D. H. Lawrence.* Denver, Colo.: Swallow Press, 1950.
Widmer, Kingsley. *The Art of Perversity: D. H. Lawrence's Shorter Fictions.* Seattle: University of Washington Press, 1962.
Worthen, John. *D. H. Lawrence and the Idea of the Novel.* London: Macmillan Press Ltd., 1979.

Yudhishtar. *Conflict in the Novels of D. H. Lawrence.* Edinburgh: Oliver & Boyd, 1969.
Zoll, Alan R. ''Vitalism and the Metaphysics of Love: D. H. Lawrence and Schopenhauer.'' *DHLR* 11 (Spring 1978): 1–20.

Index

INDEX

INDEX